TRADITION
and MODERNITY

TRADITION
and MODERNITY

Philosophical

Reflections

on the

African

Experience

KWAME GYEKYE

New York Oxford
Oxford University Press
1997

Oxford University Press

Oxford New York
Athens Auckland Bangkok Bogota Bombay Buenos Aires
Calcutta Cape Town Dar es Salaam Delhi Florence Hong Kong
Istanbul Karachi Kuala Lumpur Madras Madrid Melbourne
Mexico City Nairobi Paris Singapore Taipei Tokyo Toronto Warsaw

and associated companies in
Berlin Ibadan

Copyright © 1997 by Kwame Gyekye

Published by Oxford University Press, Inc.
198 Madison Avenue, New York, New York 10016

Oxford is a registered trademark of Oxford University Press

All rights reserved. No part of this publication may be reproduced,
stored in a retrieval system, or transmitted, in any form or by any means,
electronic, mechanical, photocopying, recording, or otherwise,
without the prior permission of Oxford University Press.

Library of Congress Cataloging-in-Publication Data
Gyekye, Kwame.
    Tradition and modernity : philosophical reflections on the African
experience / Kwame Gyekye.
        p. cm.
    Includes bibliographical references and indexes.
    ISBN 0-19-511225-3.; ISBN 0-19-511226-1 (pbk.)
    1. Africa, Sub-Saharan—Civilization—Philosophy. I. Title.
DT352.4.G94 1997
    960.3'01—dc20   96-23814

9 8 7 6 5 4 3 2

Printed in the United States of America
on acid-free paper

For Maame,

Asantewa,

and Abena

Preface

The study undertaken in this book is a philosophical interpretation and critical analysis of the African cultural experience in modern times, an experience that is clearly many-sided, having resulted not only from encounters with what one might regard as alien cultures and religions but also from problems internal to the practice of the indigenous cultural values, beliefs, and institutions themselves in the setting of the modern world. Thus, the study is, in part, a critical evaluation of values and practices of traditional culture. It stresses the normative grounds of criticism, with a view to exploring the relevance or irrelevance of those indigenous and "alien" values and ideas to modern life. Its significance lies in its illumination of the dilemmas confronting the African people as they attempt to enter or create modernity in their own ways and evolve forms of life symphonic with the ethos of our contemporary world, while suggesting alternative ways of thought and action.

The problems confronting the African people and their societies in the modern world are legion. To the extent that some of the problems are cultural—in the sense that they are causally related to cherished practices, habits, attitudes, and outlooks that derive from the inherited indigenous cultures—it can be said that such problems predate, and can hardly be said to have resulted from, the imposition of European colonial rule with its concomitant introduction of European cultural values and institutions. But it can also be said that some of the problems derive from attempts to grapple with, and adjust to, the aftermath of colonial rule and its institutions. Perhaps it is the complex sources of the problems that have made them more intricate, daunting, and resilient.

Among the problems on which philosophical attention could be brought to bear are the following:

- problems of reappraising inherited cultural traditions to help come to terms with the cultural realities of the times and, thus, to hammer out a new modernity on the anvil of the African people's experience of the past and vision of the future;

- problems of nation-building—of integrating and welding together several ethnic (or, as I prefer to say, communocultural) groups into a large cohesive political community called "nation-state" (or, more appropriately, multinational state) to help eliminate communocultural conflicts and transfer ethnic or local loyalties to the new central government;

- problems of evolving viable and appropriate democratic political institutions that will be impervious to sudden and violent disruptions by the military or the imperious will of a corrupt and tyrannical ruler and will, in consequence, inaugurate an era of political stability and certainty;

- problems of evolving appropriate, credible, and viable ideologies for contemporary African nations;

- problems of inculcating political morality and, thus, to deal a death blow to rampant political corruption;

- problems of dealing with traditional moral standards that seem to be crumbling in the wake of rapid social change.

The resiliency of these and other problems of postcolonial Africa has brought confusion to African life and left many to wonder why. In such times of wonder, confusion, frustration, and anomie, fundamental questions and inquiries need to be pursued, responses to which are likely to clarify situations and present suggestions for new or alternative modes of thought and action. The pursuit of fundamental questions constitutes the stock-in-trade of philosophy. By clarifying issues and, thus, helping to understand them more fully, and through well-considered suggestions and recommendations, philosophical activity can help resolve issues.

Philosophy—that intellectual enterprise concerned with raising fundamental questions about the human experience—is indeed widely believed to be essentially a cultural phenomenon. The reason is that human experience is most directly felt within some specific social or cultural context; also, philosophical thought is never worked out within a cultural or historical vacuum. Thus it is that philosophers grapple at the conceptual level with the problems and issues of their times, providing conceptual and critical responses to and interpretations of the experiences of those times: this fact immediately embeds philosophy in human affairs. These convictions of the place of philosophy in grappling with human affairs have led me to undertake this study.

I devote chapter 1 to a discussion of the role of philosophy in human affairs, dwelling at great length on the career of the philosophical enterprise in the experiences of Western societies and cultures where the conceptual responses to concrete historical experiences are most amply manifested. The interaction between the philosophical activity and human affairs in the development of Western societies can, thus, be regarded as a paradigm case of the role philosophy can play in human affairs in Africa and elsewhere. I argue that the fact that philosophy takes off from experiences that may be said to be specific to cultures or historical situations does not necessarily detract from the universality of (some) philosophical ideas, arguments, proposals, or conclusions. In this connection, however, I make a distinction between what I call "essential universalism" and "contingent universalism." Essential universalism refers to fundamental values or characteristics of human nature that are intrinsic to human functioning and fulfillment. Philosophical inquiries into such fundamental human values should be of interest to all. Contingent universalism refers to a cultural value or practice created in, or by, a specific culture that, by reason of its quality or power of conviction or historic significance, is embraced by the rest of the peoples and cultures of the world and so attains the status of universality.

In chapter 2, "Person and Community: In Defense of Moderate Communitarianism," I take up the intractable problem of the most appropriate type of relation that should exist between the individual and society. I discuss the notion of personhood from the normative perspective, highlighting a moral conception of personhood, and distinguish person from individual, regarding the latter as socially detached and the former as embedded in, but only partially constituted by, the community. I argue that communitarian thought should have equal concern for individual rights and social responsibilities. I conclude that a moral and political theory that combines the appreciation and pursuit of individual rights with commitments and responsibilities to the community and its members will be a most plausible theory to defend.

I discuss matters relating to ethnicity, nation-building, and the emergence of national culture and identity in the context of a modern multinational state constituted by a plethora of communocultural groups in chapter 3, "Ethnicity, Identity, and Nationhood." Initially I distinguish two senses of the concept of nation—as ethnocultural community and multinational (multicultural) state. I deploy arguments to demonstrate that the common descent or kinship basis on which the notion of ethnicity has been erected is genealogically, if not straightforwardly, false in view of the complex genealogies of the individuals composing a particular cultural community and, therefore, that ethnicity is an invention. Thus, it will be more appropriate to speak in terms of communocultural, rather than ethnic, group. The suspicions or skepticisms about the simplicity of the genealogical background of individual members of a so-called ethnic group, however, should facilitate the move toward nation-building. Among the arguments I advance in pursuit of multicultural nationhood is a theory about the character of the modern nation-state in Africa and elsewhere. This theory I call "metanationality": it states that the multinational state is constituted primarily by individual human beings (who happen to share certain cultural and historical experiences) rather than by "ethnic" groups. The metanational state is another, a third, sense of nation.

In chapter 4, "Traditional Political Ideas, Values, and Practices: Their Status in the Modern Setting," I examine claims about the democratic features of the traditional African political practice by delineating the contours of political thought and practice of the Akan society of Ghana, adding references to the political practices and values of some other African societies. I try to delineate what may be regarded as the democratic features of the traditional political thought and practice, stressing the need to adapt what has been inherited from the colonial and traditional practices to suit political life in a large, complex, heterogeneous, modern political community. I advocate a comprehensive conception of democracy that will be strongly committed to both political and economic rights of citizens to make the notion of political (or social) equality a reality. But the main thrust of the chapter is to suggest a thorough and critical examination of the traditional ideas and values of politics and to give a modern translation to those that can be considered worthwhile in pursuit of the democratic political practice in the modern setting.

In chapter 5, "The Socialist Interlude," I demonstrate that the traditional African communal idea or practice that the apostles of the ideology of "African socialism" such as Kwame Nkrumah, Julius Nyerere, and Léopold Senghor identified with modern socialism (Marxism) and from which they derived and justified their choice of the socialist ideology was tendentiously misinterpreted (for that idea was essentially a socioethical idea, not particularly economic); that the traditional idea of economic management bears both individualist and communitarian features; that there are acquisitive and capitalist elements in the African character that seem to have been ignored by the advocates of African socialism; and that what was meant by "socialism" was humanism, a doctrine concerned crucially with human well-being, which is espoused in African moral thought but does not seem necessarily to mandate a socialist economic order. I also present a brief analysis of the concept of ideology and its relation to philosophy.

The problem of justifying the exercise of political power by the military following a series of coups d'etat in African nations of the postcolonial era constitutes the background of the discussions of chapter 6, "Quandaries in the Legitimation of Political Power." Political legitimacy, I point out, is a complex issue, its complexity stemming from several factors, including the circumstances in which individuals or groups have come to assume political power, the nature of the adequate expression or translation of popular consent, the whole question about what constitutes majority vote or decision, the relation (if any) between legitimacy and economic performance or effectiveness of a government. This complexity generates quandaries in the consideration of whether a political power is legitimate. In this chapter I distinguish between formal and informal legitimacy, and between legitimacy of power and justification of power. I argue against effectiveness as a criterion of legitimacy. I argue also that, even though military overthrow of a repressive, authoritarian regime is justifiable on moral grounds, military rule as such will not be legitimate.

I take up the problem of political corruption, rampant in the politics of postcolonial African states and destructive of efforts to develop their societies, in chapter 7, "Political Corruption: A Moral Pollution." I try to clarify the notion of political corruption, and I examine the manifestations of political corruption in the traditional setting as well as the effects of traditional African cultural practices on contemporary political behavior. In contrast to the causal explanations of social scientists that highlight the political, economic, and legal circumstances of political corruption and generally ignore, or regard as peripheral, the moral circumstances, I argue that political corruption is fundamentally a *moral* problem; hence the subtitle "A Moral Pollution." Therefore I stress the need for what I call "commitmental moral revolution"—for fundamental (radical) changes in the attitudes and responses of the individual members of society to the moral values, principles, and ideals cherished by the society. In my view the moral is the ultimate, and therefore we must pay serious attention to matters of personal integrity and character.

In the longest chapter of the book, chapter 8, "Tradition and Modernity," I deal with a complex of issues. I open with an analytical discussion of the notion of tradition: what is tradition? I cast serious doubt on the widely accepted view of tradition as any cultural practice or value that has been "handed down" or "transmitted" from the past to a present, and I attempt to provide a new definition. I point out that the dichotomy between tradition and modernity cannot be well founded because there are many traditional elements inherited, cherished, and maintained by modernity. I also reject the view that tradition has an inherent authority, just as I reject the view of an invented tradition. In a discussion of different attitudes toward a cultural past, I argue against both the wholesale, uncritical, nostalgic acceptance of the past—of tradition—and the wholesale, offhanded rejection of it on the grounds that a cultural tradition, however "primitive," would have positive as well as negative features. The grounds of rejection or acceptance will have to be normative or practical. In a discussion of the relevance or irrelevance of the values, practices, and institutions spawned by the traditional African cultures to the modern situation, I point up, using the Akan experience as a paradigm, some of what I consider to be negative features of our African cultures: these include the traditional attitude toward science and technology and some aspects of the traditional social and moral practice, such as the inheritance system. The humanistic ethic—the ethic of concern for the welfare and needs of others—is among the features of the cultures I consider positive. In a discussion of the notion of modernity as held in Western societies that created it, I point out that some features of Western modernity may not be appropriate for African and perhaps other nonwestern societies and cultures. I emphasize the urgent need to pursue a critical reinterpretation and reevaluation of inherited cultural traditions.

In the concluding chapter, "Which Modernity? Whose Tradition?" I deal with the creation of modernity in Africa. I set out from the need to understand the whole process of "modernization" and argue that it would be wrong to equate modernization with Westernization, because modern or developed nonwestern cultures may not be enamored of all features of Western modernity. Thus, a monolithic conception of modernity is highly contestable. I suggest not only that it should be possible but also that it would be desirable to create a modernity appropriate to particular cultural traditions. From this standpoint, I suggest further that African modernity must creatively draw on Africa's complex cultural experience. I highlight the need to cultivate science and technology, including upgrading traditional technologies through the development of indigenous technological capacities, as a significant aspect in creating modernity in Africa. In this connection, I argue that the notion of the "transfer" or "transplant" of technology must be replaced by the notion of the "appropriation" of technology. The creation of modernity in Africa will also require radical changes in some of the old "things," if not their abandonment, as well as the maintenance and pursuit of those features of traditional culture—a number of them discussed here (and thus deferred from the previous chapter)—that may be regarded as positive and harmonious with the ethos of the contemporary culture. If African modernity is to endure and really to mean something to its practitioners, I conclude, it must be a *self-created* modernity—forged and refined in the furnace of conversations between African intellectual creativity and Africa's complex cultural heritage.

One final note: Because I consider the postcolonial experiences of the African people—experiences in dealing with problems attendant to transition to a new era or phase of development—to be largely common, I have made the whole of the sub-Saharan Africa (rather than a specific nation or region of it) the focus of my attention in this book. When it comes to practices of traditional African societies, however, I draw most of my examples from the traditional Akan society of Ghana. In the light of the multiplicity of African cultures and the diversities among them, one need not generalize the details and nuances of an idea or practice worked out within one cultural context for other cultures. Yet what may be true is that in many instances the different cultural forms or practices can be said to be essentially variations on the same theme. There is no denying that contiguous cultures do influence one another; and the cultures of dominant groups have influenced those of smaller groups. This is the reason why a number of scholars recognize the existence of common features or commonalities among the cultures of Africa. On the controversy over the use of the term "African," see my *An Essay on African Philosophical Thought: The Akan Conceptual Scheme,* rev. ed. (Philadelphia: Temple University Press, 1995), pp. xxiii–xxxii and 189–212. There is no denying the fact that the postcolonial experiences of the African people are largely common.

Acknowledgments

E ven though I wrote drafts of some of the chapters of this book before I went to the Woodrow Wilson International Center for Scholars, Smithsonian Institution, in Washington, D.C, in September 1993, I can say, nevertheless, that I wrote this book during the next twelve months when I held a fellowship at the center. Not only did I write the remaining chapters there, but I reworked the previously written drafts of some of the chapters there as well, in one of the most congenial and hospitable centers for academic work in the world. The coterie of world-renowned men and women of outstanding erudition that gathers there is indeed itself a great source of inspiration for a research scholar.

It is with the greatest pleasure, therefore, that I express my profound gratitude and appreciation to the Board of Trustees of the Woodrow Wilson Center for offering me a fellowship from September 1993 to August 1994 that enabled me to embark on the research for the publication of this book. Among the staff of the center who made my stay there most enjoyable and memorable, I wish to mention Charles Blitzer, the Director; Ann Sheffield, Director of Fellowships; James M. Morris, Director of the Division of Historical, Cultural, and Literary Studies (the division to which I belonged), and his assistant, Susan Nugent; Richard Cranston, the computer specialist of the center; Lindsay Collins, the receptionist; and Benjamin Arah (then a Lecturer in Philosophy at Howard University), who was my research assistant. I deeply appreciate the assistance of various kinds I received from them.

In bringing this book to its present form, I have benefited a great deal from the critical and penetrating comments and suggestions of a few people who were generous enough to find time to read and offer me their views on various chapters of the book in draft. At the Woodrow Wilson Center, Philip Selznick, a Co-Fellow and an Emeritus Professor of Sociology and Law at the University of California at Berkeley, discussed his written comments on chapter 2 with me, and so did Seymour M. Lipset, Senior Scholar at the center, with chapter 6. On chapter 2, I received detailed comments also from Eliot Deutsch (University of Hawaii), Will Kymlicka (University of Ottawa), Alasdair MacIntyre (University of Notre Dame), Stephen Mulhall (University of Essex, England), and Amitai Etzioni (George Washington University). The late Sir Ernest Gellner (Cambridge University and the Center for the Study of Nationalism, Central European University in Prague) sent me comments on chapter 3. Lawrence E. Cahoone (Boston University) offered comments on chapters 8 and 9. Following a public lecture at the University of Kansas based on chapter 3, I received written comments from Ann E. Cudd. I must also thank the two anonymous readers selected by Oxford University Press for their comments, queries, and suggestions.

Needless to say, I found these comments and suggestions extremely helpful: they not only compelled me to clarify and amplify my own position and hone some of my arguments but also directed my attention to other aspects of the subjects I was dealing with which I had either neglected or not given enough treatment to. I am deeply indebted to these distinguished scholars and philosophers.

I benefited tremendously from philosophical conversations I had regularly over a two-year period with Anita Allen, Professor of Law and Philosophy at Georgetown University Law Center, on some of the subjects discussed in this book.

I must also express my appreciation to my student Matthew McAdam, then an undergraduate senior at the University of Pennsylvania, who took my seminar "Ethnicity, Identity, and Nationhood" and also had an independent study with me on related subject matters and whose intelligent questions and insightful remarks at private tutorial sessions helped me to clarify portions of chapter 3.

Parts of chapters of the book were presented in public lectures: parts of chapter 3 were given in public lectures in several places, including the Institute of Philosophy and Public Policy, University of Maryland at College Park, Brown University, Haverford College, and the University of Kansas. Parts of chapter 2 were presented in a philosophy colloquium at the University of Pennsylvania. Parts of chapter 8 constituted the subject of the first Annual Humanities Lecture delivered to the Ghana Academy of Arts and Sciences in May 1993 under the title "Philosophical Inquiries into the Presence of the Past in the Present." The section on the notion of tradition was presented in public lectures at Temple and LaSalle Universities and at the University of Pennsylvania. I found the discussions that followed my presentations helpful, and I would like to record my gratitude to the various audiences.

But since this is *my* work, I alone am responsible for its shortcomings and defects, which merely reflect my own limitations.

I made the final revision of the manuscript when I was a Visiting Professor of Philosophy at the University of Pennsylvania during the 1995–96 academic year. I would like to express my gratitude and appreciation to Gary

Hatfield, Philosophy Department Chairman, who made the offer of appointment to me, and Sandra Barnes, Professor of Anthropology and Director of the African Studies Center at the university. They helped to make my stay at the University of Pennsylvania most worthwhile in terms of both teaching and research.

Finally, I wish to express my gratitude to Deborah A. Stuart, whose meticulous and competent copyediting of the final manuscript resulted in many stylistic improvements. At Oxford University Press, Cynthia A. Read, Executive Editor, and Robert Milks, Production Editor for this book, placed at my disposal their advice and rich experience in book production. I am most grateful to them both.

University of Ghana, Legon, Ghana   Kwame Gyekye, FGA
University of Pennsylvania, Philadelphia, Pa.

Contents

TRADITION
and MODERNITY

1

Philosophy and Human Affairs

The nature, purpose, methods, and relevance of philosophy are widely misunderstood. In consequence, philosophy has come to be burlesqued and travestied by most people outside this intellectual discipline. The misunderstanding or misconception has in some people matured into prejudice and resilient skepticism about the relevance of philosophy to public affairs in particular and human purposes in general. Philosophers have been charged with a preoccupation with abstract theoretical concerns, with elitism, apriorism, and uninvolvement in the practical affairs of life: philosophy has in fact been regarded by most nonphilosophers as the quintessence of ivory towerism and irrelevance. Thus, almost invariably, philosophy is the first discipline to be stretched on the Procrustean bed when budget directors consider cutting or withdrawing grants or subventions to university departments:[1] in many universities, particularly in Third World countries, philosophy as an academic discipline exists only marginally, if at all.

The primary cause of the misconception is widespread ignorance about the nature of philosophy and the past achievements that philosophy and philosophers through the influence of their work can be said to have made. While most people are aware of, and can identify, the subject matters of such generally distinct and fairly well defined social science disciplines as sociology, economics, and psychology and may even have some idea of what these disciplines have achieved and what they are capable of achieving, they are almost totally ignorant of the subject matter—whatever it is—of philosophy, of how, that is, this discipline is pursued or tackled, and what philosophy is ever capable of achieving, if anything. Hence the unrelenting cynicism or skepticism about the relevance of philosophy to the affairs and problems of human society. The skeptics are not, to be sure, unaware of the critical and analytical powers that the pursuit of the philosophical enterprise can develop in the individual who undertakes it. But to them these analytical powers are misapplied because they are not directed at grappling with the concrete and existential problems of human society. And so the skeptics repeatedly ask, what is the relevance of such intellectual powers and endowments to the needs and problems of humankind? Yet, even though the skeptics may disdain philosophical activity for being irrelevant, they are not necessarily scornful of philosophers as such; they tend in fact to respect the intellects of philosophers—to see philosophers as individual sages or wise persons. It may indeed be said that in all cultures, and throughout history, thinkers are given due respect and admiration; it is only that their intellectual pursuits are often supposed not to be germane to the negotiation of the practical problems of life.

The misconception of the relevance of philosophy to the problems of human life results also from the impression most philosophically untutored people have that the ideas and arguments of philosophy are incomprehensible. The seemingly technical, or perhaps esoteric, language in which the ideas and arguments of philosophers are generally expressed makes philosophy intellectually inaccessible to most people. In consequence, philosophy has come to be regarded by its critics as a cloistered intellectual enterprise that merely arouses the intellectual interest of its practitioners, who themselves are unable or find it difficult to climb over their intellectually cloistering walls and venture out into the extramural world of real life, where they might communicate their ideas and arguments to ordinary people. Those who are skeptical about the relevance of the philosophical enterprise are aware of the highly technical, professional, and esoteric language of science and economics, for instance; but they would quickly point out that, despite their recondite languages, these intellectual disciplines, unlike philosophy, have achieved practical results in the past and continue to do so in the present and thus have amply demonstrated their capabilities to achieve more in the future.

Some philosophers in the past were preoccupied with the vexing conundrums of language as an end in itself, narrowly interpreting or translating conceptual analysis—an outstanding feature of the philosophical enterprise—as no more than linguistic analysis. This is most probably what led A. R. Lacy, for instance, to make the following inaccurate assertion: "In particular, philosophy avoids using the senses and relies on reflection. It is an a priori study."[2] It is not true that philosophy entirely avoids the senses. If philosophy were a wholly a priori intellectual activity, then it would hardly bear any relation to human experience or the practical problems of human life. This conception of philosophy tends to impress it with marks of aridity and jejuneness and thus to confirm the charges that it is irrelevant.

In the foregoing, I have attempted, if briefly, to understand the nature and grounds of the criticisms and cynical attitudes taken by nonphilosophers regarding the relevance of the philosophical enterprise. But this is not intended to imply by any means that the criticisms and skepticisms are well grounded and sustainable. I have noted the ignorance of most nonphilosophers as a cause of the misconception of the purpose and relevance of this intellectual enterprise. I have noted also that some of the ways the enterprise has been conceived and executed in the past by several of its practitioners seem to have removed it from the theater of human affairs and practical concerns, making it an esoteric and cloistered enterprise with some arcane aims, doctrines, and methods accessible only to the initiate. My intention here, however, is to argue the *relevance* of the philosophical enterprise to human affairs and to the development of human culture with a brief clarification of the nature, purpose, and methods of philosophy and by indicating, with a historical overview, what this intellectual enterprise is capable of achieving. I hope to dispel the misconceptions that have befogged the relevance of the philosophical enterprise. I shall end with some thoughts on how philosophy can be considered relevant to an understanding and interpretation of the postcolonial world of Africa and how philosophy could be harnessed to help deal with its problems.

1. The Nature and Purpose of Philosophy

Even though philosophers, whether from the same culture or from different cultures, are not in complete agreement on the definition and methods of their discipline, a close examination of the nature and purpose of the intellectual activities of thinkers from various cultures and societies of the world reveals nevertheless that philosophy is essentially a critical and systematic inquiry into the fundamental ideas or principles underlying human thought, conduct, and experience. Ideas, which include the beliefs and presuppositions that we hold and cherish, relate to the various aspects of human experience: to the origins of the world, the existence of God, the nature of the good society, the basis of political authority, and so on. With regard to the human society, for instance, we would be right in saying that every human society consists of some arrangements and institutions—social, political, legal, and so on—established to meet the various needs of the society. These arrangements clearly are based on ideas, for we know they were not thoughtlessly established, nor did they occur randomly. The institution of punishment, for instance, is based on the assumption that human beings are free agents and are, therefore, free to choose their actions, and hence that they are morally responsible for those actions. The assumption of human free will upon which the ascription of both moral and legal responsibility is based is thus a fundamental assumption that can critically be—and in fact is—examined by philosophy. Thus, philosophy is essentially concerned with the critical inquiry into the most basic of our ideas, beliefs, and assumptions.

These ideas often appear in the form of issues and problems. That is to say, an idea may result from, or be wrapped up in, a problem; thus, problems generate philosophical speculation. Philosophical problems about political obligation might arise because some citizens raised questions about the conditions under which they should obey their government that could not be satisfactorily answered; problems about knowledge, human free will, moral conflicts, and death and immortality might arise because someone raised questions that could not be adequately answered. Philosophy grapples with problems such as these, problems that cannot be solved by empirical methods, even though they have their origin in human experience. I am certain that no rational being could quarrel with philosophy's concern with clarifying and critically appraising our fundamental ideas or rationally disentangling basic human problems; for such an enterprise, if successful, could form the basis of a satisfactory way of life. For instance, the knowledge that our actions are free or not free is relevant to the question of the justifiability or unjustifiability of the ascription of responsibility. Philosophy thus invites us to be self-critical and to know what things are most worthwhile. If the skeptics and critics seriously considered these purposes of philosophy, perhaps they would not subject it to so much questioning.

Although these same skeptics and critics may consider it appropriate and useful to seriously examine the fundamental ideas that shape and influence our lives and to rationally unravel basic human problems, philosophy, to them, deals with abstract matters, and so philosophical activity, they erroneously infer, is unrelated to the practical concerns of humankind, concerns that are concrete and specific. It is, indeed, part of the method of philosophy to operate at an abstract level, but the conclusion that has been drawn from this by nonphilosophers is misguided. The abstract level at which the philosopher operates is perhaps unavoidable inasmuch as philosophical questions are very often general. Whenever two people—they may not even be trained philosophers as such—are disputing about whether or not a particular action of their government was just or democratic, and one of them, perhaps wanting to be clearer about the concepts involved in the dispute, asks: "what is justice?" (or "what is it to be just?") or "what is democracy?" (or "what is it to be democratic?"), he would be raising a philosophical question. And, if both of them attempted to answer the question in a sustained manner, they would immediately and necessarily involve themselves in abstract thinking, aimed at clarifying some concepts, an activity that might well prove helpful to the resolution of the dispute. And so it is that the abstract level at which the philosopher operates is intended to offer her a vantage point from which to beam her analytical searchlight on the inarticulate and woolly beliefs and thoughts of people. So that the abstract reflections of the philosopher need not—should not—detract from the relevance and value of the philosophical enterprise in the search for answers to at least some of the problems of human society.

Perhaps the most outstanding method of philosophy is reflection. But we must try to understand what the reflective process is or involves. What does the philosopher reflect on, pure concepts or general human experience? And how does reflection proceed? I think that the point of departure of philosophical reflection is the whole gamut of human experience: fears, desires, beliefs, conduct, thoughts, observations, institutions, hopes and aspirations, failures and successes, problems and enigmas of life, and so on. On this showing, the reflective analysis—and hence the philosophical enterprise—cannot dispense with experience. This is not to say, however, that philosophical problems and issues can be solved by empirical methods, for no amount of observation can determine whether or not the universe has a purpose and whether, and in what sense, human beings have free will; it is not to say either that philosophy directly derives its conclusions from experience or observation. What it means, rather, is that philosophy raises fundamental and profound questions *about* experience in order to explore its meaning and construct from it a synthetic and coherent picture of ultimate reality. The position taken here is at variance with a widely held view that philosophy is a wholly a priori intellectual activity—as suggested, for instance, in the quotation from Lacy, an activity that can be pursued prior to, and hence can dispense with, experience. Here I make a distinction between a philosophical concept, such as justice or free will, and a logical concept, such as validity or consistency: it is the logical concept that may in some sense be said to be a priori, based purely on the activity of the mind, despite the fact that it derives from certain features of language—and language is a social fact.

The critical and systematic examination of the fundamental ideas underlying human experience, involving the clarification of those ideas, is usually referred to as conceptual analysis. Many twentieth-century philosophers in the West regard conceptual analysis as the main task of philosophy. It is undoubtedly the most important and fundamental aspect of the philosophical enterprise inasmuch as the other important approach to philosophy, the speculative or substantive (normative), depends on it, as the elements of the latter approach would need to have been given prior clarification. Thus, the quality of the speculative approach presupposes considerable attention to the analytic. For this reason, speculative philosophers necessarily give adequate attention to conceptual analysis.

Conceptual analysis, as such, cannot be undertaken entirely in isolation from some social or cultural or political or intellectual context. It can most satisfactorily be pursued within some sociocultural context and with reference to that context; it is in fact inspired by that context. One cannot analyze the concept of justice or liberty, for instance, without taking into consideration a whole range of human experience—experience that has allowed us to observe what constitutes human nature, what political systems are or ought to be, and what suffering or inhuman treatment governments or public officials have caused or meted out to individuals or groups; experience that has allowed us to gain empirical knowledge of societal problems; and experience that has filled us with yearnings to see put in place the necessary social arrangements that would allow everyone to fully realize his or her potential as a human being—all this and more comes into play in the analysis of such a concept as justice. Thus, philosophical or conceptual analysis cannot be undertaken in a social or cultural or historical vacuum; it has an experiential background and connections. This is not to imply by any means that philosophical analysis is an empirical inquiry; analysis includes a rigorous form of reasoning, which is an a priori activity. What all this means, then, is that there is a dynamic practical relationship between the a priori and the empirical, within the framework of the enterprise of conceptual analysis; one is indispensable to the other.

This is the reason I find a great virtue in W. V. O. Quine's rejection of the analytic-synthetic distinction.[3] This rejection is also a rejection of the distinction between the conceptual and the factual (empirical) and results in the subversion of the conception of philosophy as a purely second-order, a priori intellectual activity. Quine's thesis can be exploited to support my conception of conceptual analysis, and of the nature of philosophy itself. It is a conception that makes the philosophical enterprise relevant to the concerns and problems of humankind. But, remember, it is a conception of philosophy that has been held and practiced by most philosophers of the Western tradition from Socrates on: the essential task of philosophy is to speculate critically about human experience with its many-sidedness, including the experience we have in using language. Thus, for me—and judging from the content of their works, for many others—it would be an oversimplification to consider philosophy or philosophical analysis a purely and wholly a priori intellectual activity.

It is true that a great number of the philosophical problems that have exercised the minds of thinkers with different linguistic and cultural backgrounds arise from human experiences, a great part of which may be said to be common to humankind, while some others arise from the fact that human beings live in communities and share desires, aspirations, lifestyles, and life projects. In dealing with such problems—anchored as they really are in human experience—attention will necessarily have to be paid to experience, if the conclusions of conceptual or philosophical pursuits are to be relevant to the resolution of some of the issues and problems facing human society.

2. Philosophy: Not a System of Beliefs?

Wittgenstein claims that "philosophy is not a body of doctrine but an activity."[4] Brenda Almond claims that philosophy is "not a system of beliefs," and that it must be regarded "as a method rather than as a system of beliefs."[5] And Gilbert Ryle observes that "philosophy is not adherence to a tenet or membership of a church or party. It is exploration. Only a Terra Incognita is interesting."[6] The view that philosophy is not a system of beliefs is another widely held view of the nature of the discipline. It is this view that I would like to examine in this section. The key phrases in the statements quoted above are "a body of doctrine," "a system of beliefs," and "adherence to a tenet." I take it that they all mean the same thing roughly, and that their authors, along with many others, share a common view of the nature or mission of the philosophical enterprise. But what is really meant by saying that philosophy is not a system of beliefs?

Ryle's reference to "membership of a church or party" provides a clue to understanding the meaning of his statement. In religion there is a well-organized or established corpus of doctrines or beliefs that, once enunciated, not only attain the status of orthodoxy, but also, in the wake of that reason, ossify into a monolithic doctrinal unity, exercising a powerful influence on the life and thought of the religion's adherents or devotees and holding them captive perhaps for life. Politics or ideology may induce similar attitudes in the members of a political party, attitudes that may result in a serious and perhaps lifelong commitment to specific political or ideological beliefs, a commitment that may in turn cause each party member to defend those beliefs tooth and nail, to resist any seemingly far-reaching changes in them, and perhaps to fight and die in their cause. Ryle sees religion and political ideology as exhibiting similar characteristics, evoking similar attitudes in their adherents. Ryle's main intention is of course to point out that there is a strong contrast between religion and political ideology on one hand and philosophy on the other hand. The contrast is that while religion and political ideology may hold the individual devotee or adherent in thrall—and perhaps for life—philosophy does not do so for its practitioners. And while there is a substantial element of tenacity and dogmatism in religious and political (or ideological) commitments, there is none, or very little of that, in philosophical pursuits.

Let me say, parenthetically, however, that it seems to me that there is an element of exaggeration in the claim about the unrelenting or lifelong commitment to religious beliefs. For there are cases of some members of a church or religious faith abjuring their original faith and taking up new ones altogether: cases of Christians converting to Islam or Hinduism or Buddhism; Muslims converting to Christianity or Buddhism; adherents of these religions abandoning their faith altogether and becoming atheists or agnostics. New religious sects, with different doctrines, which proliferate in most societies of the world, draw their membership mostly from already existing religions. So that, even within the territory of religious people, that is, some individuals, do "travel" (to use Ryle's word): commitment in this territory is not as unrelenting as it might be supposed. Similar features may be seen of political or ideological beliefs: the fate that has befallen Marxism or Communism in the last few years, and the well-known phenomenon of individuals moving from one political party to another in democratic political communities—these are clear cases that involve ideological "travels." But, having said all this, I think one has to grant that the contrast Ryle intends to establish between philosophy and religion and political ideology is real to a very large extent. I think that the inebriation often induced by religious faith in its adherents, the petrified commitment often demonstrated by people in regard to religious beliefs, and the emotional and even bellicose responses generated by serious challenges to those beliefs have no parallels in philosophy. In the latter intellectual enterprise, the immediate awareness of the need for rational response introduces intellectual sobriety rather than physical or emotional belligerency.

To grant the appropriateness of the contrast between religious and philosophical beliefs is not, however, to deny by any means, as others are wont to do, that philosophers do demonstrate commitment to their ideas, beliefs, and arguments. Ryle, for instance, thinks that "we have to renounce the supposition that Plato was the lifelong warder or prisoner of a tenet. Plato *travelled*."[7] Elsewhere he says that "we have to recognize that Plato's thought *moved*."[8] The implications of Ryle's assertion that Plato traveled—intellectually, of course—and that his thought moved are that Plato was not intellectually sclerotic, that he made progress in his philosophical travels (hence Ryle's title, *Plato's Progress*), and that he never thought of establishing a philosophy that was to be a system of beliefs to be cordoned off and warded against the logic and persuasiveness of new or future intellectual discoveries or superior arguments either of his own or of other thinkers. Yet it may be true that one can intellectually travel a long distance without necessarily jettisoning the ideas or beliefs seriously held in the early days of one's philosophical journey. It all depends, of course, on how persuasive or compelling one's earlier intellectual or philosophical positions were, how seamless the previous arguments. Progress is not necessarily achieved by a total abandonment of previous intellectual positions; it could be achieved, rather, by building on previous positions, or refining them. And when Ryle says that philosophy is an "exploration," it must be noted that the explorer hopes to achieve something substantial: to explore a problem is not merely to clarify or analyze it but, more important, to search for a solution to it; to explore a territory is to try to discover something—something substantial.

It would be instructive to know what individual philosophers say late in their philosophical careers about their attitudes toward doctrines they had held earlier. Quine, in his autobiography written well toward the end of his very active philosophical career, makes frequent references to "my philosophy."[9] He says that at some public lectures held in Oxford on mind and language, he observed that other speakers were dwelling so much on his work that he thought, "I might do better to present a more central statement of *my* philosophical position."[10] And, as if to affirm a celebrated doctrine of his, propounded thirty-five years earlier, he states: "My challenge of the boundary between analytic and synthetic statements is notorious, and I have been *at pains* to blur the boundaries between natural science, mathematics, and philosophy."[11] In the autobiography the eminent American philosopher admits giving lectures on the same themes; he presumably presented the same ideas. This fact can be taken to imply that Quine was, to use Ryle's expression, a "warder" of his doctrines. Surely any philosopher who constantly talks of "*my* philosophy" must mean to imply a commitment to the ideas and doctrines of his philosophy.

All philosophers in their philosophical exertions aim at dealing with an issue or a problem or set of issues or problems. They think and hope that

they have, or can spawn, ideas and can advance arguments that will clarify
the issues and so help in their resolution. In all this, the ultimate aim is to
search for truths about the issues involved. They deploy arguments and evi-
dences of various kinds in search of the truth as they see it. In response to
fresh ideas and arguments derived either from their own further reflections
or from examining those of others, they may refine and prune in the course
of their philosophical sojourns: all this in pursuit of the truth. We would be
right in saying, however, that there are cases of total rejection of previous
philosophical ideas or arguments by their authors; but there are also cases
of refinement and improvement on previous ideas or positions. All philosophers have unflagging commitments to truth about the specific issues of
their philosophical concerns. If this were not so, what would be the point of
the elaborate and complicated arguments philosophers incessantly put forward? Sooner or later, philosophers become convinced of the correctness of
their ideas and the validity of their arguments, and, a fortiori, of the truths
embodied in those arguments. At this point, then, it may be said that their
reflective exertions have resulted in a body of assertible truths. Others may
become convinced of those truths. It is these truths or convictions that in
due course distill into 'isms': thus, Platonism, Aristotelianism, Kantianism,
Marxism, and so on, these 'isms' referring specifically to the philosophical
doctrines of celebrated individual philosophers. Thus, if someone calls himself a Platonist or Kantian, what he means, surely, is that he is convinced of
the truths he sees in Plato's or Kant's philosophy, that he has come under
the spell of that philosophy and has, consequently, become its adherent or
disciple, even though he may not necessarily be taken in by all aspects of
Platonism or Kantianism. In the light of the existence of philosophical adherents to an accepted body of truths that may be said to be embodied in
the philosophies of some individual thinkers, it would not be wrong to claim
that philosophy is in some sense a *system of belief*, even though the nature
of belief here will not be the same as that of a belief in a religious or ideological system.

Moreover, the history of philosophy acquaints us with such phenomena
as neo-Platonism, neo-Aristotelianism, neo-Thomism, neo-Kantianism, and
neo-Hegelianism. Now, what are these neo-isms? And what is the relevance
of the existence of such phenomena to the pursuers of the philosophical
enterprise? It would be correct, I think, to say that the neo-isms are new
forms of the old 'isms', that their starting points are the old 'isms', that
they are (therefore) based on them, and that, consequently, they are greatly
influenced or inspired by the old isms. Neo-isms may, therefore, be said to
be interpretations and developments on the erstwhile philosophical 'isms' of
individual philosophers: to invert the old biblical expression, neo-isms can
be said to be essentially the old wine in new wine bottles. It would not be
wrong, then, to claim that there is a basic intellectual or doctrinal affiliation
between a neo-ism and an old 'ism'.

In Antony Flew's view: "the passages in *The Republic* about the Forms of
the Good have had a remarkable influence. It was from them that Plotinus

in the 200's of our era derived the central notion of the philosophy which was later to become known as Neo-Platonism, and the ideas of Plotinus for centuries played a part in shaping the intellectual traditions first of Christianity and then of Islam." [12] And a foremost scholar of ancient philosophical tradition says of neo-Platonism, "The movement itself was regarded by its exponents as the direct continuation of Platonic thought. To themselves and to their contemporaries these men appeared simply as Platonists." [13] And, according to A. H. Armstrong, "Platonism in the second and early third centuries A.D. was very much alive, and by no means merely stereo-typed and superficial: and the thought of Plotinus in many ways continued along lines laid down by his predecessors." [14] Now, to be so influenced or inspired by the ideas and arguments set out in a philosophical system as to embark on interpretations of them—interpretations that generally turn out to be positive, favorable, and supportive and are thus intended to extend, amplify, or deepen the understanding of that system—is to accept or believe quite firmly in those philosophical ideas (for a radical rejection of Platonism, for instance, will surely not result in neo-Platonism). Whether the acceptance or belief is going to be lifelong or not depends on both the profundity and the logical force of those ideas and arguments and on the intellectual outlook of the individual philosopher or group of philosophers concerned. It is perhaps undeniable that there have been some Marxists or neo-Marxists whose beliefs in the doctrines of Karl Marx were lifelong. It is, also, possible for some philosophers who are tremendously enamored of the ideas of the Absolute One, of the Divine, of the immortal soul, of the mysteries of the postmundane world, and of conceptions of life uncluttered by the impurities of the sensible or sensual world to entertain a lifelong belief in the philosophy of Plato and of neo-Platonism, or some important aspects of them. In all this, the inclinations, orientations, intuitions, outlooks, and, if you like, natures of the individual philosopher are very relevant. It would, therefore, be an oversimplification to assert with confidence that philosophy is not at all a system of belief.

Related to neo-isms in philosophy are other phenomena with which the literature is replete; these are known or referred to as philosophical traditions. We read or know of the liberal tradition, the analytic tradition, the empiricist tradition, the pragmatist tradition of American philosophy, and so on. What are these traditions, and what do they add to the idea of philosophy as a system of beliefs? It can be said at once that, as traditions, they must have been not only bequeathed by previous generations of philosophers but also accepted, maintained, and cherished by subsequent generations of philosophers (see chapter 8). A generation receives a corpus of philosophical doctrines from a previous one, derives from it what it considers worthwhile, maintains and refines it, and then hands it on to the next generation. The corpus of philosophical doctrines thus received influences, or is allowed to influence, the intellectual and other aspects of the lives of the members of the receiving generation. The corpus of the doctrines received— that is, those philosophical traditions—would have long been abandoned if they had not been accepted by successive generations as a body of doctrine that they consider worthwhile adhering to. It would thus be correct to consider some philosophical doctrines that in the course of time constitute themselves into a philosophical tradition as constitutive of a system of belief as well. Human beings do believe in traditions when they have convinced themselves of the worth of those traditions, cherish them, and allow them to influence their lives. On this showing, believing in a philosophical tradition may be equivalent to taking that tradition as a system of belief.

I think there is yet another way of characterizing the notion that philosophy is not a system of belief. A system of belief, like a system of religious belief, is such as would influence and guide individuals or groups of individuals or generations of people in their lives. Can philosophy provide *such* a system of belief? One celebrated view of philosophy held by philosophers and hallowed and elevated to the status of a testament is the view that philosophy is an activity, a pursuit, as it is asserted in an already quoted statement of Wittgenstein's. The view that philosophy is an (intellectual) activity goes back in the Western tradition to Socrates. The activity is the activity of rational examination and analysis of human thought and action with a view clearly to understanding them or coming to have self-knowledge of them; it is an activity of search and of raising questions, challenging assumptions and beliefs hitherto held as true or taken for granted. The position of some twentieth-century philosophers in the West has been that clarity of thought is all that is required of philosophy. It is not the business of philosophy to establish a system of well-laundered and definite doctrines to guide people in their lives; nor is it its business to prescribe ways of life: it is only to point up alternative courses of action for choice by the individual. Many philosophers, however, including the ancient Greek philosophers Socrates, Plato, and Aristotle, have held, or at least implied, that clarity or elucidation cannot—must not—constitute the terminus, the cul-de-sac of the philosophical activity, and that philosophy can offer more for the life of the individual and for human society and its affairs.

Socrates tenaciously maintained that "the unexamined life is not worth living." [15] In the thought of Socrates, the only life that is worthwhile for human beings or human society is the life whose basis and goals have been thoroughly and critically examined, searched out. It is therefore the task of philosophy to subject our lives—our ideas, beliefs, actions, values, and goals—to serious critical examination if we should be what we want to be and know what things are most worthwhile for our lives. In proclaiming that philosophers should be kings, Plato was alluding to the application of theoretical wisdom to practical human affairs. And Aristotle described as the aim of his investigations into moral phenomena a similar application: "we are inquiring not in order to know what virtue is (that is not just to understand the meaning of virtue), but in order to *become good*, since *otherwise our inquiry would have been of no use.*" [16]

A number of contemporary moral philosophers, however, insist that they should confine their activity to metaethics, that is, to the analysis of the language of morals, the elucidation of moral terms and the logical structure of moral reasoning and moral judgment, maintaining that it is not their business to suggest how people ought to live their lives. But by refusing to pursue the practical implications of their ethical inquiries, metaethicists—but not normative moral philosophers—merely scotch the snake, and, thus, perform an incomplete act. The analysis of moral concepts is an important pursuit, to be sure; but to shy away from making prescriptions or normative suggestions to guide people in their lives is to hide our philosophical lights under a bushel. After all, a good number of the questions philosophers raise involve substantive issues of human experience. If theologians, sociologists, psychologists, social workers, and others feel they have the warrant to offer moral recommendations or advice to guide people in their lives, then philosophers, professionally given to making profound and critical examination into various aspects of human nature and the basic principles of human action, could make the claim of having insight into morals sufficient to provide them with some justifiable basis for offering moral prescriptions, and for passing moral judgments on human conduct. Similarly, even though philosophers operate within cultural frameworks and their thoughts may be said to be influenced by their cultures, they can, and often do, make criticisms of those frameworks on normative and other grounds.

Humanism, a philosophy to which human interests and purposes are central, is certainly a system of beliefs tenaciously adhered to by those who see it as offering a guide to the lives of individual human beings. According to one of the outstanding exponents of the humanist philosophy, Corliss Lamont, there are "ten central propositions in the Humanist philosophy." He goes on to describe the doctrines in which humanism *believes,* using the phrases "believes in" and "Humanism believes that." [17] It is a philosophical system put forward, argued, and defended by philosophers of different intellectual outlooks and persuasions. Only a truncated or impoverished conception of philosophy would deny that humanism *is* a philosophical system.

Before I conclude this section of the chapter, I would like to make some observations on Wittgenstein's characteristically aphoristic statement, "The philosopher is not a citizen of any community of ideas. That is what makes him into a philosopher." [18] This statement might turn out to be at variance with the views I have expressed in the immediately preceding paragraphs. But we must first determine the meaning of the first part of the statement, which is not very obvious. It may mean that the philosopher must be radically detached from the ideas, beliefs, or presuppositions of his society if he is to pursue his intellectual activities effectively. If this is what the statement means, then it can be supported, for if insight and objective truth are to be achieved by philosophical analysis, the philosopher must be detached, even though he operates within a cultural setting. But if this is indeed the correct interpretation of the statement, as Michael Walzer in fact thinks,[19] then the statement is innocuous and would, in fact, be on all fours with the accepted methodological approaches of the philosopher.

I think Wittgenstein means something more radical than this interpretation suggests. The notion of "citizen" in the statement is quite suggestive of Wittgenstein's intentions. If we take it that a citizen is someone who generally accepts the values, beliefs, practices, and institutions of his community, one who is involved in, and committed to, the pursuit and promotion of those values and practices and shares many things (values, beliefs, etc.) with other members of his community, we would have some insight into what Wittgenstein might mean by his statement. By saying that the philosopher is *not* a citizen of any community of ideas, he probably means: (1) that the philosopher is not committed to any body of ideas, (2) that he does not (have to) share any ideas with others, and (3) that, in consequence, he is so radically detached from his cultural or intellectual milieu that his ideas are unique and idiosyncratic to him, bearing no relation whatever to those of his community of thinkers, past and present. If this last interpretation of Wittgenstein's statement is correct, then, the statement is, in my view, in the extreme, and would not, perhaps for that reason, be entirely true. For even though it can be conceded that a philosopher can break new ground, spawn new ideas, and critically reevaluate received ideas, this fact, nevertheless, does not detract from the idea of a philosophical tradition or philosophical discipleship, or the idea of neo-isms in philosophy that we noted as clear phenomena in the history of philosophy. The idea of philosophical traditions would not make sense if a philosopher's ideas and arguments were not shared, followed up, maintained mutatis mutandis by a new generation of philosophers and then handed on to another generation; if, that is to say, there were no philosophers who were *fellow citizens of a community of ideas.*

To conclude this section, then: the view that philosophy is not a system of beliefs must be explored (1) from the perspective of the individual philosopher's commitment, or lack of it, to her philosophical ideas or doctrines; and (2) from the perspective of the extensive and enduring currency and influence gained by the ideas or doctrines of an individual philosopher that may eventually result in a philosophical tradition (e.g., Kantian or Platonic tradition) influencing the thoughts and perhaps the actions of those under the spell of that tradition. Even though an individual philosopher may not be totally immersed in the ideas or doctrines that may issue from her philosophical reflections, as adherents to religion usually are with religious doctrines, nevertheless, she does frequently demonstrate some enduring commitment to at least some of those ideas and arguments that she may, with compelling reasons, see as embodying some truths, truths that she is almost always prepared intellectually to defend. And to the extent that those truths may form the basis of a moral, social, political, and intellectual life, they may be regarded as constituting a system of beliefs. And so it can be maintained that philosophy provides people with a fundamental system of beliefs to live by.

It may be the self-effacing diffidence or a sense of modesty or an oversimplification of the mission of that enterprise that makes many philosophers shy away from making explicit conclusions implicit in their philosophical arguments that will offer rational and practical guidance on questions of individual action or public policy. But the reticence displayed by some philosophers about the direct consequences of their enterprise on life does not in any way detract from the worth of that enterprise as a system of beliefs.

3. Philosophy as a Conceptual Response to Human Situations

I would now like to undertake a discussion of a very important aspect of the philosophical enterprise, which unmistakably gives the lie to the view of that enterprise as an ivory tower intellectual pursuit, unrelated to the practical problems and concerns of human society. This aspect reveals philosophy as a conceptual response to human situations or basic human problems that arise in any given human society in a given era. And I would start off by briefly examining the significance of the celebrated allegory of the cave in Plato's undoubtedly most well-known philosophical dialogue, *the Republic.* For the allegory is illustrative of how the intellectual ascent, beginning in the world of the ordinary human being, toward the attainment of philosophical knowledge or understanding or appreciation or insight is (to be) followed by a *return* to that world for the purpose not only of enlightening its inhabitants but also of helping to deal with concrete problems thereof, such as the problem of ruling.

3.1. The Return to the Cave

In the allegory,[20] Plato supposes human beings to be living as prisoners in an underground cave and chained in such a way that they see only what is in front of them, which consists of images or shadows of material objects cast on the wall of the cave by firelight behind them. Their situation makes them accept as true or real the shadows or appearances they perceive before them. The system of the cave, Plato says, describes the general human condition in matters of education (or enlightenment) and knowledge. He invites us to suppose that one of the prisoners is released and made to stand up and turn his head around and walk toward the light. Initially the released prisoner displays some misgivings about the reality of the new things he is perceiving in his "liberated" condition. In further ascent from the cave, however, the former prisoner becomes gradually habituated to the world outside the cave, reconsiders the condition of the cave from the outside, is now able to distinguish shadows from realities more easily, and considers himself happy and his fellow prisoners pitiful. If the released prisoner descended again into the cave and delivered his opinion on those shadows (i.e., the unrealities, superficialities, of their circumstances), he would be misunderstood and even ridiculed. Plato then explains that the prison dwelling, that is, the cave, corresponds to the region revealed to us through the senses, in this particular case the sense of sight; while the ascent to see the things in the upper world represents the upward journey of the mind into the region of the intelligible, the world of Forms (or, Ideas), which, in the epistemology of the *Republic,* constitute the objects of knowledge.

It would have been natural or expected that, having been released from their intellectual thralldom and set on the pursuit of pure philosophical knowledge and contemplation, the released prisoners, that is, the philosophers, would be reluctant to return to sully themselves with the life of the society of the cave—a life characterized by ignorance, unrealities, superficialities, material impurities, and lack of enlightenment—but would prefer instead to remain on the heights, in ivory towers, in order to enjoy a purely intellectual life uncluttered by the unfortunate and shallow circumstances of the cave society. But Plato denies them the pure life of philosophical contemplation unrelated to, having no impact on, the practical affairs of society. Plato does aver, rather, that, having looked upon the Form of the Good, which, according to him, is the highest object of knowledge, the philosophers (i.e., the released prisoners) "must not be allowed, as they now are, to *remain on the heights,* refusing to come down again to the prisoners or to take part in their labors and rewards, however much or little these may be worth."[21] And, as if he were exhortatively addressing philosophers, Plato asserts:

> [Y]ou have been better and more thoroughly educated than those others and hence you are more capable of playing your part both as men of *thought* and as men of *action. You must go down, then, each in his turn, to live with the rest and let your eyes grow accustomed to the darkness. You will then see a thousand times better than those who live there always; you will recognize every image for what it is and know what it represents, because you have seen justice, beauty, goodness in their reality.*[22]

Plato in this passage is emphatic that, having attained knowledge and truths about the nature of human society and its values, the philosophers must *return* to the cave, the world of the ordinary nonphilosopher, and participate in the organization of its affairs. They will, in due course, "grow accustomed to the darkness" of that world and thus get acquainted with its defects, its problems, and the unrealistic ways by which its affairs are executed; they will, thus, be in the position to introduce light (i.e., enlightenment) into that "dark" world. Plato is deeply concerned about the welfare of the society as a whole, a welfare the attainment of which, he thinks, can be bolstered by applying the theoretical insights of the philosopher to matters of public policy: "You have forgotten again, my friend, that the law is not concerned to make any one class specially happy, but to ensure the welfare of the commonwealth as a whole." He adds, almost immediately, that the "purpose in forming men of that (philosophical) spirit was not that each should be left to go his own way, but that they be *instrumental* in binding the community into one."[23] For this reason, argues Plato, "there will be no real injustice in compelling our philosophers to watch over and care for other citizens."[24]

For Plato, then, philosophical knowledge and insight should benefit the society as a whole, not the philosophers personally. The message of the allegory of the cave is so important to Plato that later, after the main passage on the cave, he reverts to it.

> For after that they must be sent down again into that Cave we spoke of and compelled to take military commands and other offices suitable to the young, so that they may not be behind their fellow citizens in experience. . . . [T]hose who have come safely through and proved the best at all points in action and in study must be brought at last to the goal. They must lift up the eye of the soul to gaze on that which sheds light on all things; and when they have seen the Good itself, take it *as a pattern for the right ordering of the state and of the individual,* themselves included.[25]

The message of the allegory embodied specifically in the return of the released prisoners to the cave is pretty clear: philosophical wisdom and insight should be applied to the practical problems of human society. Our philosophical lights should not be hidden under a bushel; they should, rather, be used to illuminate—and hence dispel—the woolly and inarticulate thoughts of human beings and the beliefs, practices, and institutions that derive therefrom: thus, Plato regards the philosopher as a guide. It is certainly not part of Plato's message that the philosopher, even though he or she engages in abstract thought, should permanently remain at that (abstract) level without relating his or her thought to the concrete world of human problems. The philosopher should not ignore the sensible world but should take interest in it. Plato regards the ascent from the cave (i.e., the sensible, practical world) not at all as a way of getting away from it without looking back on it but as a way of searching for a vantage point from where a better view can be taken of it, and a better or deeper analysis made of its problems.

We must remember that prior to the philosophical ascent, the philosopher was already acquainted with, and involved in, the experiences of the life of the society and cannot be said to be oblivious to those experiences, even though he is (now) 'poised aloft' philosophically. The return to the cave signifies the dynamic relationship that, according to Plato, ought to exist between philosophy and human or societal affairs, the intelligible and the sensible, the world of thought and the world of action, between theory and practice, analysis and synthesis. It can thus be concluded that Plato eschews ivory towerism, or "remaining on the heights," as he puts it in his dialogue. The allegory of the cave is a clear case of a metaphysical odyssey that ends up by demonstrating concerns for the practical affairs of society, a metaphysical (abstract) soaring that descends mainly for the purpose of illuminating the ideas of human beings and thus the concrete facts of life based thereon.

3.2 Conceptual Analysis and Human Affairs: A Historical Overview

Now if one were to examine the cultural and historical setting of the intellectual focus, concerns, and direction of the individual thinker, one would be convinced, beyond doubt, that philosophy is a conceptual response to the basic human problems that arise in any given society in a given epoch. Such an examination would reveal that philosophers grapple at the conceptual level with problems and issues of their times, even though this does not mean that the relevance of their ideas, insights, arguments, and conclusions is to be tethered to those times; for, more often than not, the relevance of their insights and arguments—or at least some of them—transcends the confines of their own times and cultures and, thus, can be embraced by other cultures or societies or different generational epochs. In other words, a philosophical doctrine may be historical, that is, generated originally in response to some historical events or circumstances, without our having to look on it as historicistic, without our having to confine its significance simply to those times of history when it was actually produced. (I shall in due course indicate a reason for the transcultural, transgenerational, and transepochal relevance of philosophical insights and doctrines.) But the fact that the philosophers who produced the ideas and arguments were giving conceptual response and attention to the experiences of their times needs to be stressed and constantly borne in mind: it was the problems of the times that constituted the points of departure for their reflective analyses, just as it was the problems and experiences of the society of the cave that, remember, initiated the philosophical ascent from the cave. We are told in fact that "Plato meant the dialogues to apply to the problems of his own time."[26] In this section, I intend to embark on a historical overview of how the philosophical concerns and arguments—and hence conceptual analyses—were engendered and influenced by the problems and issues of their times.

G. C. Field, in his study of life and thought in ancient Greece in the fourth century B.C., makes the following noteworthy observations: "Plato grew up in a period when the established order and accepted standards seemed on the verge of dissolution under the pressure of political events and theoretical criticism. . . . [H]e turned to philosophical speculation as the only direction from which help might come. From one point of view, indeed, the chief aim of Plato's philosophy may be regarded as the attempt to re-establish standards of thought and conduct for a civilization that seemed on the verge of dissolution."[27] It would most probably be true to say that Plato's theory of Forms (or Ideas)—the warp and woof of his philosophical system—was his theoretical approach to dealing with the crisis of values occasioned by the intellectual, moral, and political situations of the contemporary society. Even though the thrust of Plato's philosophical speculations was generally metaphysical (thus, the theory of Forms was essentially a metaphysical theory, that is, a theory about reality or being), its ultimate aim, nevertheless, was the search for standards (Greek: *paradeigmata*) in social, ethical, aesthetic, political, and epistemological matters with a view to reforming society.

It may be said that Plato's excoriation of democracy in the *Republic* resulted from his interpretative analysis of his observations and experiences of the politics of Athens during the Peloponnesian war between Athens and Sparta. The war is said to have broken out in 431 B.C. and to have ended in 404 B.C. Plato was born in 427 B.C., that is, four years after the outbreak of the war. Thus the first twenty-three years of his life were lived in times of war, political instability, and uncertainty. Athens, Plato's city-state, was constantly being defeated in the various battles of the war, the result, as Plato saw it, of the confusion and weakness of the 'democratic' form of government, where 'democracy', the rule of the people, was practiced in accordance with the literal meaning of the term. Plato thought that it was the rule *(krateia)* of the people *(demos)* that had led to the bitter experiences of Athens, and there was therefore some justification to revolt against democracy. For him, governing is a science better left to the experts, just as navigation or practicing medicine should better be left to sailors or doctors. Democracy, as Plato understood it, is a rejection of science in government. Hence, his advocacy of the rule by the philosopher-kings, the rule of the intelligentsia, in his famous proclamation:

> Unless either philosophers become kings in their countries or those who are now called kings and rulers come to be sufficiently inspired with a genuine desire for wisdom; unless, that is to say, political power and philosophy meet together . . . there can be no rest from troubles for states, nor yet, as I believe, for all mankind; nor can this commonwealth which we have imagined ever till then see the light of day and grow to its full stature.[28]

Plato denies that it is "conceivable that the multitude [i.e., the people] should ever believe in the existence of any real essence, as distinct from its many manifestations." For this reason, "the multitude can never be philosophical."[29] It is only the philosopher, who has knowledge of essences (i.e., the Forms), not just the many particular sensible things, who should rule. Even though Plato's advocacy of rule by the intelligentsia can hardly be justified, what I am really concerned to point out is the fact that his thesis takes its rise from, and is influenced by, the peculiar circumstances of his society. Plato was giving conceptual response to the problems of government in his day.

Aristotle's work on moral and political philosophy was a conceptual response to the events and beliefs of his time. In his moral inquiries, Aristotle makes the current views about what happiness or virtue is his starting point: "It is enough," he writes, "if we take the most common opinions and those that seem reasonable."[30] Aristotle's description of particular virtues and vices is, according to W. F. R. Hardie, "an analysis of contemporary society and ideas;"[31] "his moral ideas and moral ideals are, in some degree, the product of his time."[32] And W. D. Ross also asserts that what Aristotle presents with respect to the virtues and vices is "a lively and often amusing account of the qualities admired or disliked by cultivated Greeks of Aristotle's time."[33] Hardie, thus, rightly concludes that "Aristotle in the *Nicomaechean Ethics* is at least in part an interpreter of Greek experience,"[34] a view supported by Bertrand Russell in his observation that "Aristotle's opinions on moral questions are always such as were conventional in his day."[35] When philosophical analysis comes to grips with the issues of the day, it can make a direct impact on the beliefs, practices, and problems of contemporary society.

There are many philosophers in the modern world whose ideas and insights have had direct and immediate impact on political and socioeconomic circumstances (to mention only the conspicuous areas) in their own societies or age, or on later generations. It should suffice to mention a couple of examples. The social contract theories developed by the seventeenth- and eighteenth-century European philosophers were a reaction to the basis for political authority claimed by the European monarchs of those times. Many kings of Europe had been claiming divine right as the basis of or justification for their political authority, a claim that directly led to the exercise of political power without the consent of the people; other rulers, who also exercised despotic powers, claimed that, even though their system of rule was not based on the consent or will of the governed and thus excluded popular participation, it was nevertheless legitimate inasmuch as it was "enlightened" or "benevolent" because it resulted, so they claimed, in an improvement in the social and economic conditions of the governed. The social contract theories were intended to establish the fact that government should be by the consent of the people, the only basis for the legitimate exercise of political power. The contract theories developed by the European philosophers had a great intellectual impact on the political or ideological arguments that preceded the American and French Revolutions of 1776 and 1789, respectively. Thus, it can be said that the ideas and arguments of the philosophers in seventeenth- and eighteenth-century Europe played important political roles. But it must be pointed out that this was so because those philosophers were responding at the conceptual level to the political circumstances of their times.

One of the proponents of the social contract theories was the seventeenth-century English philosopher John Locke, who is best known for his contributions to epistemology and political philosophy. But Locke was concerned also with economic problems of his time and paid attention to the philosophical foundations of economic activity. He made significant contributions to economic theories, anticipating and influencing another philosopher, Adam Smith. Locke set forth theories of value, prices of commodities, money, interest, rent, foreign exchange, and foreign trade. He argued against price regulation: "Experience will show that the price of things will not be regulated by laws, though the endeavors after it will be sure to prejudice and inconvenience trade, and put your affairs out of order."[36] He argued for minimal state intervention, through legislation, in the operation of the economy, a position that was in keeping with his philosophical arguments for the creation of a minimal state. Locke's advocacy for private property is well known: for him civil society was created to protect economic achievement and was to be subordinate to it. In the opinion of Karen I. Vaughn, "Locke was a far more sophisticated economist than most historians of economic thought have given him credit for being."[37] She also thinks that "Locke was in many respects an early social scientist with a consistent view of social action in both his economic and political writings."[38] The view that Locke was an early social scientist is also held by Joseph A. Schumpeter.[39]

Adam Smith, the high priest of the doctrine of free market economy, who was very much influenced by Locke in his economic theories, was a moral philosopher (*not* an economist) at Glasgow University. Before being given the chair of moral philosophy (which, according to Robert L. Heilbronner,[40] included political economy), he had held the chair of logic (a purely formal study); and, before writing the book for which he is known to the world, he had written a book on moral philosophy entitled *The Theory of Moral Sentiments* (1759). These philosophical insights into human nature and the most satisfactory way of running human society, as well as his views about morality, led to the publication of his classic *The Wealth of Nations* (1776), in which he examines such notions as division of labor, wages of labor, profits of stock, and natural and market prices of commodities. Smith's moral philosophy had a great impact on his ideas on political economy. David Ricardo, the economist who put capitalism (the free enterprise system) in the classical form that has come to us today, revised and trumpeted Smith's ideas from the perspective of the world of business. Smith's philosophical insights into the socioeconomic conditions of his time constitute the basis of the economic thought and practice of many developed and developing nations of the world today, two centuries after the publication of his book.

The philosophical responses to the consequences of the French Revolution may be briefly mentioned. It may be said that the modern social and political philosophy of the West dates from the French Revolution. Before this historic event, modern political philosophy had concerned itself with the classical problems of who should rule and how. The French Revolution posed new problems not only in France but throughout the Western world. One of the consequences of the revolution was the birth of a new species of political and social philosophy: this was the idea of the welfare state, the idea that the object of the state is to secure the well-being or happiness of the people. Philosophers like Marx, Hegel, August Comte, Victor Cousin, and Claude-Henri de Saint Simon were all convinced that the French Revolution had ruptured the political and moral fabric and basis of European society, and that it was an opportune time to use philosophy constructively to serve as the basis for a moral regeneration of society on which alone a stable political edifice could be rebuilt. Hence, the torrent of socialist credos of nineteenth-century Europe.

The utilitarian moral philosophers of nineteenth-century England were thinkers committed to social reform. The distinguished philosopher Jeremy

Bentham, for example, was more concerned with practical than with purely theoretical issues. A leader of a group called the Philosophical Radicals, whose activities led to the formation of the British Liberal Party, his aim was to modernize Britain's social and political institutions. His philosophical arguments as well as his personal involvement played some significant role in the eventual passage of the Reform Bill of 1832, which radically reformed British politics by removing the control of Parliament from the aristocratic class and putting it in the hands of the urban middle class. The other well-known utilitarian philosopher, John Stuart Mill, also devoted the whole of his life to programs of social reform and thus pursued the tradition of the Philosophical Radicals. It should be noted that Mill was also a logician, involved in purely formal studies. The practical concerns demonstrated not only in the philosophical arguments but also in the personal involvement of some philosophers in sociopolitical reform programs clearly contradicts Marx's view that "Hitherto philosophers have only interpreted the world in various ways, but the real point is to change it."[41] As already observed, Plato, Aristotle, Bentham, Mill, and others set themselves the task of reforming the societies in which they lived. Moreover, changing the world involves having well-defined goals, and philosophy can be of great assistance in defining and articulating those goals.

In a discussion of the practical consequences of philosophical insights, I cannot forget to mention the insights of the contemporary American philosopher John Rawls, whose monumental work *A Theory of Justice* (1971) has had an enormous influence on legal treatises as well as on discussions of social policy, particularly in the United States.[42] It may be said that Rawls was at least in part responding conceptually to the American sociopolitical experience in the wake of the civil rights movements and the debates about the controversial status of certain disadvantaged groups in the United States, as well as the anti–Vietnam War movement in the 1960s.[43] These movements or events threw into relief basic questions about the fairness of sociopolitical institutions and the distribution of the resources and burdens of society. Rawls's ideas on justice have been extensively discussed in journals not only of philosophy but also of political science, social theory, economics, and law.

These examples of the impact of philosophical arguments and insights on human affairs, examples that can be multiplied, are intended to clear up the misconception about the relevance of philosophy to practical human concerns and support the conviction that the ultimate goal of philosophizing is—and ought to be—the determination of the nature of human values and how these can be realized concretely in human societies. Philosophy must be concerned, directly or indirectly, with the problems of human value.

To round off the discussions of the foregoing sections: I have indicated that, on the basis of the concerns and activities of philosophers, it can be said that the ultimate purpose of philosophy is to speculate about human experience, that conceptual analysis—an important way of doing philosophy—is not, and cannot be pursued as, an a priori activity in isolation from experience, that philosophy is in some sense a system of beliefs, and that philosophy is a conceptual response to the problems and circumstances of a given society in a given epoch. The last-mentioned feature of philosophy immediately embeds it in the problems of those times and suggests that it should address those problems from the conceptual level. Philosophers, who not only make inquiries into fundamental principles underlying human experience but also undertake analytic interpretation of that experience, will, I believe, have something relevant and important to say about that experience that can influence or guide individual action, public policy, and the development of human culture.

4. Philosophy and the African Experience

One of the main points or conclusions made in the foregoing sections is that philosophy speculates about the whole range of the human experience: it provides conceptual interpretation and analysis of that experience, necessarily doing so not only by responding to the basic issues and problems generated by that experience but also by suggesting new or alternative ways of thought and action. I have so far dwelt at great length on the career of the philosophical enterprise in Western cultures and societies. This is deliberate; but it is also unavoidable in view of the fact that the historical career of the philosophical enterprise—the role it has played in human affairs, in the development of human culture—is undoubtedly most amply manifested in the development of Western cultures. Furthermore, to make the career of that enterprise in the development of Western cultures my starting point is not irrelevant to my purposes here, for I believe that how philosophy can and should conceptually interact with the African experience is no different from how this has been done for other societies and cultures. It must be conceded, however, that much of the importance and thrust of that conceptual interaction will depend on the kinds of ideas, issues, problems, or concepts that attract the attention of the African philosopher. Even though I do not want to undercut the pretensions of philosophy to universality in respect of doctrine, I maintain, nevertheless, that it is certain fundamental problems posed for a given society or era by new situations or experiences that give rise to philosophizing as well as the choice of problems on which attention may be focused. On this showing, problems and concepts that occupy the attention of groups of philosophers need not be the same, even though they could be in many instances.

It is a well-known fact that since the early euphoric days of postcolonial rule, African nations and peoples have had all kinds of experiences that have embraced practically all aspects of human life. Some of these experiences, to be sure, predate the era of postcolonial rule. But the real nature of the problems generated by those experiences has come to the fore as the African people themselves attempt to "modernize" their societies or evolve forms of life in harmony with the ethos of the contemporary world. The attempts to develop or modernize or, as I prefer to put it, to situate themselves most satisfactorily in the social, political, and intellectual formation of the contemporary world, have, however, been beset by daunting problems, failures, and frustrations.

Some of these problems or experiences may be recounted briefly: many African nations since attaining political independence have been beset by political corruption and instability. A symptom of this political instability is reflected in the inauguration, almost throughout sub-Saharan Africa, of authoritarian governance: the politics of authoritarianism and military dictatorships in which political power is concentrated in a leader (or in a coterie of like-minded power-seekers) who is insulated from the pressures of accountability to the people and yet insists on their immediate obedience to his authority. The authoritarian ruler surrounds himself with a cordon of security men and women and would strive to hold on to power for as long as possible. Criticisms of his rule are to all intents and purposes nonexistent.

The disruption of the democratic, constitutional process by the military has been a feature and pattern of governance in Africa since the dawn of postcolonial rule. The justification for military rule—as if military rule is ever justifiable—needs to be examined. But it seems pretty clear to me that military rule in Africa has certainly not enhanced the political or economic well-being of the African people; it has not had a salutary effect on the development process and has in practically all instances halted the march toward political and economic advancement. Military regimes, like their civilian counterparts, are intolerant of criticism but are less amenable to public opinion and feel very jittery if that opinion is negative. It has sometimes been supposed by those who care or try to find some justification for military rule that only a military regime can adopt and pursue the bold and austere economic measures so urgently needed for resuscitating the African economy. This assumption or interpretation strains credulity: many African nations have been ruled by the military for more than half—in some instances three-quarters—of the period since political independence, and none of these has developed a stable or healthy economy. The truth of the matter, in my view, is that civilian administrations can also take, and are prepared to take, bold and austere economic measures but for the fear of military intervention.

Political corruption has afflicted every postcolonial African nation. It is an outstanding feature of the postcolonial African political experience. It is one of the major causes of military intervention in African politics, with very damaging consequences to the process of democratic politics. Political scientists have made extensive investigations into this phenomenon of political corruption. And it is appropriate for philosophers also to help clarify the issues involved with a view to finding some realistic and enduring way of dealing with this problem.

Because of the dynamic relationship between politics and economics, bad,

unstable, and corrupt politics, in the long run, usually begets bad economics. Hence, it is not surprising that, economically, African nations have fared
disastrously in the postcolonial era. Despite the constant infusion of capital
and other forms of assistance from the developed nations of the world and
international organizations, Africa is in a deep development crisis. The
causes of the crisis are legion.

Choosing an appropriate and effective ideology has been a besetting
problem. The ideology pursued by a very large majority of the African political leaders on attainment of political independence was socialism, but they
preferred to refer to it as "African socialism" because they regarded it as
having African ancestry. The pursuit of socialism by African political leaders
was aggressive and unrelenting, but with disastrous consequences that, in
the course of time, led—or rather forced—some of them to change their
ideological choice or direction. Thus, it can be said that African nations in
the postcolonial era have been groping through an ideological labyrinth.
Philosophical insights might serve as Ariadne's thread out of this labyrinth.

It would be correct to say that no human culture has remained pure since
its creation, free from external influences. But the most important thing is
what to do with the ideas, concepts, and institutions that come from different cultures, particularly when, as in Africa, these are foisted on an existing
culture without its having, or being given, the opportunity to select or adopt
what it considers desirable or worth its while and adapt it to suit its own
circumstances. It seems to me that Africa must deal most seriously with the
ideas, values, practices, and institutions that sub-Saharan Africa has received
from other cultural sources, if the cultural situation of Africa is to be vitalized and made a viable framework for development. The viability of a cultural framework for development is determined by the characteristics of that
culture. Several characteristics of African cultures can be considered obstacles to development. This would make the cultural framework for development in Africa unstable. The traditional cultural values and institutions of
African societies will need to be reexamined from a critical and fundamental
perspective.

Science and technology do not seem to have fared well in African societies of the postcolonial era. The emphasis has been on the transfer of technology from the technologically advanced countries of the world. But without firm grounding in the scientific principles of the technologies, the
transfer of technology has not had any real impact on African economic and
industrial development. Perhaps the whole approach to the cultivation of
technology has been misconceived. For Africa to participate meaningfully in
the promotion and cultivation of science and technology, which, clearly, are
not only important engines of development but are becoming the outstanding features of the global culture, serious examination must be given to the
traditional African perceptions of science, technology, and the external
world.

An important feature of the African colonial and postcolonial experience
that has had enduring effects is the mentality acquired by the African people

regarding their perceptions of the "African way of life" compared with the "European way of life." That mentality almost invariably leads many Africans to prefer European things—values, practices, institutions, and so on— even if a closer look might suggest that the equivalent African "thing" is of comparable worth. Thus, that mentality—colonial mentality—engenders apism and so subverts originality and creativity, because it makes people look outside rather than inside for standards of judgment. It seems that the most enduring effect of the colonial experience on the African people relates to their self-perceptions, to skewed perceptions of their own values—some of which (values) can, on normative grounds, be said to be appropriate for life in the modern world.

Confronted with a deep and resilient development crisis, with frequent military disruptions of the democratic political process resulting, inevitably, in political instability, uncertainty, and confusion, and with a poor demonstration of political morality resulting in pervasive and rampant political corruption; riven by almost incessant communocultural (or "ethnic") turmoil that threatens national unity and integration; filled with a colonial mentality that hamstrings the cultivation of an endogenous innovative spirit; and bedeviled by aspects of their cultural traditions that thwart attempts to evolve forms of life in harmony with the ethos of the contemporary world, while those aspects of the traditional culture that can be considered relevant have not been given adequate recognition in the creation of modern political and economic institutions, African life on the eve of the twenty-first century is not only confused but at a low ebb. And many wonder why.

In times of wonder, confusion, instability, and uncertainty, in times when the definition and articulation of values and goals become most urgent, in times when the search for fundamental principles of human activity becomes most pressing and is seen as the way to dispel confusions and unclarities as well as the way to draw attention to new or alternative modes of thought and action—in such times, the services of the intellectual enterprise called philosophy become indispensable. For philosophy, as explained in earlier sections of this chapter, is a conceptual response to the problems posed in any given epoch for a given society or culture. It would therefore be appropriate, even imperative, for contemporary African philosophers to grapple at the conceptual level—as has indeed been done by philosophers of other cultures—with the issues and problems of their times.

4.1 Universalism and Particularism in Philosophy

It is instructive to note that philosophers such as John Locke, Adam Smith, Jeremy Bentham, and John Rawls, whose socioeconomic, political, and moral ideas and arguments had telling influence on social and cultural values and institutions of their societies, were grappling at the conceptual level with the issues and problems of their times. They were giving conceptual interpretation to the contemporary experience, primarily of their own people. In saying that philosophy responds conceptually to issues and problems,

I have used such expressions as "a given society," "a given culture," "a given epoch," "their own times," and other kindred expressions to indicate the historical or cultural relations and matrices of philosophical ideas, arguments, and proposals. And one will also agree with the assertion by the German philosopher G. W. F. Hegel that "Philosophy is its own *time* apprehended in thought."[44] Now does all this mean that the relevance of the ideas, insights, arguments, and conclusions of philosophers—who necessarily have to belong to some time, culture, or society—is to be tethered to those times, cultures, or societies? The answer to this question turns on whether one perceives philosophical ideas or doctrines as particular, that is, as relative and relevant only to the times and cultures out of which they emerged, or as universal, that is, as transcending the times and cultures that begat them, and hence of transparticular (universal) applicability. Both particularist and universalist theses have been put forward by African philosophers.

The particularist thesis maintains the particularity of philosophical ideas or doctrines: it holds that the historical-cultural moorings of philosophical ideas and proposals are sufficient evidence of their particularity and of the inappropriateness of applying them universally to other cultures or societies, that those ideas—and the problems that gave rise to them—derive from experiences that are specific to cultures or historical situations, and that, consequently, philosophers unavoidably focus attention on issues and problems that interest them or relate to the experiences of their particular cultures and histories, unconcerned seriously to engage reflectively on the problems and issues of other peoples and cultures. The thesis appears to be bolstered by the assertions of some philosophers who make no bones about contextualizing their philosophical concerns by referring to the social, ideological, or cultural circumstances to which they were giving philosophical responses. The distinguished American philosopher John Rawls in his writings on the theory of justice describes his own work as having specific application in the American context.[45] Rawls observes: "In particular, justice as fairness is framed to apply to what I have called the 'basic structure' of a modern constitutional democracy."[46] In his article on the principles of equality, Joseph Raz writes: "The starting point [i.e., of his thesis] is the existence within the western cultural heritage of an egalitarian tradition."[47] References to such specific cultural or ideological contexts made by philosophers as the focus of their philosophical activity can be multiplied. Such approaches to the pursuit of the philosophical enterprise would seem to provide support for the particularist thesis.

One advocate of the particularist thesis is K. C. Anyanwu, an African philosopher from Nigeria, who rejects the notion that philosophy has a universal character. He writes: "I am saying that . . . African philosophy is a particular instance of philosophy as a cultural product. It is definitely unphilosophical to subordinate the different visions of all cultures to the European world-vision alone, and this is what the 'perennial' and the 'universalist' philosophers are trying to do. . . . I argue that every philosophy is relative to its basic assumptions about the nature of experienced reality as well as its epistemological attitude or method. . . . And furthermore, different assumptions and models of experienced reality lead to different philosophical doctrines."[48] The particularist thesis is sometimes mischaracterized or misunderstood. Odera Oruka, an African philosopher from Kenya, who rejects the particularist thesis and takes a universalist view of philosophy, to be explained presently, says: "Some wish to deny critical rationality, at least as it is understood in the West, to African Philosophy, claiming indeed that it is precisely lack of critical reasoning that helps to distinguish African philosophy from Western philosophy. Yet others think that philosophy, whether *African* or not, is not worth the name if rationality and logicality are ejected from it."[49] (By "others," Oruka is referring to those, like himself, who subscribe to the universalist thesis.) Oruka further says that whatever is the difference between African philosophy and Western philosophy, "it does not qualitatively lie in the use of *reason*. Reason is a universal human trait. And the greatest disservice to African Philosophy is to deny it reason and dress it in magic and extra-rational traditionalism."[50]

But the question is: does the particularist thesis deny rationality and the place of logic in African thought in the traditional setting? Of course, not. Neither Anyanwu nor any advocate of the particularist thesis would deny the place of rationality in human thought, African or non-African. The point of the particularist thesis is that the concept of rationality as understood in philosophy is a product of Western culture and that the way it is understood in that culture may not (necessarily) apply to other cultures, such as the African. But to say this is not, by any means, to imply a denial of the rational or logical character of African philosophy; what may be meant is simply that it should be possible or appropriate to provide a different understanding of, or meaning for, the concept of rationality. There have, in fact, been some discussions about whether or not rationality is a culture-dependent concept.[51]

I think that the particularist-universalist thesis is best confined to the *content* or *product* of a philosophy: to the ideas, insights, proposals, arguments, and conclusions of a philosophy, all of which can only be arrived at through *rational* and *logical* discourse. African traditional thought was not— could not have been—pursued without the underpinnings of rationality.[52] And discourse, even ordinary conversation, would not be mutually intelligible in a literate or even preliterate society without the minimum understanding and application of logic, even if one were not conversant with its formal rules. This is not an empirical but an a priori truth. Now, the universalist thesis.

Peter Bodunrin, an African philosopher also from Nigeria, says that, along with his fellow "professional philosophers" from Africa, he takes "a universalist view of philosophy," by which he means that "Philosophy . . . must have the same meaning in all cultures although the subjects that receive priority, and perhaps the method of dealing with them, may be dictated by cultural biases and the existential situation within which the philosophers operate. According to this school, African philosophy is the philosophy done by African philosophers whether it be in the area of logic, metaphysics, ethics or history of philosophy. It is desirable that the works be set in some African context, but it is not necessary that they be so."[53] The universalist thesis, thus, holds that the relevance of philosophical ideas, insights, and arguments can transcend the limits of the cultures and times of the philosophers who produced them, despite the fact that those philosophers were giving critical attention to the intellectual foundations of their own cultures, their cultural and historical experiences providing the setting for their conceptual explorations. The thesis does not deny the historical or cultural specificity of philosophical ideas or insights; but it maintains that this fact does not detract from the relevance of those ideas or insights to other cultures and times, and that they can therefore be considered universal.

I find the universalist thesis quite attractive. The universality of philosophical ideas may be put down to the fact that human beings, irrespective of their cultures and histories, share certain basic values; our common humanity grounds the adoption and acceptance of some ideas, values, and perceptions, as well as the appreciation of the significance of events taking place beyond specific cultural borders. This being so, problems dealt with by philosophers may be seen as *human* problems—rather than as African, European, or Asian—and, hence, as universal.

In critical response to the universalist thesis, however, I wish to say this: human problems are of course human; but this statement, as a logically necessary statement, is in itself innocuous. The main point, however—and this is a strident implication of the particularist thesis—is that human problems can invariably be contextualized, for they arise in, or out of, certain historical or cultural situations. This being so, the approach to solving them need not be the same; different ideas and therapies may be required, even though one need not deny that the required ideas and therapies may in fact be adopted from the experiences of other peoples and cultures. Also, to regard the problems of the various peoples of the world as simply human, and hence universal, is to imply that there are necessary or historically structured modes of societal development and approaches to tackling the problems of human societies. This is to endorse the doctrine of historical determinism that is belied by the fact that the mode of development of a colonized people, for instance, will most probably not be the same as that of a colonizing people: the problems of establishing stable democratic institutions in most developing, formerly colonized, nations of the world are a clear case in point. A straightforward adoption of the institutions of a developed nation may not be adequate in solving the problems of a developing nation. Different peoples, cultures, and nations have historically developed differently; the ideas that led or supported their development must, at least in some respects, have been different. The universalist thesis cannot, therefore, be unqualifiedly true.

In earlier sections of the chapter, I attempted to indicate that philosophy speculates about and interprets human experience. It is pretty clear that human experience is excessively varied: the cultural and historical experiences of human beings do differ in some respects. The experiences of colonized and subjugated peoples would differ in most respects from those of the colonizer and the conqueror. If, in fact, the subject matter of philosophy is human experience, and human experiences differ in some respects, then we would expect the contents and concerns of the philosophies produced by thinkers with different cultural or historical experiences to differ in some respects. This is what I consider the essential point of the particularist thesis. And therefore, I believe the particularist thesis cannot be set aside cavalierly.

This is not to say that the particularist thesis is free from defects and wholly supportable; it is not. For one thing, it denies the possibility—and sometimes the necessity—of exploiting the ideas, values, and institutions of other peoples and cultures, where necessary, relevant, beneficial, and practicable, for dealing with the problems of a people. Because of our common humanity and because the values, experiences, and characteristics of human beings can in *some* respects be said to be common (as I discuss later), that possibility cannot be reasonably denied. For another, to insist on particularism is to imply that a thinker from one culture cannot understand, appreciate, and feel convinced of the content of a philosophy produced in another culture and give a positive assessment of it; but this is surely not true. For a philosophical idea to emerge from the experiences of a particular culture or people does not necessarily mean that there is no possibility of its taking on (sooner or later) a universal character; nor does it mean that its significance is necessarily tethered to its original cultural ambience. Even though the potential for universality of a philosophical idea—any philosophical idea— would depend very much on its quality and power of conviction, that potentiality cannot unconscionably be rejected a priori, as the particularist thesis seems to imply. Particularism fails to give due cognizance to the historical fact of cultural borrowing in the wake of contacts between peoples of different cultures (see chapter 8, section 1).

In the circumstances of our common humanity, a particular idea or fact, irrespective of its cultural or historical origin, may potentially be an exemplification of a universal principle. And those philosophers who do specify the cultural or ideological or social context that gave rise to their philosophical responses still entertain the hope, nevertheless, that their theses will some day have wider application. Thus, Rawls, after the second statement referred to above, adds: "Whether justice as fairness can be extended to a general political conception for different kinds of societies existing under historical and social conditions, or whether it can be extended to a general moral conception, or a significant part thereof, are altogether separate questions. I avoid prejudging these larger questions one way or another."[54] Thus he does not rule out the possibility of his theory having a wider, even a universal, application. Even though the concept of 'mentanationality' that I introduce in chapter 3 (section 3.1.2) as a new philosophy of the nature of the nation-state is inspired by reflections specifically on the African ethnic situation, I certainly expect my analysis, nevertheless, to be universally acceptable and applicable.

Now, having made negative remarks about both the universalist and the particularist thesis regarding philosophical ideas and their relevance or irrelevance to peoples and cultures, I wish to maintain that, in the light of our common humanity, which forcefully suggests a common denominator of basic values and goals, the universalist thesis appears to be of greater intuitive appeal. One may therefore come down on its side. Human experiences or problems may not be shared by all humans. But the fundamental mundane *goals* of human beings can be said to be held, *ultimately*, in common by all. This fact of sharing in ultimate goals, in my view, makes the universalist thesis more convincing.

I deem it appropriate, however, at this point, to deploy a distinction between two concepts of universalism, a distinction that is rarely made. I distinguish between what may be called "essential universalism" and "contingent universalism." (The former may also be called "constitutive universalism" and the latter "functional universalism.") By essential universalism, I am referring to certain basic values and attributes so intrinsic to the nature and life of the human being that they can be considered common to all humans. The statement I have just made insinuates the notion of the objectivity of human values and will immediately be countered by those philosophers who maintain the subjectivity or relativity of values. But can it be seriously denied that there are values that human beings, irrespective of their societies or cultures, hold and cherish, values whose violation by, or in, some societies will provoke utter outrage and scandal in other societies? Surely not. Friendship, knowledge, happiness, respect for life, the avoidance of pain would be among such values. Any human society that fails, for example, to pursue the ethic of respect for human life cannot survive as a *human* society for any length of time. It is the existence of, and belief in, such commonly (universally) held values that grounds the legitimacy and justifiability of criticisms of societies or nations that violate them: otherwise, what moral right or justification would one human society have to condemn violations of such values by another? Essential universalism thus appeals to certain fundamental values of humanity. And a philosophical inquiry into such human values should be of interest to all people irrespective of their culture.

By contingent universalism, I have in mind the notion of a philosophical idea or a cultural value, practice, or institution becoming so attractive and influential as to be embraced in the course of time by practically the rest of the peoples and cultures of the world. Such an idea or value or institution attains the status of universality by virtue of its historic significance or relevance or functionality or power of conviction or some such quality. The difference between the contingent and the essential universal is that, whereas the latter's universal status is immediate, being, as it were, intrinsic to human nature or purposes, the former acquires the status of universality in time, as peoples outside the cultural origin of the idea or value become increasingly enamored of it for several reasons and accept, appropriate, and exploit it for their own purposes. (An example is the idea and practice of the free market economy.) At this point that idea or value or practice would have become metacontextual, for it would have transcended its original cultural or historical context and would thus have, by reason of its quality or power of conviction, gained the widest currency elsewhere: an originally vertical idea or practice would thus have become horizontal. The notion of the contingent universal is the justification or explanation for the dominance of the ideas, values, and institutions fashioned by some particular peoples, cultures, or times of history. But it presupposes that the field of universality, to be populated by contributions from the various cultures of humankind, is open. Thus it makes it possible for every culture to make a contribution to the global system whether in the field of ideas, values, institutions, or some other, and for that contribution to gain appreciation and recognition far beyond the confines of its origin.

Within the framework of the distinction between essential and contingent universalism, an idea, value, or institution that masquerades as an essential universal may in fact be a contingent universal. A particular idea or value that fails to attain the status of contingent universality would continue to remain a particular idea but will continue also, of course, to be cherished by the culture that originated it. Particularity, then, would not be eliminated by the distinction between essential universalism and contingent universalism.

I conclude, therefore, that African philosophy, like the philosophies produced by other cultures, will have characteristics of both universality and particularity, for it will be concerned with ultimate goals that can be said to be shared by all human beings irrespective of their cultures and nationalities, *and* with social and cultural experiences and problems some of which may, in some sense, be said to be peculiar to the African people.

5. Conclusion

In this introductory chapter it has been my purpose to point out certain features about the intellectual discipline of philosophy in order to dispel misconceptions about its relevance to grappling with the problems of human life and of human society. I have claimed that philosophy does not—cannot—dispense with experience or observation, despite its abstract character, and that the abstract approach to dealing with its issues and problems is to enable it to see them in the clearest light and at the fundamental level considered most relevant, effective, and enduring in understanding and negotiating those problems. I have pointed out that even though the philosophical reflection is invariably inspired immediately by—and is thus a conceptual response to—the cultural and historical experiences of the philosopher, it nevertheless does not necessarily follow that the worth or significance of philosophical ideas, doctrines, propositions, and conclusions is to be tethered to their cultural or historical contexts. For the significance of many such philosophical ideas or doctrines can gain considerable plausibility and currency beyond the confines of their cultural or historical origin.

I have explained at some length, with the support of concrete historical evidence, the role philosophy has played in social, religious, political, and economic affairs of Western societies and in their cultural development. In those societies the relevance of the philosophical enterprise to human or societal problems can be seen at its highest. Yet the fact that this intellectual enterprise is essentially a cultural phenomenon, responding at the conceptual level to issues and problems unleashed by cultural or historical situations, suggests a strong conviction that it *is* most appropriate for African philosophers to conceptually respond to the various problems of their societies. The impulse to this conceptual response is not only the cultural character of the philosophical enterprise but also the conviction of its relevance to human or societal problems. While human nature or our common humanity will underpin the universality of some of their philosophical theses, the peculiarity of some of the problems that will attract them will underpin the particularity of some of their philosophical ideas, arguments, or proposals. Hence I distinguish two kinds of universalism: essential universalism, which responds to and takes its rise from problems related to our common human nature, and contingent (or functional) universalism, which elevates an originally particular philosophical idea or proposal to the status of universality because it contains features of such high quality as commend themselves to, or are appreciated by, others outside the immediate cultural or historical environs of that idea or proposal. African philosophers can make contributions to the global philosophical experience in both of these ways.

2

Person and Community

In Defense of Moderate Communitarianism

The most appropriate type of relation that should exist between the individual and society has been an intractable problem for social and political philosophy. The problem arises because we believe, on one hand, that the individual human being has autonomy, freedom, and dignity—values that are considered most worthwhile and ought therefore to be respected by the society; we believe, on the other hand, that the individual not only is a natural member of the human society but needs society and all that it makes available for the realization of the individual's potential, and for living a life that is most worthwhile. The sort of relation that should exist between the individual and the society is reflected in conceptions of social structure evolved by a community of people. The existence of a social structure is an outstanding, in fact, a necessary feature of every human society. A social structure is evolved not only to give effect to certain conceptions of human nature but also to provide a framework for both the realization of the goals, hopes, and potentials of the individual members of the society and the continuous existence and survival of the society. It seems that the type of social structure or arrangement evolved by a particular society reflects—and is influenced by—the public conceptions of personhood held in the society. These conceptions are articulated in the critical analyses and arguments of its intellectuals.

Questions raised by intellectuals, especially the moral and political philosophers among them, relate, in this connection, to the metaphysical and moral status of a person (or, self). The metaphysical questions are about whether a person, even though she lives in a human society, is an atomic, self-sufficient individual who does not depend on her relationships with others for the realization of her ends and who has ontological priority over the community, or she is by nature a communal (or, communitarian) being, having natural and essential relationships with others. Moral questions, which may, in some sense, be said to be linked to, or engendered by, metaphysical conceptions of the person, relate to, (1) the status of the rights of the individual—whether these rights are so fundamental as cannot be overridden under any circumstances, (2) the place of duties—how, that is, the individual sees his socioethical roles in relation to the interests and welfare of others besides his own, and (3) the existence and appreciation among the individual members of the society of a sense of shared life or common (collective) good. Moral or normative matters may be expressed in sophisticated and elaborate conceptual formulations; but they do, as practical matters, have their best and unambiguous articulation or translation in the actual way of life of a people—in the way individuals are expected or not expected to respond to one another in times of need, in the way individuals are expected or not expected spontaneously to care for one another, and so on.

My intention in this chapter is to explore the above questions, which bear on personhood and community, making, as my point of departure, how the concepts feature and are understood in African cultures. In an earlier publication,[1] I discuss the concepts of individuality and communalism as they are understood in Akan philosophy in the traditional setting. In this chapter, however, I focus my attention mainly on the normative features of personhood and community.

1. Communitarianism in African Moral and Political Theory: Moderate or Radical?

The communal or communitarian (I use the two words interchangeably) aspects of African moral and political thought are reflected in the communitarian features of the social structures of African societies. These communitarian features, which have been the subject of much scholarship involving the cultures of Africa, are held not only as outstanding but also as the defining characteristics of African cultures. The sense of community that is said to characterize social relations among individuals in African societies is a direct consequence of the communitarian social arrangement. This sense of community, according to Kwesi Dickson, is a "characteristic of African life to which attention has been drawn again and again by both African and non-African writers on Africa. Indeed, to many this characteristic defines Africanness."[2] Regarding the traditional life in Kenya, Jomo Kenyatta makes the following observation: "According to Gikuyu ways of thinking, nobody is an isolated individual. Or rather, his uniqueness is a secondary fact about him; first and foremost he is several people's relative and several people's contemporary."[3] Elsewhere he observes that "individualism and self-seeking were ruled out. . . . The personal pronoun 'I' was used very rarely in public assemblies. The spirit of collectivism was [so] much ingrained in the mind of the people."[4] On the same phenomenon, John Mbiti also writes that in African societies, "Whatever happens to the individual happens to the whole group, and whatever happens to the whole group happens to the individual. The individual can only say: *'I am, because we are; and since we are, therefore I am.'* "[5] These descriptions of African culture make clear its communitarian nature. What they do not make clear, however, is what type of communitarian notion is, or can be said to be, upheld in the African moral and political theory: radical or moderate?

It is possible for people to assume off-handedly that by emphasizing communal values, collective goods, and shared ends, a communitarian social arrangement necessarily conceives of the person as *wholly* constituted by social relationships. It might be thought that in doing so, such an arrangement tends to whittle away the moral autonomy of the person—making the being and life of the individual totally dependent on the activities, values, projects, practices, and ends of the community—and that, consequently, that arrangement diminishes his freedom and capability to choose or re-evaluate the shared values of the community.

Indeed, this view of the interaction of the individual and the community is well accepted by many scholars of African thought systems. Making Mbiti's statement, "I am, because we are; and since we are, therefore I am," his point of departure, the African philosopher Ifeanyi Menkiti, from Nigeria, for instance, infers that the African view asserts the ontological primacy of the community, that "as far as Africans are concerned, the reality of the communal world takes precedence over the reality of the individual life histories, whatever these may be."[6] From this inference, he makes three further inferences: first, that in the African view, "it is the community which defines the person as person, not some isolated static quality of rationality, will, or memory"[7] (here he contrasts this with the Western view); second, that the African view supports "the notion of personhood as acquired"[8]—not merely granted as a consequence of birth; and third, that "[a]s far as African societies are concerned, personhood is something at which individuals could fail."[9]

While I believe that the metaphysical construal of personhood in African thought such as Menkiti's and Mbiti's is overstated and somewhat misleading, such views or beliefs did provide the ideological groundwork for the so-called African socialism chosen by most African political leaders in the early days of postcolonial rule. For, the advocates of the ideology of African socialism, such as Kwame Nkrumah, Leopold Senghor, and Julius Nyerere, in their anxiety to find anchorage for their ideological choice in the traditional African ideas about society, argued that socialism was foreshadowed in the traditional African idea and practice of communalism. Thus, Nkrumah observed that "If one seeks the socio-political ancestor of socialism, one must go to communalism. . . . In socialism, the principles underlying communalism are given expression in modern circumstances."[10] And Senghor also said that "Negro-African society is collectivist or, more exactly communal, because it is rather a communion of souls than an aggregate of individuals."[11] (For a discussion of the so-called African socialism, see chapter 5.) These statements clearly suggest the conviction of these African leaders or scholars that the traditional African social order was absolutely communal and would, perhaps for that reason, easily translate into modern socialism. Hence the euphoric and unrelenting pursuit of socialism by most African political leaders for more than two decades following the attainment of political independence.

But here I want to point out that inasmuch as all of the scholars referred to do not appear to have fully recognized the status and relevance of individual rights, their views patently model the notion of radical and unrestricted communitarianism. (Perhaps the position of Senghor may be excepted in the light of another view of his I examine later.) This notion of communitarianism I would find hard to support.

It is true, of course, that an individual human being is born into an existing human society and, therefore, into a human culture, the latter being a product of the former. As the proverb of the Akan people states, "When a human being descends from heaven, he [or she] descends into a human society." The fact that the individual human being is born into an existing community must, it seems to me, suggest a conception of the person as a communal being by nature. This communitarian conception of the person implies that, since the human being does not voluntarily choose to enter into a human community, community life is not optional for the individual. It also suggests that he cannot—perhaps should not—live in isolation from other persons, that he is naturally oriented toward other persons and must have relationships with them. It suggests, further, that the person is constituted, at least partly, by social relationships in which he necessarily finds himself.

The fundamentally relational character of the person and the interdependence of human individuals arising out of their natural sociality are thus clear. This attribute of relationality or sociality in some way makes up for the limited character of the possibilities of the individual, a limitation that whittles away the individual's self-sufficiency. Thus, an Akan proverb states, "A person is not a palm tree that he [or she] should be complete or self-sufficient." It is evidently true that in the social context, in terms of functioning or flourishing in a human society, the individual is not self-sufficient, her capacities, talents, and dispositions not being adequate for the realization of her potentials and basic needs. Human beings have needs and goals that cannot be fulfilled except through cooperation with other human beings. Our natural sociality—and hence our natural relationality—provides the buttress indispensable to the actualization of the possibilities of the individual.

All this presupposes the priority of the cultural community in which the individual human being finds herself. Yet, it might be supposed that if a community consists of individuals sharing interests and values, would this not imply that the individual has priority over the community and that therefore the community existentially derives from the individuals and the relationships that would exist between them?

We may here turn briefly but critically to an Akan proverb that says,

"One tree does not constitute a forest." That is to say, for there to be a forest there will have to be several individual trees. In the context of the relationship between the individual and the community, this means that one individual does not constitute a community. Just as we would not speak of a forest where there is only one tree, so we would not speak of a community where there is only one human being. Although communities can vary in size, not even the smallest is constituted by only one individual. A community emerges, that is, comes into existence, according to the proverb, with the congregation of several individuals: the priority of the individual, vis-à-vis the derived status of the community, appears implicit in this proverb. And one might be tempted to emphasize the apparent individualist aspect of this proverb by pointing out that a tree can be conceived of as prior to the forest, and thus too, the inference is, with a person. But giving in to such a temptation leads to a misinterpretation of the proverb.

The reason is that the analogy the proverb seeks to establish between the forest and community is defective. Whereas the individual tree can grow in a lonely place in isolation from other trees and, thus, without any relationship with, or assistance from, other trees, the individual human being cannot develop and achieve the fullness of her potential without the relationships of other individuals. And, whereas the individual human being is born into an existing human community, not into a solitary wilderness, and is naturally oriented toward other individuals, the individual tree can sprout from, or be planted, in a lonely place. On the analogy of the proverb, the reality of the community is derivative: secondary, not primary.

The ontological derivativeness of the community, however, cannot be upheld. The reason is that the view of the priority of the individual, logically implied in the notion of the ontological derivativeness of the community, makes the individual's choice of membership in the human community merely contingent and optional. Such a view is clearly at variance with the notion of the natural sociality that is held as a fundamental feature of the human being. It also makes the emergence of the community a contingent matter, for, where membership of the community is optional and dependent on the choice of the individual, individuals may not have to come together to form a community, even though in pursuit of their own interests they most probably would. The community, that is, a cultural community, not only is a basis both for defining and articulating the values and goals shared by several individuals but alone constitutes the context, the social or cultural space, in which the actualization of the potentials of the individual can take place, providing her the opportunity to express her individuality, to acquire and develop her personality, and to fully become the kind of person she wants to be. The system of values that the individual inherits as she enters the cultural community and the range of goals in life from which she can choose—these are of course not anterior to a cultural structure but the function of the structure itself: they are therefore posterior to—indeed the products of—the cultural community. Thus, insofar as the cultural community with its complex of social relationships constitutes the context or medium in which the individual works out and chooses her goals and life plans, and, through these activities, ultimately becomes what she wants to be—achieves the status and goals in life she wants to achieve—the cultural community must be held as prior to the individual.

Having said all this, I would like to refer to some other proverbs which, examined in contradistinction to the ones already quoted, can be interpreted as implying, not a radical, but a moderate communitarianism, the model that acknowledges the intrinsic worth and dignity of the individual human person and recognizes individuality, individual responsibility and effort. The recognition is most appropriate, for, after all, the naturally social human being has will, personal initiative, and an identity that must be exercised, if his or her individuality is to be fully expressed and actualized.

Before I bring up some proverbs that, on my interpretation, model the notion of individuality, however, I wish to refer to the views of the Senegalese intellectual (and political leader) Léopold Senghor, which suggest a moderate communitarian position. Senghor writes: "Negro-African society puts *more* stress on the group *than* on the individual, *more* on solidarity *than* on the activity and needs of the individual, *more* on the communion of persons *than* on their autonomy. Ours is a community society." [12] I am in sympathy with Senghor's relativistic language, which certainly insinuates at least the relative status of individuality and does not ignore it. Although Senghor also subscribes to the ideology of so-called African socialism, his position—as it appears in the above quotation—is unlike that of the other African writers I discuss, for it suggests a moderate, not radical, communitarianism. I shall indicate shortly, however, where my own position differs from Senghor's.

The notion of individuality in African social thought is expressed in many African proverbs. The Akan proverb states:

> The clan is like a cluster of trees which, when seen from afar, appear huddled together, but which would be seen to stand *individually* when closely approached.

In drawing an analogy between the clan (or community) and a cluster of trees, this proverb says that, even though some of the branches of a tree may touch other trees—an analogy to the natural relationality of individuals—the individual tree is separately rooted, has its own separate identity, and is therefore not totally absorbed in the cluster. According to the proverb, then, individuality is not obliterated by membership in a human community.

Proverbs such as the following:

> Life is as you make it yourself.

> It is by *individual* effort that we can struggle for our heads.

> Life is war.

> The person who helps you to carry your load [i.e., who places the load on your head] does not develop a hump.

One does not fan [the hot food] that another may eat it (expressed also as:

Nobody cracks palm kernels with his [or her] teeth for another).

The lizard does not eat pepper for the frog to sweat.

These proverbs express the idea that as individuals we are responsible for our situations in life, that our individual effort is a necessary condition for fulfilling our needs and reaching our goals, that human life is a continuous drama of struggles—of successes, failures, and frustrations—that demand a great expenditure of effort if we are to succeed, and that even a helper (whether or not he or she is a member of the family) cannot completely take over our burden, so that in the end each one of us—every individual—will have to bear our own burden and be responsible for our own well-being. These proverbs are part of a body of evidence that the espousal of communal values does not in any way involve the rejection of individualistic values. And, to the extent that the moderate communitarian view accords due recognition to individuality, the above proverbs, examined in conjunction with ones already referred to, support that view. It is the view that I would defend.

The view seems to represent a clear attempt to come to terms with the natural sociality as well as the individuality of the human person. It requires recognizing the claims of both communality and individuality and integrating individual desires and social ideals and demands. The recognition appears implicit in Senghor's employment of relativistic language in his statement about African life. The relativistic language—the use of the expression "more . . . than"—in connection with the claims or status of individuality and community seems to suggest that no human society is absolutely communal or absolutely individualistic, and that it is all a matter of emphasis or of priority or of basic concern or perhaps of obsession with one or the other. There is some truth in the view that communalism or individualism as applied to a social arrangement is a matter of degree. For this reason, we should expect a human society to be either more individualistic than communal or more communal than individualistic. But, in view of the fact that neither can the individual develop outside the framework of the community nor can the welfare of the community as a whole dispense with the talents and intitiative of its individual members, I think that the most satisfactory way to recognize the claims of both communality and individuality is to ascribe to them the status of an equal moral standing.

2. Community, Social Relationships, and the Common Good

Communitarianism immediately sees the individual as an inherently communal being, embedded in a context of social relationships and interdependence, never as an isolated individual. Consequently, it sees the community as a reality in itself—not as a mere association based on a contract of individuals whose interests and ends are contingently congruent, but as a group of persons linked by interpersonal bonds, which are not necessarily biological, who consider themselves primarily as members of a group and who share common goals, values, and interests. The notion of shared life—shared purposes, interests, and understandings of the good—is crucial to an adequate conception of community. What distinguishes a community from a mere association of individuals is the sharing of an overall way of life. In the social context of the community, each member acknowledges the existence of common values, obligations, and understandings and feels a commitment to the community that is expressed through the desire and willingness to advance its interests. Members of a community society are expected to show concern for the well-being of one another, to do what they can to advance the common good, and generally to participate in the community life. They have intellectual and ideological as well as emotional attachments to their shared goals and values and, as long as they cherish them, they are ever ready to pursue and defend them.

I have said that, for the individual, community life is not optional—an assertion that follows from the natural sociality of the person and from the fact that she is embedded in a set of necessary social relationships, some of which (relationships) are certainly essential to the development of her individual personality and potentials. In stressing social relationships, however, I do not mean to equate with the community, as such, those social relationships that can be said to be truly essential for personal development. For, the creation of social relationships is mostly a function of the community, and hence a cultural product. Social relationships are, thus, mostly a feature of the cultural community. They are expressed in, and consciously shored up by, reciprocities, comprehensive interactions, and mutual sympathies and responsibilities.

Of course not all social relationships are essential for personal development; some of them can surely be regarded as optional, in the sense that a person would not be harmed if such relationships were to wane or disappear; but there are some relationships that can surely be said to be positively harmful to the individual's development and interests, relationships, for instance, that are built on slavery, domination, humiliation, or discrimination. The last category of social relationships represents the weaknesses and imperfections in the institution of community; but these relationships more truly reflect the defects in the human moral character. And human aspirations and struggles have, it can be said, been aimed at the eradication of such inhuman social relationships. Yet, the alternative to relationships built on false or defective moralities is not to advocate a social world of atomic individuals, as anticommunitarians (in the West) are wont to do. The reason is that it is possible for stronger individuals even in the socially atomistic world—unconstrained by deep moral convictions—to impose the same inhuman relationships on weaker individuals. It can be expected, however, that in a community characterized by its ethic of mutual sympathies, reciprocities, and concerns and responsibilities for others inhuman social relationships will be dealt with more satisfactorily.

But there is more to community than social relationships. Sharing, as I said, an overall way of life is most essential and basic to any conception of a community. Sharing a way of life implies the existence and acknowledgment of common roles, values, obligations, and meanings or understandings. In the social context of the community, each member recognizes a loyalty and commitment to the community and expresses this through the desire to advance its interests in a way that cannot be fully expected in a social context in which individuals are concerned solely and primarily with the promotion of their own interests, ends, and well-being and pay attention to the common good of the society only sporadically and only in the face of danger or crisis situations that are seen as potentially deleterious to their personal well-being. Thus, in a noncommunity social context, neither the advancement of the common good nor the demonstration of concern for the well-being of others is normatively perceived as a socioethical testament, principle, or requirement. Also, the community constitutes the context for the creation and development of a person's identity. A person comes to know who she is in the context of relationships with others, not as an isolated, lonely star in a social galaxy. Such a context is of course a cultural context, made possible by the practices and traditions (i.e., long-preserved cultural values; see chapter 8) that themselves resulted from—in fact were made possible by—the activities of a (past) community of people living and acting together, collectively. A person's identity derives, at least in part, from a cultural context, that is, a community. Thus, in the articulation of a deep sense of personhood as well as of individuality, the community plays an important and indispensable role.

The notion of the community, then, is a notion of particular social settings and networks characterized by such social and normative features as have been delineated in the immediately preceding paragraphs. These social settings and networks are of different forms and shapes: thus, the family (both nuclear and extended), clan, village, tribe, city, neighborhood, nation-state—all these are kinds of community. (We even talk about 'the international community'.) Since a person participates in a variety of communities—for she would be a member of an extended family, village or town, and a nation-state—it would follow that she would participate also in a variety of social relationships. Thus, a person's essential social relationships are by no means coextensive with only one community. People are therefore members of many different communities, different in size and operating at different levels, and are likely to develop different aspects of their sociality in the various communities. Consequently, a person's well-being may be tied up with the existence of social relationships at many different levels, some of which extend far beyond her proximate community. Within this range of complex relationships in which a person is embedded, there are likely of course to be some social relationships that do not promote—and may in fact damage—her well-being and that she, as a being with moral and intellectual capacity, has to deal with in some satisfactory way. But despite a person's membership in different communities that operate at different levels, and given the purposes of the discussions of this chapter, it would be enough to note that at each level the person would be *participating in a community life* essential for the development of her well-being, identity, and potential.

In attempting to provide a specification for a relevant community, I equate "the community" with "the cultural community." The reason is that culture—defined comprehensively as the entire way of life of a people and expressed by the complex of values, practices, and institutions (see chapter 3, section 4)—constitutes the greatest portion of our necessary social context. But the equation raises the question of what defines a "cultural community." Many scholars argue that sharing a culture requires a shared language. And since there are so many languages in most larger communities, such as nation-states, there would therefore (have to) be as many cultural communities. Yet, culture as a complex phenomenon is constitutive of numerous elements, of which language is one, albeit a very important one. Because of the numerous constitutive elements of a culture, it should be possible for people to share many aspects of a culture without a shared language, if they happen to participate in the activities, goals, aspirations, and the fate of a larger community; such a participation is, and should be, possible even without a shared language. The members of a large multilingual community will not live a strongly unified cultural life; nevertheless, they can be said to live a unified cultural life in some (weak) sense. (I distinguish between a strong and a weak sense of a unified cultural life in chapter 3, section 4.) In Ghana, for instance, despite the multiplicity of languages, there are many habits, outlooks, practices, institutions, and cultural values that can certainly be said to be shared by people who speak the different languages of the state. Even though it would be plainly false to compose such a slogan as "One people, one language, one culture" for a multicultural society or a multinational state, nevertheless, there are features of the cultures of peoples speaking different languages that do coalesce. Also, given at least a fair amount of tolerance, people with different religious beliefs and practices can share many aspects of a culture and can, thus, participate in one cultural community.

In the light of such an empirical truth, it would be more appropriate to regard shared (nonreligious) values and practices, rather than language, as the defining feature of culture. In most communities, it is possible to find people who speak the same language but profess different religious beliefs: thus, while language unites, religion divides. Alternatively, there would be people who affirm the same religious beliefs but speak different languages: in this case, while religion unites, language divides. And so on. Thus, to search for a cultural community in which the participants are culturally homogeneous *in all respects* is to pursue a chimera. But the interesting thing to note is that, while a person may not need to share the religious beliefs of (some) members of his community—he may not even hold any religious beliefs—or speak the same language with other members of the community, nevertheless, he would need to have food, shelter, security, goodwill, friendship, and self-respect if he is to have access to the goods or the basic needs indispensable to the fulfillment of life, basic goods that can be said to be commonly, universally, required by all human beings irrespective of their religious or linguistic affiliations. And this brings me to a discussion of the notion of the common good.

Intrinsically connected with the notion of a community is the notion of the common good, a notion that seems to be a bugbear to individualist thinkers and has consequently been maligned and burlesqued by them. (I prefer the term "individualism" to "liberalism" because the latter has different meanings to different people; the former is a more accurate description of the society that stresses individual interests and rights and is more appropriate in a discourse on the relation between the individual and the community.) These thinkers maintain that the pursuit of a common good in an individualistic society will do violence to the autonomy and freedom of the individual and fetter her ability to choose her own good and life plans. But not only that: for they would also say that the pursuit of the common good will result in intolerance of other conceptions of the good and inappropriate use of political power to realize the common good.

Much of the individualists' fear or suspicion of the notion of the common good stems, however, from their own conception of the common good as the aggregate of the particular goods of individual persons, which, like individual rights, ought to be respected. Thus, the nineteenth-century British individualist thinker Jeremy Bentham identifies the common good with "the sum of the interests of the several members who compose it" (i.e., the community).[13] And a contemporary individualist thinker, Will Kymlicka, also observes that "[i]n a liberal society, the common good is the result of the process of combining preferences, all of which are counted equally (if consistent with the principles of justice)."[14] To understand the individualist one must understand the normative or ideological impulse to that notion: individualists start out by considering the individual to be prior to the community and equipped with conceptions of the good perhaps totally different from the purposes of the community, individual conceptions of the good *wholly* and *always* arrived at independently of the system of values available in a community. Yet, the common good, properly understood, is not reducible to an artificial combination of individual interests or preferences.

The common good literally and seriously means a good that is common to individual human beings—at least those embraced within a community, a good that can be said to be commonly, universally, shared by all human individuals, a good the possession of which is essential for the ordinary or basic functioning of the individual in a human society. It is linked, I think, to the concept of our common humanity and, thus, cannot consist of, or be derived from, the goods or preferences of particular individuals; thus, the common good is not a surrogate for the sum of the different individual goods. If, in fact, the common good were the aggregate of individual goods, it would only be contingently common and might, on that score, not be achieved, or might only partially be achieved. The notion of the common good is a notion of that set of goods that is essentially good for human beings as such; it may, in fact, be characterized as human good. On this showing, there should be no conceptual opposition or tension between the common good and the good of the individual member of the community: for the common good can be conceived as embracing the goods of all the members of the community. It should be understood that by "the goods of all the members" one is referring only to what can be regarded as the basic or essential goods to which every individual should have access. There is no human being who does not desire peace, freedom, respect, dignity, security, and satisfaction. It is such a political or moral notion—not an exotic or weird notion—embracive of fundamental or essential goods, to which all individuals desire to have access, that is referred to as the common good. The insistent advocacy and pursuit of such concepts as sympathy, compassion, social justice, and respect of persons make sense *because* of beliefs in the common good. The pursuit of social justice is intended to bring about certain basic goods that every individual needs if he is to function as a human being.

It can be said that the concept of the (civil) society implies the recognition and existence of a substrate of commonly shared values and self-understandings. It is this (substrate) that underpins the thoughts and activities of people who live together in an organized human society. Otherwise, what would be the point in the search for, and the establishment of, moral, legal, economic, political, and other institutions? Isn't the establishment of such institutions inspired and guided by a system of shared values—a common good? Aren't these institutions set up to achieve certain commonly shared values and goals? And aren't these values and goals the kinds of desirable and cherished things that the community would like to make available to all of its members? The institution, for instance, of a government or a social order is a common good. So that, if there is a human society, if human beings can live together in some form of politically organized settings despite their individuality—despite, that is, their individual conceptions of the good life, individual ways of doing things, and so on—then the existence of a common good must be held as the underlying presupposition. The common good can, thus, be regarded as that which inspires the creation of a moral, social, or political system for enhancing the well-being of people in a community generally. I think that the differences in individual conceptions of the good are often exaggerated by individualist thinkers; such an exaggeration does not, however, chime with the implications of the commonly accepted notion of our common humanity.

Finally, let me say that there are some individualist thinkers—minimal and "night watchman" theorists of the state—who argue that many of the essential social relationships will sustain themselves through voluntary choices of individuals in civil society and so would not require the assistance of the communal structure or the state. Even the common good, however it is understood by them, need not, it is argued, be promoted by the state, since it is expected that in the individualist state the common good will be adequately promoted by the individuals themselves. These thinkers do recognize, however, that there would be a need—albeit a minimum need—for the state or the community. This individualist position, as optimistic as it sounds, cannot be fully endorsed. The optimism about the ability of essential social relationships to sustain themselves through the voluntary activities of individuals without the support of the state exaggerates the moral virtues or capacities or volitions of the individual to have deep, extensive, and consistent concerns for the well-being of others; thus, the individualist optimism unreasonably discounts or underrates the self-interested proclivities of the individual. (I do not, however, deny the human capacity to [sometimes] demonstrate love, compassion, and other forms of altruistic behavior.) Also, those social relationships that, as I said earlier, are built on domination, slavery, and discrimination and that are positively detrimental to the development and interests of the individual can be dealt with most adequately by the state through its panoply of political and legal institutions. The elimination of social and other evils, such as injustices and discriminatory practices, cannot be made dependent solely on the goodwill and voluntary choices of individuals in the civil society. Thus, the individualist idea of promoting the common good through the voluntary choices of individual members of the civil society does not appear to be well anchored.

3. Communal Structure and Personhood

The claims, made in section 1, about the natural sociality of the human being, the ontological primacy of the community, the organic character of the relations between individuals, and the relevance of the community to the total well-being or realization of the potentials of the human being can certainly give rise to a hyperbolic and extreme view of the functional and normative status of the community. The characterizations of the nature and status of the community just provided may be true; in fact they are true, to my mind. Yet one could err in at least some of the conclusions one may draw from them by overlooking the logic or relevance of the attributes that can be delineated as belonging essentially to the human individual. In this connection, a consideration of other features of human nature would certainly be appropriate and helpful.

The individual is by nature a social (communal) being, yes; but she is, also by nature, *other* things as well; that is, she possesses other attributes that may also be said to constitute her nature. The exercise or application or consideration of these other attributes will whittle down or delimit the "authoritative" role or function that may be ascribed to, or invested in, the community. Failure to recognize this may result in pushing the significance and implications of the individual's social nature beyond their limits, an act that would in turn result in investing the community with an all-engulfing moral authority to determine all things about the life of the individual. In short, one could easily succumb to the temptation of exaggerating the normative status and power of the cultural community in relation to those of the person and, thus, obfuscating our understanding of the real status of this cultural structure as well as the complex nature of the human person who is to function in that structure. Those who express extreme or radical views on the status of the community, such as Mbiti, Menkiti, and most of the advocates of the ideology of African socialism, are victims of the temptation. Menkiti, a philosopher, has presented elaborate arguments on personhood in African moral and political theory, and I will make his views the point of departure for my analysis.

3.1 Personhood in African Thought

In his analysis, Menkiti makes at least three characterizations of personhood. But, in my view, only one characterization is of philosophical interest or relevance; it is also the one that does not seem to involve itself in a morass of confusions and incoherences. This characterization adumbrates a moral conception of personhood, and I find it interesting. Menkiti states:

> The various societies found in traditional Africa routinely accept this fact that personhood is the sort of thing which has to be attained, and is attained in direct proportion as one participates in communal life through the discharge of the various obligations defined by one's stations. It is the carrying out of these obligations that transforms one from the it-status of early child-hood, *marked by an absence of moral function, into the person-status of later years, marked by a widened maturity of ethical sense—an ethical maturity without which personhood is conceived as eluding one.*[15]

I would, in general, agree with this interpretation of personhood in African thought, but Menkiti clutters up this moral conception of personhood with other assertions or arguments that introduce some confusion to his analysis. He says that personhood is achieved through social incorporation: individuals "become persons only after a process of incorporation . . . into this or that community."[16] As part of the process of socialization, the individual in the African society goes through different rites of incorporation. Only after these rites, according to Menkiti, does he or she become "a full person in the eyes of the community."[17] But it is not clear whether this way of achieving personhood involves morality at all, as the extensive quotation above suggests. It is true that at the time of their initiation into adulthood, young people are reminded and seriously instructed in the moral values or virtues of the society (as they are instructed in other social customs). But, if leading a satisfactory moral life is an important determinant of personhood, it is difficult to perceive how this can be manifested at the stage of social incorporation through mere rituals.

Menkiti's analysis becomes more perplexing when he asserts that "*full* personhood . . . is attained after one is well along in society" and this "indicates straightaway that the older an individual gets *the more of a person* he becomes." [18] The notions of "full personhood" and "more of a person" are as bizarre as they are incoherent. How does one know exactly when a person becomes a "full" person, whatever this word means as applied to a person? And, when, and how, does a person become "more of a person"? On the basis of a maxim Menkiti refers to, the answer to both questions will be: when a person has become elderly or old, at which stage he or she would, according to Menkiti, have attained "the other excellences considered to be definitive of full personhood." [19] It is not clear what these excellences are, specifically. (Earlier on he speaks of "the full complement of excellences seen as definitive of man").[20] But let us assume that the attainment of the excellences represents an individual's success in her moral life, an adequate practice of moral virtues. This assumption accords with a conception of moral personhood derivable from the extensive quotation above.

But, if the assumption is a legitimate assumption, it raises at least one major difficulty. The difficulty is in considering elderly people as necessarily moral, or as necessarily having the ability or disposition to practice moral virtues satisfactorily. For, surely there are many elderly people who are known to be wicked, ungenerous, unsympathetic: whose lives, in short, generally do not reflect any moral maturity or excellence. In terms of a moral conception of personhood, such elderly people may not qualify as persons.

Thus, Menkiti's analytic account of personhood in African thought is befogged with confusions, unclarities, and incoherences. With all this said, however, this aspect of his account adumbrates a moral conception of personhood and is, on that score, interesting and relevant to the notion of personhood important for the communitarian framework. But I will now turn my attention to a conception of a person held specifically in Akan moral and political thought.

In delineating the moral features of personhood in Akan thought, I will start off by making some disquisition on the word used for "person" in the Akan language, undoubtedly the most widely spoken language in Ghana (and my native language). The word used for "person" in Akan is *onipa*. But this word also means "human being," and the plural form of it can also mean "people." Thus, *onipa* is a highly ambiguous word. As with ambiguous words in many other languages, it depends on context for its meaning. Thus the meaning of the word in reference to "person" can be delineated from the context of its use, and an analysis of a concept of a person linked to that meaning can be made. When an individual's conduct consistently appears cruel, wicked, selfish, or ungenerous, the Akan would say of that individual that "he is *not* a person" *(onnye onipa)*. Two important things can be said to be implicit in this statement. The first is that, even though that individual is said not to be a person, he is nevertheless acknowledged as a human being, not as a beast or a tree. A clear distinction between the concept of a human being and a concept of a person is thus deeply embedded in that statement: an individual can be a human being without being a person.

Second, implicit in that statement is the emphatic assumption that there are certain basic norms and ideals to which the behavior of an individual, *if he is a person,* ought to conform. The language expresses the notion that there are moral virtues that an individual is capable of displaying in his conduct. Considering the situations in which the judgment "he is not a person" is made about individuals, these moral norms and virtues can be said to include kindness, generosity, compassion, benevolence, and respect and concern for others; in short, any action or behavior conducive to the promotion of the well-being of others. And the reason for that judgment is that that individual's actions and conduct are considered as falling short of the standards and ideals of personhood. I must add, though, that the individual to whom the judgment "he is not a person" is applied would be one whose conduct is known to the community to be generally unethical, not one who occasionally experiences moral lapses or failure of moral commitment. There is no implication, however, that an individual considered "not a person" loses her rights as a human being or that she loses her citizenship or that she ceases to be an object of moral concern from the point of view of other people's treatment of her. Only that she is not a morally worthy individual.

Also, if a human being lives an isolated life, a life detached from the community, he would be described *not* as a person but as an individual. A life detached from the community would be associated with an egoistic life. An individual detached from the community would not be considered a responsible moral agent. Thus, a distinction is made also between the notion of a person—a concrete being situated in a social context—and that of an individual—a being detached from the community.

The judgment that a human being is "not a person," made on the basis of that individual's consistently morally reprehensible conduct, implies that the pursuit or practice of moral virtue is intrinsic to the conception of a person held in African thought. The position here is, thus, that: for any *p*, if *p* is a person, then *p* ought to display in his conduct the norms and ideals of personhood. For this reason, when a human being fails to conform his behavior to the acceptable moral principles or to exhibit the expected moral virtues in his conduct, he is said to be "*not* a person." The evaluative statement opposite to this is, "he *is* a person" means, 'he has good character,' 'he is peaceful—not troublesome,' 'he is kind,' 'he has respect for others,' 'he is humble.' "[21] The statement "he is a person," then, is a clearly moral statement. It is a profound appreciation of the high standards of the morality of an individual's conduct that would draw the judgment "he is truly a person" (*oye onipa paa*). A rider is required here: while children are actual human beings and are members of the community, they are persons only potentially and will achieve the status of personhood in the fullness of time when they are able to exercise their moral capacity.

Now, the moral significance of denying personhood to a human being on the grounds that his actions are known to be dissonant with certain fundamental norms or that he fails to exhibit certain virtues in his behavior is extremely interesting for communitarians. Personhood, in this model of humanity, is not innate but is earned in the ethical arena: it is an individual's moral achievement that earns him the status of a person. Every individual is capable of becoming a person inasmuch as he is capable of doing good and should therefore be treated (potentially) as a morally responsible agent.

An aphorism or belief of the Akan people holds that "God created every individual [to be] good." The meaning of this statement is ambiguous. The ambiguity is between an individual's actually doing good, that is, actually behaving morally or virtuously, and an individual's being capable of moral choice, that is, having the moral sense to distinguish between good and evil or right and wrong. It is thus not clear whether the statement means that the human being has been determined to do good—to actually pursue virtue—or that he is merely endowed with a sense of right and wrong and the capacity for virtue. How do we interpret the meaning of the statement then? In view of the evil and unethical actions of individual human beings, the first interpretation cannot be accepted as the correct meaning of the statement, for it is plainly contradicted by our putative moral experience. The correct interpretation of the view that the human being was created good, then, will be that the human being is a being endowed with moral sense and, so, has the capacity for both moral judgment and virtue. The human being can then be held as a moral agent: not that his virtuous character is a settled matter, but that he is capable of virtue, and hence of moral achievement. (Let us note that if the human being were created or determined actually and always to do good, we would never have had a concept of evil or vice, since no human being would, in that kind of moral scenario, commit a vicious or evil act.)

The moral conception of personhood finds concrete expression in the attitudes of members of Akan and other African communities toward the funeral of an individual member. The type of burial, the portion of the community involved in the funeral, and the nature and the extent of grief expressed all depend on the community's assessment of the deceased's moral life.[22] People, including wealthy people, who do not satisfy the society's moral criteria may be given simple funerals and attenuated expressions of grief. By contrast, those individuals whose moral achievements are admired by the community are given elaborate burial ceremonies with ritualized grief regardless of the financial means of their families.

I must point out that there are some situations when an individual who considers himself at the bottom rung of the social ladder, often lacking the wherewithal to make ordinary living bearable, unsuccessful in many of his endeavors, feeling miserable and helpless, but who, nevertheless, has not abandoned all hope of succeeding and improving his present conditions—such an individual, rapt in thought and wonder, would ask himself the following rhetorical question: "Am I going to be (or, become) a person"? *(Se me be ye onipa ni?).* The question, in the context in which it is raised, gives the impression that personhood in the Akan thought is conceived in terms also of social or economic success or achievements. Yet, social success or economic achievements will by themselves not—from the perspective of the wider community—confer personhood on an individual, *if* that individual's conduct frequently falls short of the moral expectations of the community, if he fails, for instance, to demonstrate moral sensitivity to the welfare of others. Thus, achieving economic success or status is one thing; achieving personhood is quite another. The former is not automatically followed by the latter. The latter is clearly a function of the concrete demonstration of the individual's moral virtues and responses. Incidentally, that rhetorical question suggests that an individual participates in the determination of her personhood and identity and therefore that personhood is not fully defined or constituted by the communal structure: achieving personhood is not a function solely—or fully—of the communal structure.

Thus a moral conception of personhood is held in African thought: personhood is defined in terms of moral achievement.[23] Personhood conceived in terms of moral achievement will be most relevant to the communitarian framework that holds the ethic of responsibility in high esteem: the ethic that stresses sensitivity to the interests and well-being of other members of the community, though not necessarily to the detriment of individual rights (as I point out later).

I have a difficulty, however, not with the notion of moral achievement per se, but with how to bring it about, how, as it were, to achieve moral achievement. If moral achievement is the actual consequence of the successful exercise of an individual's moral capacity, how is it that some individuals succeed in this enterprise and so attain the status of personhood, while others fail in their moral endeavors and, thus, fail to attain that status? Since achievement here clearly involves a dynamic interplay between potentiality and actuality, the problem relates to the actualization of the potential. An examination of this problem, within the context of morality, would involve a discussion of such concepts as trying, moral will, and moral weakness, which is beyond the scope of my present purposes.

3.2 Communal Practices and Individual Autonomy

Radical or unrestricted communitarianism, which seems to give short-shrift to individual rights or individual autonomy, while maintaining the primacy of the community to the hilt, would hold that personhood is fully defined by the communal structure. Mbiti's already quoted statement, "I am, because we are; and since we are, therefore I am," strongly endorsed by Menkiti, as I said, suggests such a view. And when Menkiti asserts that "in the African understanding human community plays a crucial role in the individual's acquisition of *full* personhood," [24] he can be taken as implying that personhood is fully defined by the community, a view that would have deleterious consequences for individual autonomy. Indeed, Menkiti makes this assertion as he contrasts what he calls "the African understanding" with the "Sartrean existentialist view," which is, he says, that "the individual alone defines the self, or person, he is to become." [25] The point of the contrast is that just as the individual alone defines the self in one system, so does the community alone define the self in the other. I disagree with Menkiti on this aspect of his interpretation of personhood in African moral and political thought. But the disagreement is not just hermeneutic; it is philosophical or conceptual.

Now, despite the natural sociality of the human being, which at once places him in a system of shared values and practices and a range of goals—which, in short, places him in a cultural structure—there are, nevertheless, grounds for maintaining that a person is not fully defined by the communal or cultural structure. I have made the observation that, besides being a social being by nature, the human individual is, also by nature, other things as well. By "other things," I have in mind such essential attributes of the person as rationality, having a moral sense and capacity for virtue and, hence, for evaluating and making moral judgments: all this means that the individual is capable of choice. If we do not choose to be social—because we are social by nature—neither do we choose to be intelligent or rational beings or beings with a moral sense (or, capacity for virtue). Let us use the expression "mental feature" as a shorthand for all these "other things." It is not the community that creates this mental feature: this feature would not be natural if it were created by the community. The community only discovers and nurtures it. So that, if the mental feature plays any seminal role in the formation and execution of the individual's goals and plans, as indeed it does, then it cannot be persuasively argued that personhood is *fully* defined and constituted by the communal structure or social relationships. There is no denying the community's role in the complex process involved in the individual's realization of her goals and aspirations, though; yet, even so, the communal definition or constitution can only be partial.

It is true that the whole gamut of values, practices, and meaningful options in which the individual is necessarily embedded is a creation of the cultural community and is part of its history and tradition. For this reason, it can be said that some of our goals are set by the communal structure. Yet, the following questions may be asked:

1. Is it possible for the communal structure to set the whole or a seamless set of values, practices, and ends of the individual that will perfectly reflect the complexity of human nature, values, and practices at least some of which, we know, do change in response to new experiences or situations and so cannot be considered monolithic?

2. Does the communal, and therefore cultural, character of the self really imply that the self is ineluctably and permanently held in thrall by that communal structure?

3. Does the ethos of the communal structure preempt a possible radical perspective on the communal values and practices that may be adopted by a self? That is, does the communal structure make reevaluation of inherited values and practices absolutely impossible?

All of these questions can be answered in the negative.

The reason is that individuals, as participants in the shared values and practices and enmeshed in the web of communal relationships, may find that aspects of those cultural givens are inelegant, undignified, or unenlightened and would thoughtfully want to question and reevaluate them. The reevaluation may result in the individual's affirming or striving to amend or refine existing communal goals, values, and practices; but it may or could also result in the individual's total rejection of all or some of them. The possibility of reevaluation means, surely, that the individual is not absorbed by the communal or cultural apparatus but can to some extent wriggle out of it, distance herself from it, and thus be in a position to take a critical look at it; it means, also, that the communal structure cannot foreclose the reality and meaningfulness of the quality of self-assertiveness that the individual can demonstrate in her actions. The creation and historical development of human culture result from the exercise by individuals of this capacity for self-assertion; it is this capacity that makes possible the intelligibility of autonomous individual choice of goals and life plans. The fact that changes do occur in existing communal values—for some new values are evolved as some of the old, inherited ones fall into obsolescence—is undoubtedly the result of the evaluative activities and choices of some autonomous, self-assertive individual human beings. That is, changes in culture often reflect, or at least begin in, the self-assertive enterprise. This phenomenon can be perceived even in a tradition-centered culture, for no human culture is absolutely and eternally unchanging (see chapter 8, section 1). It would be correct to say, though, that in tradition-centered cultures changes that result from the activities of self-assertive individuals are slow in permeating the existing culture.

The capacity for self-assertion that the individual can exercise presupposes, and in fact derives from, the autonomous nature of the person. By autonomy, I do not mean self-completeness but the having of a will, a rational will of one's own, that enables one to determine at least some of one's own goals and to pursue them, and to control one's destiny. From its Greek etymology, "autonomy" means, self-governing or self-directing. It is thus essentially the freedom of the person to choose his own goals and life plans in order to achieve some kind of self-realization. The actions and choice of goals of the individual emanate from his rational and moral will. Thus, the self-directing (or, self-determining) will also be self-assertive. Autonomy must be a fundamental feature of personhood, insofar as the realization of oneself—one's life plans, goals, and aspirations—greatly hinges on it, that is, on its exercise. Autonomy is, thus, valuable in itself.

I do not think, as does Joseph Raz, that autonomy is valuable only when it is used in pursuit of the good: "Autonomy is valuable only if exercised in pursuit of the good. The ideal of autonomy requires only the availability of morally acceptable options. This may sound a very rigoristic moral view, which it is not." [26] According to Raz, "Autonomy requires that many morally acceptable options be available to a person. . . . Autonomy requires a choice of goods. A choice between good and evil is not enough." [27] I find it difficult to understand why the concept of autonomy should be given an entirely moral garb. I would agree with Raz that "the autonomous person is a (part) author of his own life."[28] But, surely, life is not all moral. There are at least two senses in which an agent may be said to be moral: an agent may be said to be moral in the sense that he has the moral sense or capacity to distinguish between the good and evil; but he may also be said to be moral in the sense that he does that which is good, that his actions conform to the existing moral values or rules. An autonomous person can be said to be moral in the first sense; but he is moral in the second sense only if he does that which is required by the moral rules.

Even though the concept of autonomy cannot be said to be morally neutral, it can nevertheless be said to be only partly moral. Moreover, the variety of options made available to the individual by the cultural community are not necessarily moral in their entirety; nor are all of them morally acceptable to every individual: the available options presented by the community may include practices and patterns of behavior, such as polygamy, homosexuality, divorce and inheritance rules, and certain social rituals and customs, which may not be agreeable to some members of the community. I do not see any conceptual link between autonomy and acting morally. There is, however, a conceptual link between autonomy and freedom, since a self-directing agent necessarily has the freedom to direct himself or herself. But it is of course possible—isn't it?—for an individual to use his or her freedom to pursue the wrong things. If Raz is merely prescribing that the autonomous person *ought* to use his or her autonomy to pursue the good, I would support that moral recommendation. But, if his position is to regard the pursuit of the good as a conceptual feature of autonomy, I would demur.

The most that, in my view, can reasonably be said in this regard is that autonomy presupposes some basic moral competence—competence to pursue the right thing, and that the autonomous person, thus, has moral competence or capacity. But, having said this, we must admit that it would not necessarily follow that the autonomous person *always* exercises, or is *always* able to exercise, that moral competence or capacity in pursuit of virtue, to do the right thing. A moral choice always has to be made. Yet, if in fact it were true that the autonomous person always exercised, or had to (in the sense of being predetermined to) exercise, her moral capacity in pursuit of the good, then she would be considered as having been morally determined to pursue the good; her moral inclinations to pursue the good would have been settled or determined beforehand. Raz's position on autonomy would, thus, clear the way for moral determinism. And the consequence of this is the subversion of the reality of moral freedom and choice, and, alas, of autonomy itself. The consequence is a reductio ad absurdum of the view that autonomy must be exercised in pursuit of the good. To avoid that consequence requires modifying that view.

In the light of the autonomous (or near-autonomous) character of its activities, the communitarian self cannot be held as a cramped or shackled self, responding robotically to the ways and demands of the communal structure. That structure is never to be conceived as reducing a person to intellectual or rational inactivity, servility, and docility. Even though the communitarian self is not detached from its communal features and the individual is fully embedded or implicated in the life of her community, the self nevertheless, by virtue of, or by exploiting, what I have referred to as its "mental feature" can from time to time take a distanced view of its communal values and practices and reassess or revise them. Moral idealism and vision result from the communication between this feature of the person and her experiences of the community in which she lives. The ideals or visions of the individual can be subversive or demolitionary of existing societal values, practices, and institutions: what is called a revolutionary action can thus be understood generally as the activity of an idealistic or visionary individual (or, a group of idealistic or visionary individuals). Even though it would be correct to say that it is the community in which people live that to a great extent shapes their identity and serves as the locus of their values, it nevertheless would also be correct to say that the development of human culture—itself a product of a human community—is shaped *through* the activities of idealistic or visionary individual human beings. To the extent that the individual also can be said to help in shaping the cultural and social (including political) forms of her society and its institutions, to attribute the constitution of her identity and the impulse to the choice of the entire range of life forms or plans she can lead or prefer *solely* or *wholly* to the community (as some communitarian thinkers tend to do) would be an exaggeration. The autonomous character of the person, which is the ground of her capacity to choose her specific goals, is certainly worth being given adequate consideration.

Raz says that the whole concept of autonomy makes sense and becomes valuable only within the context of cultural structures that make available a variety of valuable options, and that the actions of autonomous individuals derive their significance from social forms or the communal structure. Raz thus writes:

> Autonomy is only possible if various collective goods are available. The opportunity to form a family of one kind or another, to forge friendships, to pursue many of the skills, professions and occupations, to enjoy fiction, poetry, and the arts, to engage in many of the common leisure activities: these and others require an appropriate common culture to make them possible and valuable.[29]

In the absence of an adequate range of valuable options—the presence of valuable options being a feature only of the community—a person cannot, on Raz's showing, be autonomous. He adds:

> It is not that a person cannot, through the development of his own variations and combinations, transcend the social form. People can, and sometimes do, do this, but inevitably in such cases the distance they have travelled away from the shared forms is, in these cases, the most significant aspect of their situation. It more than anything else then determines the significance of their situation and its possibilities for those people.[30]

I have a great deal of sympathy with the claims made by Raz. Nevertheless, it would also be correct to say, I think, that the availability of a range of options makes possible only the actual exercise of the individual's autonomy, that the availability of a variety of options does not ipso facto imply that a person would be able to make a most meaningful and satisfactory choice of the best option if his autonomy were not satisfactorily exercised. The existence of a variety of options is certainly important; but equally important is the satisfactory exercise of a person's autonomous capacity to make the best choice from those available options. For, after all, it is the individual who makes the choice: a particular choice made by the individual is not foisted upon him by the community.

The existence, through the activity of the community, of a variety of valuable options with respect to life forms or goals is one thing; the capacity to adopt the best approach to those options is quite another—that capacity may be said to be linked to the autonomous character of the person: for, the capacity to choose one's ends is a fundamental feature of personhood, even though this does not mean that capacity is always exercised, or always exercised in the most effective, appropriate, and satisfactory manner. Autonomy subverts robotism, even though I do not at all want to imply by this that the autonomy of the individual has no bounds. For, social and political life, however it is articulated—whether by individualist or communitarian thinkers—places limits on the directions of the exercise of individual autonomy. Autonomy is, thus, already dented somehow by civility or natural human sociality. Even so, it can still be exercised to the extent that is possible.

Also, I do not think that the range of options made available by the community can be said to be exhaustive of all conceivable options. If it were, it would make nonsense of the viable and telling pursuits of individuals who can appropriately be described as idealists, visionaries, or revolutionaries. That is to say, if the range of options were circumscribed, these individuals would have had to operate within the given or available framework of options. But we know that this is not so, and that idealists and visionaries can, and do, go beyond the available framework.

People often say of some visionary leader, "He [or, she] was *ahead* of his [or, her] times." What they mean by this utterance is that that individual's visions, actions, thoughts, arguments, and prescriptions were not comprehended or appreciated by her contemporaries, as they perhaps were by later generations. But it may be noted that even though such thoughts and actions may be interpreted as significant (with the benefit of hindsight), their significance may not, by reason of their newness and originality, initially be appreciated by the contemporary community. A visionary leader may inaugurate new moral, ideological, or intellectual paradigms, immediately considered subversive and looked at with askance by his contemporaries, who in due course, however, may come to appreciate and accept them. The inauguration of new paradigms in the wake of the intellectual or moral pursuits of a visionary or idealistic individual indicates ipso facto that it is possible for the individual to climb over the existing cultural walls and to ruminate on extramural matters. Thus, an available cultural framework may not be as cloistering as it might be supposed. It is clear that ideals and visions as such result from the moral and intellectual activities of some individuals and are consequently accepted and adopted, in whole or in part, by the cultural community or by later generations of it. There is no reason why such a visionary individual cannot emerge from a communal milieu.

The acceptance by the cultural community of new paradigms would be appropriate for several reasons. First, in the light of human limitations, no human community could be considered perfect in terms of all of its norms, values, practices, and institutions. Reforms may have to be undertaken to improve matters or forms of life for the members of the community. Perfectibility thus requires that due attention or recognition be given to new ideals and visions. Second, no human community, however conservative it considers itself to be, would consider its system (moral, political, social, etc.) as ossified, self-sufficient (or, self-complete), and unchanging. And, third, the development or improvement a human community would like to experience depends very much on its readiness to come to grips with new ideas, values, and institutions. Autonomous individuals have a lot to do in the origination of ideas and ideals; and much of their moral or intellectual activity results from their normative communication with existing ideas, values, and practices, which may be found to be riddled with ambivalence, incongruities, obsolescence, dysfunctionality. All of such ideas and practices would need to be questioned and critically examined and reevaluated. The growth of culture as well as modifications in the cultural heritage of a people is invariably due to the intellectual and moral activities of some autonomous individuals with their unique qualities and endowments.

What characterizes the kind of innovation embarked upon by individuals who provide visionary leadership for their own communities (and, perhaps, for other communities) is presumably twofold. First, the individual who provides such leadership is intentionally offering her innovation as a contribution to the life and conversation of her community, framing her thoughts and arguments in terms that generally (only generally) acknowledge—mutatis mutandis—the continuities in the past development of the community. I use the word "generally" advisedly: to indicate that in certain specific cases the innovative thoughts of the visionary individual will in fact deviate from what may have gone on in the past. But, even so, the innovative activities of such an individual are intended to extend and enrich, rather than entirely break with, certain aspects of the community's history. Second, it is, in retrospect, possible in many instances to understand how what was presumably new and innovative in some respects was nonetheless rooted in the community's past, at least in terms of its basic or original normative trajectory. It is these features of the innovative activity that make for and sustain the integrity of a system or tradition and, hence, of a community and thus destroy any impression regarding the tentative character of a particular tradition.

Now, the fact that it is possible to reevaluate existing or received values of a community and to inaugurate new ones implies that the self can set some of its goals and, in this way, participate in the determination or definition of its own identity. The upshot is that personhood can only be partly, never fully, defined by one's membership in the cultural community. The most that can be said, then, is that a person is only partly constituted by the community. This view is an amendment to the unrestricted or radical communitarian view that the community fully defines personhood. That view differs from the one I am putting forward, which is that of a restricted or moderate communitarianism. It seems to me that moderate communitarianism offers a more appropriate and adequate account of the self and its relation to the community than the unrestricted or extreme or radical account, in that the former sees the self both as a communal being *and* as an autonomous, self-assertive being with a capacity for evaluation and choice, while the latter sees the activity of what I have referred to as the "mental feature" of the person as *wholly* contingent upon, and determined by, the communal structure itself. Extreme or unrestricted communitarianism fails to give adequate recognition to the creativity, inventiveness, imagination, and idealistic proclivities of some human individuals in matters relating to the production of ideas and the experience of visions. The powers of inventiveness, imagination, and so on are not entirely a function of the communal culture; they are instead a function of natural talents or endowments, even though they can only be nurtured and exercised in a cultural community.

Let me conclude this section by making some animadversion, if briefly, on the position maintained by American communitarian thinkers that the individual member of the communal society, bound to the social meanings, understandings, and practices of the community and to his social roles, will be unable to detach himself from the communal ties or practices in order to evaluate (or, criticize) and revise those practices. Michael Sandel, for instance, makes the following observation:

> As a self-interpreting being, I am able to reflect on my history and in this sense to distance myself from it, but the distance is always precarious and provisional, the point of reflection never finally secured outside the history itself.[31]

And Alasdair MacIntyre also states:

> For the story of my life is always embedded in the story of those communities from which I derive my identity. I am born with a past; and to try to cut myself off from that past, in the individualist mode, is to deform my present relationships. The possession of an historical identity and the possession of a social identity coincide. Notice that rebellion against my identity is always one possible mode of expressing it.[32]

What the two passages are saying, as I understand them, is that an individual whose life is anchored in a community cannot really detach or distance herself from her historically grounded identity or social roles. The position depicted in these passages seems to reflect the version of communitarianism I have characterized in preceding sections of this chapter as radical or extreme (even though I believe that not all features of their position can be so characterized). And it is clearly at variance with the moderate communitarian view I have attempted to articulate in this section.

Both passages demonstrate a clear consciousness of the impact of history—of the past—on the identity or social roles of the self. For Sandel, the individual cannot distance himself from his history on any permanent basis. This view can hardly stand up to scrutiny. First, if the statement "He [or, she] was ahead of his [or, her] times" can truly be asserted of an individual, then what this means is that the thoughts and actions of that individual can be said to have in at least some respects been "outside the history itself." Also, Sandel's view totally ignores influences on the intellectual and moral horizons of the individual that often result from the encounter with other cultures, that is, with processes outside an individual's history itself. (On cultural encounters, see chapter 8, section 1.) Sandel's point will be true only in a community that is totally burrowed into its particularities and totally insulated from other cultures and their histories. As far as our knowledge of human history goes, there has never been such a human community. No human community is a closed society, totally impervious to external influences. The point, then, is that cultural contacts may lead an individual to think and act outside his history. It can be said, furthermore, that an individual's distancing himself from his historical background is not necessarily or "always precarious," as Sandel says. It is all a matter of an individual's moral intuitions or moral sense, not every aspect of which can be said to be cramped by his membership in the community, otherwise moral vision or idealism would never have been a feature of some individuals in historical societies. A moral visionary, intensely convinced of his moral discernment, which reflects his perception of humanity and the quality of human or social relationships, would hardly suppose that the reformatory moral enunciations he is articulating are precarious. For him, the new moral enunciations are well anchored, based on unshakable convictions. The historical emergence of moral visionaries or idealists in societies is an eloquent testimony that the moral hands of (some) individuals are not tied by the communal structure.

Now, in asserting that rebellion against one's identity "is always one possible mode of expressing it," MacIntyre is saying or implying that the individual cannot rebel against her historically grounded identity and social roles. I think, however, that the truth of this assertion depends on the nature of the consequences of the rebellion. If the consequences are radical and far-reaching, the rebellion can be doing much more than merely expressing or acknowledging an existing identity: it can in fact disrupt the existing contours of an individual's identity and thus introduce sensitive changes in her particular identity. MacIntyre also says that an individual inherits from her familial, communal, and cultural antecedents "a variety of debts, inheritances, rightful expectations and obligations." These, he says, "constitute the given of my life, my *moral starting point*. This is in part what gives my life its own moral particularity."[33] MacIntyre's view that our cultural or historical antecedents constitute a moral starting point is instructive and noteworthy. But the implication of the view should not be that what one starts with becomes a permanent feature of one's moral thought and conduct throughout one's life, as the last part of the quotation seems to imply. For it is possible for an individual to start off from a set of given (i.e., inherited) moral assumptions or beliefs but to reject (some of) those beliefs in the course of her life. The possibility is not only theoretical but also practical or empirical. That is to say, such a rejection of inherited moral beliefs is true in real life. There are, to be sure, many individuals brought up in racially bigoted families and towns who in the course of their own lives have come to reject (some of) the moral beliefs they had come, or were made, to hold as children and young adults. European—and, also, American—advocates of the abolition of slavery and the slave trade in the late eighteenth and early nineteenth centuries were nurtured in slave-owning cultures and societies that engaged in those inhuman and immoral practices. Some of the advocates may have indeed come from slave-owning families or may even themselves have been slave owners. Their advocacy of the abolition of those evil practices clearly implies a rejection of the moral practices and beliefs they had inherited. Moral starting points, thus, do not constitute a basis for permanent moral particularities.

I think that radical communitarian thinkers generally tend to exaggerate the impact of history and cultural and communal structures on the exercise by the communal self of his moral or intellectual autonomy. Two historical examples belie such an exaggerated position. It must be borne in mind that the European societies from which individuals emerged in the twilight of the medieval period and contributed ideas that spearheaded the rise of Western modernity were *communal* societies. And so were the ancient Greek societies that spawned Socrates, Plato, Aristotle, and others whose critical intellects knew no bounds and some features of whose intellectual activities can be said to have been demolitionary of the existing ideas, values, and practices of their societies. For me, it is moderate communitarianism that, in the final analysis, adequately reflects the claims of both individuality and communality, both of which need to be recognized morally and functionally.

There are, to be sure, other reasons for preferring moderate or restricted communitarianism over unrestricted, extreme, or radical communitarianism, which I discuss in the sections that follow.

4. Rights, Responsibilities, and the Communal Structure

It might be supposed that proponents of communitarianism, with its emphasis on, and concern for, communal values, will have nothing to do with rights, for the "natural" home of rights is said to be individualistic moral and political framework. Yet there is some truth in that supposition, for there indeed are communitarian thinkers who either deny the ontology of rights and so ignore them or reduce rights to some secondary status. Advocates of African socialism do not, as I have said, generally entertain the notion of rights in their political or ideological schemes. Others, such as Menkiti, would reduce rights to a secondary status. Menkiti writes: "In the African understanding, priority is given to the duties which individuals owe to the collectivity, and their rights, whatever these may be, are seen as secondary to their exercise of their duties."[34]

Nor is the short-shrift given to individual rights a feature only of (some) African communitarian thinking in the (recent) past. Leading communitarian thinkers in the West, such as Sandel, MacIntyre, and Charles Taylor, also fail to accommodate the appropriate status of rights in their systems; for them, rights are not really essential or such as should be given priority in our political thought and practice. Sandel holds a "remedial" conception of rights: rights are invoked only when satisfactory communal relations have been corrupted. In a communitarian society in which "a spirit of generosity" prevails, rights would not be important and would therefore not be invoked or insisted on.[35] Taylor wonders why we should "find it reasonable to start a political theory with an assertion of individual rights and to give these primacy."[36] He asserts that "the whole effort to find a background for the arguments which start from rights is misguided."[37] Taylor of course rejects the view of the primacy of rights. And, for MacIntyre, "the truth is plain: there are no such rights, and belief in them is one with belief in witches and in unicorns."[38] He asserts in fact that "natural or human rights . . . are fictions."[39] Most communitarian thinkers in the West share the view that the "politics of rights" should be given up and replaced with the "politics of the common good." For me, such claims or assertions are in the extreme.

It is true, I think, that in a communitarian society rights may not be asserted or insisted on with belligerency, for communal values such as generosity, compassion, reciprocities, and mutual sympathies may be considered more important than one's rights. Even so, this is far from saying that rights do not exist as part of the structure of a people's moral beliefs or values, or that rights are fictional or not at all essential in the communitarian moral and political theory and practice. Rights belong primarily and irreducibly to the individual. They are a means of expressing an individual's talents, capacities, and identity, even though the expression, arguably, can best be accomplished within a social framework. Individual autonomy—which is acknowledged in communitarian conceptual scheme—must involve recognition of the ontology of rights: indeed individual autonomy and individual rights persistently appear as conceptual allies. A communitarian denial of rights or reduction of rights to a secondary status does not adequately reflect the claims of individuality mandated in the notion of the moral worth of the individual. Such a position would be extreme and would be at variance with the moderate communitarian view that I think is defensible.

The supposition that communitarianism will have no or very little place for rights will be false in both theory and practice. Communitarianism—of the moderate kind—will not oppose the doctrine of rights for several reasons. First, communitarianism cannot disallow arguments about rights that may in fact form part of the intellectual activity of a self-assertive, autonomous individual possessed of the capacity for evaluating or reevaluating many of the practices of her community. Some of such evaluations may touch on matters of rights, the exercise of which a self-assertive individual may see as necessary for the fulfillment of the human potential, and against the denial of which she may raise objections.

Second, the notion of respect for human dignity—a natural or fundamental attribute of the human being—which cannot be set at nought by the communal structure, should generate regard for personal rights in a communal context. That is, the dignity or worth of the individual cannot be diminished by his natural membership in the community. Some conceptions of human dignity are anchored in theism, in the conviction that the dignity of the individual is a natural endowment by some supernatural creator of humankind. One proverb of the Akan people, whose social structure is communal states, for instance, "All human beings are children of God; no one is a child of the earth." The insistent claim that every human being is a child of God does seem to have some moral overtones or relevance, grounded, as it must be, in the conviction that there must be something intrinsically valuable in God. Human beings, as children of God, by reason of their having been created by God and possessing, in the African belief, a divine element called soul, ought to be held as of intrinsic value, as ends in themselves, worthy of respect. A concept of human dignity can be linked with, or derived from, the concepts of intrinsic value and respect. Also implicit in the proverb is the equality of the moral worth of *all* human beings—of all the children of God. Concepts of human dignity, intrinsic value, and equal moral worth generate a notion of moral rights that, as deriving ultimately from God or as belonging fundamentally to every human being as a creature of God, could be linked with the notion of innate or natural rights, that is to say, a human rights concept can certainly be said to be already involved in conceptions of human dignity. The conception of human dignity compels the recognition of rights not only in an individualistic but also in a communal setting.

It is thus possible to derive a theory of individual rights from conceptions of the intrinsic worth of a human being that are themselves based on theism. One conception of rights famously known to be grounded on an act of God is in the preamble of the American Declaration of Independence (1776): "We hold these truths to be self-evident, that all men are created equal, that they are *endowed by their Creator* with certain inalienable rights." The presumption here is that rights are an endowment of a creator.

It is also possible to derive a conception of human dignity—and hence individual rights—not from theism but from reflections on human nature, particularly on the qualities that will dispose the human being to function at his best in human society and realize his potentials to the full. Thus, the eighteenth-century German philosopher Kant, on the basis of his rational inquiries into human nature, grounds the notion of human dignity or intrinsic worth on human capacity for moral autonomy, that is, rational freedom. Thus conceived, argues Kant, the human person ought to be treated as an end in himself: "Now I say that man, and in general every rational being, exists as an end in himself, not merely as means for arbitrary use by this or that will: he must in all his actions, whether they are directed to himself or to other rational beings, always be viewed at the same time as an end."[40] Kant thus states his famous Categorical Imperative, which to him was the supreme principle of morality, also as: "Act in such a way that you always treat humanity, in your own person or in the person of any other, never simply as a means but at the same time as an end."[41] This leads Kant to a notion of moral rights, which he refers to as "innate rights" but which belong to everyone by nature and so could be called natural rights—our fundamental moral end. Thus, a conception of human dignity—and moral or natural (human) rights that concomitantly flow from it—can be reached through a purely rational reflection on human nature. But, however the conception of human dignity or rights is derived, whether from theistic considerations or from sources independent of God, that conception is linked with, and in fact compels, the recognition of rights, and not only in an individualistic but also communitarian setting. In other words, the derivation of individual rights from naturalism (humanism) or supernaturalism cannot be confined to an individualistic framework; the derivation is not an activity or a characteristic or a possibility solely of an individualistic moral or social ambience.

Third, at both the theoretical (conceptual) and practical levels, communitarianism cannot set its face against individual rights. For, implicit in the communitarianism's recognition of the dual features of the self—the self as an autonomous, assertive entity capable of evaluation and choice *and* as a communal being—is a commitment to the acknowledgment of the intrinsic worth of the self and the moral rights that can be said necessarily to be due to it. The recognition by communitarian political morality of individual rights is thus a conceptual requirement. It is also a practical requirement: at the practical level communitarianism would realize that allowing free rein for the exercise of individual rights, which obviously includes the exercise of the unique qualities, talents, and dispositions of the individual, will enhance the cultural development and success of the community.

On this showing, communitarianism's absorbing interest in the common good, in the provision for the social conditions that will enable each individual to function satisfactorily in a human society, cannot—should not—result in the willful subversion of individual rights. This is because, even though rights belong primarily to individuals, insofar as their exercise will often, directly or indirectly, be valuable to the larger society, their status and roles will nevertheless (have to) be recognized by communitarian theory. If communitarianism were to shrug off individual rights, not only would it show itself as an inconsistent moral and political theory, but also it would, in practical terms, saw off the branch on which it was sitting. It can be said, however, that restricted or moderate communitarianism is a consistent and viable theory, one that is not opposed to individual rights, even though it will consciously and purposively give equal attention to other values of the community, all (or some) of which it may occasionally regard as overriding. The foregoing discussion, then, clearly shows, I hope, the falsity of the view that moderate communitarianism will have no or very little place for individual rights.

With all this said, however, it must be granted that moderate communitarianism cannot be expected to be obsessed with rights. The reason, which is not far to seek, derives from the logic of the communitarian theory itself: it assumes a great concern for communal values, for the good of the wider society as such. The communitarian society, perhaps like any other type of human society, deeply cherishes the social values of peace, harmony, stability, solidarity, and mutual reciprocities and sympathies. For, in the absence of these and other related values, human society cannot satisfactorily function but will disintegrate and come to grief. The preservation of the society's integrity and values enjoins the individual to exercise her rights within limits, transgressing which (limits) will end in assaulting the rights of other individuals or the basic values of the community. An individual exercising the right to free speech or expression, for instance, cannot be allowed to run berserk and engage in verbal or physical vandalism, such as vandalism of a synagogue or church building—an action that not only subverts the right of others to freedom of worship but also disrupts the communal value of social peace and harmony. In the ethnically heterogeneous state whose goal is clearly national integration and cohesion, the right to form an ethnically based political party should not be upheld; such political parties will have to be banned in order to avoid fanning the flames of ethnic conflict. In such political contexts, some political rights will have to be abridged in the interest of national integration and social stability and peace.

There are likely to be acts or lifestyles, such as homosexuality or the production and display of pornographic material, that may or in fact will offend the moral or aesthetic sensibilities of some members of the communitarian society. Will these also be banned by the communitarian society? Here, we have to make a distinction between actions or behaviors that affect others, that is, the public, and those that affect oneself. From the moderate communitarian perspective, only the former are to be banned or restricted in order to prevent the disruption of the community. Individual rights to expressions that are of a strictly private nature may not be disallowed, unless there is overwhelming evidence that such expressions can, or do, affect other innocent members of the society.

Individual rights, the exercise of which is meaningful only within the context of human society, must therefore be matched with social responsibilities. In the absence of the display of sensitivity to such responsibilities, the community will have to take the steps necessary to maintain its integrity and stability. The steps are likely to involve abridging individual rights, which, thus, will be regarded by the moderate communitarian as not absolute, though important. The possession of rights becomes nearly inconsequential if a viable framework for their meaningful exercise does not exist.

To the extent that the meaningful and continuous enjoyment of one's rights is a function of the appropriate conditions of a social context, an overwhelming concern for the viability of that context is surely legitimate. That context is constituted by the shared, communal values or ends of the society.

I have indicated, if briefly, when the common good of the society justifiably trumps individual rights. But the moderate communitarian view suggests that the claims of individuality and community ought to be equally morally acknowledged. For, the community needs the individual and the individual, having natural links to the community, can hardly function properly outside the framework of the community.

It is conceivable that individuals in the communitarian society that espouses social morality or the ethic of responsibility may not be obsessed with insisting on their rights, knowing that insistence on their rights could divert attention to responsibilities that they, as members of the communitarian society, should strongly feel they have toward other members. Communitarianism requires a great demonstration of moral sensitivity and expenditure of moral effort by the individual. The communitarian society will thrive on the high sense of the morality of the individual. This is because of the attention given to the notion of responsibility in the communitarian political and moral theory. Rights and responsibilities are not polar concepts, even though they could be: if I insist on my rights to all my possessions or to all that has resulted from the exercise of my endowments, I may not be able to show sensitivity to the needs and interests of others, even though showing sensitivity to the interests of others is an important plank in the moral platform of the communitarian political morality. The danger or possibility of slipping down the slope of selfishness when one is totally obsessed with the idea of individual rights is, thus, quite real. In a social situation that, as a matter of ethical testament, stresses the importance of social relationships and such communal values as concern and compassion for others, insistence on rights (some rights) may not always be necessary or appropriate. In terms of the communitarian morality, then, love or friendship or concern (compassion) for others may be considered the first virtue of social institutions, rather than justice, which is fundamentally about, or crucially allied to, rights. Questions of social justice may not constantly arise in a society whose practices are shored up by communal values and other moral virtues.

The communitarian ethic acknowledges the importance of individual rights but it does not do so to the detriment of responsibilities that individual members have or ought to have toward the community or other members of the community. Concerned, as it is, with the common good or the communal welfare, the communitarian moral theory considers responsibility as an important principle of morality. By "responsibility," I mean a caring attitude or conduct that one feels one ought to adopt with respect to the well-being of another person or other persons. Such responsibilities include the responsibility to help others in distress, the responsibility to show concern for the needs and welfare of others, the responsibility not to harm others, and so on.

Responsibilities to the community as a whole or to some members of the community would not derive from a social contract between individuals. The social contract theory is a contrivance for voluntary, not natural, membership in the type of society that is regarded by some people as a mere association of individuals convened (hypothetically) to determine the moral and political principles that would govern a political order they envisage; it is a launching pad for a civil society or a political community. In a communitarian framework, however, there would be no place for the social contract theory to articulate and formalize the responsibilities some individuals will have or will fulfill with respect to others. The responsibilities will derive from the communitarian ethos and its imperatives.

A question may be raised, however, about the justification for giving equal attention to responsibilities in the communitarian political morality. The justification derives from our understanding of what social and solidaristic life requires. The relational character of the individual by virtue of her natural sociality immediately makes her naturally oriented to other persons with whom she must live. Living in relation to others directly involves an individual in social and moral roles, obligations, commitments, and responsibilities, which the individual must fulfill. The natural relationality of the person thus immediately plunges her into a moral universe. Social life itself, thus, prescribes or mandates a morality that, clearly, should be weighted on responsibility for others and for the community, a morality that should orient the individual to an appreciation of shared, and not only individual, ends. Social reciprocities that are (or, should be) an essential feature of communitarian morality mandate concern for the interests of others, including recognizing the rights of other individuals. The communitarian morality should therefore be an altruistically freighted morality.

The success that must accrue to shared or corporative living depends very much on each member of the community demonstrating a high degree of moral responsiveness and sensitivity to the needs and well-being of other members. This should manifest itself in each member's pursuit of his responsibilities. Thus, the community life itself constitutes the foundation for moral responsibilities and obligations. Also, the common good of shared relationships, which is an outstanding goal of the communitarian political morality, requires that each individual should work for the good of all. The ethical values of compassion, solidarity, reciprocity, cooperation, interdependence, and social well-being, which must be counted among the principles of the communitarian morality, primarily impose responsibilities on the individual with respect to the community and its members. All these considerations elevate the notion of responsibilities to a status equal to that of rights in the communitarian political and moral thought. Neglect of, or inadequate attention to, the status of responsibilities and obligations on one hand, and the obsessional emphasis on, and privileging of, rights on the other hand, could lead to the fragmentation of social values and, consequently, of social relationships and the integrity of society itself. Responsibilities, like rights, must therefore be taken seriously.

It is often said that rights are correlated with responsibilities, that, if there are rights, then there must be corresponding responsibilities. This hackneyed statement does not seem to me to be *wholly* true, certainly not true in aspects of moral relationships between individuals, or in cases where individuals feel they ought to fulfill some responsibility to their community. It is true that if I have a right to education, then it is the responsibility of someone—a parent or a local authority or the state—to provide what is necessary for my education; similarly, if I have the right to work, it is the responsibility of the state to make jobs available to me. In such cases, where rights are asserted against the state or against some persons in specific social or political or public roles or positions, the correspondence or correlation between rights and responsibilities will clearly be on track. But it is possible for a person to carry out a responsibility to some one else without our having to say that the responsibility was carried out *because* of the right of this other person, that is, the person for whose sake some responsibility was fulfilled. If I carry out a responsibility to help someone in distress, I would not be doing so because I think that that someone has a right against *me*, a right I should help defend or realize. If I give my seat on a bus to an older person, I do not do so because this older person has a right against me. In such situations, the fulfillment of responsibility would not be based on the acknowledgment of someone's right. I would be carrying out that responsibility because I consider that person worthy of some moral consideration by me, someone to whose plight I ought to be morally sensitive. The kind of moral responsibility I am referring to here will be different from the responsibilities enjoined upon persons by reason of certain specific social or public roles, positions, or statuses they occupy in the society.

When we want to fulfill some responsibilities, such as providing aid to someone in distress, conferring benefits on individuals unrelated to us, we do not first ask ourselves whether the persons whose well-being we should care for have any rights against us and whether we should carry out those responsibilities *because* of those rights. People in societies in which the concept of rights has not gained (much) currency in their moral or political language and behavior would carry out their responsibilities to their fellow human beings, yet without the conviction that the latter have rights against them. Responsibilities to such fellow human beings, then, are not grounded on their rights. In other words, it is not so much a consciousness of the rights of others as our moral responsiveness to their particular situations or needs that impinges on our moral decision to carry out our responsibilities to them. This, I think, is generally true and would be very much so in a political context, like the communitarian, which does not lay any obsessional stress on rights.

A rider, however, is required here. There are certain things that we should not do: we should not harm others; we should not rob or kill others. Let us call them "negative moral imperatives." These invariably do have corresponding rights. For, one's right not to be harmed imposes a responsibility on others not to harm one. But, as regards our moral responses to an individual's situation or needs, the correlation between rights and responsibilities arising out of positive moral imperatives collapses. For, as I said, there are responsibilities that are not based on the recognition of others' rights.

The position I am maintaining is clearly at variance with one that is widespread and maintains that our "duties," that is, responsibilities, are based on the rights of others. Raz, for instance, asserts: "Since a right is a ground for duties there is a good deal of truth in this kind of correlativity thesis." [42] He says also that "[r]ights are the grounds of duties in the sense that one way of justifying holding a person to be subject to a duty is that this serves the interest on which another's right is based." [43] The well-known thesis of correlativity can generally be upheld, to repeat, only with respect to positive "duties" enjoined upon state authorities or upon individuals who occupy specific roles in the society or state; it can be upheld also with respect to negative moral imperatives enjoined on all individual members of the community. We would be right in saying that in all such cases rights enjoin corresponding responsibilities. But positive moral imperatives acted on by "free" persons ("free" in the sense of not occupying any specific social or public role in the society) generally do not have their grounds in the rights of others. In our moral world, to act in accordance with free-floating positive moral imperatives is always in demand or required: positive response to them appears to be the touchstone of moral integrity. For, unlike negative moral imperatives, which often overlap with, and so are enjoined by, the law, free-floating positive moral imperatives are acted on by individuals who are sensitive to moral principles or moral ideals. The upshot of the foregoing, then, is that it is possible for the communitarian morality to hold the moral status of responsibilities in high esteem without our having to say that this (communitarian) attitude toward responsibilities is mandated or induced by a consciousness of the rights of others. The communitarian attitude toward responsibilities to others is mandated rather by consciousness of the *needs* of these others.

Yet, in paying due regard to responsibilities people feel they owe to the community and its members, the moderate communitarian political and moral theory does not imply, by any means, that rights are not important; nor does it deny responsibilities to the self. As pointed out earlier in this section, moderate communitarianism acknowledges the intrinsic worth of the individual and the moral (natural) rights of the individual that the acknowledgment can be said to entail. As an autonomous, self-assertive being, the individual should, within limits, care for her own well-being or needs just as she cares for the needs of others. Altruistic concerns cannot obliterate responsibilities to the self. This is because the concern for the interests and needs of others cannot imply the dissolution of the self. For, after all, the individual has a life to live and so must have plans for her life and must see to the realization of those plans—a goal the attainment of which imposes on an individual the responsibility to develop her natural abilities and talents.

Therefore, the responsibility an individual has toward the community and its members does not—should not—enjoin her to give over her whole life, as it were, to others and be oblivious of her personal well-being.

What the communitarian ethic would enjoin, then, is dual responsibility, a proposal—or, better, an imperative—that will reflect an attempt to respond adequately to the problem of the relation between the individual and society, a problem I referred to at the outset of this chapter. The successful pursuit of the individual's dual responsibility requires that, through the development of her capacities and through her own exertions and striving—and hence through self-attention—the individual should herself attain some appropriate status, socially, economically, intellectually, and so on. I am not saying that all the needs or interests of the individual should be taken care of before she embarks on her responsibilities and commitments to others. Yet, it is surely a necessary requirement that the individual be in a position to fulfill her responsibilities to others: and hence the need to carry out responsibilities to herself. If the notion of responsibilities to self—if self-attention—makes sense even in a communitarian context, as I maintain it does, so would the notion of individual rights, which, as a reflexive notion, must be conceptually linked to that of self-interest or, as I prefer to say, self-attention.

5. Communitarianism and Supererogationism

Communitarian moral and political theory, as I said, advocates the politics of the common good; it is concerned with the communal welfare—the well-being of every member of the community. This kind of moral ethos will, as argued in the foregoing section, set great store to moral responsibility: it will consider responsibility as an important plank in its moral platform. That consideration will itself be underpinned or inspired by such fundamental moral values as love, friendship, and sensitivity to the welfare of others. In the communitarian moral universe caring or compassion or generosity, not justice—which is related essentially to a strictly rights-based morality—may be a fundamental moral category. In a moral framework where love, compassion, caring, friendship, and genuine concern for others characterize social relationships, justice—which is about relations of claims and counter-claims—may not be the primary moral virtue. Since individual rights would not be a special focus of the communitarian morality, as pointed out in the preceding section, and since the basic communitarian moral structure can to some extent—or in many ways—absorb or take care of those claims and counter-claims, claims made in pursuit of fair or equal distribution can be expected to be reduced to the minimum. Moreover, the pursuit of the politics of the common good may not require excessive insistence or emphasis on individual rights, which often lie at the foundation of individual claims and counter-claims and elevate the value of justice to a priority status.

In indicating a reason why equal attention ought to be given to responsibilities in the communitarian theory, I said that social life, which follows upon our natural sociality, implicates the individual in a web of moral obligations, commitments, and responsibilities to be fulfilled in pursuit of the common good or the general welfare. The scope of the responsibilities and obligations will expectably be extensive and not clearly circumscribed. Thus the communitarian concept of moral responsibility will encompass what are known in other moral theories as acts of supererogation. And, further, the communitarian political morality will not make a distinction between moral responsibility and a supererogatory act, the former being obligatory and the latter nonobligatory or optional, but instead will collapse the two. Before moving on, however, let us try to clarify what a supererogatory act is.

A supererogatory act (*super* in Latin means "above") is generally defined as an act that is beyond the call of duty, that is, over and above what a moral agent is required to do. Among the implications of the definition are that an act of supererogation is neither morally obligatory nor forbidden, that its omission is not wrong and hence does (or, should) not draw moral sanction or criticism, that it is morally good and commendable by virtue of both its intrinsic value and its consequences, that it is an optional act, done for the sake of another person's good and is, thus, a meritorious act.[44] The characterization of the supererogatory act sets it off from moral responsibility, properly called. In being described as good, or morally commendable, or pursued for the welfare of another person, the supererogatory act is clearly a moral act, which, *as such,* ought normally to be performed. Yet, according to many moral philosophers, its optional, nonobligatory character makes it a different sort of moral requirement, one that may or may not be performed or, put differently, a requirement whose moral force or "oughtness" is a matter for the individual moral agent to decide. We would normally think that a morally good or right act ought to be done, that there is a moral link between "good" and "ought": if an act is morally good, then it ought to be done. This kind of equation would normally be taken to be correct in a moral context. According to theories of supererogation, it is correct but applicable only to moral responsibility "proper," not to an act that is beyond the call of duty. In regarding an act as morally good and yet as belonging to a different sort of moral responsibility, one that does not exact obligation, the supererogationist is clearly faced with a dilemma.

Implicit in supererogationism is a clear assumption that there are limits to what we, as human beings, can reasonably consider as our legitimate moral responsibilities and obligations, those responsibilities that we naturally feel we are morally obliged to fulfill. We cannot fulfill, or are not prepared to fulfill, those responsibilities that we think are beyond our limits. The problem that immediately arises is: how do we set the limits, that is, what criteria are we to establish in order to set those limits, to demarcate responsibilities from those responsibilities that are sort of quasi-responsibilities and, thus, beyond the call of duty? In other words, how do we come to decide that such-and-such acts are beyond the call of duty?

One major set of criteria will relate to the practicability of certain acts, that is, whether or not those acts are such as we, as human beings, have the ability or are in a position to perform. Thus, the desire or wish to give help to some people in distress who are so physically distanced from us may not be fulfilled; similarly, the desire or wish to provide financial or other forms of aid to people experiencing famine, whether near or far, may not be fulfilled because we are financially handicapped ourselves. The impracticability of such acts, or rather our inability to perform them, tends to make us feel that those acts are beyond the call of duty. I think, however, that it would be necessary to distinguish acts that we should regard as moral responsibilities but which for some practical or other reasons we cannot carry out from those moral responsibilities the fulfillment of which is relatively easier. Yet our inability to fulfill the former set of responsibilities does not—should not—make them supererogatory. There are indeed some responsibilities that we recognize as *within* our moral limits, that is, not "beyond the call of duty," but which, nevertheless, we are *not* able to carry out (hence the problem of incontinence, moral weakness); but we do not say that they are supererogatory by reason simply of our inability to carry them out. So, our incapacity to fulfill a responsibility, however complicated it may be, cannot be a legitimate ground for our shrugging it off as supererogatory.

Another criterion may fasten on those actions or rules the pursuit of which makes social life possible or tolerable. J. O. Urmson maintains that we should be concerned to prohibit "behavior that is intolerable if men are to live together in society," and to demand "the minimum of cooperation toward the same end."[45] And, for Urmson, all that is required for the achievement of a tolerable basis of social life is a set of "basic rules" or "basic duties"[46] that, being basic, must be severely limited in scope. Urmson's concern about social life, about human beings living together in society, about cooperation among human beings who live (or want to live) together, would certainly titillate the moral palate of the communitarian moralist. But it is precisely because of the creation of a viable and tolerable social life that the communitarian moralist would wish to argue against circumscribing the responsibilities that people who live together in society ought to carry out with respect to others. A harmonious cooperative social life requires that individuals demonstrate sensitivity to the needs and interests of others, if that society is to be a moral society. The reason is that the plight or distress of some individuals in the society is likely to affect others in some substantial ways. If social arrangement is to maximize the good for all, then that arrangement will have to include rules the pursuit of which will conduce to the attainment of communal welfare. In this connection, such moral virtues as love, mercy, and compassion will have to be regarded as intrinsic to satisfactory moral practice in the communitarian society.

Yet, another criterion that may be established to set limits to moral responsibility derives from conceptions of the autonomy of the individual, so crucial to the well-being of the individual. Related to the concept of individual autonomy is of course that of individual rights, as I said in the preceding section. Thus, David Heyd observes that "supererogation is justified by showing that some supererogatory acts must exist because society cannot require of the individual every act that would promote the general good, and because the individual has the right to satisfy his wants and to achieve his ends and ideals regardless of their social utility (with some obvious limitations, of course)."[47] What Heyd is saying is that the existence and exercise of the individual's autonomy and rights justify supererogationism, for they set limits to what the individual, concerned with the fulfillment of his own needs and welfare, can be expected to do in meeting the needs of others. The implication here is, thus, that the denial of supererogationism will lead to the inappropriate extension of the individual's moral responsibility and the consequent sacrifice or subversion of his autonomy and personal needs. And, for John Rawls, if moral responsibility is allowed to contain supererogatory acts, it would involve risk and loss to the agent: "It is good to do these [supererogatory] actions but it is not one's duty or obligation. Supererogatory acts are not required, though normally they would be were it not for the loss or risk involved for the agent himself. A person who does a supererogatory act does not invoke the exemption which the natural duties allow. For while we have a natural duty to bring about a great good, say, if we can do so relatively easily, we are released from this duty when the cost to ourselves is considerable."[48]

The views expressed by Heyd and Rawls in the above quotations, which are the common views of the advocates of supererogationism, reflect a certain conception of the nature of morality or moral conduct: that moral conduct is essentially to be confined to acts that human beings can or want conveniently to perform and that will promote their own individual ends. It is not that supererogationists necessarily think that morality is self-regarding and that all self-sacrifice should be expunged from morality. It is rather that they think that *some* form of self-sacrifice cannot be required of any and every moral agent. But the question is: which form of self-sacrifice can or should be required of the moral agent, and how do we determine that? For some people, providing the slightest assistance of any kind to someone in distress will be a self-sacrifice; others, however, will not consider such acts as sending huge amounts of money to help people in famine-stricken areas within their nation or outside it, or helping to get someone out of real danger, as self-sacrificial or heroic or saintly. What all this means surely is that the field of our moral acts should be left open: the scope of our moral responsibilities should not be circumscribed. The moral life, which essentially involves paying regard to the needs, interests, and well-being of *others*, already implies self-sacrifice and loss, that is, loss of something—one's time, money, strength, and so on. There is, in my view, no need, therefore, to place limits on the form of the self-sacrifice and, hence, the extent of our moral responsibilities.

On this showing, there is no justification for Heyd to think that "a doctor who goes to a remote tribe to cure a rare disease is doing a supererogatory act." In Heyd's view, the doctor who acts in this way "goes beyond his natural duty, which in that case is confined to the fulfillment of his social duty as a doctor in *his* community."[49] In opposition to Heyd's view, I wish to say that morality requires us to look beyond the interests and needs of our own selves, and that, given the beliefs in our common humanity—with all that this concept implies for the fundamental needs, feelings, and interests of all human beings irrespective of their specific communities—our moral sensitivities should extend to people beyond our immediate communities. The concept of our common humanity clearly lies at the base of references to "the international community," "the world community," "the global community" frequently made by diplomats, politicians, and world leaders of different national or cultural communities. The relevance and significance of the references to the highest level of human community suggest the understanding and conviction that all human beings, irrespective of their local communities, are *also* members of a single large human community. This fact, at least in principle, clearly and insistently grounds the need to extend our moral concerns and responsibilities to members of "other" communities—distant strangers. The communitarian ethic could be a vanguard in this enterprise.

Also, as a riposte to whatever is meant by "natural duty" (a term used by both Rawls and Heyd), it may be pointed out that morality is generally conceived of as a device for countervailing or "straightening up" our natural inclinations. In most instances our "natural duty" would have been responsibility to oneself. But this is not what morality requires of us. Urmson also says that as part of the notion of duty, "I may demand that you keep your promises to me . . . and I may reproach you if you transgress. But however admirable the tending of strangers in sickness may be, it is not a basic duty, and we are not entitled to reproach those to whom we are strangers if they do not tend us in sickness."[50] It seems surprising that Urmson should say that tending strangers in sickness is not a basic responsibility (or duty) the transgression of which should attract censure, when he holds that "morality . . . is something that should serve *human needs*."[51] Most people, I think, will agree that to tend a stranger in sickness is to serve a *human* need and hence should be considered a basic moral responsibility. We would be blunting our moral visions, or demeaning our moral and personal autonomy, if we considered "human needs" to be the needs *only* of people in our own neighborhood or local or proximate community.

It seems to me that supererogationists conceive human nature to be warped from the moral point of view. They seem to think that only a few human beings have the capacity to practice such basic virtues as love, charity, benevolence, and sensitivity to the needs of others, and hence only a few people—those consumed with moral ideals or, in the words of Urmson, "the higher flights of morality"[52]—can pursue a certain category of acts, that is, supererogatory acts, which, for supererogationists, are separable from basic moral responsibility. Consequently, they speak in terms of a supposed dual nature of morality: basic responsibility and ideal (moral) responsibility. Thus, Heyd: "Many ethical theorists believe in the dual nature of morality:

on the one hand, there is the morality of duty, obligation, and justice, which is essentially social and formulated in universal principles. . . . On the other hand, there is ideal morality, the morality of love, virtue, and aspiration, which is not formulated in universalizable principles."[53] The supererogationist distinction between responsibilities ("proper") and ideals seems to be predicated on the assumption, which I have already referred to, that only a few human beings can be idealistic, which is to hold a low opinion of the moral quality of humankind. I think, however, that human beings could be conceived generally as not lacking the capacity to demonstrate love and altruistic sensitivity in favor of other human beings *without* thinking that doing so goes beyond the call of duty, or that they are doing what most other human beings cannot or are not disposed to do, or that they are being simply idealistic. The communitarian moral theory that I espouse would not consider most human beings as drained of the virtues of love, benevolence, and other "moral ideals," required in the communitarian pursuit of the common good.

Communitarian moral theory, concerned with the welfare and needs of people, would see no real distinction between moral responsibility and moral ideals, the latter regarded as the basis of supererogationism. It would hold that moral responsibility already contains moral ideals. Thus supererogationism will have no place in the communitarian moral theory. If supererogationism is allowed a status in our moral thought and behavior, it will diminish the moral quality or status and perfectibility of humankind. In our world in which human beings, as human beings, can be assumed to share certain fundamental needs, values, desires, and aspirations, such statements as "it is not my business," "I do not want to be involved," "each for himself," and so on, made by someone as the grounds for refusing to help another person in distress, or to demonstrate regard for the interests of others generally, will be considered by the communitarian moral theory as morally reprehensible. The incapacity to perform certain moral responsibilities, erroneously regarded as moral or saintly ideals, does not make those responsibilities supererogatory. From the point of view of morality, devised in pursuit of cooperative living and human well-being, there cannot really be any act such as can be said to go beyond the call of duty. No act that is morally good in itself or that will conduce to the well-being of some individual or group of individuals should be considered morally optional, to be morally shrugged off or unconscionably set aside. The fact that such an act may be beyond our immediate capacity to perform is irrelevant: what is important is to recognize that act as in principle *within* the pale of our moral responsibility.

6. Conclusion

Communitarian moral and political theory, which considers the community as a fundamental human good, advocates a life lived in harmony and cooperation with others, a life of mutual consideration and aid and of interdependence, a life in which one shares in the fate of the other—bearing one another up—a life that provides a viable framework for the fulfillment of the individual's nature or potential, a life in which the products of the exercise of an individual's talents or endowments are (nevertheless) regarded as the assets of the community as such, a life free from hostility and confrontation: such a life, according to the theory, is most rewarding and fulfilling. To my mind, it is the moderate or restricted version of communitarianism that is defensible and that I support and argue for in this chapter. But apparently it is the radical or extreme version of communitarianism that has hitherto been espoused in the writings of some African scholars of the postcolonial era. The position I take is therefore in many ways at variance with the views expressed by those scholars, which insist on the moral primacy of the community and reduce individual rights to a secondary status. A strong and unrelenting insistence on the moral primacy or prerogative of the community can lead (and in postcolonial African has led) to tyranny, political intolerance, and authoritarianism.

Moderate or restricted communitarianism gives accommodation to communal values as well as to values of individuality, to social commitments as well as to responsibilities to oneself. In its basic thrust and concerns, it pays due, and adequate, regard to responsibilities to the community and its members and would, I think, consider the so-called supererogatory acts as belonging to the category of moral responsibilities, though not to the detriment of individual rights whose existence and value it recognizes, or should recognize, and for a good reason. I believe strongly that a moral and political theory that combines an appreciation of, as well as responsibility and commitment to, the community as a fundamental value, *and* an understanding of, as well as commitment to, the idea of individual rights, will be a most plausible theory to support. Guided by the assumptions about the dual features of the self with an implied dual responsibility, it should be possible to deflate any serious tension between the self and its community.

3

Ethnicity, Identity, and Nationhood

When someone asks whether Ghana or Kenya or Yugoslavia (as it was then) is a nation, he is, I believe, not asking about whether or not any of these states or countries has a government or a central political authority or sovereignty; nor is he asking about the political or economic system that has been established by that state. What, then, would he be asking about or looking for? What is a nation? What is it for a state or a country or a community of people to be a nation? Why should a state seek to become a nation? Is it not enough to be a state, an independent state at that? What does a nation have that a state or a country does not have? How can a state become a nation or, put differently, how can a nation be built if it *can* be built? What is the real nature of the ethnic group that, in one sense, becomes a nation and, in another, becomes a component of a nation (i.e., a multinational state)? And, finally, how do we understand the notions of national culture and national identity? And how can these notions manifest themselves in concrete situations? I intend to explore these questions in this chapter.

It is a well-known fact that a very substantial number of the states of the contemporary world are ethnically and culturally heterogeneous societies. Each state is constituted by a medley of ethnic groups. The historical explanations for the ethnically plural structure of many of the states in today's world need not occupy our attention for the moment. One of the nagging and resilient problems unleashed by the ethnically plural structure of modern states is how to weld the constituent ethnic groups into a new, certainly larger, form of sociopolitical association for the benefit and welfare of all the groups, how to solder the component parts together to make a whole—how to create a unity out of plurality: in short, how to integrate the constituent ethnic groups into a nation, at least some of whose goals, characteristics, and systems of functioning would be different from those of a component ethnic group. (I argue later that, in my opinion, "communocultural" would be a more appropriate term than "ethnic.") The failure effectively to negotiate the problem of sociopolitical integration or fusion may give rise to apathy, disenchantment, feelings of not belonging or of neglect, inter-ethnic conflicts and, ultimately, disintegration and the demise of the whole, that is, the nation (or, nation-state).

Awareness of the disintegrative force that could be released by the failure to deal effectively with the problem of fusing the diverse ethnic elements into a new and vibrant political whole called "nation" is what gives rise to the search for national unity, national culture, national loyalty, national identity, national integration, and so forth. It can safely be assumed that in such expressions as "national culture," "national identity," and "national integration," "national" is being contrasted with ethnic or local or provincial (or, regional). Hence, the political or ideological importance of these expressions. The use of these expressions presupposes some understanding and appreciation of the concept of a nation. But it is instructive to note that these expressions are used—often exhortatively—despite the fact that those who use them already live within a territorial boundary called state or country. This suggests the conviction that a nation is distinguishable from a state or country, that our conception of a nation would differ from our conception of a state or country, that, given that understanding, nationhood is a project, a badly needed project, the achievement of which, in the circumstances of the modern nation-state, is in the womb of time. What, then, is nationhood?

1. Nation as an Ethnocultural Community

I shall set out by distinguishing two senses or conceptions of nation, the first or original sense, which is simpler, and a second sense, which is complex. The first conception of nation derives from the etymology of the word "nation." Its etymology provides it with the meaning of "a birth group," "a blood-related group." Let us dwell for some moments on the implications of this original meaning of nation, a meaning that has not been abandoned even in the modern world and in fact is still influential. Perhaps the eighteenth-century German philosopher G. W. Herder was guided or attracted by the etymology of "nation" when he made the following observation: "A nation is as *natural* a plant as a family only with more branches. Nothing therefore is more manifestly contrary to the purpose of political government than the unnatural enlargement of states, the wild mixing of various races and nationalities under one scepter; . . . such states are but patched up contraptions, fragile machines, for they are wholly devoid of inner life."[1] Herder would thus strongly object to the idea of forming a multinational state, for he would consider such a political formation "unnatural." But Herder's view of "nation" as natural, by which he most probably means that members of a nation are consanguineous and that a nation is therefore one vastly extended family, is surely an exaggeration. Consanguinity among the entire membership of a nation is more a matter of feeling or belief than of historical or genealogical fact; consanguineous feeling is sometimes the result also of demagogic indoctrination and sleight of hand or chicanery.

In the wake of its first or original sense, "nation" has come to be used to refer to a group or community of people who not only share a common culture, language, history, and possibly a territory but believe that they hail from a common ancestral background and are therefore closely related by kinship ties. But whether members of a nation share kinship or blood ties or not, it would be correct to assert that relations between them are characterized by the ethos of cohesion, solidarity, fellow-feeling, and mutual recognition, sympathy, and understanding. Thus, ethnicity—the feeling or consciousness of belonging to a group that shares certain common sociocultural elements—is the most outstanding feature of a nation; it may in fact be said that nation in the first sense is coterminous with ethnocultural community. That is to say, "nation," in this sense, may (roughly) be held as equivalent to an ethnic group. (I explain below why the ethnic group is essentially a cultural group.) Thus, an individual's nationality is occasionally expressed in terms of her ethnic affiliation even in a modern state composed of diverse ethnic groups or nationalities: thus, the statement "I am Welsh" may be uttered by a Welsh person in the United Kingdom; "I am Yoruba" by a person in Nigeria; "I am Jewish" by a person in the United States. The connection between nation and ethnic community suggests a connection between nation and people, whether the people have a well-defined territory or not. Thus the Jewish people referred to themselves as a Jewish nation centuries before the creation (in 1948) of a Jewish state. And, one often hears of such utterances by Arab political leaders as "the United Nations wants to destroy the Arab *nation*," or "Sadat's visit to Jerusalem was a disgrace to the Arab *nation*." In such statements, "nation" is being used to refer to people—Jewish, Arab, or other, who believe that they are bound together in many ways. What holds a nation together is a combination of factors: beliefs about a common ancestral background, culture, language, history, and possibly a territory. All, or some, of them constitute the identity conditions for nation.

It may be said that the idea of culture or language as constitutive of nation goes back particularly to the German philosophers, such as J. G. Fichte, Friedrich von Schlegel, and Herder, who wrote toward the end of the eighteenth century. Fichte observed: "It is true beyond doubt that wherever a separate *language* is found there a separate *nation* exists which has the right to take independent charge of its affairs and to govern itself." [2] And Schlegel also remarked that "the older, purer and unmixed is a tribe, the more customs it has . . . which are genuinely persisted and adhered to, the more it becomes a nation." [3] In fact, for Schlegel, the concepts of customs

(Sitten) and nation *(Nation)* "hang together."[4] Thus, nation was defined in terms (also) of cultural continuity and identity, an essential ingredient of which is language. A contemporary German scholar, Ludwig von Mises, also thinks that language is synonymous with nationality, that "the essence of nationality lies in language."[5] Indeed, as I discuss below, the link between language and nationality—a sense of common nationality and national identity—is an essential step toward nation-building in a multinational (multi-ethnic) situation.

During the peace negotiations at the end of the First World War (1919), matters concerning nationalities came to the fore. President Woodrow Wilson of the United States proclaimed and espoused the doctrine of national self-determination, intended to raise the status of every nation (i.e., nationality, ethnocultural community) to that of a state, an independent state. The League of Nations, which was created in the wake of the war to help bring about and maintain peace in the world, was very much concerned about minority cultural groups, that is, nations, nationalities, in the multinational states of Europe, in which the political community was obviously not coextensive with only one ethnocultural community. For there were several cultural structures within the multinational state. Questions of minority cultures and their protection were of paramount importance to the League of Nations. In the conceptions or understandings of the times, "nation" was used to denote an ethnocultural community of people who have a sense of belonging together. Thus, writing in the days of the League of Nations, the British philosopher L. T. Hobhouse observed that "the problem of dealing with minority nation is the hardest that statesmen had to solve."[6] The context of the statement indicates that by "nation" Hobhouse meant an ethnocultural community, a (minority) culture. Nation, as thus understood, was perhaps not coterminous with state, for the ethnocultural community was generally not in possession of well-defined and recognized territorial boundaries and a system of government; but it could become a state. I shall refer to this conception of nation as N_1.

On the other hand, however, the term "nation" in the name League of Nations did not refer to an ethnocultural community; it referred to a state—a political entity, like Great Britain or the United States, embodying several nations. Hence the ambiguity in the application of the term "nation."

Inasmuch as N_1 is a community of people who believe themselves to be bound by some intrinsic ties, and inasmuch as it is possible for such a community of people to have no territory with well-defined boundaries or government with a central authority, N_1 may be regarded generally as a social (or sociological) concept, rather than as a political concept. If we regard the state as a sovereign political entity with territorial boundaries and a government that has ultimate central authority, then N_1 may not be a state, even though it is possible for it to develop into one if it is able or has the opportunity to create the apparatus of statehood. Thus, while N_1 is originally or essentially not a political concept, the state is at once a political concept, a political entity. Nationhood in the sense of N_1 suggests essentially the idea of cultural homogeneity, while statehood suggests the idea of the concentration of sovereign political power at the center. Thus, a political community with a culturally homogeneous citizenry *and* a sovereign power concentrated at the center to which all the citizens are subject and owe loyalty will be a nation-state. This in fact is the most appropriate meaning of the political concept of nation-state: a nation, that is, an ethnocultural community that has evolved into a state, having acquired the relevant appurtenances of statehood. (It must be noted, however, that in the language of modern politics "nation" is used synonymously with "state" or "nation-state," e.g., "African nations," while the term "nation-state" has been used where the most appropriate term would be "multinational.")

Now, what are the great virtues or essential characteristics of nation conceived as ethnocultural community (N_1)? The fact of the linguistic homogeneity of the members of the ethnocultural community is perhaps the most outstanding feature of N_1. It facilitates and fosters interpersonal communication, understanding, and mutual recognition of close ties that generally exist among people who speak the same language. It also forms a basis for unity. The social character of N_1 makes for sharing, solidarity, interdependence, commitment to the cause of the nation, and sensitivity and responsiveness to the interests of fellow members of the nation, while evoking natural sentiments of loyalty. Cultural homogeneity is another virtue of ethnonationality: it enables members of the ethnic community to share basic values and meanings that constitute the ground by which they understand themselves and interpret their experiences. The basic values and shareable meanings of the culture also constitute the context of social identity and induce national consciousness and a sense of belonging together. Thus, loyalty, solidarity, social commitment, cultural and linguistic homogeneity, a sense of belonging and of common life: these are among the virtues of N_1 that tend to make it an ideal model of human community and relationships and ought to underpin or characterize or influence human relationships and attitudes even in an ethnically and culturally plural state.

2. Nation as a Multinational State

Now, the concept of a nation has been applied also to complex, ethnically and culturally plural political communities called states. This is clearly a comprehensive use of the concept, for the states themselves are almost invariably multiethnic, multinational, multilingual, and multicultural. Thus, there is an organization comprising a large number of independent states or countries of the world, the United *Nations* Organization; there is also the Commonwealth of *Nations;* and there was the League of *Nations.* These nations are mostly multinational, each of them being a conglomerate of several nationalities or ethnocultural communities. The concept of a nation has thus taken on a new meaning, a complex and comprehensive meaning, which I shall refer to simply as N_2. Thus,

$$N_2 = \Sigma\ N_1 a + N_1 b + N_1 c + N_1 d \ldots + N_1 n$$

where "Σ" stands for "the totality of." The set of N_1 constituting N_2 will of course have to be finite. For a concept that was originally applied to nationalities, ethnocultural communities as single or simple entities to be applied to a complex of these indicates how far it has moved from its original semantic moorings. The concept of a nation is now commonly and widely understood as N_2, a multinational state. So that, in terms of our current conceptions, almost all N_1, which were originally nations and are now constitutive of N_2, have thus become subnations or subnationalities.

N_2, as a complex entity, is of course to be distinguished from N_1, which is a simple entity. N_2, however, is to be assimilated to a state, for, in the process of becoming or emerging or being created as N_2, it would have taken on political configurations (with a government, central authority, well-defined territorial boundaries, etc.) that characterize a state. That is to say, N_2 would have become a political concept. But if N_2, now with the status of a state, comprises a number of nations (N_1), why should the problem of nation-building arise for a state, for N_2? The answer is twofold. First, even though N_2 (i.e., multinational state) is constituted by several N_1, it nevertheless at once lacks the virtues or the essential characteristics of an N_1 discussed earlier. Second, the component N_1 would have their own peculiarities and idiosyncracies: in terms of its cultural structure, N_1 is essentially homogeneous, while N_2 is heterogeneous. The problem that would unavoidably be generated by this kind of political arrangement would be how to weld the constituent N_1 into a whole, so that N_2 will emerge as a genuine amalgam of several N_1, ultimately taking on the characteristic features of an N_1.

The formation of the modern nation-state, a heterogeneous ethnic and cultural conglomerate with a concentration of sovereign power at the center, resulted in some cases from the movement of neighboring peoples toward larger political units for mutual benefits of all kinds; in others it resulted from the conquest by some invading peoples who forced several neighboring nationalities, that is, ethnocultural communities (N_1), into larger political communities called states—multinational states. The conquerors who shepherded different nationalities into nation-states failed to realize that it is one thing to make Ghana or Kenya or Yugoslavia; it is quite another to make Ghanaians or Kenyans or Yugoslavs. The nation-state, which for the citizens is a new experience and a new political concept, is surely not the same as a nation (N_1), which is essentially a sociocultural concept. Consequently, one of the besetting and daunting problems confronting a modern state in Africa, as elsewhere, is simply how to create or build a nation within a state that is politically independent. It is interesting to note that the talk—and therefore the concern—has always been about *nation*-building rather than *state*-building or *country*-building. Thus, Nelson Mandela, the distinguished political leader and statesman of South Africa, made the following statement on the eve of the first multiracial elections in his country: "This is, for all South Africans, an unforgettable occasion. . . . We are starting a new era of hope, reconciliation and *nation-building.*"[7]

The use of the term "nation-building" is, to my mind, not merely a matter of locution or idiom. There must surely be a reason why we talk of nation-building rather than "state-building" or "country-building." (Of course we can, and often do, talk of building a state or country, but the sense of "building" here is different from the sense of "building" in nation-building.) State-building essentially means developing the state by providing, for example, physical infrastructures. This sense of "building" forms only a part of the sense of "building" in nation-building, as I point out shortly. But for the moment it must be noted that the need to understand the idea of nationhood has become urgent, for to seek to attain the characteristic features—and hence the status—of a genuine nation (N_1) has in fact become a *moral* need, something worthwhile to attain. Nationhood has become a normative concept in that it has come to describe a desired level of ideal political arrangement embodying ideal or satisfactory human relationships. And so it is, that the ultimate goal of every multinational state (N_2) is to become a nation, to build a nation (in the sense of N_1). It is in pursuit of the moral, social, and cultural virtues of N_1 that nation-states (i.e., multinational states) seek to build themselves into nations.

What, then, is nation-building? Before I attempt to answer this question, I would like to critically examine Walker Connor's view that nation-building is a "misnomer." "Since most of the less developed states contain a number of nations," observes Connor, "and since the transfer of primary allegiance from these nations to the state is generally considered the *sine qua non* of successful integration, the true goal is not 'nation-building' but 'nation-destroying'."[8] Connor's statement equivocates on the term "nation" here; for, in nation-building, "nation" clearly refers to N_2—a multinational state, whereas in nation-destroying it clearly refers to N_1—an ethnocultural community. By "nation-destroying," I think Connor means eradicating ethnic consciousness or identity or ethnic nationalism that, according to the thesis of his lengthy essay, has been a barrier to political integration in the multinational state, an impediment to attaining the essence of nationhood (N_1). Connor's causal analysis, however, is, in my opinion, only partly correct: ethnicity is only part of the problem of achieving nationhood, even though it can hardly be denied that it is the most intractable part. Even so, ethnicity constitutes the tip of an iceberg whose base is perhaps much more complex, as I shall indicate presently. But let me say, now, that even though it makes sense to suggest that in the attempt to pursue nationhood, ethnic identities and their concomitant primary allegiances will have to be seriously deemphasized or curtailed, one should also recognize that at least some of the elegant aspects of the component ethnic cultures will (have to) feature in the new national identity and culture that will be created by the new multinational state, and need not be destroyed. What should instead be destroyed is ethnic nationalism (including the languages of some of the ethnic groups), which bedevils attempts at political integration at the level of N_2. In the enterprise of creating a nation-state (N_2), one most important thing is to find ingenuous ways by which primary allegiances can be transferred from the ethnocultural community to the state, that is, from the parts to the whole. One such way would be the kind of politics that will be practiced at the national (N_2) level, how, that is, political power is to be shared or used.

Thus, the political behavior of the government and public officials will be crucial to the maintenance and smooth functioning of the nation-state. If the political behavior tends to be negative and destructive of the aspirations of most people from the component groups, frustrations and negative sentiments will begin to well up that will not be a good presage for the burgeoning nation-state. Thus, the lack of fairness in the distribution of the resources and burdens of the state, which is the function of governmental authority and policy, for instance, is, in my view, a major causal factor in the disintegrative politics of many a nation-state, because it directly and deeply affects the economic, and ultimately, political welfare of the members of the constituent groups of the state who may feel cheated and unfairly treated. Citizens so treated are made to feel that they do not belong to the new state; nor is their future prosperity guaranteed by the new sociopolitical dispensation. If such aggrieved citizens happen to come from specific ethnic groups, they could begin to think of ways to safeguard their interests, ways that might include secession—an act that will lead immediately to political disintegration. What the new state will have to do is to find ways to keep the lid on the seething cauldron of discontent by assuaging fears and suspicions and opening wider the windows of opportunity for all the citizens of the new nation-state. Thus, the political role of the state is most crucial to maintaining the integrative political structure of the multinational, multiethnic state. Bad policies of the government may lead to the separation of the nations (N_1) and, ultimately, the collapse and possible demise of the nation-state (N_2). If a congenial political climate could be created by the new nation-state, the component ethnic groups would adapt themselves to their new social and political circumstances and seek to advance their economic interests and social status as parts of the whole.

Before discussing matters relating to nation-building, we must deal with the question, what is nation-building? I would like at once to distinguish nation-building from nation-developing (or, national development), for the two ideas or concepts are not, to my mind, coextensive or logically equivalent. National development, pursued by every state, is almost invariably confined to the development of the economy: provision for roads, water, schools, hospitals, electricity, and other material comforts that make ordinary life livable and bearable. If national development is pursued, however, in such an equitable manner as to benefit each region or ethnic community in the state, it will contribute to bringing about cohesiveness, which is what I think nation-building essentially means. Thus understood, national development is clearly a dimension or an aspect of nation-building or, perhaps better, a step toward nation-building, but only a step, because it is possible for a nation-state to be developed and yet fall short of the ideals of nation-hood.

The idea of building something suggests or requires putting parts together into a whole. We put stones and sand and wood and cement and other materials together in order to build a house. But the structure, that is, the house, that results from the composition is a unity; but not only that: it is also a *new* thing, which is neither a stone nor sand nor wood. Nation-building can be conceived on this analogy, even though the analogy may be defective in some respects in dealing with situations of conscious, rational, and moral beings, like human beings, who have values, goals, desires, and aspirations.

The question that immediately follows is: are nations built? This question can be answered both yes and no. In terms of the conception of a nation as an ethnocultural community speaking one language (i.e., in terms of N_1), nations are of course not built. From the circumstances of its emergence, N_1 is a more cohesive, less artificial sociocultural, possibly also political, community. With respect to N_1 there are no parts (i.e., ethnocultural parts) to be welded together into a whole. For, thanks to a shared cultural life and the belief—whether real or fictive—of the members of the nation that they are related by kinship ties, there is already a palpable manifestation of unrelenting unity, cohesion, solidarity, and fellow-feeling among them. The concept of nation-building, then, will not be applicable to N_1. A caveat may be entered here, however: a nation (N_1) that has, for whatever reasons, suffered breakdown for decades or centuries in its unity, cohesion, or solidarity, and hence in its consciousness of belonging together as a people will need to embark on nation-building. But it must be recognized that the task of nation-building with respect to N_1 will not be as arduous as that to be undertaken by N_2. This is the reason why "nation-building" is invariably used in reference to the multinational (or, multiethnic) state, not to nation in the pristine sense of N_1.

Thus, in terms of N_2, the answer to the question I posed is an unqualified yes: nations are built, just as parts are consciously and purposively put together to make a whole, a unity, to make a new object. The parts to be welded together into N_2 are of course the several N_1's. Nation-building is thus a conscious and purposive attempt to bring different peoples together to think, act, and live as if they were *one* people belonging to one large ethnocultural community, that is, as if they belonged to an N_1. The approach here is thus clearly instrumental. It will be seen at once that there is a clear element of artificiality about the character of N_2, particularly when the parts are welded into a whole as the result of wars and the implementation of the imperial designs of an imperial power superior in arms. The artificiality of N_2 probably bears the potential of disintegration, which could eventually erode the new multinational state.

Yet, historically, the coming together of several neighboring ethnocultural groups to form a nation-state (i.e., N_2) often could not be avoided. If a group of neighboring ethnocultural communities was not already forced by an external power—as was most often true in the colonized parts of the world—into forming a nation-state, then several considerations would have gone into the decision for a group of such ethnocultural communities to come together voluntarily to form a larger political community. Such considerations would have included, for coping effectively with the problems of human existence and for sheer survival, the need to establish a strong cordon of security and the desirability of establishing a strong political power or entity. Hence, the creation of larger political communities appears to be historically inevitable, and hence the ethnocultural plurality of many a modern state.

Basil Davidson, the well-known British writer and historian of Africa, has characterized the institution of the nation-state in Africa as a "curse" on Africa.[9] The reason for his view is certainly because of the intractable problems and frustrations of nation-building experienced by postcolonial Africa; such as recurrent ethnocultural conflicts, evolving national (N_2) culture and identity, and transferring loyalties and commitments from the ethnocultural groups to the new nation-state. These problems of nation-building are of course not unique to African states, even though they seem to be much more rampant and resilient in Africa than elsewhere. Yet, despite these problems, there is nevertheless a real need for the formation of the larger and stronger political units called nation-states. Nation-statism would have emerged in Africa even without colonialism. There is evidence that nation-statism was in fact in the process of emerging in Africa on the eve of the forcible imposition of colonial rule and the shepherding of communities (or, states) of diverse cultures into single nation-states. Davidson himself made the following remarkable observation: "The Europeans who first came in close contact with Asante, increasingly in the nineteenth century, certainly thought and wrote of Asante as a *nation-state* . . . because it had all the attributes that justified the label. It had a given territory, known territorial limits, a central government with police and army, a national language and law, and, beyond these, a constitutional embodiment in the form of a council called the Asanteman. . . . The Asante polity proceeded to behave in the best accredited manner of the European nation-state."[10] Given the historical truth of Davidson's observations and my own view of the historical inevitability of different people's forming themselves into larger political units for reasons adumbrated in the preceding paragraph, it would not be correct to say or imply that nation-statism is a "curse" for groups of people of diverse cultures. What *is* a curse, one might say, is the imposition of the type of nation-state tendentiously designed for the African people by the colonial powers, a type that did not take into account the cultures and characteristics of the peoples forcibly placed within the same territorial borders and ordered (or expected) to evolve a common form of cultural and political life: a design that to all intents and purposes eliminated the element of choice on the part of the different communities (or, states) shepherded into the new colonial nation-state.

But despite the apparently intractable problems of nation-building, the

concept of the nation-state (multinational state), in the context of the existential goals, conditions, and aspirations of human beings, is a useful and
appropriate concept to evolve, perhaps also necessary. How to translate it
into concrete and functional terms, however, appears to be a herculean task.
Even so, the concept should not be regarded as a misty ideal; nor should it
be considered a curse or bogus.

3. Beyond N_2: Toward Nationhood

Having shown that the idea of nationhood is useful and worthwhile, and its
concrete pursuit a political and moral need, the next question to be grappled
with relates to how to build a nation, that is, how to build an N_2 such that
it can become an analogue of N_1. Becoming an analogue of N_1 is the telos
of the pursuit of nationhood. To review, N_2 has (or must have) two features,
the descriptive feature, which simply describes the multinational state as a
political community constituted by several nations (N_1), and the normative
feature, which relates to what the (ideal) character of the multinational state
ought to be. For purposes of clarity, let us use N_2 for the descriptive feature
and introduce N_3 for the normative ideal of nationhood, which represents
the successful goal of nation-building. Notice, however, that there is something common to the two features: both are based on the assumption that
the multinational state is constructed from the diverse materials of several
N_1's.

N_3 represents the multinational state that has evolved through a transformative process aimed at welding together diverse nations (N_1) and thus
achieving some kind of unity and cohesion. Thus, the process is a moral
and political one, for it is an attempt not only to enhance the political well-
being of the culturally conglomerate state but also to insure the welfare,
survival, and interests of the citizens of the state. N_3, which represents a
stage beyond N_2—beyond, that is, the mere act of forming a single state out
of diverse national groups (N_1)—will have thus successfully progressed along
the path of nation-building and may be said to have achieved a reasonable
measure of social, cultural, and political unity and cohesion and a (or, some)
sense of common national identity (i.e., identity at the multinational level).
Thus, N_3 would look as follows:

$$N_3 = \Sigma\ n_1a + n_1b + n_1c + \ldots n_1n.$$

It must be noted that in this equation the N used after the equation sign in
N_2 to denote the national constituents (i.e., N_1) now appears in lowercase.
The use of the lowercase (n) here is intended to point up the fact of the
deemphasis of the N_1 identities at the level of N_3. For, in order to form a
new social entity above the particularities of the diverse N_1's, the distinct,
particularistic forms of identification would have to lose much of their
meaning to the new, larger sociopolitical dispensation. The primary affiliation is, to a considerable extent, now to N_3.

As already noted, the use of the lowercase *n* merely represents deemphasis of particularistic identities, not the total riddance of the presence or influence of the national (that is, ethnocultural) groups, the various constituents of the multinational state. This means not only that there are still subloyalties but also that the pristine, more particular group identities may continue to play a role in one's public and private life, even if those subloyalties and identities may, at this level, be innocuous and not particularly disintegrative of the whole. But what this means is of course that nationhood is not completely achieved at N_3. Yet, N_3 may emulate some of the virtues of N_1 and thus come to possess a satisfactory amount of unity and cohesion.

From the point of view of nationhood, however, N_3 may be said to be incomplete because of the presence and role of N_1 subloyalties. In pursuit of nationhood as a moral and political ideal to be achieved through the creation of a real and abiding sense of national identity analogous to that of N_1, I will, later in this section, propose a new theory of the multinational state that is not to be perceived necessarily as composed primarily of nations or ethnocultural groups, whether N's or n's. I call this theory "metanationality" and identify it with the symbol N_4. For the moment, however, I would like to put forward some thoughts regarding the pursuit and attainment of nationhood.

Before I do so, however, let me dispose of an idea some people espouse about ethnicity: that ethnicity can be a means for mobilizing the masses of a people for a struggle of some kind, that it can be a resource base for pursuing positive actions in support of the goals and welfare of the members of a particular (ethnic) group. Thus, ethnicity is perceived as a positive political and, perhaps also, social value. Obviously this perception of the political and social value of ethnicity can be held only in heterogeneous, multiethnic states in which ethnic affiliations may serve as a rallying point for political purposes and for providing help, support, and goodwill for members of a particular group. But it is precisely the exploitation of ethnicity for such purposes that turns it into a political disvalue, just as it makes it a morally unacceptable basis for appointment to public or official positions. Efforts to mobilize a relatively small ethnic group for national politics, that is, for winning political power in a multiethnic state, will fizzle out if they discount the other, perhaps larger, ethnic groups. But, even though the mobilization of the dominant ethnic group will most probably succeed in winning political power, it might end up disaffecting the minority groups politically and, consequently, economically as well. Thus, such a political perception of ethnicity makes it inherently fissiparous and disintegrative and, thus, at once poses problems for nation-building. It therefore makes political and moral sense to reject the perception of ethnicity as a political and social value in a multiethnic situation. I shall now suggest steps that may be helpful in the attempt to build a nation.

First, a profound consideration of the virtues or essential attributes of nation conceived as an ethnocultural community (N_1) will be fruitful and relevant in our attempt to understand not only what the nature of the nation-state ought to be but also how people will have to think and act in the large, multicultural, and complex environment of the nation-state. I have already made it clear that despite the fact that N_1 is a simple concept, while N_2 is a complex one (and so also is N_3), nevertheless N_1 spews out certain norms, ideals, outlooks, and attitudes from which N_2 as well as N_3 can benefit. Thus, it can be said that, despite the ethnocultural plurality of the modern state, considerations of the common interests or the collective good of the citizens of the nation-state can be a basis for the unity, cohesion, solidarity, and commitment of the citizens. Natural sentiments of loyalty and communal identities and consciousness that characterize the socioethical thought and action of the members of the single ethnocultural community ought to feature prominently in the thought and action of the citizens of the multinational state. Cultural homogeneity, which is an outstanding feature of the ethnocultural community, is of course not an intrinsic feature of the multinational state, which is by definition a culturally plural society. Even so, cultural pluralism does not necessarily preclude the possibility of horizontal relationships and fruitful interactions among component ethnic cultures. Ways will have to be found by the new multinational state to create a sense of cultural belonging or identity in all the citizens. Reflecting on the essential features of N_1, therefore, can be relevant to our appreciation of the nature of the multinational state and the expectable behavior of its multiethnic citizens.

Second, it seems to me that the ethnoculturally plural nature of the multinational state strongly suggests the creation of an open society. An open society is a democratic society in which the interests of every citizen, irrespective of ethnocultural background, are expected to be given equal consideration; a society in which merit, achievement, and credentials, rather than ethnocultural background, are considered the basis for the offer of a job or a rank; a society in which the idea of the equality of opportunity is appreciated by all and is given practical translation in the allocation of awards, public offices, and educational facilities—and hence allows room for social mobility—and, thus, gives no cause to an individual to feel cheated because of her ethnocultural affiliation: a society that insures the full equal rights of all the citizens; a society that, holding democracy in high esteem and considering it the principle of public political thought and behavior, avoids and resists tyranny; a society that cherishes not only open government and public accountability but also consensual politics—the politics of participation, accommodation, and compromise to which every citizen can contribute. In the open society to be created by the multinational state, political power must be shared satisfactorily among the constituent ethnocultural communities, for the political domination by any one single group will be perceived as a threat to the interests of minority groups and hence to national integration. The open society allows for the existence of alternative doctrinal or ideological frameworks competing for the cognitive or intellectual allegiance of the people. If a multicultural society endorses this kind of political philosophy or ideology, it will, I think, be on its way to providing a considerable degree of political satisfaction for all of its members. One of the important consequences of social mobility created in an open multinational state is that people will feel bound to one another more by social and professional interests than by ethnic considerations. Those sentiments that give rise to the nostalgic and exotic intra-ethnic relationships and fellowships of individuals in N_1 may reappear and characterize the inter-ethnic relationships of the citizens of N_3, if the latter could create an open, fair, democratic society.

In connection with political participation at the highest level and satisfactory power sharing, I wish to suggest that the political system or constitution of the multinational state be designed in such a way that the presidency or the highest political authority rotate among the various ethnocultural groups. This will make it possible for the president of the state to come from a minority ethnocultural group. The president will of course have to be elected. But when the turn comes to a particular group to provide a president for the entire multinational state, the various political parties— which themselves are expected to be national (N_3)—will each nominate one person from that particular ethnocultural group as their presidential candidate to stand for formal election, on the basis of his or her credentials, by the entire state at the polls. In time, the highest political office of the state will have been held by persons from all the various groups of the multinational state. This political dispensation will be a potent factor in promoting a sense of belonging and relationships of mutual trust, recognition, and respect among the component groups of the multiethnic state and will, thus, greatly help to maintain its integrity. Where the minority ethnocultural groups feel that, by reason of their small numbers, they are eternally condemned to the political periphery, and therefore to impotence—unable really, and ever, to influence affairs of state in any important and noticeable ways—the cauldron of discontent and disenchantment will never cease to seethe, with consequences that may threaten the future integrity of the multinational state. All the members of the state will have to be made to feel that they are equal citizens and are politically important and relevant.[11]

Third, national development, even though it is conceptually not equivalent to nation-building, as I said earlier, will, nevertheless, be a step in the direction of building a multinational state. But for it to have the greatest impact on the pursuit of nation-building as such, national development will have to be pursued equitably, fairly. This means that the allocation of development resources and projects must be horizontal, spread across the board, with no one district or region of the state—and hence no one ethnocultural community—left in limbo. One effective way of achieving this is to adopt and pursue a vigorous and well-meaning policy of decentralization. A decentralized system will promote adaptability and sensitivity to the special needs of particular localities or districts in the state. In these ways, a decentralized system would promote the exercise by members of the various ethnic communities of their talents and endowments; it would engender participation in the national (N_2 or N_3) effort to develop the state and induce euphoric sentiments of being political members of the state, having a real share in the national (N_2) wealth.

Decentralization will be an important factor in promoting democracy because of the political and economic consequences that it will bring about. Politically, decentralization will lead to power-sharing, as political power will trickle down to the localities. Economically, the interests of the component ethnic groups will be treated equally with respect to, at least, the provision of infrastructural facilities. It is appropriate—in fact, imperative—that serious and sustained attention be given to the economic interests of all the component ethnic communities of the state. For, this action or policy will help nip in the bud ethnocultural conflicts and problems that most often are political as well as economic: such conflicts are often generated both by the concentration of political power in the hands of a single component group and by the existence of economic inequalities. People from different ethnocultural groups can hardly live peaceably if they have reason to believe that they are not given equal economic treatment. Economic justice, then, to the attainment of which a decentralized system can contribute, is an important factor in the pursuit of nationhood.

Fourth, in the interest of achieving nationhood, social and moral attitudes of members of the component ethnic communities toward one another ought to be positive and conducive to the promotion and maintenance of good neighborly relationships. Despite the fact that members from different ethnocultural communities live cheek by jowl with one another, they nevertheless quite often perceive one another as "strangers." It seems to me that in those perceptions, the stranger is not just anybody you do not know or have not seen before, but the person who does not belong to your own ethnic group, whether you know him or not, whether you went to school with him or not, whether you are both employees in the same organization or not. He is a "stranger"—an "outsider"—inasmuch as he does not belong to your ethnocultural group, distinguishable from the "insider,"—a member of your own group. The latter is of course not a stranger; he is a "brother." Thus, people who are supposed to be fellow citizens in a new multiethnic state regard one another as strangers. Attitudes toward the stranger are often not charitable. Fear, distrust, suspicion, and sometimes antipathy are evoked by the presence of the stranger. Can a multinational state be built on the basis of such perceptions of its citizens? Hardly. The moral perceptions and attitudes of the citizens in the ethnically plural state will have to be profoundly revised if nationhood is to be achieved.

Fifth, an important step toward the creation of nationhood is the due consideration and respect that ought to be given to the dignity of every individual member of the state. Every human being, irrespective of her cultural background or status in society, does entertain feelings of dignity and self-respect and expects members of the wider society to acknowledge and respect those feelings. Members of a component group may be able, legally, to share in the economic benefits that accrue to the state; yet, if they have reason to feel that their dignity is constantly lacerated because of their membership in a particular ethnic or cultural group, the assault on their sense of dignity will derogate from their sentiments of fully belonging to or being part of the state. Violation of the dignity of members of a cultural group will hardly advance the course of nationhood.

Sixth, the most daunting, intractable, and resilient problem in the attempt concretely to realize the concept of nationhood arises from the fact that any form of nation-building—any attempt toward nationhood—however well-intentioned, will unavoidably privilege one ethnocultural group or certain ethnocultural groups over others. This privileging will derive from, or rather will be connected with, the numerical, cultural, or political superiority or dominance of one group or certain groups. (In the context of military rule, the ethnocultural group to which the military leader of the government belongs will invariably assume a privileged status, even though that group may neither be numerically superior nor culturally or politically important in terms of the level of cultural sophistication and achievement of the membership of the nation-state as whole.) The privileging will, in turn, inevitably bring about ethnocultural conflicts, divisions, and discontents. Unless some realistic way is found around it that could, for instance, head off the full impact or implications of the presence of a privileged group in a state of many nations (N_1), the privileging of some ethnocultural components of the nation-state over others will torpedo even attempts at establishing democratic politics and an open society, which otherwise could have been potent remedies against enduring ethnocultural conflicts.

The fact is that the various component groups would consider themselves culturally and politically equal, even though they may not be really equal in size of population or level of educational and political development or cultural sophistication. But in a context where an ethnocultural group did not really choose to join an already existing, autonomous political state, as would occur in a colonial context, one component group would be right in arguing that it did not enter the new, larger political community, that is, the multinational state, on the terms of any of the component groups. For this reason, the group will argue, the assumption by some groups of privileged positions cannot be justified and will have to be resisted. The question of language—selecting one language as a national language—is one outstanding step that will clearly privilege one group or some linguistically related groups.

It can hardly be denied that the most outstanding feature of a multinational state is multilingualism. Practically all nation-states contain a multiplicity of languages, even though the actual number of languages of course differs from one state to the next. Members of the ethnocultural community (N_1) speak the same language (or dialects that are mutually intelligible), while the citizens of the multinational state speak different languages. Questions that may be explored, within the context of the pursuit of national (N_3) identity, include the following: Will there be a need for a common or national (N_3) language, or should the languages of the various ethnocultural groups be allowed by the state to survive? How is such a common language to emerge or be developed, if it is considered desirable? Should the state adopt a policy of promoting one language as a potential common language for the entire state? And, if it should, how is this (promotion) to be done?

Given the importance of language as a vehicle of culture, it might be supposed prima facie that it will be desirable to allow the different languages to survive so as to provide a medium for cultural expression and development for the different groups in the state. Yet, this policy will be counterproductive in terms of the ultimate cultural and political goals of the nation-state. Integration of the different ethnocultural groups is undoubtedly the ultimate goal of every nation-state. Integration involves the creation or development of common language, national culture, and national identity. The goal of integration would surely be frustrated if all the languages were officially recognized and allowed to develop vertically. The language groups would remain the focus of people's sense of national (N_1) identity, a situation that will thwart not only the development of a sense of national (N_3) identity—the kind of identity that is really expected to emerge in a multinational state—but also the transfer of their allegiances and loyalties to the larger state. In that circumstance, it would be difficult for a common sense of nationality (N_3) among the various language groups to emerge. Consequently, the goal of a common language would be difficult, if not impossible, to attain.

Yet, in the light of the crucial importance of a common language for the development of a sense of national (N_3) identity essential for national integration, it would be necessary for the state to involve itself in deciding which language (or, languages) will be given official support. Giving official support to a language will insure its special status and survival. That language will become the official language of the schools, of the courts, of bureaucracy, of the army and police, of radio and television, and of other public services or organizations. It can be expected that the state's language policy will be resisted tooth and nail by other language groups and will generate conflicts. But the state should not cave in in the wake of the resistance and accommodate or recognize the use of the other languages in all government (or, public) organizations. The reason is that this kind of language policy will eventually—after several generations—bring about a real, meaningful, and enduring sense of common nationality (N_3) and determine the reality of integration in the multilingual nation-state. (The role Kiswahili has played in the development of a national identity in Tanzania is noteworthy.)[12] The alternative is to retain all the languages of the state—a situation that simply will enable each language group to maintain itself as a separate ethnonation (N_1) and, thus, have its sense of separate ethnonational identity strengthened, but that will thwart a most important and fundamental goal of the state, political unity and survival as a nation-state. This alternative, then, cannot be entertained.

Another question arises immediately, however: will or should integration at the language level lead to the destruction of other cultural features of the groups whose languages will eventually not survive, such as their aesthetics—especially artistic productions? If we answer yes then we are saying that nation-building requires, and will have to lead to, the subversion of cultural plurality, which will, in turn, lead to the emergence of drab cultural unity or uniformity: the previously existing cultural tapestry will thus disappear, to be replaced by a monochromic culture. This situation will stunt the development of the aesthetic culture of the nation-state. Therefore, we do not need to answer yes to that question.

Even though language is certainly an important aspect of a culture, people whose languages will eventually disappear can express themselves culturally (aesthetically) through the medium of the new common language of the state. Aesthetic productions—in dance, music, the visual arts (such as painting and sculpture), the verbal or literary arts (such as epic, dramatic poetry and storytelling); other crafts such as carving, pottery, basketry, cloth-weaving, gold-smithing, and leather and metal works—all these will continue to be created by those (from the withering language groups) who have the various artistic talents, endowments, and capacities. Their cultural productions of different kinds will be appreciated and enjoyed at the national (N_3) level. In this connection, I might mention, as an example, that one of the most famous Ghanaian musical and verbal artists, Euphraim Amu (1899–1995), whose native language was Ewe, produced his most important and lasting musical pieces in the Akan language (undoubtedly the most widely spoken language in Ghana), which he had thoroughly mastered in his youth. One of the songs he wrote in the Akan language has, in fact, been elevated to the level of a national (N_3) anthem, appreciated and enjoyed by the entire state. Artistic productions will surely not disappear with the disappearance of some of the languages of a state. So that, even with the withering away of all but one language, it will be possible and appropriate for the citizens of the state, though they come from different ethnocultural backgrounds, to feel that they are not only political citizens but also cultural members.

I might also mention that the Akan people of Ghana, who speak the Akan language, comprise several groups or subgroups (Asante, Akim, Akuapem, Fante, Kwahu, Bono, Assin, Denkyira, Ahanta, Aowin, Nzima; there are Akan people also in the eastern sections of the Ivory Coast, placed there as the result of the way the colonial rulers drew the boundaries of African states over a century ago). Akan is indeed a general name of a family of closely related and generally mutually comprehensible languages: Twi, Fante, Bono, Nzima, Ahanta, and others. Even though all the groups of the Akan people may be said to speak the Akan language, not all aspects of their cultures are similar; many of them are. This indicates that it is possible for groups of people to speak the same language while some features of their cultures differ, notwithstanding the existence of many other features that may be similar. Thus, the cultures of the various subgroups may be regarded as cultural tributaries that, from one point of view, feed into the greater stream of the Akan culture and, from another point of view, take off from that greater or main Akan cultural stream. The discussion of the Akan language and its various speakers is intended to highlight a point, implicit in the immediately preceding paragraph, that the development or emergence of a common national (N_3) language will not necessarily sweep away some cultural features or productions of those ethnocultural groups of the new multinational state whose languages will eventually not survive, and that such groups will continue to contribute to the cultural life of the new state.

Finally, the course of nationhood will, I have reason to believe, be very much advanced if the new conception of the nation-state I propose in the next section—based on a philosophy of "metanationality"—is accepted and becomes an integral part of the social and political consciousness and behavior of the citizens of the new state. For metanationality will make ethnocultural borders (within a multinational state) much less distinct, clear-cut, and defined. In this way, metanationality will nip in the bud the emergence of a privileged "ethnic" group, since no particular group would be a (an ethnically) well-defined group. Moreover, metanationality will require the state to think and act in terms of the interests, not of particular groups as such, but of all the individual citizens of the state, irrespective of their ethnic or cultural backgrounds. The metanational state will not essentially be a nations-based state, like N_2 or N_3. Since the individual citizen of the metanational state will, in many cases, have multiple identities, his sense of allegiance or loyalty to a (i.e., one) particular group will be weak indeed. It will thus be easier for such an individual to transfer his loyalty and sense of national (N_1) identity to the larger state. And, since the individual citizen's commitment and allegiance to a particular ethnocultural group would not be strong, the state's decision to give official support to one language and to nurture it to become the common language of the state will not be met with unrelenting resistance from the other language groups. Another reason is that, by virtue of their multiple or complex ethnocultural backgrounds, some of the members of these other language groups may already, culturally and linguistically, be part of the officially elected language. The metanational state will of course not be free of conflicts and divisions; but these will be engendered rather by class and ideology than by strong ethnocultural affiliations.

Now, nation-building can of course be said to be coextensive with creating a sense of national identity, which is invariably a problem for the ethnically or culturally heterogeneous state of the modern world. In this section, I have explored conditions that could dispose the citizens of the multinational state to identify with the state. Before I conclude the section, I wish to deal, albeit briefly, with the philosophical question, what is it to identify with something, with, say, state, culture, religion, ideology, association, or political party? To identify with something involves several things. It involves feeling that one is inextricably a part of it, having both intellectual and emotional attachments to it, acknowledging and demonstrating one's commitments, obligations, and loyalties to it, doing what one ought to do to enhance its goals, ideals, welfare, and advancement, supporting and defending it to the hilt (though not necessarily to be unmindful of its weaknesses or defects), being personally distressed by its failures, and acknowledging—and behaving in a way that suggests—that much of one's life and much of one's future is anchored in the unity, survival, and integrity of the state. These, essentially, constitute the contours of the notion of identifying with something. And they must all be involved in the notion of national identity, in having a sense of national identity.

3.1 A New Conception of the Nature of the Nation-State

Toward the attainment of nationhood, I wish also to put forward a new philosophy or conception of the nature of the multinational state. The background, as well as the impulse, to this new philosophy is sociological/historical as well as normative. With respect to the sociological/historical background, I intend to look closely at the notion of common ancestry, a notion that has been proposed as the basis of ethnicity: ethnic membership, identities, loyalties, and so forth. With respect to the normative, I argue that it is the individual, worthy of dignity and respect, not the ethnic group, who ought to be considered the fundamental or primary unit in the composition of the multinational state.

3.1.1 The Invention of Ethnicity. It is said that members of an ethnic group have common ancestry and can trace their pedigrees to one ancestor. This is a common assertion of most social scientists, and I crave the indulgence of the reader to quote the words of a few of them. Max Weber describes ethnic group as "those human groups that entertain a subjective belief in their common descent."[13] To David Miller, "Ethnicity involves two elements: first a belief in common descent, leading to a historically given identity."[14] In a more recent publication, he observes that "an ethnic group is a community formed by common descent."[15] E. K. Francis says, "Identification with an ethnos comes essentially from a belief in a common origin."[16] George de Vos also refers to the sense of "common ancestry or place of origin."[17] And so it is, that ethnicity has been defined in terms essentially of common ancestry or descent, that its basic constitutive element is said to be common ancestry. I argue, however, that this definition of ethnicity is incorrect, for its essential element, common ancestry, is itself not coherent, well-defined, or historically transparent.

As a preliminary to my objection, I would like to quote the definition of the Greek word *ethnos,* from which "ethnicity" is derived: "a number of people living together, company, body of men; nation, people; class of men, caste, tribe."[18] What appears to be suggested by the Greek word is essentially the idea of people living together, an idea that does not directly imply a sense of kinship and common ancestral ties. To Anthony Smith, in fact, "ethnos would appear to be more suited to cultural rather than biological or kinship differences; it is the similarity of cultural attributes in a group that attracts the term ethnos."[19] In Smith's view, the Greek word *genos,* rather than *ethnos*, "appears to have been reserved for kinship-based groups."[20] His belief that the term *genos* was used for kinship or biological ties seems to me to be correct because of its etymological affiliation with the Greek root *gene*, which is translated variously as "birth," "nativity," "race," "ancestor," and "kin."[21] Even though Connor is correct in saying that ethnicity is derived from *ethnos*, he is wrong in saying that *ethnos* is "the Greek word for nation in the latter's pristine sense of a group characterized by common descent."[22] Connor seems to see some semantic parallel between the Latin etymology of "nation" and the Greek etymology of "ethnicity." I doubt very much, however, that there is any such parallel. Whereas "nation," as we said earlier, originally (etymologically) connotes the idea of a birth-group and thus of kinship or blood ties, ethnicity has no such connotation.

I believe that the basis of the claim to a common ancestry can be justified for the early descendants of an ancestor, but not for subsequent generations of people. The history of humankind tells us of the movements of peoples from place to place in the wake of wars of invasion and conquest and of enslavement of people with their consequent adoption or incorporation into the communities of the victorious groups, and in the wake also of the pursuit of commercial intercourse and the search for better economic lives elsewhere. As a result of these movements, ethnic interpenetration resulting from inter-ethnic marriages and cohabitation would have been unavoidable: children would have been born of parents from different ethnic groups. This sociological phenomenon will characterize relations particularly among neighboring ethnic groups, which are invariably the components of the nation-state (N_2). The phenomenon itself is historical, implying that ethnically split parentage, with its implications for people's ethnic identities, is not a feature unique to contemporary societies; it has antecedents in the past history of humankind. In the light of such historical or sociological facts, the concept of common ancestry cannot be regarded as simple, straightforward, well-defined, and easily comprehensible; it is a complex concept. One can trace one's pedigree to some ancestral roots; but these roots may be so ramifying that it would hardly make sense—hardly be justifiable—to claim identity with a particular ethnic group and to give a firm allegiance to it. If all this is true, claims to belong to one ethnic group can, to say the least, be doubted for the most part.

Smith is most probably right when he observes that "generally speaking, ethnic communities are far too large to possess any kinship basis; their sense of common descent is only a myth, albeit a powerful one."[23] Donald Horowitz and Igor Kopytoff also speak of the incorporation and amalgamation of groups into other, perhaps larger, groups.[24] It follows that the kinship or common ancestral basis of an ethnic group expanded through amalgamation and incorporation would be weak or loose: consequently, amalgamated and incorporated groups would certainly not share a genuinely common ancestry among themselves or with the groups into which they are incorporated. Thus, Horowitz rightly speaks of "imputed common ancestry,"[25] and Kopytoff of "a ramifying and mostly fictitious genealogy."[26] A fictitious genealogy would be an invented genealogy. Thus, ethnic affiliation acquired through amalgamation and incorporation would not generate a simple and unique genealogical identity. What we would have would instead be a community of people bound, not by kinship or intrinsically ancestral ties, but by goals, values, ideals, sentiments, and aspirations that the members of that group would have come to share by living together. In time, they would share a common sense of history and culture, perhaps a common language, and other characteristics concomitant to a shared life in a cultural community.

To explain in some concrete terms how the basis of ethnic belonging or identity would be most ramifying or complex and therefore tenuous from the perspective of clear or strict identification of an individual's ethnic membership, let us take an example of an individual's complex ethnic background from Ghana: Odartey is of ethnically split parentage. His father is a Ga and his mother an Ewe. His father's mother (i.e., Odartey's paternal grandmother) is an Asante whose grandfather was a kola trader from Hausaland (in the north of the country) who settled in Kumasi (the Asante capital) in the nineteenth century. His maternal grandfather is Fante and his maternal grandmother is a Ga. And so on and so forth. I must state that, even though this particular case is imaginary, it is not by any means an unrealistic example: for there are a good many people in Ghana and, I have reason to believe, in other multiethnic states with this kind of ramifying ethnic or ancestral background.

Now, with this complex, weblike ethnic background, it would simply be false for Odartey to claim that he is a Ga or Ewe or Asante or Fante. Being of multiethnic extraction, he has multiple identities. We can of course appropriately speak in terms of his ancestries, but this only means that we can genuinely speak only in terms also of his ethnic identities or ethnic groups (i.e, we have to speak in terms of a plethora of identities). Considered on objective grounds (in this case, historically), therefore, an individual's historically complex ancestry strictly places him not within one specifiable ethnic group as such, but within several ethnic groups. (I am not talking here about common ancestry supposedly shared by members of an ethnic group. I am talking, instead, about the several ancestries that, on my showing, can be said to constitute the [complex] ethnic background of *an* individual.) The generally complex historical dimensions of an individual's genealogy undermine the appropriateness of the concept of ethnicity—of an (i.e., a single) ethnic group of which many individuals are members, and thus make its use as a social category somewhat suspect and not particularly credible.

Even though, given the arguments of the immediately preceding paragraphs, the claims of individuals about their specific ethnic belonging may not stand up to profound and extensive historical inquiries, an individual nevertheless may choose to identify with a particular ethnic group on the grounds that she was raised in that group. Odartey can claim to be a Ga despite his ancestral (kinship, ethnic) ties with some members (relatives) from other groups. His ethnic identity then becomes a matter of personal belief or choice. Actually, however, being raised in a particular group can be grounds for claims about *cultural,* rather than ethnic, identity. A distinction, then, must be made between cultural and ethnic identity. (Strictly speaking, the expression "ethnic identity" should be "ethnic identities" as I argue in this section.) Culturally, Odartey can claim to be a Ga; ethnically, however, he is clearly a person of several—perhaps many—ethnic parts. Cultural identity is, thus, not coextensive with ethnic identity. It is possible for people from different ethnic backgrounds to share at least some features of a culture. While kinship ties are certainly indispensable—and in fact relevant— to ethnic identities, they are generally dispensable in matters of cultural identity. What is often called "ethnic" identification is almost invariably cultural identification.

Cases of individuals of multiethnic extraction, and hence of complex ethnic background, are, I believe, innumerable in ethnically plural societies in Africa and elsewhere. If we were to trace the lineages of individuals in an ethnically plural society far back in history, we would discover that most individuals hail from a complex ethnic background, and that in terms of descent it is all a potpourri. I am not at all denying the importance of the notion of ancestry; human beings of any generation (except the very first) of course have ancestors. What I am at pains to point out—in fact, my thesis—is that our ancestries are so complex and intricate that "ethnic" (i.e., kinship) grouping or membership cannot be founded on them.

About the individual's ethnic membership or identification, one might say, as a riposte to my thesis, that ethnic belonging is based initially on membership in a clan or lineage, a subethnic group, and that each culture has a well-established custom for placing individuals into particular lineages and then into ethnic groups. My response would be that the customary basis for ethnic identification or belonging is itself rationally questionable. The reason is that it is on the basis of some myths, or hardly rational beliefs, that some individuals are said to belong to the lineage of the father in some cultures, and to that of the mother in others. This is the whole basis of the notions of patrilineality and matrilineality. The dichotomization of the individual into patrilineal and matrilineal categories hardly makes sense; there is really no rational or moral justification for it. If an individual is an offspring of a man and a woman, as he naturally is, why should he be placed in the lineal category of either the father or the mother? Why should he be excluded from one or the other category? It seems in fact that nature had already determined the offspring to be placed in the lineal categories of both parents. The duality of direct lineage should also mean, rationally, that an offspring immediately belongs to two lineal categories and hence to two direct ethnic groups, where parentage is inter-ethnic. Given the historical reality of the phenomenon of inter-ethnic marriages, the duality augments the complexity of the supposed ancestral basis of the individual's ethnic identity: the genealogical tree will be so massive and extensive that the attempt to trace one's specific lineage all the way down will most probably not succeed.

But, then, one may raise the question whether we need to go all the way down in tracing or deciding on an individual's ethnic membership. Wouldn't it be enough, one might ask, just to make reference to the ethnic group (or, groups) to which the parents and grandparents belong? My response to this question is that inasmuch as kinship (blood) relationship is held by most people as the most essential element of ethnicity and inasmuch as genuine (not mythical) descent or ancestry is based on blood relationship, it would not be enough, in tracing one's ethnic membership, to stop with one's parents or grandparents. Indeed, in trying to impress others about how important or how noble or how great their lineage or ethnic background is, individual members of a present generation would—and with gaiety, confidence, a sense of self-importance, and (sometimes) hubris—refer to their great-great-great grandfathers and grandmothers! These distant forebears, it must be noted, may have sprung from ethnic groups different from what an individual currently claims as her own ethnic group. The claims may not necessarily be dubious or false; but the truth or genuineness of those claims merely establishes the complexity of the individual's ethnic background.

The foregoing analysis, then, whittles away the whole basis of ethnic identity: it may well lead us to consider ethnicity as an invention, constructed out of not-well-founded beliefs and assumptions that members of an "ethnic" group are related by kinship ties. There is no doubt that ethnicity, defined in terms solely and essentially of common ancestry, has no firm foundation in historical or genealogical reality. Yet, the proposition that ethnicity—the social grouping of individual human beings on the basis of imputed common ancestry or descent or blood kinship—is an invention may be met by many with belligerent skepticism, even scandal, particularly when we know that states (or, multinational states) in Africa and elsewhere are replete with recurrent conflicts often described as ethnic conflicts. The reason is that individual persons believe—or have been made to believe—that they share a common ancestry with many others and therefore belong to one specific "ethnic" group. But the proposition that ethnicity is an invention, I believe, has the warrant of history and sociology. As human beings, not only do we have ancestors—who are the originators of our cultural traditions—but also we have a sense of ancestry and origins. And even though this fact places an individual human being into some social group, it does not, however, necessarily shepherd her into a specific and an unambiguously identifiable "ethnic" group to which she permanently owes (or, should owe) her allegiance or loyalty. The identity of the group into which an individual enters in consequence of her ancestry is not uniquely or necessarily ethnic, one that is founded on kinship relationships.

Against the background of the foregoing analysis, I would endorse the observation made by the eminent American sociologist Talcott Parsons that "it seems to be generally agreed that what we call ethnicity . . . is an extraordinarily elusive concept and very difficult to define in any precise way."[27] He calls the ethnic group "a diffusely defined group."[28] And Harold Isaacs also speaks of "the identity derived from belonging to what is generally and loosely called an 'ethnic group'."[29] Thus some social scientists have had serious misgivings about the definite character of what is called "ethnic" group or "ethnic" identity. The characterization of the ethnic group or ethnic identity as "loose," "general," "diffuse," "imprecise," and "elusive"— grounded in, and thus justified by, the genealogical backgrounds of individual human beings—indicates the invented or constructed nature of ethnicity. The characterization, however, should favor or facilitate the pursuit of nationhood, for the looseness or diffuseness of ethnic identity will (or should) weaken loyalties and commitments to particular ethnic groups while concomitantly enhancing their transfer to the larger political community—the multinational state. Thus, the importance or effect of deconstructing ethnicity is that it lends great support to the efforts toward nation-building by diminishing, if not removing, a historically robust and significant barrier.

I wish to end my attack on the concept of ethnicity by saying this: even though human communities may have had their beginnings in extended families, they have not, in their completeness, emerged as a result necessarily of the belief that members of those communities are bound by kinship or ancestral ties. (Here, I take the community to be something larger than, and thus different from, the extended family, among whose members one may expect some kinship relationships.) Several different extended families, among whom there may be no kinship relationships at all, have historically come together, for several reasons, to form a larger social—and, later, political—group. In time, the descendants of the members of the group come to consider themselves as related through descent from a common ancestor, even though there will not have been any biological bonds between all of them as such. That group will, thus, not be an "ethnic" group—a group standardly defined by common descent or biological ties. But, even so, the members of the group will come to share—and to be bound by—common goals, values, and practices, a common language, a sense of history and of solidarity, and other features concomitant to a shared life lived over a very long period of time. Such a group comes to assume a collective name and is identified as "the Akan," "the Yoruba," "the Luo," "the Zulu," and so on, a collective name that gives the impression—albeit false—that the Akan (or Yoruba or Luo or Zulu) are a people who are linked by kinship ties and can unmistakably trace their descent from a single ancestor. But what would have emerged, surely, is a cultural, not particularly an ethnic, group. It seems, therefore, that what we have is more appropriately a concept of cultural community than a concept of ethnicity.

3.1.2 Metanationality. Even though I would reject the notion of a specific ethnic identity, I would certainly not deny that an individual belongs to a community of individual human beings. But individual human beings do not have to be related by kinship ties or to have specific ethnic affiliations before they can be members of a cultural community. People do not have to have a common ancestry or descent before they can have common history or live together in a shared territory or develop common culture and a sense of solidarity. Individuals, even though they may not have a basis in common descent, can be bound together by a sense of shared goals, values, and mutual sympathies and understandings. Thus, while our real ancestry is so complex that a claim to one's specific (or, monolithic) identity cannot be rested upon it, the fact that one is an individual human being cannot at all be denied. Such an individual is of course born into, and so belongs to, a community. Thus, from here on I use the term "communocultural" rather than "ethnic" group and the word "ethnic" only in quotation marks.

My conception of nationhood, then, results from a reflection on the "ethnic" situation of the "ethnically" plural state. The view that ethnicity is invented should bring to the fore the uniqueness of the individual in reckoning the composition of the multinational state. The new philosophy therefore calls for a revision of our conception of the multinational state (N_2). As now held, N_2 is said to be constituted by a complex of several "ethnic" communities. I propose that the conception of (N_2) as composed of "ethnic" communities be abandoned and replaced with a conception of it as a metanational entity (*meta* in Greek means "beyond," "behind"). By metanational conception of the modern nation-state, I am referring to a view of the nation-state constituted, not by communocultural groups (or, nations, in the original, first sense of N_1), but primarily by individual human beings who happen to share certain cultural and historical experiences with some other human individuals in a given, well-defined territory. The conception, thus, suggests going beyond the existing view that a nation-state consists of communocultural entities, that the latter constitute the basic units of the modern nation-state. I refer to the metanational conception of the nation-state as N_4.

$$N_4 = \Sigma \; v_1 + v_2 + v_3 + v_4 \ldots + vn$$

(where "v" stands for individual.

When I introduced the notion of N_3 to refer to the multinational state that has achieved a considerable degree of social cohesion, I pointed out its failures or defects in terms of the attainment of nationhood. Despite its failures, however, N_3 as an intermediary step shows that, in time, through social cooperation in all facets of social life, a certain amount of social cohesion can come about and that, in time, this cooperation can prepare the consciousness of the citizenry for the acceptance of a proposal, such as the metanational one, that will bring them to full nationhood. At N_4 citizens will cooperate as *individuals* rather than as groups. On this showing, N_4 can be said to embody many of the virtues of N_1 and thus to exemplify the idea of nationhood.

One most telling shortcoming of N_3 is the failure of its citizens—still inward-looking in several aspects of their lives and, thus, unable to wean themselves totally from particularisic subloyalties and obligations—to do away with such social and moral evils as discrimination and harboring low opinions of persons from other groups and suspicions and distrust of fellow citizens from different groups. N_4 is a step that comes to grips with the moral aspects of N_3 by drawing attention to the need to recognize the moral worth of others and placing the exercise of our moral sentiments and responses on a broad—rather than particularistic—basis, across the board ethnoculturally.

Metanationality, as I conceive it, requires that we consider every citizen of the nation-state, irrespective of the family, clan, or communocultural group into which she happens to have been born, as an individual of intrinsic moral worth and dignity, with a claim on others to respect her. The moral worth of the individual human being should be the basis of any treatment—social, political, legal—that is to be meted out to her. No one knows how she came to belong to some natural family or group. Contingency has placed individual human beings into different families, clans, or communocultural groups, but this fact should not detract from the intrinsic moral value of the individual human being; nor should it be presumed as bearing tags of inferiority, superiority, or special status in society. Our humanity, not our particular "ethnic" background, should constitute our fundamental identity. This fact underpins the conception of the metanational state. Inasmuch as metanationality is intended to supersede the conception of the composition of the nation-state that has been held in modern times, it may be regarded as a postmodern conception of the nation-state.

Metanationality, in addition to being a theory about the composition of the modern state in a culturally plural setting, is a theory about the moral worth of the individual. It is to be distinguished from metaphysical individualism, which sees individuals as self-sufficient beings, not dependent on social relationships for the realization of their goals and potentials. It is to be distinguished also from moral individualism, the view that it is only the interests of individuals that should form the basis for designing sociopolitical institutions. The metanational conception of the nation-state is neither of these. For, it does not deny that the individual self is dependent on, and is partly constituted by, social relationships and communal ties; nor does it affirm that only the interests of individuals should count in designing sociopolitical institutions, to the detriment of communal interests and goals. While it insists on the just and equal recognition of the moral rights of all the individual members of the nation-state, it also recognizes the important role of the cultural community in the life of the individual. But, even though it recognizes the equal worth and dignity of every individual member of the community, metanationality does not necessarily hold that individual rights are invariably to be privileged over communal interests and goals. This is where my theory of metanationality differs from Western individualist (liberal) theories that generally insist that individual rights invariably trump the collective welfare of the community. But, remember, the community as conceived here is not the "ethnic" community as such but the larger political community, that is, the nation-state.

In the metanational state communocultural (i.e., "ethnic") boundaries, in the form of collective names and "identities," may continue to exist—albeit in some hazy forms, but their toxic effect on the moral and political thinking of the citizens would have been seriously neutralized, to the point of hardly influencing the attitudes of some individual members of the state toward others. The word "hazy" is significant and is used here to clinch the idea, implicit in much of what I have already said, that the boundaries of specific communocultural entities will be porous, ill defined in view of the putative multidimensional cultural identities of most individual members of the nation-state. (The multiplicity of the cultural identities of the individual members derives, remember, from their complex "ethnic" backgrounds.) The individual person who refers to himself as an Akan, for instance (in Ghana), may in fact, strictly speaking, also—in terms of his cultural background—be an Ewe, Ga, Fante, and others.

The consequence of all this will be that an individual's "ethnic" badge, accidental as it is, will (and should) determine nothing about him; it is instead his moral worth or value, intrinsic to him as an individual human being, as well as his personal character that will determine or influence people's attitudes toward him. A metanational conception of the state, then, will contribute to the building of a cohesive nation (N_2) in which the interests of one individual would not differ essentially from those of the other individuals. This fact can eliminate conflicts, prejudices, and stereotypes, while creating structures of mutual understanding necessary to the integrity, solidarity, and cohesiveness of the nation-state.

Metanationality may be considered by others—but wrongly—as an ideal or a normative principle that cannot be realized in practice. It is indeed a theoretical ideal in that it does not reflect the character of any contemporary multinational state. Even so, I would claim that it is a normative ideal that is realizable if individuals only recognized that, as citizens of the multinational state, they share certain basic interests and that they have no moral rights to deny other fellow citizens—who are of equal intrinsic moral worth—goods that they desire for themselves. To suppose that metanationality is impossible of practical realization is to imply that human beings are incapable of recognizing other human beings as of equal value and deserving of equal dignity and respect, and that they are incurably insensitive to the distress of others—implications that, most people would agree, are wrong. I think myself, however, that "ethnicism" has contributed in no small measure to blunting the moral visions of most people who believe—or have been made to believe—that, as individuals, they belong to certain specific "ethnic" groups, beliefs that have led to the adoption by members of one "ethnic" group of certain morally reprehensible attitudes toward members of other groups. "Ethnicism," that is, has led to the adoption of inward-looking moral attitudes: individuals generally tend to take the appropriate and expected moral attitudes toward members of "their" own group. But when the artificially—or, rather, less naturally—constructed walls separating the various communocultural groups tumble down, most people would morally reach out to other fellow human beings from "the other groups" in a more spontaneous manner. On the metanational theory of the nation-state, certain moral and mental attitudes that originally were features of the people within the boundaries separating the various communocultural groups will diminish into the otiose and the inconsequential. And citizens of the nation-state will feel "liberated" from the constraints imposed by not-well-grounded beliefs in "ethnicism" to exercise their capacity for moral virtue with respect to members from "the other groups."

Because metanationality discounts ethnicity and aims at giving consideration to the individual (rather than the group) as the basic unit of the nation-state, one might suppose that it will deprive the individual of cultural roots, a basis of identification, and other social relationships essential for the enhancement of her general well-being. Such a supposition would be legitimate and credible only if the subversion of ethnicity (membership in a specific ethnic group) were concomitantly to result in the eradication of a cultural framework. But this surely would not happen. If common ancestry or kinship relationships are removed as the essential plank in the constitutive platform of ethnicity—what results is a cultural community. In consequence, we can sensibly talk only of "Akan culture" rather than "Akan ethnic group." An individual is born into a family (nuclear and extended) and a lineage that are already embedded in a culture. Thus, from the very outset the individual is embedded, not only in a cultural community having traditions and practices, but also—if for that reason—in some essential social relationships: she would therefore not be culturally deracinated. The cultural community is a basis (one of the several bases) of her identity. But the cultural community, remember, is not an "ethnic" group. Metanationality will thus not lead to the subversion of the identities of individuals. In many respects, then, N_4 will bear many of the marks of N_1.

Also, because in the metanational state communocultural boundaries are expected to become much less defined, it might be supposed that metanationality will eliminate cultural diversities, which is important for the growth and elegance of the national (N_2) culture of the new nation-state. Such a supposition, however, will have no real basis. First, as I have already argued, what is labeled an "ethnic" group is in fact a cultural community, comprising people between whom there may or may not be kinship bonds. Second, culture, as I point out later in this chapter and also in chapter 8, is an enactment of a community of people, despite the fact that some specific cultural products are actually created by some individuals; but the people do not have to be related ethnically, that is, in terms of kinship ties. People or groups have created cultures not because they are related by kinship or ancestral ties but because they have lived together for decades and in the doing have evolved common forms or ways of life: cultures. Thus, the creation of a culture is not a function particularly of what is called "an ethnic group." It would not be correct to say that individual contributors to culture, such as artists, owe their natural talents and endowments to their membership in a particular ethnic group, notwithstanding the fact that the realization of their talents would have been made possible through their membership in a community; but that community, remember, is not necessarily an "ethnic" community. The metanational state will encompass various cultural communities, creative individual members of which will exercise their talents in the creation of cultural products. Cultural diversity will thus not wither away or ossify into some jejune cultural unity or uniformity.

To conclude: metanationality, as a social and political theory, is a normative theory aimed essentially at setting up standards of behavior for public officials in their treatment of individual citizens of the state as well as for the entire membership of the state in their attitudes toward one another. The inauguration of new paradigms of moral and mental attitudes will be the greatest virtue of metanationality. This is not to say, however, that metanationality promises a nation-state that will be devoid of conflicts; it will not by itself eliminate conflicts among citizens of the multinational state. There would be conflicts in the metanational society. But, even if such conflicts are between communocultural groups, the basic causes of the conflicts would be essentially political (or, ideological) or economic rather than "ethnic."

4. National Culture and Identity

The metanational state (N_4) is, in my analysis, a state composed primarily of individuals who naturally belong to cultural communities. This means that in the metanational state communocultural identities may in fact coexist with the future national culture and identity, even though it can be expected that their political venom will diminish considerably and become innocuous in the fullness of time. Despite the existence of communocultural identities, however, creating or developing an awareness of a national culture and identity would be most desirable for several reasons: the need for national integration, national cohesion, and solidarity; the need for having a common perspective on national problems and common approaches to their solution; the need for a people to appreciate the significance and meanings of events taking place in their society; and the need for providing an easily comprehensible interpretation of societal experiences and for eliciting shareable responses and reactions to those experiences. These needs or goals, which indeed are among the desiderata of nationhood, do give rise to the concern for evolving and promoting a national culture. (I use "national" in the sense that relates to the concept of metanationality; unless otherwise indicated, I have in mind this sense of "nation" or "national" hereafter.)

The need for a national culture clearly would be felt more in a heterogeneous or multicultural society, one constituted by a medley of communocultural groups, than in a homogeneous society whose culture can be said largely to be homogeneous or national; for, homogeneity (but not heterogeneity) with respect to a culture immediately makes for the horizontalization of meanings, outlooks, perspectives, and so forth. Thus homogeneity facilitates, if it does not condition, the development and emergence of a national culture. Thus the need or search for a national culture seems to be a problem for a nation of heterogeneous communocultural groups. But before we attempt to characterize a national culture, we must first understand what culture itself is.

According to the etymology of the word "culture," it derives from the idea of tilling or cultivating land, a process that involves helping crops to grow by giving them the needed care and attention. Culture thus involves care, nurture, promoting the development of something. As it has evolved, the word has come to refer to patterns of thought and ways of acting and behaving that have been created, fostered, and nurtured by a people over time and by which their lives are guided and, perhaps, conditioned. The culture of a people thus includes their systems of values; their beliefs, social practices, and legal and sociopolitical institutions; and their manners (i.e., habits and customs), etiquette, and fashions. Another significant aspect of culture relates to the act of developing the intellectual faculties: in this sense works of art (music, dancing, sculpture, and painting), and of science, philosophy, and literature (oral and written) are things of the culture. As a creation of a community of people, culture is a complex of shared meanings that people in a given society derive from or attach to their experiences, the ground by which they understand themselves and interpret their experiences. It is the specific embodiment of a people's way of life in its totality. People tend sometimes to hold a truncated, and hence impoverished, conception of culture by thinking of it in terms solely of the performing and fine arts (music, dancing, sculpture, and painting).

Now, what is a national culture? What is it for a culture to be national? The notion referred to of shared meanings of cultural products and experiences may be taken as constitutive of culture, whether local, provincial, or national. This is because culture is the product of a community of people, not of an individual. A national culture, then, is a culture whose meanings have become homogenized and can, thus, be said to be generally shared by all the citizens of a nation, one whose basic values are cherished by the citizens and considered as constituting the social context within which the individual citizen perceives herself as an individual with goals, hopes, aspirations, and life projects, It is the system of values, practices, and institutions with which, in the context of a metanational state, all the individual members from the component communocultural groups can identify, to which they spontaneously feel they belong, which they regard as theirs, and in the appreciation and enjoyment of whose products they all participate. A national culture is thus essentially a participatory culture in the particular sense that it opens itself up for appreciation and identification by all the citizens of the metanational state, and to whose development and evolution they can all contribute. Now, is such a national culture possible for a nation (N_2 or N_3) that is a conglomerate of several communocultural groups?

I have said that a national (N_1) culture easily emerges in a society that may be said to be largely homogeneous, for in such a society the values, practices, and institutions of the culture are more easily horizontalized, homogenized. Even though the emergence of a national culture would not be easy for a heterogeneous society, such as the metanational state, I think, nevertheless, that homogenization of cultural values can come off also in a heterogeneous society. An outstanding feature of the heterogeneous society is its cultural pluralism, the obvious consequence of its "ethnic" configuration. Yet, cultural pluralism does not necessarily eliminate the possibility of horizontal relationships between the cultures of the individual component groups: it is thus possible to observe common or underlying affinities among the plural cultures of a metanational state. These common features may have resulted from several factors—social, historical, linguistic, and purely existential. It is conceivable that some amount of cultural interpenetration may have taken place among groups of people who have lived cheek by jowl for decades or centuries; or, to put it differently, it is inconceivable that groups of people would share a geographic area for a very long time without their adopting at least some of the ways of life of one another. The dynamics of human interaction plainly disclosed to us by the history of the development of human cultures cannot be disregarded: the cultures of groups of people who speak the same language or dialects of a language are most likely to share some common elements. It can be safely assumed that within the territorial boundaries of the emergent nation with a dominant group, the dominant group will exert influence on the cultures of the minority groups, with the consequent diffusion of the cultural values and practices of the dominant group among the minority cultures.[30] It is possible for the culture of the dominant group to be not merely replicated but also transmuted in a different cultural setting. Just as an idea, even though it is the product of an individual mind, gains currency among other people, so culture (i.e., a set of cultural values, beliefs, and practices), even though it is the product of a particular group or community of people, can gain currency or adoption among peoples beyond the borders of the community of its origin.[31] The conclusion, then, is that the culturally plural metanational state may not necessarily lack elements of a common culture, a fact that would facilitate the conception and creation of a national culture.

The creation and development of a national culture may, I think, proceed in two ways. The more difficult way would be to nurture the putative common elements of the component cultures. Here, one can focus only on what may be referred to as the material aspects of culture, such as music, dancing, sculpture, painting, and crafts. It is of course the elegant aspects of the component cultures that should be featured and developed to the national level and with which all the citizens of the nation can identify. This will not be an easy way because it will involve selection; and the problem that this procedure will raise relates to the criteria of selection that will be established: the possibility exists of riding roughshod over the cultural sensibilities of some component cultural community. And yet, there would be aspects of the component cultures that can be said to be crude, dross, bizarre, and outmoded: such aspects will have to be pruned away.

I use the word "elegant" in this chapter in reference to aspects of the cultures of the component communocultural groups that may feature in a national culture to be forged by the new national state. I use the term to indicate that not every aspect of the cultures of the diverse groups will be worthy of respect, accommodation, and a place in the new national culture, and that such features of those cultures as cannot, on some reasonable grounds, be regarded as worthy of recognition and respect, such as lack of respect for human life and dignity, will have to be abandoned.

I have said that a national culture is essentially a participatory culture: one that is participated in by all the citizens of the metanational state irrespective of their original communocultural matrices. One great virtue of this conception of national culture is that it makes it possible for artistic forms and other cultural products originating from particular communocultural environments of the state to stimulate a lasting national aesthetic appreciation and enjoyment. In this way, the cultural products of a particular communocultural origin, paradoxically, will become *less* particularistic or local: those products will in fact become national, as most other citizens across the nation come to appreciate and identify with them. Because of the attraction and interest those local cultural products may hold for the wider society, they will in time shed much of their local or regional identity and take on a national identity. The conception of a national culture in terms of participatory culture will allow the development of local artistic forms and, in this way, promote individual creativity.

A national culture can be forged in another way by the new metanational state. In addition to revitalizing aspects of the received component cultures and elevating their elegant features to a national status, the new state will have to build national institutions, create new values and patterns of attitude and behavior, create new symbols and myths about a common past, promote and urge new outlooks and self-definitions, new hopes, goals, and aspirations, facilitate cultural contacts between the component cultural groups: all these and other activities that transcend local or regional orientations will have to be created by the state. Some of these will come through formal education if the appropriate curriculum structures are designed. Inevitably, through contacts with the cultures of other peoples, some of the cultural values, practices, and institutions would already have pervaded and taken root in the cultural life of the citizens of the new state and might already have assumed a national status.

In the creation and development of a national culture, the intellectuals of the new state who are producers of ideas will have seminal roles to play. Whereas culture is a creation of a community, not of individuals, ideas are productions of individual intellectuals. How, then, would the productions of individual intellectuals fit into the creation of a (national) culture? The answer to this question is simply that the ideas of the intellectuals would gain currency among the wider society and influence the thought and action of the citizens of the nation. This is how ideas have generally come to form the basis of the entire cultural life of a people. The intellectuals are those individuals in the society who consciously and systematically employ the mind and are irresistibly attracted to, or fascinated by, ideas, apply themselves with unrelenting assiduity to conceive and produce them, argue them, and battle with them, always prepared to abandon their own intellectual positions in the face of the superior ideas or arguments of others—doing all this in the pursuit of truth and the promotion of values. The category of intellectuals includes artists, academics, and literary persons (such as poets, novelists, playwrights, and journalists). What is common to all these different intellectuals is their passion for ideas and the effective way they deal with them.

It can be said that throughout history and in all societies, developments and advances in culture, new—and sometimes radical—values, orientations in mental outlook, ways of interpreting human experience, and so on, have been the results of the work of intellectuals, that is, persons who have the capacity to produce ideas and handle them effectively. It is the intellectual who argues either for or against the continuation of existing practices, institutions, value systems, and modes of thought, just as he argues for the inauguration of new systems of value, modes of thought, and so on, to replace the old. His ideas and arguments may gain acceptance among the wider society and, in this way, directly or indirectly, come to affect the cultural life of the people.

Since the intellectual in the metanational state necessarily belongs to the culture of a component group, was nurtured in that local culture, and operates or works out his thought within the context of that culture, why, one might ask, would he not be held in thrall by his cultural ambience, unable intellectually to release himself or break loose from that ambience, culturally to rock the boat, as it were, and embark on more challenging intellectual enterprises? The reason is this: the intellectual in the metanational state may spring from one of the constituent cultures, yet it is expected that in the exercise of his intellect he will be able to soar above the limits of his local culture, orient himself to exploring the total culture, and focus his intellectual gaze on the culture of the whole as such. We must also note that an individual intellectual of the metanational state, by reason of his multiple "ethnic" backgrounds, will most likely belong to more than one culture.

Let me illustrate this point with examples from the history of cultural developments in Western Europe. The ancient Greeks were given to explaining natural phenomena in mythological and supernatural terms, terms that later Greek thinkers, those in the sixth century B.C., considered irrational and unscientific. By insisting that natural phenomena be explained in rational and scientific terms, these early Greek thinkers succeeded in making inroads into the pristine mentality, effecting a transition from *mythos* to *logos* (from mythical to rational explanation), and setting up new explanatory paradigms. Also, the phenomenon known in medieval European history as the Renaissance, which was a series of cultural changes that began in Italy in the fourteenth century A.D. and spread to the rest of Europe by the late fifteenth century, affecting many fundamental assumptions about art, literature, and morality—this phenomenon was an intellectual movement, the work of scholars and artists. The Enlightenment in Europe in the eighteenth century, also an intellectual movement, was initiated by such French intellectuals (the "Philosophes") as Voltaire, Diderot, and Montesquieu. Its thought was essentially social and was concerned with social ends, values, and reforms. The members of the movement argued for the establishment of new social and political values in the period before and after the French Revolution.

The reference to the foregoing cases in history is intended to show that the intellectual can transcend the limits of his particular culture and make an objective, critical assessment of the values, beliefs, and practices of that culture, reaching conclusions that may either affirm existing values or suggest revision or amendment to them, or suggest their total abandonment and replacement by new ones. In the development specifically of national culture, the intellectual or methodological possibility of transcending the limits of one's culture provides the grounds for the belief that the intellectual from a communocultural group would not necessarily anchor his intellectual exertions in his local cultural milieu, but that he would be able to take an intellectual flight onto a higher cultural plateau—the level at which his focus or concerns will be the wider society, that is, the nation.

The intellectual, it can broadly be assumed, has a vision of the kind of society he would like his own society to become. The sources of an intellectual's vision may include his insights into human nature generally, his reflections on the historical and cultural experiences of his people and perhaps of others, his critical evaluation of the values, practices, and institutions of his society, and his conception of the nature of the good society and the possibilities of its survival. The intellectual may develop commitment to the ideals of his vision and may even pursue ways of realizing those ideals. But the commitment to those ideals will not, I believe, be sufficiently strong to detract from the ideal of detachment to which he, as an intellectual, is also committed if he is to achieve some objectivity and truth in his analyses and judgments and to persuade others to his points of view. Thus, through the perceptive actions of the new metanational state and the activities of its intellectuals, a national culture can in time be evolved.

It can be expected, however, that the metanational state will manifest a cultural tapestry, for there will be diversities in its cultural make-up. The concept and development of a national culture cannot thrive on drab unity, which will result only in stifling individual creativity, originality, and innovativeness. Cultural diversity can be said to derive from cultural richness and thus has aesthetic merits. The pursuit of the values of human inventiveness and creativity in the various areas of culture will invariably result in the emergence of diverse elements in aspects of a national culture. Diversities in the culture of a people, then, reflect the creative endowments of some talented individuals of the nation—artists and other intellectuals. If ideas of art, science, philosophy, and literature are included—as indeed they are—in the phenomenon of culture, then diversities can hardly be eliminated from a national culture. Thus, it makes no sense to harp on the diversities in the culture of a people. There are some people, however, who think—erroneously—that the culture of a nation must be free of diverse elements, that for a culture to be national or to be the culture of a nation, the citizens of the nation must wear the same type of dress, cook the same way, eat the same type of food, dance the same way, and so on. It is the existence of same or unified features in the ways of life and thought of the individual citizens from the various communities of the nation that, in the view of such people, justifies the characterization of a set of cultural values and practices of a people as national. This way of characterizing a national culture is, to my mind, misguided and unwarranted. The reason is that a national culture does not necessarily mean cultural unity or cultural uniformity or conformity.

Now, it might be supposed that the existence of diversities in a national culture runs contrary to the notion of a cultural identity at the national level, the reason being that a national culture constitutes part of the basis of national cultural identity. A national cultural identity is defined by a set of values, practices, and outlooks commonly shared by the citizens of the nation. This is the set of values, practices, and outlooks that individuates the culture and makes it the unique culture it is, that the users identify with and acknowledge as theirs, and that others outside the culture also acknowledge as the culture of a particular people. Cultural identity is thus both a subjective and an objective phenomenon. It is worth noting that even though culture is a communal structure, it is possible within a culture to distinguish between public and private aspects.[32] Political, social, economic, and legal values and institutions would be included in the category of the public, while aesthetic perceptions, such as styles of dress, tastes in food, and forms of music and dance, would fall into the category of the private. Diversities in a national cultural identity are likely to be most visible in the private category of the culture and as such are not likely to tear down the national cultural fabric. The public dimension of a national culture, on the other hand, would evince only a minimal diversity, if any at all, and would thus present a most reliable and enduring basis of national unity and integration.

This leads me to a discussion of an important idea, which begins with the question, do people in a given cultural milieu live an absolutely unified cultural life? Given the fact that culture encompasses the entire life of a people and that some aspects of culture are a response to environmental or even climatic conditions, this question will have to be answered in the negative.

I would like, however, at this point to make a distinction between a strong and a weak sense of the idea of a unified cultural life (or cultural unity). The strong sense of the idea would imply that in literally all aspects of their cultural life, people in a given cultural environment live the same way: eat the same food, wear the same clothing, share the same tastes, have common political, religious, and moral beliefs, think, act, and react in the same way, and so on. Thus, in terms of the strong sense, if people speak the same language but do not share common religious or political beliefs, they cannot be said to live a culturally unified life; similarly, people who speak the same language, eat the same of food and wear the same clothing cannot be said to live a culturally unified life if their religious beliefs, for instance, are different; and so on. Therefore, in terms of the strong sense of the idea, then, it is impossible to expect people of any culture to live a totally unified cultural life. In short, there is no such thing as a purely or absolutely unified cultural life.

On the other hand, the weak sense of that notion would be defensible both conceptually and empirically. It does not imply or suggest a monolithic cultural life for a people who live in what may be described as a shared cultural environment. Instead, it allows for the expression of individual or group tastes, sentiments, preferences, and ways of responding to local or particular experiences. Social stratification, occupational differences, and differences in individual talents, endowments, desires, and aesthetic perceptions insistently constrain the homogenization of particular forms of cultural life even in the same cultural milieu. To say this, however, is of course not to deny that people belonging to the same cultural environment would generally share certain fundamental values—a proposition that logically derives from the notions of culture and community. It is this weak sense of the notion of a unified cultural life that can be defended in a discourse on the cultural life of a people. Rejecting the strong sense of the notion of a unified cultural life and adopting the weak sense of that notion will not affect the idea of a national culture.

National culture is not coterminous with national identity, even though it is an important ingredient of it as well as an important determining factor; a nation is not merely a cultural configuration. National identity is a more comprehensive concept whose constituents encompass factors other than common cultural elements. National identity refers to the principles of collective belonging, to the set of characteristics by which a nation can collectively define itself and be distinctly recognized. The citizens of a state must share common characteristics that justify their belonging to a single political community. These characteristics of course include cultural elements; but they also include emotional and sedimented sentiments of loyalty and attachment, sentiments that derive from a sense of common history, of sharing a common territory and thus of belonging together, and of a common destiny, future, or goals. These characteristics constitute what is often known as "national character" and hold the citizens together.

Now, one last important question: is the development of national culture and identity really possible without a common or national language, that is, without an indigenous lingua franca? This question will have to be answered no. The discussions in section 3 about the steps toward nationhood make it clear that a common language is most essential for the development of a sense of national identity. Language is a vehicle of culture; and a common culture can best and most visibly be expressed through a common language.

5. Conclusion

I have distinguished two meanings of the concept of a nation: one applies to a communocultural group of people who share the same culture, language, and history, while the other applies to a communoculturally plural political community, that is, a nation-state, a multinational state. The latter is perceived to have two features, one descriptive and the other normative. The former is symbolized as N_2 and the latter as N_3. While the concept as applied to a communocultural group is essentially social (or, sociocultural), it is, as applied to a nation-state, a political concept. Because nation, conceived communoculturally (what I call N_1) seems to a large extent to manifest characteristics such as unity, solidarity, cohesion, cultural homogeneity, and a strong sense of identity—characteristics that we appreciate and consider most worthwhile but that seem to be largely absent from nation conceived as multinational state (what I call N_2), N_1 can be considered a paradigm—an ideal form—of human community and relationship. As an ideal form, it has come to be sought after, to be attained, by more complex political communities called states: hence the political and moral importance of the notion of nation-building. But human thought and experience indicate that it is not easy to copy or attain or adapt to an ideal, particularly when the ideal is simple and the entity (the multinational state) that is trying to copy or adapt to it is a complex phenomenon. Its complexity generates daunting problems of creating cultural and national identity: hence the plethora of problems confronting modern states seeking to achieve the essence of nationhood. If the citizens of the new multinational state would bear in mind, however, that their vital interests and fate are not only held by them in common but also linked to those of the state, that their general well-being will be enhanced, even maximized, by their membership in it, that the state is a metanational polity (N_4)—one that is constituted primarily by individual human beings rather than by communocultural communities, and that each individual citizen is of intrinsic moral worth and ought therefore to be accorded equal treatment and respect by both his government and his fellow citizens; and if the state were to create a participatory, democratic, and open society and to succeed in evolving a common language to serve as a basis for developing a sense of national identity, then it would be possible to approximate the ideal of N_1 and so achieve the essence of nationhood. I have explained the invented character of "ethnicity" by debunking the beliefs about common ancestry on which it has been based. The rejection of the common ancestry basis of "ethnicity"—of the ethnic group—leaves us with a community of people bound together by values, language, a sense of history, loyalty, solidarity, and social commitment; it also leads us to a distinction between cultural and ethnic identity (strictly, ethnic identities), the latter identity resting on kinship ties. The perception of "ethnicity" as invented should favor the pursuit of nationhood in the multinational (multicultural) state in the contemporary world.

4

Traditional Political Ideas, Values, and Practices

Their Status in the Modern Setting

It is a matter of common knowledge that since the euphoric early days of postcolonial rule, the politics of many an African nation has been blighted in several ways. The political institutions that were bequeathed to the African people by their colonial rulers, modeled, as they invariably were, on those of the colonial rulers, did not function properly. The democratic constitutions that were fashioned by the African peoples themselves suffered the same fate. This constitutional failure—the failure to rule in accordance with formally established procedures—may be explained in several ways. One explanation may be that the African people simply did not have the ability effectively to operate institutions of government that were entirely alien to them, institutions that had not taken root in—and so had not become part of—their political culture and, consequently, failed to elicit cultural understanding and legitimacy, institutions to which they had no emotional, ideological, or intellectual attachments and whose nuances could not be fully appreciated: such institutions could easily be subverted. Another explanation might be that the African people lacked certain moral or dispositional virtues or attitudes (such as patience, tolerance, moderation, incorruptibility) indispensable to the successful operation of those alien institutions. Yet another explanation might be that the political institutions—whether created by the colonial governments or by the postcolonial African governments—would have worked well but for the disruptions of the constitutional process by the military. However this constitutional or institutional failure is to be explained, its unavoidable consequence for most African nations has been political confusion, instability, uncertainty, and frustration.

In this political confusion and uncertainty, questions are being asked why viable political structures cannot be forged in the furnace of the African's own tradition of political rule. The participants of a three-day conference in

1993 on the future of Africa, for instance, agreed that "it is important that traditional cultural values be integrated into the process of developing better governance."[1] The positive attitude being evinced toward the traditional system stems from the claim or conviction of a number of people that the traditional system of government did have some democratic features that a new political system can profit by. Because of the problems African nations experienced in their efforts to establish democratic institutions since regaining their political independence, any talk of African traditions of government having democratic features will undoubtedly evoke cynicism, even scandal. But, perhaps, the facts of anthropology will shed light on these matters.

My intention in this chapter is to explore the traditional African ideas and values of politics with a view to pointing up what may be described as the democratic features of the indigenous system of government and to examine whether, and in what ways, such features can be said to be harmonious with the ethos of contemporary political culture and hence can be said to be relevant to developments in political life and thought in modern Africa. I shall set out from the observations made by anthropologists and other scholars on the democratic nature of the traditional political practices. Then, using mainly the traditional Akan system of Ghana as a paradigm for an indepth analysis, I shall give an account of political institutions and their manner of operation in the traditional setting. I shall then investigate the philosophical underpinnings of the traditional political institutions. I hope by this approach, descriptive as well as conceptual, to provide an insight into the African traditions of political thought and practice as well as an answer to the question whether or not the indigenous political system exhibited democratic features. I shall also explore the problems that will be unleashed in attempting to build a democracy on the democratic elements of the traditional African political institutions.

1. Observations on the Democratic Character of the Traditional African Political System

For more than a century scholars writing about Africa have suggested that democracy, as an idea and a political practice, is an aspect of the political culture of traditional Africa. And I crave the indulgence of the reader to assemble the observations of some of those scholars and writers. The observations cover such topics as the will of the people or rule by popular consent, freedom of expression of opinions in the conduct of public affairs, the limited power of the chief (who is the highest political authority), and checks on abuse of power.

About the turn of the century, Adolphe Cureau, a French scholar who wrote about the people of central Africa, observed that "over the free citizens, the Chief's authority is valid only insofar as it is the mouthpiece of the majority interests, lacking which character it falls to the ground."[2] Dugald

Campbell, a Briton who spent almost three decades in central Africa (including Zambia) from the latter part of the nineteenth century to the early part of this century, made the following elaborate observation: "All government is by the will of the people, whether it be the choice and coronation of a king; the selection of a man to fill a new chieftainship; the framing, proclamation, and promulgation of a new law; the removal of the village from one site to another; the declaration of war or the acceptance of terms of peace: everything must be put to the poll and come out stamped with the imprimatur of the people's will. No permanent form of negro government can exist save that based four square on the *people's will.*" [3] About forty years later, the eminent British anthropologists Meyer Fortes and E. E. Evans-Pritchard wrote, "The structure of an African state implies that kings and chiefs rule by consent. A ruler's subjects are as fully aware of the duties he owes to them as they are of the duties they owe to him, and are able to exert pressure to make him discharge these duties." [4] Recently, Jack Donnelly, writing specifically about cultural practices and universal human rights, asserted, "In fact, authentic traditional cultural practices and values can be an important check on abuse of arbitrary power. Traditional African cultures, for example, usually were strongly constitutional, with major customary limits on rulers." [5]

The constitutionality of the political practice stems not only from formal political structures and relationships that had been established but also from an awareness by the chief that his authority derives from his people, and that that fact establishes a reciprocal and, perhaps, also a contractual bond between him as the ruler and the people as the ruled. Numerous maxims clearly express the reciprocal bond between the ruler and his people. A Basotho maxim says, "A chief is a chief by the people." [6] The Lovedu of the Transvaal say, "Chieftainship is people," [7] and the Ndebele of Zimbabwe say, "The king is the people. To respect the king is to respect oneself. He who despises our king despises us. He who praises our king praises us. The king is us." [8] Among the Swazi and the Bechuana, the chief is under the law and can be tried by his own council if he breaks the law. [9] Indeed, this belief that the chief is not above the law seems to have been widely held in African communities: "Among the Yoruba, as among other African tribes," Ndabaningi Sithole, for example, writes, "the king or chief was not above the law, but under the law. The common people with whom he had to be popular were the source of all authority." [10]

It may be inferred from the observations so far made that the principle of popular government is firmly established in the traditional African political practice, for the chief has to rule with the consent of the people. In the event of the chief's failure to make his rule reflect the popular will, he could be defied or deposed. And, according to Sithole, "African history has many cases of this nature," [11] i.e., cases of popular defiance or displeasure resulting from the ruler's policies and actions not reflecting the wishes of the people. On this showing, it could be said that in traditional African politics the people—the common people—not the chiefs or kings, are the basis of all properly constituted authority. This does not mean, however, that the principle of popular sovereignty was established in the traditional African culture of politics. It was not. The right to rule is still hereditary: chiefs or kings are chosen, not directly by all the people, but by a few people; and they have to come from the royal lineage.

The will of the people is usually expressed formally in the councils of the chiefs and in other assemblies where people freely express their opinions. Speaking generally of Africa, Sithole observes: "Those who have lived in Africa know that the African people are democratic to a point of inaction. Things are never settled until everyone has had something to say. [The traditional African] council allows the free expression of all shades of opinions. Any man has full right to express his mind on public questions" and "to carry out any program required the sanction of the whole clan or tribe." [12] And Julius Nyerere, often concerned about the traditional view of things, asserts that "in African society the traditional method of conducting affairs is by free discussion." [13] Elsewhere he says: "Mr. Guy Clutton-Brock, writing about Nyasaland, described traditional African democracy as follows: 'The elders sit under the big tree and talk until they agree.' This talking until you agree is essential to the traditional African concept of democracy." [14] In the traditional African political practice, the kings' councils and other assemblies provide the forum for the free expression of opinion on public matters. The practice of "talking until you agree" implies the existence, at least initially, of *opposing* views. Thus the political concept of opposition was not unknown to the traditional political practice (see section 3 below). Let me conclude this brief survey of the observations on the democratic features of traditional African political practice with a quotation from a sessional paper produced by the Kenya government in the early years of political independence.

> In African society a man was born politically free and equal and his voice and counsel were heard and respected regardless of the economic wealth he possessed. Even where traditional leaders appeared to have greater wealth and hold disproportionate political influence over their tribal or clan community, there were traditional checks and balances including sanctions against any possible abuse of such power. In fact traditional leaders were regarded as *trustees* whose influence was circumscribed both in customary law and religion. In the traditional African society an individual needed only to be a mature member of it to participate fully and equally in political affairs. Political rights did not derive from or relate to economic wealth or status. [15]

There is, however, a dissenting view: V. G. Simiyu, a Kenyan historian, argues that the traditional African political system was undemocratic. Simiyu's denial that the traditional African political practice was democratic is premised, as I understand it, on some basic assumptions. First, he assumes that the African society was hierarchical and stratified, allowing the political and economic dominance of the lower classes by the royal and aristocratic groups: "The first general principle which seemed to lie at the base of nearly all African political systems was the concept of hierarchy." [16] Furthermore, he adds, "In some societies, the class structure prevented the development of democratic tendencies. There may have been checks and balances against the absolute authority and power of the king, but the exercise of those controlling forces was done by the immediate members of the ruling aristocracy without any participation of the commoners."[17] The second assumption, a corollary of the first, is that the traditional African society is a nonegalitarian society. This feature of the traditional system, according to Simiyu, fails to give "everyone equal opportunity to rise up in the social and political ranks."[18] Whereas a democratic system should make it possible for people to hold office or achieve some status "on personal merit,"[19] an aspiration or goal like this would be frustrated by the royal and hereditary features of the right to political power inherent in the African system. The third assumption is that a political system that promotes "gerontocracies"[20] (systems of rule by the elders) and also excludes women from "the political and judicial processes except as observers or victims"[21] is undemocratic. Thus, the alleged hierarchical, nonegalitarian, gerontocratic, and sexist features of the African sociopolitical structure: these are the assumptions upon which Simiyu erects his arguments.

Simiyu's denial of democracy to the traditional African political practice is not unqualified; it is sometimes even inconsistent. He asserts that "there were hardly any democratic traditions in the precolonial days"[22] and that in fact there were "some rudiments of democratic practice"[23] and "some rudiments of democratic principles and practices."[24] Moreover, it is logically implied in his statement that the African political tradition "was not an *entirely* democratic tradition,"[25] that more than a few aspects of the tradition were, or must have been, democratic. (What he means by an "entirely" democratic tradition, however, he does not explain.)

It must be noted that much of what Simiyu says in his denial that the traditional African political practice was democratic is in conflict with the observations made by other scholars I have referred to. What needs to be done in such a situation where conflicting or contrary positions are presented is to proffer reasons or arguments for rejecting one or the other position or for rejecting both positions. I wish to proffer reasons for rejecting the views Simiyu presents in his article. I think that Simiyu unduly expects too much of a political tradition or practice that, it can be said, was still in the process of evolving. Witness his statement, "There were rudiments of democratic principles and practices, especially in the noncentralized communities, but it would be dangerous to equate those practices with *advanced forms* of democracy."[26] He makes no attempt, however, to define or explain what advanced forms of democracy are. But his statement does imply that the traditional political practice has democratic features, albeit not "advanced" (whatever he means by "advanced forms of democracy").

As to the assumptions upon which his arguments are based, even though I would agree that African society is hierarchical and therefore not classless, I would reject the inference that a hierarchical social structure cannot spawn democracy, or that it is necessarily authoritarian. The fifth century B.C. Athenian society, famous for giving birth to democracy in the Western tradition, was a hierarchical, class-based, and nonegalitarian society. Women as well as serfs were excluded from participating in the deliberations of the Athenian assembly *(ecclesia).* Modern Western nations that have developed the democratic political practice are hierarchical—highly stratified—and not classless in their social systems. In both Western Europe and the United States the process of achieving broader political participation was one of gradual evolution. The American political scientist Dankwart Rustow admits that "universal and equal suffrage (even for males) was not achieved in most Western countries until the late nineteenth or early twentieth centuries."[27] Britain, whose democratic system may be said to have begun its development with the signing of the historic document Magna Carta in A.D. 1215 and whose political system was considered a democracy before 1927, did not give the franchise to British women until 1928. Could one describe the form of democracy practiced in Britain in the intervening centuries as "advanced"? Was the British system sexist and therefore not democratic?

In criticizing Simiyu's views, however, I do not imply by any means that the African society in the traditional setting had what he calls a "full-fledged" democratic system or that the democratic features of its political tradition were of an "advanced form." But, as I shall show in a detailed description and analysis of the political practice in traditional Ghana—using this particular practice as a paradigm—the traditional African political practice can be said to have had features or elements of democracy, in both theory and practice, elements at least some of which could be nurtured and refined for a contemporary application.

2. Chiefship and Political Authority

It is clear from the observations of scholars on the traditional political system that chieftaincy is certainly the most outstanding feature of the traditional African political structure and the linchpin of the political wheel.[28] The perception and appreciation by the chief and the people of the purpose of the institution of chiefship is thus most crucial to an assessment of the democratic character of the traditional political structure. Therefore, an inquiry into the status, nature of authority, and role of the chief and the power relationships holding between the chief and the people will disclose certain political values and ideas espoused in the political setting of traditional Africa. This will require an elaborate inquiry into the political institutions that were fashioned and their manner of operation. But I shall focus my attention on the political institutions of the Akan people, the largest communo-cultural group in Ghana. Since chiefship, as a political institution, is widely practiced in African communities mutatis mutandis, it is most likely that parallels of what I describe will be found, at least in spirit, in many other societies in Africa. In this connection, what anthropologists Fortes and

Evans-Pritchard wrote over half a century ago is worth recalling: "The societies described are representative of *common types* of African political systems.
. . . Most of the forms described are variants of a *pattern* of political organization found among contiguous or neighboring societies."[29] There is no implicit suggestion here that the various political forms are exactly the same;
only that there are similarities between them.

2.1 Traditional Akan Political Institutions

In this section, I am concerned only with the political institutions that bear
most directly on the relations between the chief and the people, that is,
between the ruler and the ruled; in other words, with the institutions that
may be said to be crucial as far as the concrete expression of the democratic
idea of the will of the people is concerned.

Every Akan town or village is made up of several clans. A lineage from
within one of these clans, probably the one whose forefathers founded that
town or village, constitutes the royal lineage from which the chiefs are
elected or chosen. The royal status of that lineage is recognized and accepted
by the people. Each clan comprises many lineages, while each lineage in
turn comprises many individuals generally supposed to be linked by blood
relationships. Each town or village constitutes a political unit. A great number of such towns and villages form a paramountcy, a state *(oman)*, such as
the Asante state or Akim Abuakwa state, whose head is the paramount chief,
the *omanhene.*

Each town or village has a chief and a council of elders, these elders being
the heads of the clans. The chief presides at the meetings of the council. In
the conduct of its affairs, each lineage in a town, or each town in a paramountcy, acts autonomously, without any interference from either the chief
(in the case of purely lineage affairs), or the paramount chief (in the case of
purely town affairs). A decentralized political system is thus an outstanding
feature of the traditional Akan political culture. Just as each town or village
has a council, so does the state have a state council, described by J. B. Danquah as "the great legislative assembly of the nation."[30] The state council,
presided over by the *omanhene*, draws its membership from the chiefs of the
towns and villages constituting the state.

2.1.1 Election of the Chief. The chief, who is the political head of an Akan
town or village, is chosen from the royal lineage by the head of the lineage
in consultation with the members of that lineage. It is necessary that the
person chosen be *acceptable* not only to the councilors, who represent their
clans, but also to the Asafo company of young men or "commoners" who
are, in effect, the body of citizens. The paramount chief is chosen in the
same way, except that his election has to be acceptable to the chiefs of the
constituent towns and villages. Thus, never is a chief imposed upon an Akan
community, *a fact of which the self-imposed military rulers of Africa today
must take note.*

Now, having been accepted by his subjects, the chief must take a public oath on the occasion of his formal investiture of power before his councilors and the body of citizens, promising that he will rule in accordance with the laws, customs, and institutions of the town or state and that should he renege on the oath he stands condemned and will be liable to deposition. At the formal investiture of power, a series of injunctions are publicly recited before the new chief. These injunctions define his political authority and the political relationship that is expected to be maintained between him and his subjects. The following are examples (taken from Rattray)[31] of the injunctions declared to the chief through his spokesman—the okyeame—and acknowledged by him:

We do not wish that he should curse us.

We do not wish that he should be greedy.

We do not wish that he should be disobedient [or, refuse to take advice].

We do not wish that he should treat us unfairly

We do not wish that he should act on his own initiative [lit.: "out of his own head," that is, acting without reference to the views or wishes of the people.]

We do not wish that it should ever be that he should say to us, "I have no time," "I have no time."

It is noteworthy that these constitutionally binding declarations are all preceded by the words "We do not wish that." The political significance of those words is enormous: the people are, in effect, telling the chief how he should govern them: the chief is thus not expected to govern his subjects in the way *he* wishes. The declarations are, in one way, an unambiguous assertion of the people's right to participate in running the affairs of their community or state, in governing themselves; they are, in another way, an indication of the confidence the people have in insisting on the exercise of a political power that will reflect their wishes. They are, in yet another way, an indication also of the people's intention to make the chief aware that he will need to depend on his people for a satisfactory and peaceful rule: this clearly implies the iffiness of the exercise of political power.

The chief (or ruler) is required by the first injunction not to abuse or insult his subjects but rather to respect them: that is, the chief should recognize their equality as human beings, even if they are not equal in directly wielding political power. The second injunction requires a reasonable sharing of the economic goods or advantages that may accrue to the community or state; it is intended to check the ruler from sliding down the path of corruption to which he could easily be led by economic or material greed. As a riposte to the inclination toward official avarice and cheat, the fourth injunction requires a fair and just treatment of the people by the chief. The most important injunctions are the third and fifth, both of which assert that the chief is never to act without the advice and full concurrence of his councilors, who are the representatives of the people. Acting without the concurrence and advice of his councilors is a legitimate cause for his deposition.[32] The chief is thus bound by law and custom to rule with the consent of his people. In the last injunction, the people ask that the chief make himself accessible to them, that he be willing and prepared to listen to their complaints or to what they have to say about any matters that concern them. It may thus be said that the Akan theory of government is a kind of social contract theory. The injunctions submitted by the people to the chief and acknowledged by him constitute a kind of contract between them. Actually, the kind of contract here is political rather than social. (I distinguish a social contract from a political contract; see page 126). The chief or king is thus to hold power in trust for the people.

2.1.2 The Chief's Council. The chief's council is the real governing body of the town. The members of this governing council are usually the heads of the various clans. The council is presided over by the chief. The councilors are the representatives of the people, and, as such, have to confer with them on any issue that is to be discussed in the council. That is to say, the councilors, to whom everyone in the town has access, have to seek popular opinion. "The representative character of a councilor," wrote Mensah Sarbah almost a century ago, "is well understood and appreciated by the people."[33] The councilor is obliged to act on the advice and with the concurrence of the members of his clan, in the same way the chief is obliged to act after consultations and with the consent of his councilors, whom he has to summon regularly.

It is interesting to note that in the Akan culture the same linguistic expression *(adwabo)* is, as Rattray also notes,[34] used for both council (or, assembly) and market. Judging from the activities or transactions that go on in markets in Akan towns and villages, the use of that expression points to the practice of bargaining, negotiation, and compromise that characterizes the deliberations and decisions of councils and assemblies organized in Akan communities.

The councilors freely discuss all matters affecting the town or state. And, in any such an atmosphere of free and frank expression of opinions, disagreements are inevitable. But in the event of such disagreements the council would continue to listen to arguments until a consensus was achieved with the reconciliation of opposed views. The communitarian ethos of African culture places a great value on solidarity, which in turn engenders the pursuit of consensus or unanimity not only in such important decisions as those taken by the highest political authority of the town or state but also in decisions taken by lower assemblies such as those presided over by the heads of the clans, that is, the councilors. And so it is that every command, every move that is adopted by the chief has been discussed and agreed upon by his councilors (who must have previously sounded popular opinion). This is the reason why any announcement made by the chief's spokesman (okyeame) about a law, decree, injunction, command, and so on, is made invariably in the name of the chief *and* his elders (that is, the councilors): "Thus say the chief *and* his elders . . ."

Having provided a brief account of the Akan traditional political institutions and how they operated, I now move on to a discussion of the democratic features of these institutions.

3. Democratic Elements in the Traditional Akan Political Practice

Defining the concept of democracy is not difficult. The famous and perhaps the most widely accepted definition is that it is the government of the people, by the people, and for the people. The notion of "the people" is central to any definition of democracy. The definition implies, as it must, that the standard by which to judge the democratic nature of a political system is the degree of adequacy allowed for the expression of the will of the people, the extent to which the people are involved in decision-making processes. The problem of democracy, however, is simply the problem of *how to give institutional expression to the will of the people*, how, that is, to make the will of the people explicit in real and concrete terms. In the nations of the Western world, such institutions as the multiparty system, periodic elections, parliaments or congresses, constitutions containing bills of rights, an independent judiciary, and others have been created to give expression to the will of the people and to guard against the violation of their political and civil rights. These are some of the ingredients of the Western democratic political systems.

Now, in what ways, and to what extent, can the Akan political institutions just described be said to have provided a means of expressing the will of the people and popular participation in the political process? Let us explore this important question.

The institution of chiefship is definitely the linchpin of the democratic process in the Akan political system. For, the nature of the political authority of the chief determines the character of the political process. The chief, as I said, is chosen from the royal lineage. Succession to the high office of the chief is thus hereditary. And this hereditary character of chiefship may be said to have imposed a limitation on the choice of rulers, though not necessarily on all other public officeholders. Four points may be made that can be said to neutralize the political seriousness and effect of this delimiting factor.

First, unlike most monarchies in the world, where the next occupant of the throne—the heir apparent—is obvious to everyone in the state, the Akan system has no obvious next candidate for chief. The reason is that there always are several eligible men in the royal lineage, and each one of them has just about equal claim to the throne. Thus, the kingmakers, who are elders also of royal lineage, have several candidates to choose from. In deciding whom to choose and present to the people, the kingmakers have to exercise the greatest judiciousness and wisdom, for their choice has to be acceptable to the people as a whole. The political history of many an Akan town or state teems with constitutional disputes arising either out of the lack of consensus among the electors—that is, the kingmakers—themselves on who would be the most suitable candidate, or out of the unacceptability of their choice to the majority of the people. But the point to be noted, for the moment, is that in putting a person forward for the position of chief, then, the electors have to convince themselves that their choice will be acceptable to the people as a whole. Thus, insofar as the people have a say in the suitability of the person chosen to rule them, it may be said that the traditional Akan political system makes it possible for the people to choose their own rulers, even if the initiative is taken by some few people, namely, some members of the royal lineage.

The second point is that just as the will of the people is of considerable weight in determining the suitability and acceptability of the electors' choice, so also is it most crucial in determining the continuity, effectiveness, and success of a chief's rulership. The common people (*mmerantee*, lit. young men) constituted themselves into Asafo companies, which are organized for social, military, and political action. "In recent years," according to Danquah, "these 'companies' have persistently claimed to possess absolute power to enstool, and chiefly to destool, a chief. This claim seems in a sense to be supported by facts of history and long-established customary practice."[35] Thus, even if the people as a whole do not have the power to choose their ruler directly, they have the power to remove him directly or to have him removed by the electors. This is another outlet provided in the Akan political system for the expression of the popular will.

The third point is that the limits of the monarchical power are clearly set both by custom and by the series of injunctions publicly declared before the chief and acknowledged publicly by him. These injunctions make it constitutionally impossible, or at least impolitic, for the chief to adhere stubbornly to his views, policies, and actions in the teeth of opposition from his councilors and subjects; they also outlaw arbitrary and autocratic government from the Akan political practice. The injunctions as well as custom so severely curtail the political authority of the chief that, in the words of R. S. Rattray, a British anthropologist in the employ of the colonial administration of the Gold Coast (now Ghana) during the first three decades of this century, "the chief in reality was expected to do little or nothing without having previously consulted his councilors, who in turn conferred with the people in order to sound popular opinion."[36] Regarding the limited character of the political authority of the chiefs, Brodie Cruickshank, a Scotsman who also served in the British colonial administration in the Gold Coast between 1834 and 1852, made the following observation: "But among none of those chiefs living under the protection of the [British] government, is their authority of such consequence as to withstand the general opinion of their subjects; so that, with all the outward display of regal power, *the chief is little more than a puppet moved at the will of the people.*"[37] The limited power of the chief is, as we have seen, a constitutional requirement, and any arbitrary and autocratic actions by him will lead to his deposition.

The injunctions listed above that are submitted by the people to the chief on the occasion of his accession to power and accepted by him constitute a kind of contract between the chief and the people. Politically, then, the relationship between the ruler and the ruled is contractual, implying of course that if the chief—the ruler—abuses the political trust, he will be removed from power. The contract involved in this kind of situation, then, is specifically political rather that social. Thus, I make a distinction between social contract, beloved of the seventeenth- and eighteenth-century European as well as contemporary American individualist political thinkers, and political contract. While a social contract is, according to seventeenth- and eighteenth-century European political thought, a contract, an agreement, generally among presocial individuals in a state of nature, a political contract is a contract of rulership or government, an agreement between people and their ruler, which constitutes the basis of the legitimate—and thus acceptable—exercise of political power. A political contract is not a social contract in that it already presupposes the existence of a real political community (yet to be established by a social contract). It is the kind of contract that may be established or undertaken in a communitarian society that sees individual human beings as naturally social, not presocial (prepolitical). A social contract, on the other hand, generally assumes that human beings are individuals, live presocial lives, and require a contract—a social contract— as a basis for the formation of a real political community. A social contract, however, is also a political contract, for the contract would include principles, political and legal, by which the future political community is to be governed. Thus, the aim of a social contract is essentially or inherently twofold.

A social contract, as conceived by European thinkers, is a hypothetical contract, an explanatory scheme. A political contract—a contract of government—however, is an *actual* contract undertaken, not by ghostly individuals, but, as in the actual case of the Akan practice, by substantial human beings already concretely situated in a sociopolitical context and ever aware of their needs, goals, aspirations, purposes, and conceptions of the good life. Also, a social contract enunciates principles from which the laws of the political community will derive, whereas a political contract deals directly with specific laws and political and moral principles that are to guide both the conduct of the ruler and the relations that ought to exist between him and the ruled. For purposes of actual governing, a political contract, which is an actual contract, is what is immediately required to keep the governor in check.

The fourth point that may be made against the view that the hereditary character of succession to chiefship might (potentially) throttle the real expression of popular will is that in any assembly, whether in the council of the chief, or in the palace of the chief—where general assemblies of all the people usually take place—or in the house of a councilor (that is, head of a clan), there is free expression of opinion. No one is hindered from fully participating in the deliberations of the councils or general assemblies and thus from contributing to the decisions of these constitutional bodies. It is thus pretty clear that the traditional Akan political structure allows for many to participate in making decisions about the affairs of the community. "Anyone, even the most ordinary youth," writes Cruickshank, "will offer his opinion or make a suggestion with an equal chance of its being as favorably entertained as if it proceeded from the most experienced sage."[38]

The observations made by Rattray about the democratic character of the politics of the Asante (Ashanti), a subsection of the Akan people, are worth noting.

> Nominally autocratic, the Ashanti constitution was in practice democratic to a degree. I have already on several occasions used this word "democratic", and it is time to explain what the term implies in this part of Africa. We pride ourselves, I believe, on being a democratic people and flatter ourselves that our institutions are of a like nature. An Ashanti who was familiar alike with his own and our [British] Constitution would deny absolutely our right to apply this term either to ourselves or to our Constitution. To him a democracy implies that the affairs of the Tribe (the state) must rest, not in the keeping of the few, but in the hands of the many, that is, must not alone be the concern of what we should term "the chosen rulers of the people", but should continue to be the concern of a far wider circle. To him the state is literally a *Res Publica;* it is everyone's business. The work of an Ashanti citizen did not finish when by his vote he had installed a chief in office. . . . The rights and duties of the Ashanti democrats were really only beginning after (if I may use a homely analogy) the business of the ballot-box was over. In England, the Government and House of Commons stand between ourselves and the making of our laws, *but among the Ashanti there was not any such thing as government apart from the people.*[39]

(I might mention that there is a striking resemblance between Rattray's account of the Asante democratic practice and G. C. Field's account of democracy in ancient Greece. "It is important," writes Field, a scholar of ancient Greek philosophy, "for a modern reader to remember that to a Greek democracy meant the continued and active participation of all the citizens in the work of government. Our modern systems of representative would have seemed to him in no sense democratic at all, because they involve the abdication to selected representatives of what should be the privilege and responsibility of each citizen.")[40]

It may be noted that neither the concept of the divine right of kings, which was asserted by the Stuart kings of seventeenth-century England as the basis of their political authority, nor the concept of enlightened or benevolent despotism, which was asserted by eighteenth-century European monarchs as the justification for their despotic rule, is known to have been asserted or claimed or pursued by the Akan or, for that matter, by more than a few of the African rulers in the traditional setting. On the contrary, interpretative analyses of anthropological accounts of their political cultures do indicate, pretty clearly, that they had created political systems that not only made real despotism almost impossible but also gave due recognition to the wishes of the governed. The participatory political process in time enabled the people to develop attitudes of personal commitment to matters of state, to res publicae.

In many traditional societies, political power could become absolute and unchallengeable because of the wealth of the ruler. In the Akan society land is held as an important source of wealth as well as political power. In order to whittle down the political power that derives from wealth, the chief is strictly enjoined by customary doctrine not to dispose of any portion of the village or communal land without the consent of his council or the elders. But not only that: like the guardians (that is, rulers) of Plato's *Republic,* the chief, until the 1930s and since then, was not allowed to have personal property. The denial of private property to the chief was to preempt conflict of interest, conflicts between his managing his own property and his managing the property of the state. The possibility of economic mismanagement was never lost sight of; but economic mismanagement was certainly not tolerated. In fact, economic mismanagement, which included adopting wrong economic measures and misappropriating public funds, was among the reasons for removing a chief. Thus Sarbah notes: "if the family finds that he [the chief] is misappropriating, wasting, or squandering the ancestral fund, it is to their interest to remove him at once and appoint another in his stead."[41] And Danquah records that "unwarranted disposal of stool property, including land, is another great cause for deposition."[42] Also, if "a chief made a habit of engaging in expensive litigations resulting in the taxation of his people," and "squandered" a substantial part of the public revenue "in unimportant affairs,"[43] he would be removed. And what applied to the chief applied also to the head of a clan inasmuch as he too was a trustee of the property of the clan. The possibility of the removal of the chief is certainly an aspect of the contractual obligations imposed on the ruler.

In the traditional political practice, the chief relies on the people for his rule despite the hereditary nature of his high office. This most probably derives from the oath that he swears on the occasion of his investiture of power and that is regarded by him and his subjects as a basis of a contractual political authority. The active participation of the people in running the affairs of the community or the state establishes a close relationship between the ruler and the ruled. It can thus be said that the traditional system of governing created no distance between the chief and his subjects, between the government and the governed. The royal palace (*ahenfie,* in the Akan language), which is the seat of political power, the seat of the traditional government, is not regarded by the citizen as an object having no reference to him personally. The citizen's way or approach to the royal palace is much easier than his way or approach to the castle, which is the seat of the colonial and postcolonial government. (Incidentally, the modern Akan word for "government" is *aban,* literally, "castle," or "fort.") In Accra (the capital of Ghana), a castle was—and still is—the seat of the colonial and postcolonial government. There is greater communication or intercourse between the citizen and the *ahenfie* because governing is more open and people have easier access to the ruler. The overall effect of this situation is that the traditional political system evokes in the individual citizen a feeling of personal commitment to the affairs of the community or the state, a sense that the government is his and therefore any harm done to the community as a whole harms him directly. The traditional ideology thus maintains that the state or government is indeed a res publica, a public thing, a matter of common concern, requiring the constant attention and interest of every individual citizen.

Decentralization, as noted by Rattray, is a fundamental idea in the Akan political and administrative structure. "Upon it, in my considered opinion," he writes, "lay the whole success and wonder of this loosely bound confederacy. . . . A Paramount Chief who endeavoured to centralize too much in olden times generally paid with his life for his folly in having allowed his ambitions to override his knowledge of his own Constitution."[44] It must be noted, however, that in the Akan political and administrative structure, the villages, towns, and other localities act autonomously in most spheres of their political life. Thus, in terms of taking decisions affecting the affairs of the localities, political power in the state *(oman)* is not centralized. "Decentralization" in a political system makes sense only when, (1) political and administrative power was previously wholly held by the center from which all political decisions flowed and, (2) devolution of power to the localities was later thought appropriate. Thus, applying the term "decentralization" to the traditional Akan political and administrative system would be inappropriate. The reason is that the creation of the state does not seem to have led to the complete whittling away of the political power of the constituent towns and villages: power (some power) was ceded rather for the *creation* and political *viability* of the state *(oman)*, not vice versa.

It could be said, in fact, that entailed in the original Akan political arrangement was the conception of the state as, to use a term familiar in Western political parlance, a minimal state, for that arrangement (see also chapter 5) allows wide latitude for the autonomous economic activities of individuals, families (or, lineages), clans, and local communities.

In all this, the Akan people *institutionally* express, in their own fashion, certain basic ideas of democracy. Foremost is the idea that the government of a people must be responsive to the wishes of the people. We have noted that although the chief is not directly elected by all the people, the electors in their choice have to consider the wishes of the people; we have noted also that the chief has to govern in accordance with the popular will. Again, the allowance made for the expression of opinion on public matters enables the people of an Akan community, or many of them at any rate, to be involved in decision making at all levels. Public criticisms of government policy and action are inevitable in a system that allows for the frank expression of opinion. Criticisms of government policy and action were made by people generally as individuals, not as members of "political parties," which were not a feature of the traditional political system.

Groupings of men and women resulting from disagreements and disputes that emerge—and not infrequently—generally over the choice of a chief, but over other matters as well, are the closest phenomena in the traditional African political system to "political parties" of the type that obtains in

Western countries. But, though such groupings can be said to be political in terms of their aims, they can hardly be described as political parties. For their aims are ad hoc and ephemeral, concerned not so much with the broad political issues of society as with the issue of the person chosen to hold the office of the chief. For this reason, such disputes and opposition never lead to ideological rifts and are submerged before long by the waves of the characteristic demands of solidarity.

Because of the nonexistence of political parties, some scholars have supposed that African political culture lacks the concept of opposition. But the existence of disagreements, divisions, and groupings along political lines in the deliberations of the traditional councils and assemblies as well as the pursuit of consensus belies this supposition. Consensus, along with reconciliation, appears in fact to have been a political virtue vigorously pursued in traditional Akan councils and assemblies, and to have become an outstanding feature in the process of reaching decisions. In all kinds of deliberations the aim is to achieve consensus, and this, inevitably, prolongs meetings; but it allows for argument and exchange of ideas. Consensus logically presupposes dissensus (that is, dissent), the existence of opposing or different views; for it is the opposing views that are, or need to be, reconciled. If there were no opposition, it would be senseless to talk of reaching a consensus. This is a conceptual truth. The appropriate conclusion, then, is that in the traditional Akan political practice there is opposition without an organized political party in opposition. Whether or not Akan (or African) political culture would have in time evolved its own brand of the party system of politics, no one can say for sure. Colonialism slammed the doors against such a possible evolution.

Consensus, as a procedure for arriving at political decisions, is born of the pursuit of the social ideal or goal of solidarity—itself inspired by a belief in the identity of the interests of all the members of the community—and of the recognition of the political and moral values of equality, reciprocity, and respect for the views of others. It must be pointed out that consensus formation operates at all political levels, from the highest level, which will involve the chief's participation, down to the lowest level, the extended family. And, irrespective of social status, every citizen—male and female—is free and has the right to contribute to consensus formation. Consensus is, with justification, considered vital to the practice of democracy in most traditional African political systems.[45] For, it allows everyone an opportunity to speak his mind and promotes patience, mutual tolerance, and an attitude of compromise—all of which are necessary for democratic practice, in which everyone is expected to appreciate the need to abandon or modify his own position in the face of more persuasive arguments by others. Through the pursuit of consensus the will of every individual is effective to a degree, and is not cavalierly set aside, as it generally is in a straightforward majoritarian decision-making system, which deprives the minority of the right to have their opinion reflected in a decision. Thus, even though consensus may not result in total agreement, it may nevertheless leave every participant in a decision-making assembly satisfied, more or less, without feeling that he has been left in limbo. Consensus must therefore be considered a democratic virtue, an ideal for any democratic decision-making body.

In most traditional African societies, it would be impolitic—perhaps also illegal—for the chief (or king) or the head of a clan to set aside or oppose a decision that has been reached through consensus. Such an action would of course frustrate the wishes of the people. In Akan political terms, for the chief to set at nought a consensus-based decision would be to repudiate two or three of the injunctions that he would have acknowledged on the formal occasion of his investiture of power. Such an action would spell political disaster for the chief or clan head.

3.1 Theoretical Expression of Democracy

In the foregoing section, I described the Akan political practice and the political institutions that made that practice possible. There is no denying, however, that political institutions take their rise from, and are molded by, a political theory or philosophy. That is to say, underlying political institutions and political practice is a political theory, a philosophy, even though such philosophy may not have been *fully* articulated or worked out. My intention in this section, therefore, is to indicate and examine the ideas underpinning the Akan political practice and how these ideas are formulated. The Akan ideas or values of politics are articulated in proverbs and art symbols. Let us begin our discussion with a well-known Akan proverb:

One head does not go into council.

This important proverb emphasizes the political value of consultation or conferring, the idea that deliberation by several heads (that is, minds) on matters of public concern is always better, more fruitful, than deliberation by just one. As a theoretical underpinning of, as well as a logical follow-up to, the injunctions formally acknowledged by the chief, this proverb says that the chief cannot—or should not—alone deliberate and make a decision or take an action that affects others, for he is (or, has) one head. Even though the proverb may not directly advocate a democratic practice, it unmistakably repudiates autocracy or despotism, which is defined here as "one head going into council." This proverb is in fact the logical consequence of another one that says:

Wisdom is not in the head of one person.

Together the two proverbs say: Because wisdom does not lie in only one person's head, then one head cannot, or should not, go into council, where the exercise of wisdom is required. Since, as the proverb clearly implies, every person has some ability to think (for every human being can be credited with some amount of intelligence)—and to think about, in this case, matters affecting the whole community or state—it would be presumptuous for one person to assume the right to think or deliberate for others. The proverb implies, then, that matters concerning the whole community ought to be thought about by all the members of the community or by as many of them as possible: neither the chief nor his councilors can alone claim the right to make decisions for the community or state without conferring with the people.

But let us explore the second proverb a bit further. The proverb implies, (1) that other individuals may be equally wise and capable of producing equally good, if not better, ideas and arguments; (2) that one should not, or cannot, regard one's own intellectual position as final or unassailable or beyond criticism but must expect it to be evaluated by others; and (3) that, in consequence of (2), one should be prepared to abandon one's position should one's own ideas or arguments be judged by others as unacceptable. The proverb underlines not only the need for but also the acceptance of criticism and compromise, just as it points up the need to respect the views of others. In the political context, it enjoins rulers to be undogmatic and tolerant of the views of others and to consider the words of wisdom and truth that may be contained in the presentations or arguments of other members of their councils or of the wider community.

There are proverbs specifically about the limited power of the chief (ruler), and the power relations established between him and his subjects.

> If a chief reprimands [rebukes, punishes] you for doing something, he does so by the authority of the citizens.
>
> It is when the state kills you that the chief kills you.
>
> It is when a chief has good councilors that his reign becomes peaceful.
>
> There are no bad chiefs [rulers], only bad advisors.

The first two proverbs express the idea that the chief (that is, the ruler) acts only by the authority of the people or their representatives. Thus, the chief cannot adopt any action without the consent or authority of his subjects. The third proverb shows the importance of the members of the chief's council, who are the representatives of the people, and underlines the dependence of the ruler on their advice for satisfactory and peaceful government. The implications of the first three proverbs are summed up in the fourth proverb. The thought expressed in the fourth proverb is that theoretically there are no bad rulers because the ruler is expected to rely solely on the advice and guidance of his advisors. The assumption is that the advice of the councilors and other lieutenants is necessarily good, well-considered, and reliable, proceeding, as it does, from many heads (minds) rather than from one head, that is, the ruler's.

The message of the fourth proverb is only theoretically plausible and may in practice be false, insofar as it is possible for a ruler to set aside the views or arguments of his advisors. The message is indeed a political ideal. But the realization of the ideal would depend very much on the character, personality, and disposition of the ruler: a stupid, arrogant, self-conceited, and strong-willed ruler may set aside even the good advice of his lieutenants, but to his own chagrin. The realization of the ideal would depend also on the extent to which the councilors and the people are prepared to insist that the ruler submit to the popular will. Even so, the proverb embodies a political ideal that, when realized, recognizes the effective role of the popular will and insures a democratic political practice.

An emblem embossed in silver or gold on top of a staff often held by the chief's spokesman at public ceremonies depicts an egg in a hand. The saying that goes with it is that holding power is like holding an egg in your hand: if you press the egg hard, you break it; but if you do not hold it securely enough, it drops and breaks. The symbol expresses an important and profound political idea: a ruler should not oppress his subjects or do anything that could cause them to revolt or rebel, for such an action could in turn lead to political chaos or the possible breakup of his kingdom. On the other hand, if the ruler fails to adopt the appropriate and judicious actions, policies, and measures such as may be required by particular circumstances, if the firmness and resoluteness that a situation demands are not shown by the ruler, his indecision, supineness, and lack of both political will and strength of purpose will equally wreck his political authority. The symbol is not intended to give the impression that a ruler's position is one of a tangle or dilemma; it is intended, rather, to express an important fact about the judicious or prudent use of political power, namely, that neither excessive action nor indolent inaction is a true mark of rulership, and that political power or authority should be exercised wisely and appropriately.

Let me say that it has not at all been my intention in the foregoing sections to claim the existence of—or to have nostalgic pretensions about—"a golden age" in the traditional Akan political practice. My intention, rather, has been only to delineate and analyze what most people are most likely to regard as *democratic* features or elements of a political practice, features at least some elements of which could be given new shape on the anvil of modern experience, demands, and aspirations in the quest for viable political structures for the contemporary political life.

4. Creating Modern Democratic Institutions

I wish to start off this section by looking at the implications of the prepositions "of" and "by" used in formulating the most famous definition of democracy as government *of* the people, *by* the people, and for the people. The expression "of the people" means prima facie that it is the people who (should) govern, or, at the minimum, it is the people who not only choose those who are to rule but also find ways to control the rulers and see to it that the way they are ruled conforms to their wishes. This can be a correct translation of the expression "of the people." I think, however, that the expression means much more than that. I think it means, equally importantly, that democracy is a government whose form of practice derives in its entirety from the historical and cultural experiences *of* a people and is is in conformity with their vision of how they want to be governed or to govern themselves; a system of government born of the hopes and aspirations of a people and in the shaping of which the people have a real say and commitment to; a political structure to which the people, in consequence, have intellectual, ideological, and emotional attachments; a system of government that is considered by the people as their own and which they are ever prepared to protect and defend to the hilt. In fine, a government *of* the people is one that has its roots in the people—in their goals, values, ideals, experiences, and aspirations: thus rooted, it is not a type of governmental system the nuances of which can be imposed on a people from outside, though some aspects of those nuances can be influenced—even borrowed—externally; but it is a system of rule that is nurtured, refined, and modified by a people to reflect their wishes, desires, and experiences. The lack of all these desiderata makes a people's appreciation of, and attitude toward, a particular form of democratic practice merely tentative and tinkering.

By "*by* the people," what is meant, I think, is that democracy is a system of government whose constitutional rules, principles, and procedures are set up by the people themselves; a system of government that allows the people to rule, that makes it possible for the people to participate in making decisions that affect their personal lives, community, or state. The central and effective role expected to be played by the people in a democracy has given rise to the notion of participatory democracy, which requires that the people be directly involved in making political decisions. The conceptual interpretation of the character of democracy I have just provided is in many ways reflected and borne up by the historical development of the democratic system of government in European nations.

As mentioned in section 1, the development of democratic political institutions in Britain, most probably the oldest democracy in the modern West, began with the signing of the Magna Carta in 1215. But it took many centuries for those institutions to evolve into their present forms, an evolutionary process that was guided by the compass of historical and cultural circumstances. The process had to jump or knock down such hurdles as autocracies, military dictatorships, claims to divine right of power, enlightened or benevolent despotisms, strong and unyielding monarchical systems, and other impediments to the establishment of democracy. These impediments to the development of the democratic process may be said to be common to the political history of many European nations. But what all this means, surely, can be summed up in four conclusions: first, that the way to the establishment of democracy was not easy for any European nation—there were in the histories of these nations revolutions and civil wars, institutional trials and errors, public executions of monarchs and public officials, adoptions and adaptations of alien political structures; second—and following logically from the first—that no democratic nation today was born a democracy and some Western democracies were until recently undemocratic and totalitarian; third—and following logically from the second—that a democracy in its mature form is built over a time; and fourth, that when democracy finally emerged, it was naturally a type that had been forged, tested, and refined in the furnace of the historical and cultural experiences of the European peoples themselves. The foregoing historical analysis provides some justification for the view that it would be appropriate for African nations to exploit their own experiences in fashioning modern political institutions that would give concrete expression to the idea of democracy. This enterprise of creation must proceed from their experience with both the traditional and the colonial elements that modern Africa has inherited.

The search for democracy in postcolonial Africa has been an odyssey, a long and arduous journey the end of which is not yet in sight. Perhaps resorting to the indigenous values and ideas of politics could be a redemptive approach. In previous sections of this chapter, some evidence and arguments have been deployed to show that ideas and values of politics such as popular will, free expression of opinion, consensus and reconciliation, consultation and conferring, and the trusteeship, and hence limited, nature of political power—all of which are ingredients of the democratic idea—are to be found in the African traditions of government and that they are, thus, by no means alien to the indigenous political cultures of the African people. The fact is, however, that these political values have not been allowed to affect and shape the contours of modern African politics. The consequences have not been palatable: authoritarian politics and illegitimate seizure of political power are the order of the day. These are features of modern African politics that can hardly be said to derive from African traditions. There is therefore a need to urge that traditional values and ideas be brought to bear on modern political life and thought. But to say this is not to be oblivious of the limitations of applying traditions of smaller and more homogeneous political communities to large, complex, and heterogeneous political settings of today.

It must be borne in mind from the outset that the conditions in which the indigenous democratic institutions operated many decades ago were different from what they are today with the emergence of large political communities (that is, multinational states) and of the ideas of a central government that controls the political power over multicultural and multilingual groups of people. The business of government in the modern world is more complex, more ramifying than of yore; we cannot go about such business in the way it was done by our forefathers. The reason is simply that certain aspects of the traditional conceptions of things, but by no means all, are incongruous with the modern situation.

For instance, the idea of a *hereditary* head of state who is not a mere figurehead but wields (or wants to wield) effective political power as in the traditional political setting will not be hospitable in a modern political community in which several individuals or groups compete for political power. Also, the concept of a regal lineage from which the chief—the highest political authority—was chosen is impossible to entertain and apply within the context of a large modern political community constituted by a medley of communocultural groups. Each of the constituent groups would want the head of state to come from within it, a desire that would, if not fulfilled, almost invariably engender political wrangles, machinations, and threats or rumblings of secession. Ethnicity—or, as I prefer to put it, the identity with one's communocultural group—has been the bane of the party system of politics in postcolonial Africa: party affiliations have generally been on communocultural lines, and communocultural identities are known to have played some role in military coups. It is thus undeniable that in the evolution of a democratic system in a large and complex political community some of the traditional African political institutions would be a hindrance. Such institutions or practices will therefore have to be expunged.

On the other hand, there are other institutions, to be sure, that would facilitate democratic political development: the town, village, or state councils that have served as instruments of political participation and involvement; the fact that wealth has never been a basis of membership in the traditional councils—so that both the rich and the poor have found themselves there; the autonomy of villages and towns (often referred to as "decentralization") as an aspect of the traditional method of taking political decisions or settling matters of local concern; the trusteeship or contractual basis of political authority; ideas of free expression of consent, opinion, popular will, consensus, and consultation; the open and accountable features of the traditional system of rule; the intolerance of misrule often demonstrated by the people; the easy approach to the seat of political power and the ease of communication between the ruler and the ruled; and the notion of the state as a res publica, as a political organization whose welfare, success, and survival are matters of everyone's concern. All these and other institutions discussed earlier are conducive to the evolution of the democratic practice even in a large modern political setting.

It must be noted that the colonial system of government created a distance between the government and the governed and that the same pattern of governing seems to have been followed by postcolonial African governments. This, in turn, has engendered attitudes of unconcern and insensitivity to the affairs of the state on the part of the governed. Consequently, the general attitude of the citizen has been that it is possible to injure the state without injuring oneself, an attitude that opens the floodgates of bribery, corruption, carelessness about state property or state enterprise, and other unethical acts deleterious to the development and welfare of the state. Traditional ideology, however, positively maintains that any injury done to the community or state as a whole directly injures the individual. Thus, the traditional system generates sentiments of personal commitment to the community that the modern state has yet to create in its citizens. These observations undoubtedly suggest the conviction that it is sensible, even imperative, to revivify those of our atavistic political values and attitudes that, evidently, are relevant to developments in modern democratic politics.

From the perspective of creating a modern democratic system of government, most people will agree that the foregoing features of the traditional political practice are positive and relevant. Yet, in the opinion of Dennis

Austin expressed in a very recent publication, "There is no alternative in
. . . African tradition" to the colonial state as the framework for building a
democratic government, and "the colonial state is the indispensable framework for any prospect of democratic government that may emerge."[46] It is
not clear what he means by the "colonial state." He is most probably referring to the colonial system of rule and its institutions, having just before the
quoted statement mentioned what he calls the "virtues" of the colonial state.
Whatever he means by the "colonial state," I think Austin overstates his case.
A few comments are therefore in order. First, it is quite surprising for Austin
to say that the colonial system of rule should constitute the indispensable
framework for any prospect of democratic government that may emerge in
Africa when he has already said that a democratic "government will have
native origins. It has been home grown in Western society and to seek to
transfer its beliefs and habits to an exotic soil will always be difficult;"[47] and
that "democracy is not a set of constitutional arrangements to be taken off
the peg for immediate use. . . . The conditions under which parliamentary
democracy evolved in the West were entirely different from those in Africa
today."[48]

Second, even though the British system of government, for instance, was
itself democratic, the colonial system of rule was not democratic: the colonial governor, who headed the colonial government, ruled by issuing decrees
(all or some of which may have originated from the colonial metropolis),
and the people (i.e., the governed) had no share in the making of the laws
to which they were subjected or in making decisions that affected their own
lives. Thus, the colonial government derived its legitimacy, not from the
governed, but from the colonial metropolis. It was almost a century later,
and well into the twilight of colonialism following the demands of African
nationalist movements for political independence, that legislative councils
and assemblies were introduced by the colonial government, assemblies that
included members elected by the native people in general elections. Long
before then, the colonial system of rule was undoubtedly a *single-party* or
autocratic government. Also, Austin, perhaps unwittingly, indicts the British
colonial government when he says: "Some African states which might have
benefitted from colonial rule, particularly British rule, came too late into its
grasp. They had too brief an acquaintance with its virtues."[49] Whatever were
the "virtues," that is, political virtues in this context, it was the responsibility
of the colonial government that ruled those states and that had already cultivated and been practicing those political virtues to introduce them in the
early days of its rule. In the Gold Coast (now Ghana), for instance, the first
political constitution to introduce a formal system of government that
would include people of the colonial territory was not established until after
more than a century of colonial control of the country, in 1946. The first
general elections were held in 1951, and the grant of political independence
came only six years later, in 1957. The Gold Coast surely did not come "too
late" into the colonial grasp; it was the political "virtues" that came or were
introduced too late. I am not suggesting, of course, that independence

should not have been granted at the time it was; no. I have introduced this brief historical note to point out, instead, that the African people were at a great disadvantage in having, on the attainment of political independence, to operate alien institutions that cannot be said to have been part of their political culture at the time and the practice of which, therefore, they were not—and could not have been—inured to.

But it is the African political leaders who took over from the colonial rulers who, in my opinion, should really be faulted for not showing interest in the creation of democratic political structures by *adapting* the traditional and colonial practices to suit the needs, experiences, and circumstances of the new African multinational state.

Now, about political institutions that must be created or strengthened in the pursuit of democracy in contemporary Africa, a couple of recommendations may be made. The guiding principle is to create institutions that will elicit local understanding and legitimacy. On this showing, those of the inherited colonial institutions that can be considered worthwhile should be appropriated, domesticated, and, consequently, allowed to acquire roots in the indigenous culture: in this way, they will in time acquire legitimacy as their virtues, relevance, functionality, and operationability come to be appreciated by the citizens of the new state.

Especially because of the participatory nature of the democratic practice and the communitarian structure of the African society, it would serve the purpose of democracy to pay close attention to the formation of town and district councils that will insure the participation of the local people in making decisions that directly affect their lives as well as engender in the local citizens the feeling that they are part of the general political process on a more or less daily basis, and not only at the time of general elections. The town and district councils must have enough autonomy to have the final say in matters affecting the localities, and they must be sufficiently large to make room for many representatives. Additionally, town or village assemblies, which must be open to all citizens who qualify to vote and where matters of all kinds—social, economic, political, and so forth—are discussed, must be made part of the democratic political process. The participation of the village and town populations in the political process will raise and sustain the high level of political consciousness required of the people in a democratic polity, but it will also make democratization a reality. It will make political participation go beyond the occasional opportunity to vote in national (or general) elections, but it will also reflect the sense of political participation Rattray describes in the statement quoted in section 3: a political tradition of active and constant involvement in the affairs of the state. It must be borne in mind that towns and villages will not disappear from a state, not even at the height of urbanization (after all, they have not disappeared from the advanced, urbanized, and industrialized states of the world). Urban centers—cities and large towns—will also develop their own "local" democratic politics. But democratic politics surely cannot be confined to urban centers; enclaves or centers of democratic political consciousness may be of any size. Participation in a democratic practice comes off well—and is at its best—when political power is decentralized and structures are put in place for a measure of local (or district) government based in towns and villages.

For there to be active and constant participation by the people in the affairs of the state in a modern setting, I believe that the referendum must be made a vital aspect of the decision-making process. In most matters affecting the people at national and local (town, district, regional) levels, the views and wishes of the people must be sought through referendums. A referendum in which only a few propositions are to be decided can be a simple method for eliciting the views of the people. But to resort to it frequently will require an efficient electoral system.

The effect of the views of the people on parliamentary or governmental decisions depends on how well a parliamentarian or representative plays his role: how well he represents the views of the people of his constituency. In this connection, ways should be found to facilitate communication between the representative and the constituents. One way of doing this is for the former to be present at village and town general assembly meetings. This kind of intercourse will give concrete meaning to the ideas of consultation, inclusion, and representation pursued in the traditional political setting. Moreover, even though an individual, having been elected by obtaining the majority of the votes, legally becomes the parliamentarian (or, deputy) of a particular constituency, it appears that his legitimacy really depends on his working with all the members of the constituency irrespective of their political affiliation. It is this approach by the representative that will insure the participation of all the members of the constituency.

The political values of consultation and consensus and—thus of inclusion—must be given institutional expression. In all decision-making councils or assemblies the consensus method of arriving at decisions should, *as far as is feasible*, be resorted to and given preference over the simple majority system of reaching decisions. I use the qualifying expression "as far as is feasible" to preempt the interpretation of my position as favoring a supermajority method of reaching political decisions. That method may hamstring the process of reaching decisions and cannot therefore be advocated without qualification. On the other hand, if it can be satisfactorily worked out, that method may be appropriate for making decisions on certain matters, especially in a multinational (multicultural) political situation. In a multinational state, the simple majority decision may (turn out to) be the decision of a dominant group or of two of the large groups, at the possible expense of the minority cultural groups whose interests also need to be protected. Unless a multinational state enjoys a high level of political and cultural integration and cohesion such as will dispose members of the dominant group to always think in terms of the national, rather than group, interests ("national" in the sense of N_2 or N_3, as explained in the preceding chapter), the interests of minority groups may eternally be ignored or not adequately protected. Yet, the need or desire to protect the interests of minority groups should not be allowed to hamstring the process of reaching decisions by a legislative body; nor should it be allowed to become a bulwark of minority privilege. So, the simple majority procedure has its virtues; but so does the supermajority procedure.

I might mention, parenthetically, that in the American democratic system, amendment to the Constitution requires at least a two-thirds, not a simple, majority; overriding a presidential veto is subject to a similar method. Implicit in the two-thirds majority—which is a supermajority—method of reaching decisions is the notion that unanimity or near-unanimity is the ideal method.

It seems to me that the democratic principle of popular sovereignty requires a *stronger* consensus than the simple majority method of reaching political decisions can offer, even though consensus formation is not easy to obtain. The simple majority method effectively excludes other citizens of the state from continuous participation in political decisions that affect their state and their own lives. The pursuit of the traditional African sociopolitical value of communal harmony—a value that is fundamental to a human polity—requires that some way be found to include "the others," that is, members of the minority political group or groups. One solution is the pursuit of consensual politics—a consensual democracy. The virtue of political inclusion is not only political but also psychological in that political inclusion invokes in every individual citizen (or representative) a sense of belonging and being a member of the political community, a virtue essential in all political settings, whether multinational or not.

The implication of the foregoing is that it should be possible, and it is appropriate, for the African people to think out and evolve political structures that can be described as democratic. In terms of its concrete or institutional expression, the concept of democracy cannot claim to be uniform or monolithic. The political institutions of Western democracies, for instance, differ among themselves, the differences reflecting the historical and cultural conditions of each country. And so also are the democratic institutions of India. Yet, they are all called democracies because the operation of their systems allows for the expression of the values and ideals of democracy. This means surely that what matters is not so much the structure of the government as whether or not a particular structure of government expresses or conduces to the realization of democratic goals, values, and ideals. This being so, the African people should be able to fashion political structures whose ultimate aim is the attainment of democratic goals, values, and practices, even if the structures themselves are different, in some respects, from those of other democracies.

5. The Need for a Comprehensive Conception of Democracy

I wish now to argue for a comprehensive conception of democracy, a conception that will give due and adequate recognition not only to political rights but also to social and economic rights of the members of the political community, and thus give sharper meaning to—and a concrete translation of—the idea of social and political equality. The conception of democracy held in Western political thought and practice places a premium on political rights and has officially failed to elevate social and economic rights to a status of concern and commitment equal to that of political rights. Thus, the state holds political rights not only as ends in themselves but also as exhaustive of the responsibilities and enduring concerns of the state. Political democracy in practice certainly does not ignore the social and economic needs of people, nor does it make those needs an important plank in the official platform of the theory of political democracy. In consequence, the fulfillment of the social and economic needs or conditions of individual members is held as a function of the enterprise of the individual and is thus to be restricted to the sphere of the private. Democracy, it is thus held, should confine its concerns to protecting and furthering the political rights of individuals and, only incidentally—not as a matter of belief or policy— to social and economic rights. This, to my mind, is a narrow conception of democracy whose focus, therefore, needs to be broadened.

There is, however, a conception of democracy that confines its focus to the social and economic rights or needs or conditions of the individual members of the political community; but it does so generally to the detriment of the political rights of the members, for it tends to pursue social equality by subordinating individual (political) rights to the economic welfare of the society as a whole. This is the socialist conception of democracy, which, by disregarding political rights, is clearly also narrow and inadequate. Underlying the two different conceptions of democracy, the individualist (or "liberal") and the socialist, is the perception that there is a conflict between individual freedom and social equality. Such a perception, however, is false. For I think that it is possible to integrate political liberty (individual freedom) and social welfare; in other words, the two values should not be held as incompatible. But it is interesting to note that both conceptions of democracy have been nested in societies whose social structures and people's moral outlooks are individualistic.

I have often wondered whether the communitarian moral and political framework is less appropriate or conducive to the development and sustainability of a democratic political order. The wonder has grown upon me because Western societies in which democracy has thrived are characterized, by and large, by individualism. Yet, Eastern European societies in which (liberal) democracy did not thrive in the last half-century or more and which in fact spawned undemocratic, authoritarian political regimes are also characterized by the individualist social and moral outlooks. So, it is neither one nor the other: the individualist socioethical outlook may, but may not, spawn a democracy; nor does it necessarily promote a concern for individual rights, as exemplified in the Eastern European politics of the recent past. But I have also wondered whether, because the failure of democratic politics and the proliferation of authoritarian politics in postcolonial Africa, there is any

relationship between communitarianism (generally espoused in African social and moral thought) and authoritarian politics. Here, again, the answer
is neither one nor the other: for authoritarian politics was pursued also
by Eastern European societies whose social outlooks are individualist and
noncommunitarian. A communitarian sociopolitical framework need not be
antagonistic to the pursuit of democracy with its panoply of rights. Democracy can thrive in an individualist social framework; it can also, if the political features of the traditional system I have already delineated are not to be
discounted, flourish in a communitarian social and moral framework.

A comprehensive conception of democracy is, in my view, badly needed
if democracy, as a system of government, is to succeed in playing the role it
is expected by its advocates and adherents to play in a political community
of human beings with multifarious—but essentially common—needs, interests, and aspirations. This comprehensive conception of democracy will be
the kind that is likely to espouse the politics of the common good, the
politics that aims at promoting a set of fundamental goods or interests held
as essential to basic human flourishing. Communitarianism, as a political
theory, is committed to the politics of the common good (see chapter 2,
section 2). I think the notion, that is, of common good, is in some sense
linked conceptually to essentialism, the view that human nature or human
life has certain basic defining features and, hence, certain basic human needs
necessary for individuals *if* they are to function as human beings. As an
advocate of the kind of communitarianism I refer to in chapter 2 as "moderate communitarianism," I am committed to essentialism. Essentialism has
consequences for politics, and particularly for democratic politics—and a
comprehensive conception of democracy at that. This is because a comprehensive conception of democracy is such as will address or explore the needs
and interests of the individual from a perspective that will give adequate
consideration to matters (or conditions) that are intrinsic to the functioning
of the human being as he or she tries to live a life in ways generally comparable to those of other human beings. The goal envisioned here for the
individual is clearly multifaceted.

But such a goal or aspiration presupposes the recognition of social and
economic rights as necessary conditions, rights that are as important for the
functioning of the human being in a human society as are political rights.
Only by giving adequate consideration to social and economic rights as well
as political rights can the concept of (political) equality really become meaningful. The reason is that economic inequalities result in undermining the
principle of equality or individual freedom important for democracy and, in
consequence, make it difficult, if not impossible, for people to exercise their
political rights. In other words, if political equality is a goal of democracy,
that goal cannot be achieved in the face of social and economic inequalities.
And, while a socialist democracy may do well in reducing social and economic inequalities and, thus, in achieving some level of social equality or
economic democracy, it cannot be commended because of its subordination
of political rights to the needs of the community. If however, equality is a

goal of democracy, then, democracy cannot—should not—be interpreted in terms only of political democracy or political rights; nor should it be interpreted in terms solely of economic rights. Political rights cannot be divorced from economic well-being: a person may be free politically and yet not free to pursue and realize his or her chosen purposes in life because the necessary conditions are denied him or her; nor should economic well-being be relentlessly pursued to the total disregard of the political rights of the individual. The conclusion, then, is that only a comprehensive conception of democracy can provide for social, economic, and political rights. The concept of democracy is thus better articulated in comprehensive terms than in the narrow terms in which it has hitherto been articulated in both Western and socialist understandings. The comprehensive conception of democracy is in fact on all fours with the famous definition of democracy (also) as government *"for* the people" because, I think, the "for" in this part of that famous definition refers to the total welfare of the people, the well-being of the people in all spheres of life.

6. Conclusion

In this chapter I have attempted to delineate the contours of political life in the traditional setting of Africa, pointing out what may be regarded as the democratic features of the traditional political life, both institutionally and conceptually. I have not lost sight of the difficulties of operating the traditional political institutions in a heterogeneous and complex political environment in a modern situation, and I have underlined the need to adapt what has been inherited from the colonial and traditional systems—where necessary and suitable. I have put forward a comprehensive conception of democracy that gives adequate consideration equally to both political and economic rights of citizens. But the thrust or upshot of the discussion of the chapter is that the ideas and values in the traditional system of government must be thoroughly and critically examined and sorted out in a sophisticated manner. Those ideas that appear to be unclear and woolly but that can nevertheless be considered worthwhile must be explored, refined, and trimmed and given a modern translation. Thus, what needs to be done, in pursuit of democracy and political stability, is to find ingenuous ways and means of hammering the autochthonous democratic elements—as well as elements inherited from alien sources—on the anvil of prudence, common sense, imagination, creative spirit, and a sense of history into an acceptable and viable democratic form in the setting of the modern world. In this task, the traditional ideas and values of politics—some of them at any rate—can be found to be of immense value to the contemporary political developments in Africa. Our culture—and our experience—may yet bring us the much needed political salvation.

5

The Socialist Interlude

On regaining the political independence of their nations, African political leaders, in search of ideologies to guide their policies and actions in matters of the development of their societies, flirted with two main ideologies: capitalism—the free enterprise economic system, and socialism—the system of public ownership of the means of production and distribution. The ideological system chosen by all but a few was socialism. But they preferred to call it "African socialism" in order to invest it with a spurious patina of African ancestry, originality, and justification. Their main argument was that socialism was foreshadowed in the traditional African socioeconomic thought and practice. The traditional system, they claimed, was entirely communal and thus was the ancestor of modern socialist thought in Africa. To adopt the ideology of socialism, then, was, so they argued, to reclaim an African socioeconomic identity. As a sessional paper of the Kenya government puts it: "In the phrase 'African Socialism,' the word 'African' . . . is meant to convey the *African roots of a system that is itself African in its characteristics.* African Socialism is a term describing an African political and economic system that is positively African, not being imported from any country or being a blueprint of any foreign ideology."[1] Similar observations are made by a Nigerian scholar, Bede Onuoha: "It is beyond doubt that traditional African society was based on a profoundly socialist attitude of mind, and governed by indigenous socialist rules, customs and institutions. But these were not the product of Marxist thinking. This is the justification for the attribute 'African' standing before the word 'socialism'. It points to the *originality* of African Socialism."[2]

It is said that European Communist theoreticians took exception to the designation by African political leaders of their brand of socialism as *African* socialism. "The idea of Senegalese or African socialism," says Mercer Cook, "is bitter gall to the Communists, who are taught to take their Marxism straight, without ice cube or aspirin."[3] Idris Cox, a socialist writer, is reported to have remarked: "To speak and write of 'African Socialism' makes no better sense than dividing the sciences into geographical compartments, for example, African mathematics, African chemistry, African biology, or African physics. There is only one socialism—scientific socialism—which belongs to the whole world and not one continent or country. Scientific socialism is not a concept limited to geographical boundaries either 'East' or 'West.' It is a universal concept of a new stage in society, applicable everywhere in the world."[4] Thus, the Communist theoreticians maintained that if we could not speak of "Senegalese mathematics" or "African physics," then we cannot speak of "Senegalese" or "African" socialism either. Since the Communist theoreticians considered Marxism as "scientific socialism," having universal validity and applicability, they thought that African political thinkers and leaders should simply apply "orthodox" or doctrinaire socialism, instead of constructing their own kind of socialism.

The arguments of the Communist theoreticians are flawed on two counts. First, the analogy they draw between mathematics or biology and socialism is false. For, while mathematics, as an exact science, necessarily has a universal validity, socialism, as a social theory, may not necessarily have a universal applicability and validity. Scientific truths qua scientific truths transcend cultural and social frontiers: hence we do not speak of American physics, French biology, Russian mathematics, African chemistry, and so on. But this observation is irrelevant when it comes to social theory, for a social theory is constructed out of a particular social or historical milieu and may therefore not have an immediate universal appeal or validity. Second, their arguments, perhaps unintentionally, imply a rejection of a basic Marxian premise. For, by "materialism" Marx meant that in constructing a socialist theory we must start with the real man and the real conditions of his life, that is to say, man's material existence. The Communist critics of the proponents of "African socialism" assumed, wrongly, that the real (existential) conditions of man in mid-nineteenth-century Europe and in mid-twentieth-century Africa are identical. The socioeconomic conditions of the industrialized countries of Western Europe provided the backdrop or point of departure for Marx's *Das Kapital;* nineteenth-century African socioeconomic conditions, with very few industries, hardly entered into Marx's scheme of things. But the African political thinkers, by stressing African conditions and historical experiences, and thus starting off with what, according to Marx, we should start off with—the real conditions of the real man, which in this instance are the real conditions of the real man *in* Africa—were, unlike their Communist critics, clearly taking their cue from Karl Marx. The mid-nineteenth century socioeconomic conditions that inspired Marx's socialist doctrines were the consequences of the industrial revolution and to Marx were evil. African socialism, as part of the African sociopolitical heritage, did not, according to the advocates of the ideology, result from the social and economic evils of an industrial revolution; nor, they would add, did it have to wait for such a revolution.

The critical remarks I have made about the communist theoretician's view of African socialism should not be taken as support for the idea of "African socialism." For I too find the idea suspect, but for entirely different reasons. In this chapter I critically examine the alleged traditional matrix of the socialist ideology in Africa, especially the communitarian thought and practice to which the ideology had been anchored. I then argue that the idea and practice of private (or, free) enterprise did exist in African culture in precolonial times (and still exists in the postcolonial era) and that the African character is not devoid of acquisitive and materialistic elements, as the advocates of African socialism would want to imply. I discuss the fate suffered by the free enterprise system during the colonial times in Africa and explore the possibility that it is the humanist features in traditional African social and moral thought that had been given the new label of "socialism." I conclude the chapter with an analysis of the concept of ideology.

1. The Alleged Traditional Matrix of African Socialism

There is hardly any African advocate of socialism in modern Africa who has not averred that socialism is deeply rooted in traditional African socioeconomic thought and practice. Assertions about the traditional matrix of socialism point especially to the communitarian thought and practice in African cultures. Those who saw modern socialism prefigured in African culture and tradition include Léopold Senghor, who observes that "Negro-African society is collectivist or, more exactly, communal, because it is rather a communion of souls than an aggregate of individuals. . . . *We had achieved socialism before the coming of the European*."[5] Julius Nyerere states that African socialism is "*rooted* in our past—in the traditional society which produced us. Modern African socialism can draw from its traditional heritage the recognition of 'society' as an extension of the basic family unit."[6] He suggests that Africans should "regain our former attitude of mind—our *traditional* African socialism—and apply it to the new societies we are building today."[7] Kwame Nkrumah believed that "If one seeks the socio-political ancestor of socialism, one must go to communalism. . . . In socialism, the principles underlying communalism are given expression in modern circumstances."[8] These samples of the views of some writers regarding the socialist character of the traditional socioeconomic system should suffice. It is this alleged socialist character that was claimed as justificatory basis for the embrace of the socialist ideology in Africa. Before examining those claims, however, I wish to take a look at the traditional concepts of ownership of the land, a fundamental property in African societies in the traditional setting.

Many writers have recognized that land was a communal property in all traditional African societies. The absolute ownership of the land was vested in the stool (a technical term for "throne" or "crown")—thus making it a public or communal property. Nana Sir Ofori Atta I, a distinguished Ghanaian traditional ruler, observes: "Land belongs to a vast family of whom many are dead, a few are living and a countless host are still unborn."[9] According to Nyerere, "To us in Africa land was always recognized as belonging to the community. Each individual within our society had a right to the use of the land. . . . But the African's right to land was simply the right to use it; he had no other right to it."[10] Jomo Kenyatta asserts that "insofar as there are other people of his own flesh and blood who depend on that land for their daily bread, he is not the owner, but a partner, or at the most a trustee for the others."[11] Dugald Campbell, the Briton who spent almost three decades in central Africa (including Zambia) from the latter part of the nineteenth century to the early part of this century, made the following observations:

> The land in every instance belongs to and is invested in the chief and people, who are only, however, tribal trustees, and have no power to sell the land. . . . This land is tribalised and belongs to the tribe in perpetuity. A man may cultivate as much as he and his wives can hoe, to supply their personal needs, but the land does not belong to him. . . . All land is nationalized, and this tribalisation of the land system obtains all over Bantuland as against the system of individual possession in vogue among European peoples.[12]

Thus, the general view is that land is communally held in traditional Africa. The chief or head of the clan, who is the occupant of the stool, is the custodian of the land. His position, however, is that of a trustee, holding the land for and on behalf of the whole community or of the clan. He is invested with the power to manage and administer the communal property, but he is under obligation to do so in the interest of the members of the community or the clan, all of whom also have the title and the right to the ownership of the land. Traditional conceptions distinguish between a subject's right to the use of the land and the stool's (that is, the community's) absolute ownership of it. But public policy toward the allocation of land to families and individuals is liberal. J. B. Danquah writes that the "the right to make farms or plantations on ancestral, family or tribal land is very liberal."[13] The trusteeship conception of land ownership with respect to stool or family lands allows the possibility of every person in the community getting a portion of the land to work on. Since livelihood depends very much on the exploitation of the land in an agricultural economy, this liberality is most appropriate. But, is it correct to say that the trusteeship principle of the African land tenure system made it absolutely impossible for an individual to hold private property in land and that the African people therefore did not have a general concept of private property? This question will be dealt with in some detail in the next section.

In the view of most of the African political leaders of the postcolonial era, the traditional communitarian practice easily translates into modern socialism: the larval communitarianism metamorphoses into the pupa of modern African socialism. The traditional matrix of modern African socialism cannot, therefore, they would argue, be seriously denied. Nkrumah thought in fact that "the underlying principles [that is, of communitarianism and socialism] are the *same*,"[14] a view that implies that he sees a logical relation—that of identity—between communalism (communitarianism) and socialism in their essentials. And in the context in which Senghor asserted that Africans "had already achieved socialism before the coming of the European," he also undoubtedly saw a relation of identity between the communitarian ethos and socialism. The identity relation that Nkrumah, Senghor, and others established between the two doctrines or systems bristles with some difficulties.

The alleged relation of identity between the two systems can logically be denied on the grounds that not everything that can be asserted of communalism can be asserted also of socialism, and vice versa. I would contend that communalism is essentially a socioethical doctrine, not particularly—or perhaps only narrowly—economic, whereas socialism, which was understood by the African political leaders as Marxian socialism, is fundamentally economic, concerned, as a matter of testament, with the relations or modes of production. The basic premises of socialism are economic. The concern of socialism with such moral values as justice and equality can be acknowledged, but this concern is certainly not idiosyncratic to it; nor can it be denied that in the states where the socialist system was established injustices and inequalities existed. On this showing, it can be said that what really or essentially distinguishes socialism from the free enterprise market system is their modes of *economic* production, including their positions on property ownership.

Also, the modern socialist conception of public (or, state) ownership is different in its nature from the traditional conception of communitarian ownership; the different conceptions of public ownership would have different consequences on the well-being of the individual. For instance, while the traditional conception of ownership of the land admits the right of the individual member of the group or lineage to use the land, though not to own it, there is no room in the modern Marxian conception of state ownership for such a right. That is, the individual in a Marxian state is not allowed a direct right to the use of the land owned by the state, as he would be in the traditional system. Thus, Nkrumah's statement that there is a "continuity of communalism with socialism"[15] is an oversimplification. It is in fact false with respect to the nature of the ownership of the land as held in the traditional African communitarian system and modern socialism: the role of a modern socialist government in matters of land ownership would not by any means be the same as that of the chief or the head of a clan. The latter, as we saw, is merely a trustee of the land and does not own it. In the modern socialist conception of state ownership, however, even if the government declared itself a trustee of the "people's" land, it would still claim absolute ownership of it. And the trusteeship principle that operates in the traditional setting disappears in both theory and practice. Thus, it is evident that the relation of communalism, as it is understood and operated in the traditional setting, to modern Marxian socialism has been misconstrued.

The African political leaders, in anchoring the rationalization of their choice of socialism in the African communitarian idea, misinterpreted the idea, in my view, in two ways. First, the kind of communitarian idea espoused by them led them to ignore or denigrate or to be oblivious of the elements of individuality and private enterprise existent in the same traditional socioeconomic milieu. The concept of private property—the hallmark of the free (or, private) enterprise system—was *not* nonexistent in the traditional African way of managing the economy. In failing to appreciate the individualist elements in the traditional social thought, the modern African political leaders may appropriately be described as unrestricted, radical, and extreme in their philosophical position on the communitarian idea, as I explain in chapter 2, section 1 (where I reject that position in favor of a moderate or restricted one). It seems to me that the view of the traditional moorings of the modern socialist ideology in Africa presents a simple and misguided picture of an otherwise complex situation.

Second, in making the traditional communitarian system a justificatory basis for their choice of the socialist ideology, the advocates of African socialism interpreted the former as an entirely economic system that can easily evolve into a socialist economy in a modern setting. The interpretation is erroneous. The reason is that the communitarian doctrine, to repeat, is essentially a *socioethical* doctrine, not markedly economic. It is a doctrine about social relations as well as moral attitudes: about what sorts of relationships should hold between individuals in a society, and about the need to take into account the interests of the wider society not only in designing sociopolitical institutions and in evolving behavior patterns for individuals in their responses to the needs and welfare of other members of the society. The communitarian doctrine, then, is conceived and pursued in the traditional setting as a fundamentally social ethic. Socialism, on the other hand, as I understand it and have said so before, is primarily an economic arrangement, involving the public control of all the dynamics of the economy, notwithstanding the fact that it genuinely cherishes the ethical values of social justice and equality.

A final point: I do not think there is a necessary connection between communitarianism and socialism; nor is communitarianism a necessary condition for socialism. The European societies that gave birth to Marxian socialism were not markedly communitarian societies; they were in fact societies characterized by the ethos of individualism.

2. Private Enterprise in the Traditional African System

Having criticized the postcolonial African political leaders for fastening onto the traditional African communitarian system for their choice of socialism and, in consequence, for ignoring the concept and practice of private enterprise spawned by the same traditional setting, I shall in this section bring up arguments to establish the fact that the concept of private enterprise or ownership is well understood and practiced in the traditional African culture of economic management. I must point out from the outset, however, that on the existence of the economic system of private enterprise in the traditional African culture, historical and anthropological opinion seems to be divided.

The British anthropologist R. S. Rattray, who researched the Asante culture (of Ghana) in the early decades of this century, concluded that "individual ownership in land did not exist."[16] Others, such as Danquah,[17] Mensah Sarbah,[18] and M. J. Field,[19] while affirming the existence of private property, seem to express doubts about its originality in the Ghanaian tradition, not knowing how far back in history the practice goes in that tradition. S. M. Molema was of the view, however, that "no race or society is really entirely communistic [that is, communal], and so we find that even among the Bantu, private property, such as cattle, existed side by side with communal property such as land."[20] Molema's statement implies that the practice of owning private property can be as old as a society itself and that it is a natural outgrowth in the economic development and life of a people—perhaps an aspect of human nature—unless it is consciously and systematically suppressed and for a very considerable length of time. Max Gluckman points out that the precolonial ownership of land by kinsmen coexisted with *individual* rights over the land.[21] And, even though Kenneth Kaunda asserts that in the traditional setting land was never bought, he also acknowledges that "it came to belong to individuals through usage and the passing of time."[22]

Matters of a sociocultural and conceptual nature need to be sorted out here. There were practices internal to the historical development of, say, the Akan societies of Ghana that would have given rise to the emergence of private property. One was the practice of mortgage *(awowa):* when it became necessary to mortgage a lineage property to pay up some crushing debt that could not be redeemed, the lineage property would become the individual property of the mortgagee, who because he was a wealthy individual could acquire that property. Second, even though it is true that in terms of the original principle governing the Akan—in fact, African—land tenure system, an individual cannot absolutely own a portion of the lineage land, the proceeds of the land allocated to him would nevertheless be *his*, not the lineage's or the community's, though he is under moral obligation to use them to enhance the welfare of the other community members. This means that a frugal, energetic, and hard-working individual can in time acquire private wealth, while working on a family land. According to Rattray's understanding of the history of the Asante, when the king or a chief returned from war, he would make grants of land—presumably conquered land—to his war chiefs *(asafohene).*[23] These grants would most probably be made to them personally and would therefore be regarded as private holdings. It can be said, then, that through such practices, free rein was given to both the vertical and horizontal development and expansion of private property.

In the early eighteenth century, according to the historian Ray Kea, writing on the history of trade and politics in the Gold Coast (Ghana), most of the gold in the state was concentrated in the hands of the *abirempon,* that is, the nobles, persons of wealth, holders of political or military office.[24] The concept and practice of private property in Ghana thus goes back in history. Also, the *abusa* system—practiced in Ghana for centuries—in which a farmer or a family gives land to a caretaker to work on and to receive one-third *(abusa)* of the proceeds is a hired-labor system. It is in fact a kind of exploitation of labor that is still practiced. Field was right in describing the *abusa* system as "capitalist farming."[25] And historical analysis leads Kea to say that the region of West Africa generally "was characterized . . . by a socio-economic system based on tributary and slave owning relations of production."[26] These facts of history contradict Nyerere's assertion that "the capitalist, or the landed exploiter, [was] unknown to traditional African society," as well as his view that in the traditional setting, "We neither needed nor wished to exploit our fellow men."[27] In critical response to Nyerere's assertions, it may be pointed out that a hierarchical social arrangement, such as the traditional African system undoubtedly was—and still is—would not be devoid of exploitation of some sort, however modest.

At the conceptual level, it must be noted that "private" is opposed to "public." "Public" means connected with or owned by or known to or affecting all the people. Thus public land is owned by a whole community or a state or government. All the members of the public have the right, at least in principle, to use of, or access to, that which is public; no individual or group has exclusive right to that which is public. By contrast, the right to use of, and access to, a private property is exclusive to the specific owner or group of owners. So understood, it is not only an individual property that can be said to be private but also a family or clan property, notwithstanding the fact that a large number of individuals (that is, members of the family) have an interest or share in it. Only the family or clan has exclusive right to the family or clan property: this fact makes that property private. (This kind of private property may be compared with *private* business corporations in the contemporary capitalist world.) It can be said, therefore, that in the traditional African culture *two* species of private ownership—individual ownership and family (i.e., corporate) ownership—existed side by side with public (or, state) ownership. The conclusion, then, is that sociocultural as well as conceptual analysis indicates the existence of the idea and practice of private ownership as an outstanding feature of economic management in the traditional African culture.

The evolution of the idea and practice of private ownership does not seem, however, to have been ardently and consistently promoted by the European rulers in Africa in the days of colonialism (see section 2.1). But it is clear that the idea of private ownership—including private property in land—had come to gain the status of a norm in the economic culture side by side with public ownership. In consequence, Sarbah, a scholar and lawyer, writing at the close of the last century, could make the following observation:

Property is designated self-acquired or private where it is acquired by a person:

(a) Through his own personal exertions, without any help or assistance from his ancestral or family property;
(b) By gift to himself personally;
(c) By superior skill in business or intellectual pursuits.[28]

A private property included "a house or land purchased or gained by a person by his individual effort or exertion."[29] Danquah also describes how a private property could be gained and owned: a private property may be held by a son as a gift from his father; it may be acquired by outright purchase. Also, "all that a trader has, all that he has bought with his own money, and all the riches amassed therefrom, are considered private property."[30] It is pretty clear, then, that Ghanaian customary doctrine allowed for an absolutely individualistic conception of property: an individual could absolutely own a property, including land. And, according to Sarbah, the individual "can sell or deal with it as he thinks fit."[31] Danquah observes that even a slave "is the absolute and entire owner of both his real and personal property, and he is at liberty to dispose of it in any way he likes."[32] S. K. B. Asante, on the other hand, thinks that private property "was impressed with a distinct social obligation which did not admit of the unfettered right to use and dispose of property in any manner the holder or holders chose and it strictly precluded the absolutist idea of the right to abuse property. This was the general signification of the trusteeship idea."[33]

Asante, a Ghanaian legal scholar, in his analytical study of the concepts of property ownership in traditional Akan society was at pains to stress (1) that "the principle of trusteeship [thus] excluded an absolutist conception of . . . individual ownership,"[34] (2) that an individual's usufruct rights over ancestral or family land are impressed with the obligation to use the resources of the land—which, after all, legally belong to the whole group—to enhance the welfare of the group, and (3) that an individual to whom a portion of the family land is allocated cannot own it and cannot therefore dispose of it. Even the chief, as a trustee, cannot dispose of the ancestral land in any manner he wishes. From our earlier analysis, the statement represented by (1) cannot be correct; the view expressed in (3) is correct, while that expressed in (2) requires qualification, to say the least. Asante appears to extend the limits of the applicability of the trusteeship principle by assimilating the disposal conditions of a privately acquired personal property to those of the ancestral or family property. Thus he thinks—but wrongly—that the operation of private property also came within the ambit of the prescriptions of the trusteeship principle. It is on the strength of the trusteeship principle with its concomitant moral postulates and imperatives that Asante thinks that the holder of a private property could not dispose of it "in any manner." But he was surely wrong.

The reason is that the trusteeship principle is essentially a legal principle, notwithstanding its moral dimensions, and it applies or relates solely to ancestral or family property. It does not spew out any prescriptions of a legal nature with respect to the disposal of a strictly private property. (In fact, to the extent that a family or clan property is a private property, it could be disposed of by the family or clan, if the members so wished.) Any obligations that attach to the use and disposal of a private property are purely ethical. And, although it is conjecturable that within the framework of the social character of the morality of the people, such ethical obligations might be observed and fulfilled by the holder of a private property, those obligations cannot, strictly speaking, abridge or whittle away his right to dispose of his private property *in any manner.* One needs here to observe a distinction between the law regarding the use of property and the morality of the use of property. The "distinct social obligation" Asante speaks of is essentially an ethical obligation, and his point can only be sustained if it could correctly be assumed that in Akan society there is no distinction between law and morality, so that what is morally wrong is also proscribed by the law. But one has to show the grounds for such an assumption.

The basis of the pragmatic pursuit or intellectual understanding of private ownership is given conceptual expression in such proverbs as, " 'It is ours' and 'it is mine' are not the same"; and "It is by individual effort that we can struggle for our heads." The first proverb clearly expresses the idea of private (personal) ownership: what belongs to *me,* distinguishable from communal (state) ownership, what belongs to us. The second proverb expresses the idea of individual effort or enterprise as a necessary condition for advancing and protecting one's interests. The notion of competition, which is perhaps an outstanding feature of the process of acquiring private property, is thus not nonexistent in the culture. Note that the *me* in this culture, as in other cultures in Africa generally, is not a detached *me* but one that is embedded in social contexts, having dynamic moral and social relations with the other members of the community, as I explain in chapter 2.

Now, underlying the pursuit of economic competition and private property is the desire for the acquisition of wealth. To discover the principles underlying conceptions of wealth and attitudes toward it, once again, I turn to Akan proverbs.[35]

> Money is sharper than the sword.
>
> When wealth comes and passes by, nothing comes after.
>
> Fame of being nobly born does not spread; it is the fame of riches that spreads.
>
> One does not cook one's nobility and eat it; it is wealth that counts.[36]

These proverbs all indicate the value and importance placed on wealth, which is appreciated and sought, for a variety of reasons. The first proverb expresses the view that wealth helps to overcome certain hurdles in life and open up opportunities. The second implies the view, perhaps an exaggerated view, that wealth is the most important thing in life; it is an ultimate possession. We must here note the acquisitive or materialistic elements in the Akan character—or perhaps the African character in general—that seem to have been ignored or denigrated by the advocates of African socialism. The third and fourth proverbs express the view that wealth brings real fame and respect, that wealth can earn a person social status and importance, and that wealth can provide a person who is not nobly born an opportunity to move up the social ladder.

The wealth by virtue of which an individual would be recognized as wealthy and that would gain him the greatest social appreciation would, ideally, be self-acquired, not inherited; that is, it would have resulted from an individual's own exertions, outside the structure of the economic activities of the extended family or clan. (An individual's wealth may have been inherited, but only from another wealthy individual.) Since generally many people, not just one person, inherit the property of a deceased person in African societies, it would be difficult for an individual to become wealthy through inheritance, unless the inherited property is augmented through the individual's own efforts. It follows, then, that the existence of a wealthy person implies the existence of private property. Thus, in Rhoda Howard's assertion that "in precolonial . . . Africa . . . there is no concept of private property, and the wealthy man is respected only if he shares his good fortune with his kin and coethnics,"[37] the first part is clearly false. The denial of the existence of the concept of private property in precolonial Africa cannot be firmly grounded. The evidence instead affirms the existence of both the concept and the practice of private property. Also, if we can appropriately talk of "the wealthy man," then, we can correctly talk also of private property. If there were no private property, there would be no wealthy *individual*. In other words, the wealthy person must be assumed as possessing private property. If the wealth or property belongs to a family or clan, then it would be the family or clan, not an individual, that can appropriately be said to be wealthy. Thus, if there were wealthy individuals in African communities in precolonial times, then, it can be concluded that there were private properties.

Wealth is highly valued in African societies because of the contribution the wealthy person can make, or is expected to make, toward the welfare of the family, community, or state. As Ivor Wilks observes with regard to the Asante—and this was in fact true generally of the Akan and other communal societies, "One model of the good citizen was the *sikani*, that person who had accumulated wealth through his or her own efforts whether privately or in public but from which the state (especially through death duties) was ultimately to be the beneficiary."[38] Hence, the proverb:

> If there is a *pereguan* worth of gold dust in a town, it belongs to the whole people.[39]

(A *pereguan* was a huge amount of gold in the traditional Akan monetary system.) This proverb does not mean or imply by any means that the wealth of a rich person is to be shared or redistributed among the members of the community; nor is it intended to encourage social parasitism. The proverb is instead a statement about the importance of private wealth or property, ultimately for the community or state. It implies in fact that the wealth of the state or community is contingent, in many ways, upon the wealth of its individual citizens. The proverb thus encourages, rather than spurns, the acquisition of private wealth.

The high value placed on wealth necessitates the need for care in the accumulation and efficient management of money. The need is reflected in the following proverbs:

> Money is like a slave; if you abuse [i.e., mismanage] it, it runs away.

> Money grows [if it stays] in the coffers of its owner.

C. A. Akrofi explains the second proverb thus: "If you look after [or, manage] your money properly, it grows and multiplies."[40] Thus the need for efficient management and saving. Indeed, the idea that saving is a precondition for capital accumulation is expressed also in the proverb:

> Money [i.e., capital] requires saving, not withdrawing [or spending].

It can thus be said that the economic ideas or values of thrift, saving, and capital accumulation are clearly understood to be important and are practiced in the management of the traditional African economy. It seems, however, that saving, thrift, capital accumulation, and efficient management of money can be practiced more at the level of the individual than of the state. At the state level, the pursuit of welfare conceptions of the state, seen, for instance, in the dispensation of largess by the chief (the ruler), would often lead to the frittering away of state finance, making capital accumulation by the state well-nigh impossible. Thus, the economic culture of our traditional society evolves and practices capitalist values and attitudes; acquisitive elements are nurtured in the African character. Wealth is sought after because of what it can do for the individual, the members of the family, and the state as a whole; and the desire to seek it did not have to await the arrival of the European on the shores of the African continent.

The acquisitive, capitalistic elements of the African character, the hankering after material welfare, the appreciation of wealth and material success: all these attitudes have reverberations in the African conception and practice of religion. In African traditional conceptions, religion is to be pursued also for its social or material relevance. Supernatural beings are to be worshipped because of the succor they could, and are expected to, provide for the human being in his this-worldly, mundane pursuits; the munificence of the gods was to be exploited for human well-being in this world. The continual obeisance to the gods was contingent upon the gods' continuing to fulfill human needs. Thus, K. A. Busia observes, "The gods are treated with respect if they deliver the goods, and with contempt if they fail. . . . Attitudes to [the gods] depend upon their success, and vary from healthy respect to sneering contempt."[41] African prayers to the Supreme Being (i.e., God) and the gods betray a deep concern for material well-being: "the prayers," observes John Mbiti, "are chiefly requests for material welfare, such as health, protection from danger, prosperity and even riches."[42] And, according to Bolaji Idowu, petitions are central to the prayers of African religions: "The petitions are largely for what may be described technically as material blessings. They consist usually of asking for protection from sickness and death, gifts of longevity, children, prosperity in enterprises . . . and abundant material things."[43]

The traditional perception of religion as a means to material success still manifests itself in the contemporary African religious world, and this in two ways: in the proliferation of local, "nonorthodox" churches (also known as "spiritual churches") most of which are preoccupied, through prayers, with helping to fulfill the material aspirations of their members and others; and in the frequent visits by many Africans who profess faith even in the orthodox religions to traditional shrines in quest for material success. It would, thus, not be far from the truth to say that the alleged religiosity of the African is closely intertwined with materiality: the intense desire for material wealth and success. This intense desire for material wealth, which can only be fulfilled through private quest or accumulation of wealth, however, appears to have been ignored or downplayed by the advocates of African socialism.

The African desire for profit and for the acquisition of wealth was to express itself also in the area of commercial activities. For, the economic history of West Africa, as elsewhere in Africa, particularly since the beginning of the nineteenth century, is replete with accounts of the activities of African traders in kola, gold, and other commodities, and their use of hired wage-laborers.[44] The trade routes from West Africa to North Africa bustled with brisk commercial activities. The traders were mostly *private* traders.

Inquiries into the traditional African cultural values, their ways of managing the economy, and the history of economic activities in previous centuries will yield the conclusion that values—and some of the characteristic behavior patterns associated with the private enterprise system—were appreciated and pursued by the African people in precolonial times. In this connection, Kea's observation is poignant: "Thus, salient features of the regional political economy in the seventeenth century included extensive trade, markets and market production, and currencies; relations of social-political domination; economic and social stratification, wealth accumulation; urban hierarchies; and a common storehouse of productive techniques in, for example, farming, metalworking, and gold mining."[45] Equally poignant is the observation made by the British historian John Iliffe: "Waddel and the abolitionists in general believed that they must convert Africans to *capitalist values, but in fact many of the values they sought to inculcate were already widely shared by Africans.*"[46] (Hope Masterton Waddel was a British missionary in eastern Nigeria in the mid-nineteenth century.)

The upshot of the foregoing discussion, then, is that a view, such as Nkrumah's, that "the presuppositions and purposes of capitalism are *contrary* to those of African society"[47] will not hold up to a close scrutiny of the ideas and practice of economic thought and management of the traditional system. Capitalism was already a palpable feature of the precolonial system of economic management. The derivation of Marxian socialism from the precolonial economic culture of Africa could only have resulted from incomplete historical, as well as conceptual, inquiries into the traditional economic culture and from a tendentious and distorted interpretation of the traditional African socioethical communitarian system. What will be more correct to say, in my view, is that the traditional economic culture exhibited features of both the "socialist" and capitalist methods in the management of the economic lives of the people.

2.1 The Fate of Private Enterprise in Colonial Africa

Historical evidence has it that the evolution of the idea and practice of the private enterprise economic system does not seem to have been ardently and consistently promoted by the European rulers in Africa during colonial times. This is because colonial governments seem to have adopted policies and measures that palpably ran counter to the ideas and values of individual enterprise and the free market system. The reasons for the attitudes they adopted in relation to the development of the free market economy in the colonial territories were mainly political. According to Iliffe, "Except in Southern Rhodesia, European governments were uniformly hostile to African rural capitalism, seeing it not only as socially and politically dangerous but as somehow improper for Africans, like guitars or three piece suits."[48] In May 1924, Iliffe reports, a British officer wrote from Kilimanjaro in Tanganyika: "The aim has been to promote coffee growing as a peasant cultivation, each one working his plot by his own industry with the help of his women and children, so that a class of native employers is not evolved" "A few years later," Iliffe continues, the colonial government in Tanganyika "deliberately destroyed the emerging African farmer-traders of the coffee-growing areas and replaced them with *state-controlled co-operative societies.*" In the Gold Coast (Ghana), the colonial government "moved the African cocoa brokers in 1939, and thereafter the official marketing boards established throughout British Africa expropriated much of the surplus which might have fuelled rural capitalism."[49] These instances of anticapitalist policies and measures of the colonial government that had the largest colonial empire in Africa should suffice. Iliffe is of course not oblivious of the fact that there were indigenous factors that also hindered the rapid progress towards rural capitalism.[50]

It must be noted from Iliffe's historical account that, (1) the European colonial governments did not appear to be enthusiastic about developing the free enterprise system in colonial Africa; that is, even though they themselves practiced the free enterprise system, they strangely enough did not want their colonial subjects to pursue that kind of economic arrangement; (2) the European colonial governments found any emerging social and political power of African business people "dangerous" and threatening; (3) the cre-

ation of state-controlled business enterprises, now called parastatals, was—
and this is surely surprising—started by the colonial rulers; and (4) state
monopoly of the market was pursued by people supposed to have been
nurtured in free market economic philosophy. It must be noted that attitudes expressed in points 1–3, which indicate the hostility of the colonial
government to the development of capitalism in Africa, showed up in the
political and economic behavior of most African governments in the early
decades of the postcolonial era. And even though it does not necessarily
follow that it was the attitudes of the colonial government that served as a
guide to the African leaders in their choice of economic policies or measures, it can nevertheless be said that at least some of the economic policies
of the colonial rulers—adopted mainly for political reasons—did not help
the course of the free market economic system in the colonial period.

3. Socialism or Humanism?

If we examine the views of the advocates of African socialism, we would find
that these advocates were not so much concerned about investigating how
the economy was really managed in the traditional setting as about the material needs or social welfare of all the members of the society that resulted
from the social or moral arrangement established by traditional society. Even
though the material welfare of the individual depends ultimately on how
much wealth is produced, it may be said that it also depends equally on
how the wealth that is produced is distributed or shared among the individual members of the society, that is, how much access the individual has to
the enjoyment of the wealth created by the society. The creation of abundant
wealth is of course the first step toward the fulfillment of the material needs
and welfare of members of a society. But the actual or eventual fulfillment
of the economic needs and welfare of the individual is certainly a function
of the social and ethical norms established by the society as a guide to individual action and social (public) policy. These norms may be established
irrespective of the actual economic system in operation, even though their
career or significance could influence, or be influenced by, socioeconomic
circumstances.

The humanist norms of traditional African society most probably were at
the base of the interpretations (or, rather, misinterpretations) of the communitarian system as a form of socialism. That the traditional morality of African societies was preoccupied with human welfare has been noted in some
studies.[51] If one were to look for a pervasive and fundamental concept in
African socioethical thought generally—a concept that animates other intellectual activities and forms of behavior, including religious behavior, and
provides continuity, resilience, nourishment, and meaning to life—that concept would most probably be humanism: a philosophy that sees human
needs, interests, and dignity as of fundamental importance and concern. For,
the art, actions, thought, and institutions of the African people, at least in

the traditional setting, reverberate with expressions of concern for human welfare. I have already noted that the humanist and social strand of the African socioethical thought and life is reflected in the African perception of the place of religion in human life. The humanist essence of African cultures is given a succinct expression in the following observation by Kenneth Kaunda:

> Our love of conversation is a good example of this [enjoyment of people]. We will talk for hours with any stranger who crosses our path and by the time we part there will be little we do not know about each other. We do not regard it as impertinence or an invasion of our privacy for someone to ask "personal" questions, nor have we any compunction about questioning others in like manner. We are open to the interests of other people. Our curiosity does not stem from a desire to interfere in someone else's business but is an expression of our belief that we are wrapped up together in this bundle of life and therefore a bond already exists between myself and a stranger before we open our mouths to talk.[52]

In references to the supposed traditional matrix of the ideology of African socialism, the language of the African political leaders and thinkers seems to indicate, pretty clearly on close examination, that it is the humanist strand of the African traditional social and moral thought and practice that they really had in mind in their discourse on "socialism." Nkrumah, for example, points out that for some African political leaders and thinkers, "the aim is to remold African society in the socialist direction; to reconsider African society in such a manner that *the humanism of traditional African life reasserts itself* in a modern technical community," and that "the restitution of Africa's *humanist* and egalitarian principles of society *requires* socialism."[53] Nkrumah thus admits that his choice of the ideology of socialism was inspired by the humanist principles of the traditional African society. His use of the word "requires" suggests that Nkrumah sees a necessary (logical) relation between humanist principles and socialism. I do not think, however, that there is any such necessary relation, for it can be argued that the same principles may require some form of the capitalist system, the system that historically has been most successful in the creation of wealth, fundamental to the fulfillment of human needs and well-being. The humanist ethic will certainly pursue a far-reaching social program, but that program will need to be fully and continually supported by a viable and productive economic system. It is doubtful, on empirical grounds, that socialism can provide such an economic system.

The claim that traditional society is egalitarian appears countered by the fact that that society is in many ways hierarchical. It would be correct to say, however, that traditional society, animated by its humanist ethic, would be a caring society, concerned about the well-being of its members. A caring society, however, is not necessarily an egalitarian society. People may not be formally equal (or, regard themselves as such), that is, equal in their characteristics or endowments, and yet can be entitled to an equal or fair share of social goods and services, essential to a tolerable and livable life.

The caring ethos of traditional African society is stressed in statements by Nyerere: "In our traditional African society we were individuals within a community. We took care of the community, and the community took care of us."[54] His perception of the traditional society as a caring society appears also in his seeing society "as an extension of the basic family,"[55] the implication being that the care and compassion demonstrated among the members of the basic family find similar expression in the sensitive attitudes members of the wider society have (or, will or should have) toward the needs of other members. Nyerere also makes the following noteworthy observation about the ethical nature of the traditional society:

> Both the "rich" and the "poor" individuals were completely secure in African society. . . . Nobody starved, either of food or of human dignity, because he lacked personal wealth; he could depend on the wealth possessed by the community of which he was a member. That was socialism. This *is* socialism.[56]

Thus, for Nyerere socialism is ministering to the needs—especially the material needs—of the individual members of the society. And when he adds almost immediately after the foregoing quoted statement that "socialism is essentially *distributive*,"[57] he is certainly alluding to the ethical, rather than the productive (economic) nature of an ideological system. This is because, as I said, distribution of the wealth of a society is the function essentially of the socioethical norms and ideals cherished by a society. Even though it may be true, as Nyerere avers, that the individual in the traditional society can depend on the wealth of the community, there is no implication whatsoever that the wealth possessed by the community is "socialistically" produced, that is, produced by the whole community into a kind of public or communal barn into which any individual can, as it were, dip her hands when she is in some material need. The individual's dependence on the wealth of the community derives from—and is an aspect of—the practice of social and humanist morality, from the fulfillment of the moral obligations of people to their fellow human beings. In his articulation of "African socialism" Nyerere employs such expressions as "caring," "familyhood," "wellbeing," "reciprocity," "togetherness," "human equality," "a sense of security," and "universal hospitality."[58] These expressions are patently and essentially socioethical, rather than economic.

On this showing, Nyerere's description of socialism as an "attitude of mind" is somewhat misleading. The expression "attitude of mind" (or, mental attitude) refers to the way an individual thinks or feels or understands. As such, the expression would refer to a psychological and, hence, a subjective state. An individual's subjective state or attitude with respect to an idea or value or situation may differ from another individual's. But this is surely not what Nyerere wants to say or imply. Within the framework of his understanding and articulation of socialism, what I think Nyerere means is that socialism is a *moral* attitude or stance, a moral attitude that, in his own words, "is needed to ensure that the people care for each other's welfare."[59]

A moral attitude is of course different from a psychological or mental attitude.

But perhaps one advocate of the ideology of African socialism who articulates his understanding of socialism in terms most stridently of the essentially ethical doctrine of humanism is Kaunda, who often prefers the term "humanism" to "socialism." Kaunda has made humanism the basis of his conception of the nature of the human being and society. Even though he does sometimes use the term "socialism," the context nevertheless indicates quite clearly that he is referring to the humanist perception of things. For instance, when he says, "In the traditional [African] society, socialism . . . has always been practiced by the village headman and the chief and his court," [60] he is most probably referring to the largess provided by the chief in support of the needs and well-being of his subjects. He does not mean that the chief alone "owned" and controlled the means of economic production. It was the obligation of the chief, as it was of other members of the community, to express sensitivity to the needs of other members of the society in concrete acts of giving. For Kaunda, "The traditional community was a mutual aid society. It was organized to satisfy the basic human needs of all its members." [61] It was this "basic needs" approach, inspired by his humanist view of man and society, that masqueraded as "socialism." Again, Kaunda:

> Just to recap, our ancestors worked collectively and co-operatively from start to finish. One might say this was a communist way of doing things and yet these gardens remained strongly *the property of individuals*. One might say here that this was capitalism. Collectively and co-operatively they harvested but when it came to storing and selling their produce they became *strongly individualistic*. Indeed, one is compelled to say a strange mixture of nineteenth century capitalism with communism . . . a strange mixture which gives the present generation the right to claim that our socialism is humanism. [62]

Clearly, Kaunda understands socialism in terms of *humanism*, in terms of the profound concern for human well-being.

I think that Charles Njonjo, a Kenyan politician, gave the most succinct expression to the perspective of the African tradition on economic management and its relation to human well-being when he made the following elliptical statement in the Kenyan Parliament:

NJONJO: I am a capitalist. I believe in African socialism. . . . I have got a three-piece suit! Does it not explain what I am?

HON. MEMBERS: Hear! Hear! Hear!

NJONJO: . . . Sir, I do not believe that this nation will be served by paupers! [63]

The point implicit in Njonjo's statement is that the acquisition of wealth, which he believes can come through the capitalist economic arrangement, is essential for meeting the needs of other people, to cater for human welfare. Njonjo was endorsing a welfarist position. The implications of his statement are congruent with the analytic interpretation I have been at pains to give of the economic management and its ethic in the traditional setting of Africa. The economic arrangement practiced in that setting is different from a Marxian socialism.

The foregoing analysis of the articulations of African socialism suggests the deep conviction that the African advocates of the ideology of socialism understood it in terms of the original sense of the Latin word *socialis,* which means "belonging to companionship, or fellowship," "fellow feeling." This root meaning of socialism suggests the idea of people living together, helping one another, caring for one another, and being just to one another. This meaning is unambiguously social or ethical but has hardly anything to do directly with an economic arrangement, such as a centrally planned economy. I am not suggesting, to be sure, that a choice of a socialist economy cannot or should not be made by an African nation. But I doubt that the premises of the arguments for such a choice should essentially be derived from the African socioethical communitarian doctrine. The socioethical sense of the word *socialis,* however, is on all fours with the communitarian and humanist interpretations provided by the advocates of African socialism in the postcolonial era. It is, as I have said elsewhere, the humanist ethic of the traditional African society that spawned the communitarian social structure; for, insuring the welfare and interests of each member of society can best be accomplished within the communitarian social and ethical framework.[64] I conclude that the use of the term "socialism" in reference to understanding the nature of the society envisaged by the African political leaders and thinkers under the inspiration of the African tradition is a misnomer. That term was undoubtedly used as a surrogate for "humanism."

4. The Pursuit of Marxian Socialism in Postcolonial Africa

African political thinkers and leaders, in their strident and unrelenting advocacy of the socialist ideology as a basis for the development of their nations, cavalierly set aside, as I point out in section 2, wittingly or unwittingly, the individualist elements in African socioethical thought and practice, the acquisitive and materialistic elements in the African character, private ownership or enterprise of a kind in the management of the traditional economy, and the traditional African society's appreciation of personal wealth. Traditional attitudes and ways of thinking and acting die hard; economic attitudes, by reason of their immediate and direct relevance to ordinary human livelihood, die even harder. And so it is that, during the heyday of the pursuit of socialism in postcolonial Africa, many individual members of the socialist parties and governments in African nations were pursuing private business interests under the aegis of their socialist parties and governments, thereby enriching themselves at the expense of the masses. In this way, the holders of political power or office became the owners of property. It was an unashamed exploitation of state apparatus to acquire private property and business interests. The strident touting of socialism was in many ways a masquerade for practicing capitalism, for the acquisition of personal wealth: as if all this resulted from dishonesty or dishonest ignorance or self-deception. But, no, it was the acquisitive, capitalistic element in the African character that was asserting itself.

From the point of view of the development of the African economy, most people will agree that the choice of socialism was a disaster. The choice has had devastating effects on the development efforts of many African nations. The failure of the pursuit of socialism led early African champions of that ideology, such as Nyerere, Kaunda, and Sékou Touré, to retreat, to retreat, though belatedly. Nyerere of Tanzania, seeing the economy of his country in ruins and without any redemption from the socialist message he had incessantly preached, abdicated the socialist throne he had occupied for a quarter of a century, his successor charting a different ideological course, having discarded the old dysfunctional or misleading ideological compass. And Sékou Touré of Guinea in the last few years of his long rule, drove a nail into the coffin of socialism in his country, and, after embracing a new ideology in his old age when realism was beginning to take over, was himself put into a coffin. Hardly had he been buried, when members of his own army, as if to say "let the dead bury their own dead," and taking their cue from their professional colleagues elsewhere in Africa, took over power and immediately established a new ideological order. Other African political leaders, convinced of the truths of other ideological doctrines as they see them operate, or compelled by the poor economic circumstances of their nations, are adopting liberal, capitalist economic policies, but then, for curious reasons, refer to these liberal policies as "pragmatic": as if the term "pragmatic" were ideologically neutral or innocuous.

It is thus clear that, since the dawn of the postcolonial era, African nations have been groping through an ideological labyrinth, the result of the lack of adequate knowledge among their leaders of the histories of economic cultures developed in their societies or the tendentious misinterpretation of the communitarian system or the lack of profound inquiries into the nature of the concept of ideology itself or the lack of appreciation of the relevant principles that guide ideological thinking and choice or inadequate knowledge of the processes of societal development or a combination of all of these.

5. On the Concept of Ideology

The causes detailed above of the ideological labyrinth suggest the need to undertake a brief philosophical inquiry here into the concept of ideology.

To begin with a basic premise, the development of human society—an activity that is consciously and purposively pursued by rational and moral beings—is guided and underpinned by a set of goals. These goals reflect the values of a society. In the development of the human society, values are generally expressed and applied through the concept of ideology, and it is necessary that we understand the concept. We would attempt to do so by first looking at the historical origins of the term "ideology."

The term is said to have been used first by the French scholar Destutt de Tracy in 1796 to mean the "science of ideas."[65] But de Tracy's motive was not just theoretical, for it was his view that the science of ideas would lead to an adequate knowledge of human nature on the basis of which we can determine the kinds of social laws, institutions, and practices appropriate for human needs. According to de Tracy, the science of ideas was to be the basis of education, morality, and finally, "the greatest of the arts, . . . that of regulating society in such a way that man finds there the most help and the least possible annoyance from his own kind."[66] Thus, ideology—the science of ideas—was to be used to improve social and political conditions of human beings through the creation of sociopolitical norms. In its origin, then, the term "ideology" had a positive connotation; as a concept ideology had a practical, normative purpose, for it was, from its inception, to be an action-oriented and morally freighted system of ideas; and ideology was to be directly linked with politics. From de Tracy's intentions and program, the following definition may be distilled: an ideology is a dominant set of ideas about the nature of the *good* society. Thus, the moral content or thrust of the concept is clear: it is intended to address the way things ought to be, not the way they actually are. If we consider that values are the good things that are continually desired and cherished by a society, we would say that an ideology is a system or cluster of ideas that define and apply, that is, make explicit, the values of a society, and thus help to bring to concrete reality a vision of the good society. The viable development of a society depends on a clear definition of its values and how these values are to be applied in the reality.

But even though the term "ideology" entered political and philosophical vocabulary at the end of the eighteenth century of our era, the preoccupation with the problems or goals covered by this concept began much earlier. Thus in the famous Funeral Oration recorded by Thucydides, Pericles, the Athenian statesman of fifth century B.C., made the following observation:

> Our constitution is called democracy because power is in the hands not of a minority but of the whole people. When it is a question of settling disputes, everyone is equal before the law; when it is a question of putting one person before another in a position of public responsibility, what counts is not membership of a particular class, but the actual ability which the man possesses. No one . . . is kept in political obscurity because of poverty. Our love of the things of the mind [that is, philosophy] does not make us soft. We regard wealth as something to be properly used, rather than as something to boast about. As for poverty, no one need to be ashamed to admit it; the real shame is in not taking practical measures to escape from it. Here each individual is interested not only in his own affairs but in the affairs of the state as well; even those who are mostly occupied with their own business are extremely well-informed on general politics: this is a peculiarity of ours.[67]

Pericles in these statements is clearly articulating the *ideology*, that is, the ideas embodying the norms, values, and ideals of Athens. Anthropological or historical inquiries into societies that existed before the eighteenth century of our era would reveal the nature of the norms and values held in those societies. Thus ideology, as a sociopolitical phenomenon, can be said not to be a creation of the modern world. Ideological thinking is undoubtedly native to humankind, even though the term "ideology," unlike the term "philosophy," was late in appearing on the horizon of the politicophilosophical language. Ideology is a characteristic feature of any socially or politically organized human community. For this reason, there will never be an end of ideology or of ideological thinking, even though the end of ideological conflicts or the softening of ideological positions of some individuals or groups in a society is conceivable, as these individuals and groups come to understand one another and see the need to integrate their positions for the common good of their society. As a system of values, ideology serves the purpose of integrating the community (see below).

But despite the antiquity of the concept of ideology and its relevance to societal functioning and development, the concept has been much travestied and burlesqued since Napoleon in the first decade of the nineteenth century ridiculed and disparaged the French ideologues for their criticisms of his authoritarian rule. Napoleon's negative attitude toward ideology was followed by Karl Marx's equally negative attitude; he considered ideology a distortion of the human understanding of social reality and, therefore, a "false consciousness" (to use a well-known expression of Marx's), that is, as a set of mistaken ideas and beliefs put forward in the interests of the ruling class. For Marx and his intellectual companion Engels, ideology reflects class interests. Ripples of the Napoleonic and Marxian derogatory and negative attitudes toward ideology have since reached the shores of contemporary understandings and interpretations of the concept. Thus, an ideological thinking or system has come to be denigrated by such terms as subjective, class-related, distorted, dogmatic, nonscientific, unrealistic, untrue, biased, partisan, nonpragmatic, closed.

The denigration of the concept, in my view, stems ultimately from the philosophical controversies surrounding the origin, nature, and place of *values* in our ethical, social, and political life and thought. For, when we talk of ideology, we are talking essentially of values. But the question that immediately arises is, whose values—those of the entire society or those of a section of the society? One would answer the question by saying "the entire society's." The question that is likely to follow at once is, is it really the entire society (i.e., all the members of the society) that created those values, and when and how? The answer to this question would be a difficult one to negotiate. It turns on how values emerge in, or for, a particular society. It would be difficult to say for sure how and when a value or a set of values emerges or comes to be established by a society. I think it is the sheer desire to live together in a stable, harmonious, and cooperative manner such as would be conducive to the realization of the goals, potentials, and aspirations of the members of a society that leads to the creation or emergence of values. It is the same desire that may lead to the adoption of new values and corresponding changes in existing values in times of crises. Thus values can be said to derive from public conceptions of what sort of society or life would be most satisfactory or worthwhile for the members of a society: what kinds of behavior patterns or attitudes of individual members of the society will make for both the most tolerable life for the members and for the continuous existence of the society.

Even though public conceptions of the nature of the good society may not necessarily converge on a particular set of values—so that there would hardly be a consensus on values in a society as such—the mere possibility of a functioning society nevertheless presupposes the convergence of (at least) a dominant set of those conceptions, which need not be the conceptions or beliefs of a particular class or interest group in a society. It is those values, spawned by public conceptions of the nature of the good society, that gain the consensus or acceptance of a large section of the society, that, in one sense, constitute the material fabric of an ideology. Thus, the philosophical controversies over the nature and origin of values need not lead to skepticism about the impartiality (objectivity) of values and negative attitudes to the concept of ideology: for the possibility of a society is grounded in the reality of a notion of a fundamental *core* of human values, a core of values that is shared by members of a society, values the observance of which makes for the continuous existence, stability, and smooth functioning of the society. It cannot be seriously denied, surely, that, for instance, there are certain things that all members of a society would *want* as rational and moral beings. This is true whether the socioethical life and thought of the society are characterized by individualist or communitarian ethos. How to achieve, or whether all the members of the society will achieve, all their wants is a different matter.

The existence of a dominant set of values to which members of a society are committed is important for a society, for it makes it possible for the members to appreciate the significance of events (public policies, individual actions, etc.) taking place in their society; it also constitutes a source of the activities and programs of viable political organizations or parties established to give those ideas or values explicit definition and concrete application.

Ideology is a way of translating ideas into action; it is, as I said, an action-oriented system of ideas. The action-oriented or action-related nature of ideology is in some sense logical, for, if ideology is to be used to make explicit the values of a society, then it would follow that what is prescribed by those values should be given concrete expression in sociopolitical arrangement. Ideology is, thus, associated from the outset with an explicit program of social and political action. But, if ideology is action-oriented, then it requires the political process for its concrete implementation. This means that it must be connected with politics. In a democracy political parties are established to pursue and to bring the values of the society to realization. The political parties may be several, reflecting the fact either that different segments of the population hold different ideologies or that different ways are evolved in the process of trying to realize the dominant set of values and ideals of the society. The former turns on the fact of the plurality of ideas and values inevitable in a human community: on this showing, it can be said that no society will be so completely dominated by a single, monolithic ideology as to have no alternative ideologies within it. But the question is, will there really be great and irreconcilable differences between the various ideologies (to be) espoused by different political parties? This question, to my mind, can be answered most often in the negative.

The reason is that in most cases the various ideologies, when closely examined comparatively, will be found either to be variations on the same basic idea, theme, or value, or, as is most likely, to be methods or programs considered by the adherents of those ideologies as most effective in translating an idea or value into action. But these programs, because they embody, or take off from, some set of ideas, are also called ideologies.

Thus, two senses of ideology may be distinguished: ideology as a framework of ideas used to define the values of a society; and ideology as a program for giving concrete expression to those ideas in the real world of politics and social action. To illustrate the distinction, we may note that the traditional American ideology, for example, is composed, according to George Lodge, of five basic ideas—ideas that derive mostly from the English philosopher John Locke, who set them down in the second half of the seventeenth century. These ideas are: individualism, property rights, competition, limited state, and scientific specialization and fragmentation.[68] Neither of the two main American political parties with their ideologies (i.e., political programs) has made deep inroads into the five basic ideas of "the American ideology." In countries such as France, Germany, and Britain, where some parties espouse the capitalist ideologies and others the socialist (or, social democratic) ideologies, certain basic ideas, such as freedom, equality, democracy, social justice, and individualism, stand as a monolith, none of the political parties prepared to demolish or subvert those basic ideas, for they embody cherished values. The socialist program of state intervention or public control of the means of production and distribution is considered by the adherents of the socialist ideology to be the most satisfactory *way* of bringing about social justice and equality, values that—it can be argued— the capitalist ideology also is intended to realize in the concrete world. It is irrelevant to me, for the moment, to dispute about which system or program will most satisfactorily attain its goals, that is, will best realize the values cherished by the society. It is enough for me to assert that the goals are in many ways fundamentally similar.

Now, a question I would like to discuss briefly is, does ideology bear any relation to philosophy? If it does, how can the relation be defined? Ideology, as has been observed, makes claims about the nature of the good society and how the good society can be brought into being. It claims, or rather assumes, that a certain type of society, or a certain type of socioeconomic or sociopolitical arrangement, is good and worthwhile. It thus assumes a set of values and attempts to find ways of defining them into concrete existence, and so to give concrete institutional expression to those values in the daily lives of the people. Ideology makes such claims about values through a cluster of *ideas*. But such ideas are generally inchoate, woolly, and devoid of clarity and hence stand in need of analysis and elucidation if they are to be coherent and well-defined. The idea of individualism or equality, for instance, stands in need of analysis and clarification; so is the idea of the good society itself. The task of conceptual analysis is of course philosophy's. It was explained at some length in chapter 1 that a major task of philosophy is critical analysis of ideas or concepts. Philosophy can thus provide coherence and articulation to ideology. Ideology requires a philosophical basis for its depth, coherence, and comprehensibility; it requires a theoretical support, which philosophy can provide.

Yet, in another way, philosophy can be of great benefit to ideology. Philosophy also attempts to give conceptual interpretation of human experience. This speculative dimension of the philosophical enterprise sets forth normative suggestions regarding fundamental principles underlying human thought and action. An aspect of this speculative enterprise is reflected in the concerns of philosophical anthropology, which is a reflective and critical inquiry into the nature of the human subject. The philosophical character of the inquiry means that its conclusions are based not simply on empirical generalizations but on systematic reflections on the reality and meaning of human nature and experience. A philosophical analysis and understanding of the nature of the human subject will help us to appreciate whether, and in what way or ways, the human subject can be said to be a moral, social, or political subject and what sorts of values and institutions ought to be evolved and put in place for the enhancement and enrichment of human life. The results (or at any rate some of the results) of this kind of philosophical thinking can be brought to bear on the actual life of the human being in society, and so can be made a basis for ideological choice, to be exploited by those concerned with the practical pursuit of ideology.

What I have said in the immediately preceding paragraphs implies that ideology is distinguishable from philosophy. This view, however, will be disputed or rejected by some people. The dispute derives from the assumption held by some people that philosophical thought or analysis is itself determined by ideology, by the range of ideas or values that the philosopher inherits and that provides the context within which he works out his thought. The assumption implies not only that ideology is already involved in philosophizing but also that the philosopher merely reflects and buttresses the values, interests, and attitudes either of her society or of her class, and that therefore there is really no distinction between philosophy and ideology.

In the light of the fact that the philosopher works out his thought within a cultural context of ideas and values, it cannot be seriously denied that ideological considerations enter into philosophical analyses and concerns. Yet, this is far from saying that ideological considerations constitute the whirlpool of philosophical thinking or that they are such as would put philosophical thinking into a straightjacket and determine its direction. For distinctions can still be made between ideology and philosophy. One way in which philosophy can be said to differ from ideology is that, whereas the ideologist argues with the view solely of endorsing or providing an intellectual prop for the ideas and values he believes in, the philosopher, even if he believes in some set of ideas and values, adopts a critical attitude to his analytical inquiries into those ideas and values with a view either to suggesting amendments or refinements to them or clarifying them or enlarging our understanding of them or suggesting their abandonment. Even if the philosopher ends off affirming those ideas and values, he would do so only after serious, profound, and critical investigations. All this means, first, that the philosopher can rise above ideology and, second, that the type of commitment the philosopher will have to his ideas will be different from that which the ideologist will have to his. I have already remarked briefly (chapter 1, section 3) that, whereas there are substantial elements of tenacity, dogmatism, emotionalism, and bellicosity associated with ideological commitments, as with religious commitments, not much of such elements can be associated with the philosopher's commitments to his ideas or arguments. The reason is that philosophers are more prepared or disposed professionally to abandon their intellectual positions than ideologists are prepared to abandon their ideological positions or beliefs. Another reason is that, while ideological thinking is characterized by the pursuit of conformity and intolerance, philosophy values diversity, tolerance, and accommodation.

Philosophy and ideology differ also in terms of their focus and concerns. I think it can generally be said that ideological thought has immediate practical orientation or implication or consequence. This characteristic of ideological thinking is involved in the meaning of ideology, already stated, as a system of ideas for defining the values of a society and for making these values explicit in the real, concrete world. This is not to say that ideology necessarily lacks a theoretical basis; it does not. Yet it would be correct to say that theoretical inquiries are pursued by the ideologist not for their own sake but for the sake of attaining practical goals directly: this is because the most important feature of ideological thought is its thrust to realize social or political goals in the real world. Also, even though ideological thinking can, like philosophical thinking, be self-consciously critical, it can nevertheless be said that the critical stance of ideological thought is aimed more at pruning its own basis or orientation than at abandoning it root and branch; that is, it is aimed at fortifying the basis of its own beliefs and presuppositions, even though new evidence or experience in the pursuit of the particular ideology may suggest radical reforms, or even rejection of that basis. Ideology thus cannot accommodate radical or subversive criticisms within itself, for that will be considered by its adherents as self-destructive. Thus, not only are the focus and concerns of ideology narrow, but ideology does not seem to be fully prepared to follow out the implications of all of its logic.

The focus and concerns of philosophical thought, on the other hand, are more comprehensive. Philosophical thought also has a practical orientation, especially as regards legal, moral, social, and political philosophy. But philosophical thinking generally pursues theoretical inquiries for their own sake, inquiries that are not directly aimed at attaining a practical goal; it aims primarily at understanding, or attaining knowledge of the truth for its own sake. Unlike ideology, philosophy can—and does—undertake radical criticisms within itself, criticisms that can be subversive and destructive of ideas, arguments, and conclusions previously held as sound and defensible. Relentless in its criticisms, philosophical analysis can reveal the inadequacies of an ideology and thus provide it with a sustainable rational support, necessary for its (ideology's) continuous survival, nourishment, and strength.

6. Conclusion

I have attempted, through historical, cultural, and philosophical analysis, to provide a new—and, I hope, a more correct—interpretation of the conception of economic management held in the traditional setting of Africa and the bearing of that economic arrangement on the socioeconomic welfare of the individual member of the society. The analysis leads to the following conclusions: that the traditional African society bears both individualist and communitarian features; that there are materialist, acquisitive, and capitalist elements in the African character; that communitarianism, as is traditionally understood and practiced, is essentially a socioethical system, not particularly economic; that the arguments of the African political thinkers and leaders in the early years of the postcolonial era to the effect that socialism (of the Marxian kind) was foreshadowed in the traditional socioeconomic thought and practice were misguided—based, as they were, on distorted and tendentious interpretations of the communitarian idea held in the tradition; that the socialism that they thought was inspired by, or anchored in, the traditional communitarian ethos was in fact a reference to the humanist principles of traditional African social and ethical thought and practice, principles that do not necessarily mandate a socialist economic arrangement. Since socialism is an ideology, I have also attempted, albeit briefly, to clarify the concept of ideology, pointing out that, to the extent that ultimate philosophical considerations bear on human aspirations and thus can provide a normative guide to human action and social policy, philosophy can contribute a great deal to an ideological understanding and choice by giving it shape, refinement, coherence, and a stronger foundation.

6

Quandaries in the Legitimation of Political Power

Political legitimacy, which can be defined as the rightful claim or title to the exercise of political power that derives from a socially *acknowledged* source of authority, does not seem to have been much of a problem in the political culture of Africa in the traditional setting. In that setting, as I explain in chapter 4, the socially acknowledged source of political power is tradition or custom, according to which a person, chosen by the kingmakers from a lineage that has historically and customarily been recognized by the entire community as the regal lineage, is installed and recognized as the legitimate chief or ruler. Even though the elected ruler has to be acceptable to the general body of the citizens—who have the moral right, in the event of the misrule or misconduct of the chief, to initiate the process of delegitimating the power of the chief to continue to rule—the principle of popular sovereignty, according to which a ruler's political authority derives directly from the consent of the people expressed through some established processes of selection such as elections, had nevertheless not been fully established in the tradition. For the chief is not directly chosen by the people. Political legitimacy became a problem for the postcolonial African state following the introduction of the important modern notion of popular sovereignty that came along with the establishment of European political institutions in Africa. The principle of popular sovereignty itself is a most appropriate principle in politics because it is appropriate that citizens should have the right directly to choose the person or persons who are to govern them. Yet the full or adequate realization of the principle, in its nuanced form and as a source of legitimacy, appears to be a problem for governments, including even liberal democratic governments. I must point out from the outset that I shall be concerned solely with the legitimacy of a political power acquired by a government or a ruler, not with the legitimacy of a social or economic arrangement such as capitalism, or the way several communocultural groups have been put together to form a single state.

Political legitimacy is not as easy to determine or establish as might be thought. This is because it turns out to be a complex concept, without a simple and easily comprehensible and applicable criterion. The complexity stems from several factors: the fact of the different ways in which governments have come to be formed or individuals (or, groups) have come to assume political power; the nature of the adequate expression of popular consent—so crucial and basic to the realization of the principle of popular sovereignty—which is itself intrinsic to the idea and practice of legitimacy; the question whether or not there is a relation between legitimacy and economic performance of a government or ruler; the fact that there appear to be both formal and informal elements involved in establishing legitimacy; and, then, the whole question about what constitutes majority—the actual source of political power in democratic states.

Governments have been formed, or have come to power, in ways that I see falling into three basic categories. That is, ways in which individuals or groups in a state have come to gain political power can be divided into three basic categories. In category A, political power is gained on the basis of the established or prescribed constitutional procedures, such as elections, or on the basis of the recognized and accepted modes of choosing and installing a king, such as was—and still is—the practice in traditional African communities and in some European nations. A political power so gained is hardly disputed and is almost invariably recognized and acknowledged by the people who live under it. In category B, political power is gained, not through the established constitutional procedures, but by a forcible overthrow of an elected government in a coup d'etat organized usually by some members of the military. In the third category, C, political power is gained as a result of a popular uprising that may result in the overthrow of an existing government, military or civilian, considered corrupt, repressive, and incompetent but that cannot be removed through constitutionally prescribed procedures. When these conditions prevail, nearly the whole population, often in concert with, or with the connivance of, the armed forces, would rise against the existing regime, succeed in overthrowing it, and set up a new government.

Governments that come into being through the established constitutional structures and rulers that are chosen and installed on the basis of tradition and custom (category A) are said to be legitimate. Military governments, which are governments that have come to power by overthrowing elected civilian governments in a coup d'etat and thus have set aside established procedures for acquiring political power (category B) are generally not regarded as legitimate. Governments that are formed after successful popular insurrections against corrupt, authoritarian regimes (category C) would probably in many instances be considered legitimate, even if after some hesitation; the legitimation of governments in category C, however, is problematic. There are, thus, some problems and quandaries in deciding on the criteria for defining particular regimes as legitimate or illegitimate. And my intention in this chapter is to attempt an analysis and understanding of the concept of legitimacy, to answer the question, what gives a regime legitimacy?

1. The Meaning of the Concept

Let us set off on our analytical journey by first looking at the dictionary meanings of legitimacy. According to the *Oxford English Dictionary*, legitimate means: "lawful, justifiable," and *Webster's Ninth New Collegiate Dictionary* says: "accordant with law or with established legal forms and requirements; conforming to recognized principles or accepted rules and standards." As elliptical as these dictionary meanings necessarily are, they require considerable conceptual unpacking as well as logical refinement. Because "legitimate" and "legal" are etymologically linked, it may be easy to establish a semantic affinity between them by simply saying that what is legitimate is legal (or, lawful), and vice versa. To do so, however, is to act with precipitation. For while a lawful government—one whose political power derives from recognized constitutional procedures—may be a legitimate government, a legitimate government may not necessarily be a lawful government by reason of its not having come to power in accordance with the established legal or constitutional procedures or principles. I elaborate and qualify this statement in section 2. But for now, I am claiming that a government can be legitimate even though it may not be lawful, that is, its power may not derive from the prescribed constitutional rules. It will be pointed out, or become clear, that legitimate means "lawful" only in a narrow sense of legitimacy, and that legitimacy is a more comprehensive concept than lawfulness (or, legality). The narrow sense of legitimacy is the sense that equates it with what I call formal legitimacy.

A government that comes to power on the basis of the prescribed legal procedures and whose authority thus derives from constitutional principles, that is, the basic law, of the state, is immediately and in practically all instances—barring genuine and justifiable complaints about electoral frauds—accepted by the citizens as legitimate and can justifiably demand their obedience. And the people on their part recognize that they have a general obligation to that government: they acknowledge the authority of the government because they consider it justifiable on some grounds. In this instance, the grounds are legal, deriving, as they do, not only from the rules of the law of the state but also from the consent of the people demonstrably expressed through their participation in choosing the government. The acceptance by the people is crucial to the notion of legitimacy. But acceptance is based on, or tied to, the justifiability of the procedures deployed in choosing the government. The people must be convinced of the grounds they provide for themselves for accepting the authority of the government. If, for instance, they have reason to believe that the electoral procedures on the basis of which a government is chosen are defective and lead to electoral rigging, they would have the right to withhold their consent and thus not accept the authority of the government. The acceptance of the people must of course be voluntary—based on neither fear nor force—if the acceptance is to be relevant to legitimacy. A government that is legally (constitutionally) elected and accepted can be considered a legitimate government. Legality and the expressed consent of the people are, thus, two important criteria of legitimacy.

In a recent book on the legitimation of political power, David Beetham distinguishes three criteria or conditions for legitimacy: legality, justifiability of (legal) rules, and expressed popular consent. Power, he says, can be called legitimate if "(i) it conforms to established rules, (ii) the rules can be justified by reference to beliefs shared by both dominant and subordinate, and (iii) there is evidence of consent by the subordinate to the particular power relation."[1] By "established rules," Beetham means established legal rules, that is, the rules of the law. What I find somewhat troubling about Beetham's threefold categorization of the factors of legitimation is his making condition (ii) a separate factor or condition. He says that the established legal rules—that is, condition (i)—stand in need of justification in terms of shared beliefs—that is, in terms of condition (ii). The reason, according to him, is that disputes about the legitimacy, about the rightful exercise, of power "involve disagreements about whether the law itself is justifiable, and whether it conforms to moral or political principles that are rationally defensible."[2] I do agree that the law itself needs to be justified in terms of some moral or political beliefs. But I think that this fact, that is, of moral or political justification, is already—to the extent possible—involved or presupposed in the making of the law; in the establishment of rules some place or consideration would necessarily have been given to shared moral or political beliefs, despite the inchoate and loosely structured nature of such beliefs. This is the reason why revisions or amendments to the law are undertaken in response, quite often, to fresh moral or political convictions, to the extent that moral and political convictions and understandings can be said to be shared among individual members of a society. This being so, I think that the first two factors of legitimacy delineated by Beetham can be collapsed into one.

1.1 Formal Legitimacy

I make a distinction between *formal* legitimacy and *informal* legitimacy. By formal legitimacy, I mean legitimacy enjoyed by a government or a ruler by virtue of having been elected, installed, or crowned in accordance with established constitutional procedures, these procedures having been approved previously and accepted by the people. "Constitutional" here must be understood in wider terms that go beyond the written, settled basic law of the state previously agreed upon by the makers of a constitution or in a referendum involving all the people. Understood in wider terms, accepted constitutional procedures that give rise to formal legitimacy would vary: a government formed by a political party that wins an election or referendum or plebiscite would be a legitimate government; the person crowned or installed as the monarch or chief in accordance with custom and tradition would be a legitimate ruler—this includes a king who claims to rule by divine right and whose claims are accepted by his subjects.

Thus, such procedures as elections as well as modalities sanctioned by tradition and custom for electing and installing monarchs can be said to legitimize a government or ruler constitutionally. There may be other structured methods of establishing legitimacy, that is, of creating a right or title to rule. The formal kind of legitimacy derives from established and publicly known procedures. The fact of their establishment—the fact that these procedures are hallowed by time and practice—means, most probably, that they enjoy the general approval of the people. So that a political action, such as usurping political power by force of arms, that flies in the face of established procedures, would be regarded by the people as unwarranted and illegitimate, because it would constitute a disruption or subversion of accepted procedures. Thus, a formal conception of legitimacy would strongly affirm a distinction between de facto and legitimate government. A military government that is formed in the aftermath of the violent overthrow of a constitutionally elected government would not be considered legitimate within the framework of the formal notions of legitimacy.

Formal notions of legitimacy make legitimacy a purely legal or constitutional matter. Its character—its formality—has some virtues: it makes for order, validity, and predictability of acceptance; it makes for the immediate and easy recognition of which of the competing political parties or candidates is to hold power, just as it makes for the immediate and easy recognition and acknowledgment of the person crowned or installed a king; it assuages fears—fears of usurpation, fraud, and unfairness, and thus is expected to eliminate dissatisfaction and misgivings; and, barring the occurrence of electoral frauds and lapses, it makes for the indisputability of the elected person's or political party's right to rule, just as it makes for the indisputability and immediate acceptability by the subjects of the election of a person as their legitimate king or chief.

An important gloss is required, however, on the very last point: it is possible for formal legitimacy, moored as it is to the anchors of legality and constitutionality, to make legitimacy merely cosmetic and window dressing. This would be particularly so in situations where democratic practice is a charade. A nondemocratic or a less democratic state may have a constitution that spells out how political institutions are to function, including those relating to electoral procedures. But having well-tailored and well-laundered constitutional provisions is one thing; having the intention, desire, and willingness to conform one's political actions to those provisions is, in a nondemocratic political situation, quite another. In nondemocratic political situations, constitutional provisions or procedures may not enjoy the respect of rulers, who may in fact set them aside if they consider the provisions as hindrances to their goals, purposes, and ambitions, but who would enthusiastically and gleefully resort to them if they consider those constitutional procedures to work to their advantage. And so it is that in a nondemocratic or less democratic system of government, the electoral process may not function at its maximum. The reason is that the constitutional provisions regarding elections may not be fully adhered to. The constitutionally required time intervals for elections, for instance, may intentionally be overlooked: and when those elections are held, they are rigged, usually by those in power, and so can hardly be said to be free and fair. The elections often result in the ruling government obtaining close to 100 percent of all the votes cast. It is a safe assumption to make that the ruling government that organizes elections does so merely to salve the political consciences of their members, or as a sop to Cerberus: that is, in response to pressures from some quarters; but the results of the elections are already a foregone conclusion.[3]

All this would be happening despite the constitution previously endorsed and accepted by the people that makes the political system that derives from it formally legitimate. Hence, formal legitimacy can, in the circumstances of a nondemocratic or less democratic political environment, become a mere window dressing, something purely ornamental. And the reason, simply, is that the prescribed constitutional procedures are not *seriously* and *truly* respected and applied to the letter.

The ultimate and most important principle of legitimacy, it seems, is the consent of the people. I say "ultimate" and "most important" because in the making of a constitution, that is, the basic law of a state, the consent of the people is either sought or required directly through referendum or plebiscite indirectly through the representatives of the people. There are, however, enormous problems or misgivings about the adequacy of the way popular consent is expressed. In all democratic political systems popular consent is most explicitly expressed through the electoral process. Yet for purposes of the adequate expression of consent—and hence as a legitimating procedure and as a way of assessing the level of legitimacy—the electoral process may have some shortcomings in the way its result are assessed and utilized. I am here referring specifically to the percentage of the total votes obtained by a candidate who is declared the winner. Let us consider a hypothetical example: In a national parliamentary election, 10,000 people are qualified and registered to vote. On the day of the election 60 percent (i.e., 6,000) of the voters actually turn out to cast their votes. Of the three political parties competing for political power, one (P_1) obtains 45 percent, P_2 obtains 35 percent, while P_3 obtains 20 percent of the total votes cast. In accordance with the electoral rules, P_1 is declared the winner and forms a government, even though it obtains 45 percent of the votes actually cast (i.e., 2,700 of the 6,000 votes). But in terms of the total number of voters (i.e., 10,000) P_1 obtains the consent of only 27 percent of the electorate. Now, will the government formed by P_1 be a legitimate government? I think not. Even though the government formed after the elections will, in terms of the simple-majority electoral rules, be a lawful government, it can hardly be said to be a legitimate government, a government to be acknowledged or justified in terms of popular consent.

Again, consider the example of two political parties contesting an election. One obtains 52 percent of the votes and so is declared the winner. The remaining 48 percent of the votes are thus discounted in the electoral equation. But, can it really be said that the party that forms the government with 52 percent of the total votes cast will be riding the crest of popular consent? But, more important, how is popular consent to be measured? Or, put differently, what are adequate criteria for the expression of popular consent? Such questions, and the difficulties in finding satisfactory solutions to them, point to some of the quandaries about legitimacy. If popular consent is to be measured solely in numerical terms—in terms of percentages—then, the percentages must, to my mind, be increased to a substantial level. To obtain political legitimation, the percentages must show that it is, in the words of Beetham, a *"mass* legitimation."[4] Beetham is right, I think, when he says: "It is this requirement of mass legitimation that forms the decisive point of difference from a traditional order, in which the right to express consent . . . was limited to the privileged or propertied section of society, whose consent was both exemplary and binding for everyone else. For political legitimation to be effective in the modern world, the expression of consent has in principle to be available to all, whether they take advantage of it or not."[5] Unless there is a mass expression of consent, there will be no real popular consent, and the absence of popular consent will have far-reaching consequences for the viability and meaningfulness of the concept of political legitimacy.

1.2 Informal Legitimacy

Despite the unsatisfactory way in which the results of an election are assessed and utilized, the electoral process appears to be the best and only procedure for establishing formal legitimacy. But, even though the electoral process is the only method for establishing *formal* legitimacy in the choosing or removing of a government or ruler in a modern democratic system of government, it is by no means the only method for establishing another kind of legitimacy, which I refer to as "informal legitimacy." This kind of legitimacy is based not on established constitutional principles for removing or installing and recognizing a government but on other principles. Informal legitimacy, I argue, like its formal counterpart, is an appropriate and meaningful concept in politics, in the power relations between the rulers and the governed.

Let us imagine a state whose politics is characterized by the following facts: The head of the state was originally elected constitutionally, through free and fair elections. Before long, love of political power leads him to abandon the constitution—the fundamental law of the state, which he had sworn to defend and to regard as the basis of all his political conduct—and to set up a repressive, authoritarian regime. He surrounds himself with a coterie of like-minded power-seekers. He is insulated from the pressures of accountability to the people and yet insists on their immediate obedience to his authority. Criticisms of his rule are, to all intents and purposes, nonexistent, for he tolerates no dent in the structure of his autocratic political power. For fear of his life and for the maintenance of his continuous rule, he establishes a security network that requires a great expenditure of money to maintain. Part of the security network consists of a phalanx of highly trained and highly paid informants and spies. They are very many, and rightly so, if they are to succeed in providing an impregnable cordon of security for the lord. Yet despite this cordon of defense and security built around him, and because of his natural concern about the continuous enjoyment of his wealth till the very end of his time on earth, he takes huge sums of money belonging to the state and has them lodged in foreign banks where the monies will be safe.

In the meantime, the economic fortunes of the state are in total decline, and living conditions are harsh and unbearable. Despite the incompetence of his authoritarian rule, he refuses nevertheless to relinquish power, hoping to hold on to it indefinitely because of his conviction—or rather his illusion—that there is no way, constitutionally or by force of arms, to bring his regime to an end. Then, early one morning a military coup d'etat, organized and executed by a group of military officers, breaks through the security cordon and succeeds in toppling the repressive and intolerable regime of this authoritarian ruler. He and his coterie of corrupt power-seekers and sycophants are arrested and summarily executed. Political power passes into the hands of the group of military officers, which decides to assume power, and so sets up a government.

Most people will agree that a military disruption of such an authoritarian regime will be justifiable on *moral* grounds. A violent overthrow of the regime will thus be morally acceptable, even though it would be illegal in every sense. A military overthrow of a constitutionally elected civilian government that becomes a dictatorship and blocks all avenues of removing it constitutionally will be morally justifiable. The action taken by the military will most probably elicit general agreement as being the morally right course to take in the political circumstances of the state. The morality of the action and thus the legitimacy of the extra-constitutional course of action is of the informal kind. The justification here is purely moral rather than constitutional: it is based on the strong moral conviction that only through this extra-constitutional course of action can gross injustices be removed, human rights abuses be eliminated, and further infliction of suffering on the citizens and further destruction of life be stopped.

But if the violent removal by the military of the authoritarian, repressive regime is hailed as acceptable or justifiable on moral grounds, would or should a government established by the military also be so regarded? Can there be a justifiable military *rule* just as, or because, there can be a justifiable military intervention? Is there a moral parallel between military intervention and military rule? These questions need to be explored.

My attempt to explore these questions begins with a statement made by Kwame Nkrumah less than a month before his overthrow by the military in Ghana. Nkrumah stated:

> It is not the duty of the army to rule or govern, *because it has no political mandate,* and its duty is not to seek a political mandate. The army only operates under the mandate of the civil government. If the national interest compels the armed forces to intervene, then immediately after intervention, the army must hand over to a new civilian government *elected by the people and enjoying the people's mandate under a constitution accepted by them.*[6]

Nkrumah's statement is a significant and powerful riposte to the assumption of political power by the military. We can certainly agree with Nkrumah that since the military has no mandate from the people, it therefore has no right, legal or moral, to rule. This means that any attempt on its part to establish a rule would be an imposition of its imperious will on the people, an action or situation hardly different from the one rejected by the military officers themselves in overthrowing an authoritarian regime.

In rebuttal of the argument, a supporter of the military setting up a rule in the aftermath of a coup d'etat might point out that even though the military had no mandate from the people in removing a monstrous regime, the action nevertheless was not only accepted by the people without demur but spontaneously and jubilantly hailed as right, and hence as legitimate. If the military had no mandate from the people in legitimately overthrowing a repressive regime to the delight of the people, why should it require the people's mandate in order for that rule to be legitimate? This is a fair question. In response, it can be argued that the justification the military officers might have for overthrowing a repressive regime is surely different from their justification for installing themselves in power and controlling and directing the affairs of a state. While the justification for the overthrow is moral as well as practical, the justification for assuming power is essentially constitutional, notwithstanding the moral dimensions of the legitimating rationale.

But, one may ask, can the spontaneous and joyous acceptance by the people of the removal of the authoritarian regime not be taken as signifying their acceptance of the new regime supervised by the military? The answer is, not necessarily. The people may merely be expressing their joy at the overthrow of a monstrous ruler. And even though their spontaneous jubilation may signify their appreciation and recognition of the heroic feat of the military officers, there is no implied commitment whatsoever to their acknowledgment of the *right* (or, *title*) of the military officers to *govern.* Enthusiastic acceptance of the removal of an intolerable regime is one thing; acceptance of an imposed rule is quite another. Emotions against the previous repressive regime may have understandably run high; but the venting of emotions against a previous regime does not necessarily translate into a positive acceptance or endorsement by the people of a regime set up by the military. The only way to ensure that the people's jubilation at the overthrow of the monstrous old political order signifies, in unmistakable terms, their acceptance of the military as their new rulers (not just saviors, redeemers, or liberators of the historic moment) is for the military to organize, through an independent electoral commission, a free and fair referendum to elicit the views of the people on the system of politics or the nature of a constitution they would prefer, to be followed by free and fair elections.

Clear popular consent is relevant here, as indeed it is in all cases of legitimacy. The mode of consent is even more crucial, the most appropriate mode being one that is structured—one that is based, for example, on elections. But in the absence of elections or referendums to test the acceptability of a military government, in circumstances in which the involvement of the people in the military's bid for political power was practically nil, how can one ever rightly or sensibly or justifiably talk of the possibility that a military *government* (distinguished from a military *coup* against a repressive regime) is or will become legitimate, notwithstanding the appearance of some sort of popular support? In situations whose outstanding features are fear, force, violence, intimidation, and lawlessness (or, at least, disdain for the law)—features that characterize practically all military regimes—in such situations, we can hardly confidently suppose the existence of a real, that is, structured, voluntary popular acceptance that would necessarily be an essential factor in making a regime legitimate. In other words, sporadic demonstrations of support—spontaneous or organized—undertaken by some sections of the population for a military regime will not amount to legitimacy.

In the context of the talk about the military redeemers' setting up a government, it might be mentioned that the justification for removing an old, decadent political regime is undoubtedly different from the justification for governing. The fact is that those who want to govern others, directing and controlling a great part of their lives, must be chosen by those who are to be governed. This, it seems to me, is a fundamental political and moral premise—a fundamental political principle that outlaws *military rule* for all time.

Now, suppose a group of military officers that overthrows an authoritarian, repressive regime forcibly sets up a government to rule the nation. And suppose that in the course of its rule most people come to agree that the military government is proving equal to the task of governing, and is performing well, particularly in matters of the economy. Would this fact of good economic performance be a basis for legitimizing the military government? Could effective performance or the amount of economic success achieved by a group of self-imposed rulers form part of the considerations for making its government legitimate? Could there be something called economic legitimacy that can lead to, or pave the way for, political legitimacy? It is prima facie difficult to say no to these questions, in view of the fact that economic achievements perhaps constitute an essential yardstick for measuring the competence and popularity of a government. Even in the stable democracies of Western nations, routinely the government that performs poorly in matters of the economy is toppled at the next general elections, its legitimacy thus withdrawn; whereas the government that performs most satisfactorily is enthusiastically re-elected by the people, its legitimacy being, thus, reconfirmed and maintained by the governed. It appears in fact that when most people are economically well-off as a result of the economic policies of a government, they tend to become less critical and more accepting of that government, their previously "con-attitudes" transforming into "pro-attitudes." And the pro-attitudes of people toward the government may constitute a recognition of its legitimacy.

Does it mean, then, that effective performance or remarkable economic achievement can be considered a legitimating principle? A good number of people are likely to say yes to this question. The reason is that a government may do all that is necessary to recognize the political and civil rights of the citizens of the state, as required by their constitution. Yet, it will certainly disaffect a great part of the population if it fails to sustain economic growth and improve the living conditions of the people. The popular disaffection that will be engendered by the failure to stabilize the economy undoubtedly demonstrates the fundamental importance or relevance of good economic performance to the popularity and esteem of a government. But the question still is, will or should effectiveness or good economic performance also establish or lead to the *legitimacy* of a government, such as a military government, that suffers from a legitimacy deficit right from the outset of its assumption of political power? Now, the answer to this question, in my view, is not a simple one. Yet, to make effective performance—even prolonged effectiveness or efficiency—a legitimating principle will introduce a more complex element into the legitimacy equation. It will make the determination of legitimacy extremely difficult, if not impossible.

The question that arises here is, at what point do we determine the legitimacy of the assumption of power by a government: at the time of the assumption of power, or in the course of the exercise of power? The performance or effectiveness argument implies that legitimacy is determinable only (or, fully) *in the course* of the exercise of political power by a government, not entirely (or, at all) at its outset. This would mean that citizens of a state will have to wait a while and observe how effectively the government performs before they can appropriately decide on the legitimacy of their government. No one knows for how long they will have to wait: until half-way through the term of the government or toward the end of its term of office? But, more important, since the performance of a government tends to ebb and flow, and the perceptions of citizens of the quality of the performance of the government also may change from time to time, at what point on the undulatory line of performance will the people feel satisfied enough to endorse the legitimacy of the government? Thus, even though effective performance can establish the popularity and high esteem of a government, it seems to bristle with problems of decision procedure if it is used as a basis for deciding the legitimacy, or the lack of it, of a government. It follows from all this that resorting to effective performance—whether prolonged or not—in making a decision on the legitimacy of a government would imply that a government cannot be considered legitimate ab initio. But this conclusion makes legality or constitutionality (including the results of an election) inconsequential in the legitimacy equation, an absurd conclusion that cannot be accepted in view of the crucial place of constitutionality among the factors that create and sustain legitimacy.

At this point, we should perhaps make a distinction between the justification of the assumption of power by a government or a regime and the legitimate exercise of that power. It seems to me that effective performance must be linked rather to the *justification* of the exercise of governmental power than to the legitimacy of that power. Suppose the leader of a military regime or a civilian government that has outlived its constitutionally prescribed term of office makes the following speech: "Look, until eight years ago when we assumed the reins of government, the economy of this country was in a shambles. . . . In short, economic growth was nil. Now, however, there have been remarkable improvements in the living conditions of our people since we took over power. The unemployment situation has considerably been reduced. But not only that: my government has streamlined the civil service and the bureaucracy. This has reduced, if not completely removed, waste in the system and has resulted also in efficiency and productivity. We have built more clinics and schools, and there are now more children in school than before. We have improved the transportation system of this country. . ."

Now, let us assume that there is adequate evidence for the truth of the claims made in the self-serving harangue of the leader of an unelected regime and hence that that regime was in many ways an effective regime. I think, then, most people will say that that regime's assumption of political power is justified—justified by its effectiveness and achievements. But, note that the effectiveness of the regime's performance can be only partial or lopsided inasmuch as it did not give—and, in fact, could not have given— any recognition to the civil and political rights of the citizens; the regime's trumpeted effectiveness may have been confined to economic matters, to the neglect of other equally important matters of life. Even though the effectiveness and success of the policies and actions of the regime may justify its assumption and exercise of power, they would not, however, legitimize its power, for not only was the exercise of power illegal but also it ignored the formal, uncoerced consent of the citizens. In other words, legitimacy must be distinguished from justification; only justification can be a function of (prolonged) effectiveness. The conflation between legitimacy and justification will be a recipe for political and moral disaster. It would mean that any group of individuals who, with inflated egos, imagined themselves capable of governing through the introduction of some needed economic reforms to resuscitate a declining economy, or through the adoption of policies that could result in harmony and peace in the multinational state, will, by hook or by crook, find a way of acquiring and exercising political power. Such an approach to acquiring political power will not only bedevil constitutionality as well as popular sovereignty as the enduring sources of legitimate power but it will also be a harbinger of unstructured—and hence unpredictable—

political life and activity, which can, in turn, only breed constant political disorder, confusion, and uncertainty.

Thus, effective performance cannot be considered a legitimating norm; any argument in support of the legitimacy of a military government on grounds that it fulfills the purposes of government, including effective economic performance, cannot be justified; nor can there be any justification for privileging what might be called economic legitimacy over political legitimacy. On the contrary, political legitimacy is a most fundamental political concept. The reason is that, where the political climate is congenial, people will still agitate for democracy—demanding, among other things, recognition of the appropriate and justifiable basis for the exercise of political authority—even when the economy is stable.

It must at this point be borne in mind that the purposes of a government are legion and cannot justifiably be reduced to economic achievements. The purposes of a government surely include the protection of the political or civil rights of the citizens: the right to participate in the choice of their rulers (that is, to vote), and the right to be involved in the decision-making processes—for instance, to have representation in the legislature and to be able freely to express opinion, critical or otherwise, on matters of common concern. Article 21 of the Universal Declaration of Human Rights speaks of every person's "right to take part in the government of his country, directly or through freely chosen representatives." It also states, "The will of the people shall be the basis of the authority of government." But a military rule, because of the manner of its assumption of the reins of government, is *by definition* a negation, in fact, a sequestration, of the political rights of the citizens. The existence of a military government is thus at once incongruent with the exercise of the citizens' political rights. And therefore some of the purposes of a government cannot simply be fulfilled by a military government, because a military government is an unelected government in a political system that prescribes and cherishes the electoral process as a mode of legitimating political power. Thus, even if legitimacy were to be partly linked to the fulfillment of the purposes of government, a military government would not be legitimate.

Thus, it is my conviction that, while there can be a morally justifiable military overthrow of a repressive government that has made it absolutely impossible to remove it constitutionally, there cannot be a legitimate military *rule.*

But if military rule cannot be legitimate, in either the formal or informal sense of legitimacy because of the nature of its origins, what about a government that is formed in the aftermath of a revolution that results in the popular overthrow of the total politicolegal system of the state? In grappling with this question, let us recall the political scenario sketched at the beginning of this section. Let us assume that the corrupt, repressive, and authoritarian government is overthrown as a result of a series of mass protests, demonstrations, and open confrontation and rebellion organized by the people with the connivance, if not with the open support, of the armed forces. The people then set up a (revolutionary) government, using some criteria for selecting the members of the government.

The criteria would not at this moment include the electoral process. One reason is that the constitution, which would stipulate how and when elections are to be held, would have been abrogated by the mere fact of the revolution; provisions regarding electoral processes would therefore have to await the promulgation of a new constitution. Another reason is that, in the wake of even a successful popular uprising, the political situation would spawn fear, confusion, intimidation, and feelings of insecurity—conditions hardly hospitable to the conduct of free and fair elections. In the circumstance, therefore, the membership of a government established by popular uprising will have to be selected from the men and women in the forefront of the revolutionary struggle or from individual citizens known and respected for their views on, and support for, such sociopolitical values as justice, freedom, equality, and democracy. Even though this arrangement would not be the best, it is nevertheless the most practical as an interim arrangement. This interim governmental arrangement can be regarded as a preliminary step toward the creation of a constitutional, democratic system of government and so can be accepted. It is expected that the interim government—informally legitimate, we might have to say—will soon hold genuine elections. This is in fact part of substantive conditions of informal legitimacy, as I point out below.

Let us note that, unlike the previous scenario, in which the overthrow of a regime results from the action of a group of military officers whose action is hailed by the people, the revolutionary overthrow of the regime results from the action of the people as a whole, intent on regaining their freedom and dignity. But, like the military coup, the popular revolutionary overthrow of the repressive regime would be justifiable, also on moral grounds, and thus largely legitimate. The legitimacy here would be of the informal kind, since the popular overthrow of the regime would not have been in accordance with the accepted constitutional procedures and principles. In the previous scenario, the military rule that was set up in the aftermath of the military coup was not considered legitimate. But the legitimacy status of the government that is set up in the aftermath of a successful popular uprising against an intolerable, authoritarian regime must, I think, be assessed differently. If we remember that this would be a government of the people *whose* consent or approval or acceptance is required to make a government legitimate—whether in the adoption of a new constitution or through electoral choice—then the newly formed government may be regarded as legitimate. The government so formed would in fact be self-legitimating, justifiably conferring on itself the right to rule. The legitimacy of the new government is informal.

One question that often comes up and engenders cynicism about the popularity of an uprising against a regime relates to the level of active involvement by the whole population in an insurrection that results in the overthrow of the existing authoritarian regime. Those who are cynical of the active involvement of the people tend to see an insurrection as the work mainly of the leaders of a movement to overthrow the existing regime. In responding to this question, I wish to say, first, that every movement requires leaders if it is to achieve its aims. This goes without saying. But the fact that leaders are required for a movement to forge ahead and succeed in its aims does not mean that the involvement of the people is necessarily precluded or inconsequential or that it is to be considered as merely token. Second, it must be noted that it is impossible to have the *whole* population as such participate in an uprising that is aimed at the overthrow of some regime. One would not normally expect those whom the existing corrupt regime has benefited—families, relatives, friends, sycophants, bootlickers, minions of the regime, and the like—to be involved in the insurrection. Also, one would expect that fear, lethargy, insouciance, and supineness may take their toll among some members of the population. These, and perhaps other factors, can affect the level of popular participation in an insurrection. I do not think, however, that such factors will diminish or depress the level of popular involvement to such a considerable degree as to cast doubt on the popularity of the insurrection itself.

The popularity of an insurrection—and hence the level of the active involvement of the people as a whole—will, it seems to me, result from the depth, extent, and intensity of the suffering inflicted on the people by a corrupt, oppressive regime. In circumstances like those in the political scenario sketched earlier in this section, where suffering of *all* kinds resulting from the oppression and incompetence of a monstrous regime is not only widespread but also great, deep, and of long duration, where the people have no reason to think that the end of their woes is in sight, and where the people are convinced that the end of their woes can be brought about *only* by the removal of the monstrous regime through the insurrection of the subjects—in these circumstances, one can easily conceive the active and spontaneous involvement of large sections of the population as well as an immediate and well-intentioned cooperation between leaders and the mass of the population. The popularity of a political uprising, then, cannot, in such circumstances, be doubted or belittled.

It must be pointed out, however, that, even though a government rides the crest of popular acceptance and endorsement, as one set up in the wake of a revolution, it will only be a de facto government and only informally legitimate. Furthermore, this informal legitimacy, as would be expected from the circumstances in which it arises, will be subject to certain substantive conditions. One such condition is that the informally legitimate government must show respect for the rights of individuals and minorities. Another very important condition is that the government must arrange for the preparation and promulgation of a constitution and submit themselves to elections within a reasonable time. Even though the government is established through popular uprising, its legitimacy would be defeasible if it failed to hold elections soon.

Now, it might be supposed that since informal legitimacy will sooner or later (have to) give way to formal legitimacy with the holding of constitution-based elections, there is therefore in reality only one kind of legitimacy, namely, formal legitimacy—the kind that derives from constitutionally established rules and expressed popular consent. Such a supposition, however, would be erroneous since, prior to holding elections, the (new) government would have been considered by the people as (informally) legitimate. Thus, notwithstanding its ephemeral and transitional nature, informal legitimacy can still be held as a politically useful and meaningful concept.

Let us now turn to the question of the legality of informal legitimacy. Generally we would say that legitimacy includes and implies legality; and this will be true of formal legitimacy. But, would the informally legitimate government set up in the wake of a popular uprising also be lawful? In section 1 I explain that legitimacy is not synonymous with lawfulness, for a legitimate government may not necessarily be a lawful government because it may not have come into existence or acquired its power on the basis of an existing constitutional framework. I now qualify that explanation because there appears to be a difference with informal legitimacy. In a situation where a (new) government has popular origins, and where the existing constitutional framework has been torpedoed long ago by an authoritarian ruler whose government has been brought to a sudden end in a revolutionary uprising, the matter is somewhat complicated. It would generate such questions as: Can the government set up by the people be considered lawful? And, how do we determine the lawfulness of that government?

These questions may be answered from either of two angles. We might say that in the revolutionary circumstances of the emergence of the government, the question whether it is lawful does not arise because the constitution—the basic law governing the state—is known first to have been rendered nugatory and dysfunctional by the deposed ruler and then to have been swept away by the revolutionary waves. In consequence, we cannot strictly talk of the action of the people conforming or not conforming to certain rules of the law (or certain provisions of the constitution). Or, we might tackle the questions from the angle of considering the people themselves as the ultimate *source* of the law, even though the law in a modern political setup is made by the representatives of the people. The implication of this supposition then is that in setting up a government in the wake of a popular removal of a corrupt, repressive, authoritarian regime, the people would in fact be promulgating a law to legalize their action. If the validity of the law can in some ways be said to be dependent on consent, then the action of the people can be considered lawful. This being so, informal legitimacy, like formal legitimacy, can mesh with legality.

2. Losing Legitimacy

The legitimacy of a government or ruler may erode and consent be withdrawn, resulting in delegitimation. Actions such as open disobedience and mass protest demonstrations by the people, clear evidence of the unfair character of elections or of the electoral procedures, legal or moral misconduct as well as ineffective performance on the part of a government or ruler: these are factors that can eventually lead to the loss of political legitimation. When, for instance, an elected government is found to be incompetent, the electorate or its elected representatives may withdraw their consent and force or insist on a premature, that is, early, election in which the legitimacy of the government may finally and formally be withdrawn by the people's refusal to re-elect it; or the electorate may, prior to the holding of elections, insist on the resignation of the government. Also, the (formal) legitimacy of an elected government or president may be called into question, may be considered problematic, if there should be clear evidence of electoral malpractice—common in less democratic states.[7] If the complaints about electoral malpractice are genuine and well-founded, they would throw the legitimacy of the elected government or political leader into serious doubt, for it would not be clear that the consent of the people has undoubtedly been demonstrated. Legitimacy in such circumstances would be doubtful and suspect and may be defeasible.

It seems to me, however, that delegitimation or the loss of legitimacy is as much a complex matter as legitimation. Legitimation requires the fulfillment of some factors or conditions. Beetham states that the three factors in his scheme, namely, legal validity, justifiability of legal rules, and expressed consent, "successively and cumulatively, are what make power legitimate. To the extent that they are present, it will be legitimate; to the extent that they are absent, it will not. Together these criteria provide grounds,"[8] that is, for legitimacy. I think it is right to say that the creation of legitimacy is a function of the presence of a set of conditions or factors. One might think that the same conditions must be considered and applied in the matter of the loss of legitimacy. That is to say, to the extent that the legitimating factors are absent, a government loses its legitimacy. (In this instance, the delegitimating factors will consist of the opposite or privation of the legitimating factors.) But herein lies a quandary: if the delegitimating factors will have to be present together, successively and cumulatively, it would mean that in the absence of even one factor, a government cannot be considered to have lost its legitimacy; its legitimacy can be considered only weakened or undermined. Thus, if such actions as mass disobedience frequently take place that may indicate the withdrawal of consent on the part of a large number of the people qualified to give consent, they would not lead to the loss of legitimacy, even though they may lead to its erosion and the consequent loss of moral authority. But this will not do.

The reason is that if a government originally elected and thus in possession of the mandate of the people to govern fails to submit itself for election at intervals prescribed by the constitution, it at once *loses* its legitimacy, for it can then claim neither to be legal nor to enjoy undoubted popular consent to its rule. The continued rule of the government would be without the people's mandate or the consent so crucial to its legitimate existence. In such a situation the loss of legitimacy will be immediate. The immediacy of delegitimation would stem from the breach of legal or constitutional validity. In the event of the breach of a constitutional provision required for formal legitimacy, the question of the adequacy or inadequacy of expressed consent of the people will not even arise; nor will the question of the unfair and unfree character of the (never-organized) election. Thus, whether the factors relevant to delegitimation are to be cumulative or not would depend on the legal or moral weight of each of the factors involved. Thus, even though mass open disobedience may—and could—eventually be an important factor in a government's coming to lose its legitimacy, the failure or refusal to submit itself for re-election will *at once* justify a loss of legitimacy. What I have said so far relates to what I have called formal legitimacy: the kind of legitimacy based on structured procedures for justifying the acquisition and exercise of political power.

Now, could an informally legitimate government also lose its legitimacy? The answer to this question is definitely yes. Because of the circumstances that give rise to an informally legitimate government, the continued enjoyment by the government of popular consent to its rule will depend very much on the quality of its rule: how well it performs and the extent to which it is able to fulfill (at least) the immediate hopes, demands, and expectations of the people—which would include holding elections; in fine, on its ability to deliver. In such situations delivering would mean enacting specific measures, not just making general or ambiguous promises. Legitimacy becomes strained in the event of the government's failure to fulfill the demands of the people for material well-being as well as for the protection of their civil and political rights.

The mandate of the people given in connection with formal legitimacy is necessarily of a general nature and thus does not detail out all the specific policies and actions to be pursued by the government. An electoral mandate merely constitutes an endorsement, roughly, of the manifesto and quality of the political party or leader elected to form the government. But manifestos themselves are of a general nature and so are usually short on specifics. Thus, a formally legitimate government necessarily has a wider latitude both to pursue such policies and actions as it may deem worthwhile and beneficial to its people and to deal effectively with emergent situations that would not have been foreseen when it presented its political agenda to the people prior to its election. By contrast, the mandate given by way of informal legitimacy for the exercise of power is much more specific: to do certain specific things, such as taking steps to restore constitutional rule, to respect human rights, to remove injustices, or to resuscitate a declining economy. Thus, the legitimacy of an informally legitimate government is at once made hostage to the quality of the performance of the government, to how satisfactorily it addresses certain specific problems in pursuit of which it was created by the people following a revolutionary uprising. An informally legitimate government would thus lose its legitimacy if it were found to rule badly, attempting to pursue policies and actions reminiscent of those of the previous repressive, authoritarian regime that would have been overthrown by popular uprising.

In the preceding section, I gave reasons why effective performance cannot be used as a legitimating principle in respect of formal legitimacy. Yet, it is expected of course that a government that exercises legitimate political power will effectively fulfill the ends and purposes—including the achievement of sustained economic growth—for which it was given a mandate by the people. Now, if such a government fails to fulfill those ends, will it not lose its legitimacy? Probably most people will answer this question in the affirmative, concerned as they would be with the enhancement of the material welfare of human beings. It would probably be right to take that position, that is, to deny legitimacy to an incompetent government. Yet, an incompetent government, with failed policies and measures, will not lose its legal validity, even though its incompetence would have seriously undermined its moral authority and esteem. But—and herein lies a quandary— since legality constitutes an important plank in the legitimacy platform (even though legality is not, as I have said, awhile ago, equivalent to legitimacy), and since legitimacy is thus not a wholly moral concept, it would not be wholly correct to delegitimate a government on the grounds that it has failed to deliver, to fulfill the ends and purposes of government. Since it is formal legitimacy that endures, and since a nonrevolutionary civilian government acquires and exercises political power only through formally established rules and procedures, the loss of legitimacy can only result from the application of those established rules and procedures. Governmental incompetence and failure, barring the committal of criminal or grave moral offenses or unconstitutional (illegal) acts that could lead to the impeachment or resignation of the government or ruler, will surely lead to the erosion or whittling away of legitimacy, but not to the complete loss of (formal) legitimacy—which, remember, can come about only through the application of established procedures.

3. Conclusion

Legitimacy involves the conviction that a group of persons have, from the point of view of the citizens of a state, a right or title to govern, that is, to initiate and form policies, to direct and run the affairs of the state, to issue and enforce commands, and so on. It thus implies a normative evaluation of the political status of a regime: whether it ought (or, has the right) to govern or not. In the African political culture, with its obsession for consensus and reconciliation, legitimacy may be regarded as a search for unanimity (consensus). Different political regimes have claimed the status of legitimacy.

I have been concerned in this chapter to point up the quandaries involved in the legitimation and delegitimation of political power exercised specifically by a government or ruler. I have distinguished two concepts of legitimacy: a formal concept and an informal concept. Formal legitimacy is anchored in legality (or, constitutionality, which would include tradition and custom) and morality, while informal legitimacy is anchored only in morality. Informal legitimacy invariably has to be propped up or firmed up by strong moral arguments because of the unsettled nature of its anchor: morality. In any discussion of legitimacy the formal concept invariably comes to the minds of most people, for it is the kind that generally is either resorted to or appealed to or that generally is valued in democratic practice. And, so, legitimacy has often been conceived in terms of formal legitimacy.

I have tried to argue that there surely is another kind of legitimacy, namely, informal legitimacy, whose conceptual status and importance in our political life need to be given their due recognition. The ultimate justificatory basis of the two concepts of legitimacy is the same: popular consent. While the formal conception of legitimacy would insist on a distinction between de facto and legitimate government, an informal conception of it would ignore any such distinction. From the point of view of the former, the fact of the existence of a government, such as a military government, does not make it legitimate, whereas, from the point of view of the latter, a government that derives its existence from a morally justified popular acceptance, as in a revolutionary situation, must be regarded as legitimate; this, however, excludes military government, which seizes the right to govern, instead of acquiring it appropriately or having that right conferred upon it by law or by the citizens. It has also been pointed out that while a military overthrow of a repressive, authoritarian government can be morally justified, military rule as such cannot be legitimized in terms of either conception. Informal legitimacy will—if, and after, elections are held—sooner or later give way to formal legitimacy; but this fact does not detract from the former's importance as a viable political concept.

Despite the structured character of formal legitimacy, it appears to be riddled with several quandaries that make the determination of legitimacy not an easy matter. Among the quandaries are the following: even though popular consent is crucial to legitimacy, it is not clear how this is adequately and unambiguously expressed and assessed; even though a regime is expected to fulfill certain ends and demands, it is not clear whether effective performance should be a legitimating factor, or whether the ineffective performance of a legitimate regime should eventually lead to the loss of its legitimacy; even though one factor may be of crucial importance to the creation and sustenance of legitimacy, it is not clear how delegitimation can be effected in the event of the privation of just that one factor, since legitimation is a function of a cumulative set of factors; because (formal) legitimacy is a complex of legal and moral factors, and because legal factors are more certain than the (often ambiguous) moral ones, it is not clear how to make a clear determination of delegitimation.

All this having been said, however, the importance of legitimacy in negotiating the power relationships between the government and the governed cannot politically be underrated or subverted by the quandaries or conundrums engendered in the application of the concept to real situations. What only needs to be recognized is the fact that ways must be found to refine the concept and make it work better in politics.

Political Corruption

A Moral Pollution

Political corruption, the kind of corruption that involves rulers and other public officials who run the affairs of a state or a political community, is a perennial problem that appears to afflict all politically organized human societies—rich or poor, developed or developing, ancient, traditional, or modern—the running of whose affairs is entrusted to a group of people called public officials. But, for several reasons, the phenomenon of political corruption manifests itself more often in some societies than in others, is more widespread or pervasive in some societies than in others, and produces more devastating effects on some societies than on others. Postcolonial Africa is undeniably among the worst victims of political corruption. For it cannot be denied that the most outstanding and resilient problem that has beset and blighted the politics of the new nations (or, nation-states) of postcolonial Africa is political corruption. It probably constitutes the most serious source of the financial hemorrhage suffered by developing nations in Africa, constantly gnawing at their development efforts; it is undoubtedly the most common cause of the military overthrow of civilian governments in Africa, with the consequent disruption of the democratic political process: thus, it is the greatest and most serious disease of governments in Africa.

A developing nation may have rich material resources; it may boast a good and viable administrative system with professionally qualified and efficient administrative officials; it may be able to produce or fashion good economic policies; it may have a leader who claims to be committed to the development of the country: all these are of course great assets that should form the basis for the nation's economic takeoff and progress. Yet, despite the possession of these great assets, a nation may still be making slow progress down the path to development, like a man trudging down a road debilitated by an unstoppable bleeding from a festering wound. Political corruption *is* the festering wound that can destroy a body politic.

My intention in this chapter is to clarify the notion of political corruption, show how it manifests itself in the traditional setting of Africa, explain how some traditional practices bear on corrupt political conduct, and argue that political corruption, despite its name, is essentially or fundamentally a *moral* problem, and that serious and profound commitment to our moral beliefs and principles will be the most adequate therapeutic response to the phenomenon of political corruption.

1. Political Corruption: What Is It?

Political corruption is the illegal, unethical, and unauthorized exploitation of one's political or official position for personal gain or advantage. The word "political" in political corruption is intended to refer to public affairs: the official goods, affairs, fortunes, agencies, resources, and institutions of the state—which is a human community with organized, public institutions. Political corruption is thus an act of corruption perpetrated against the state or its agencies by a person holding an official position in pursuit of his own private or personal profit. "Political" thus means official, public (nonprivate), or governmental. This means that a corrupt act committed against a private or nongovernmental organization will not be political corruption, even though it is indeed an act of corruption, the committal of which will justify the censure or conviction of the culprit. The victim of political corruption is invariably the fortunes, resources, and interests of the state or the body politic: thus, to say that political corruption serves the ends of the state is a contradiction in terms. It serves the personal ends of individuals or groups of individuals who involve themselves in it.

Political corruption is usually associated with the acceptance of bribe; but it is more than that. For graft, fraud, nepotism, kickbacks, favoritism, and misappropriation of public funds are all acts of political corruption when they are committed by public officials exploiting their official positions for their own advantage. The head of state who stealthily and fraudulently takes huge sums of money from his state and deposits them in foreign banks, the public official who receives a bribe from a prospective employee in return for a promise to give her a job, the official who favors a less qualified relative for a position while rejecting the candidate with better credentials, the policeman who receives a bribe and consequently abandons charges against an arrested person, the customs official who illegally reduces the customs duties on some imported goods in return for some gifts, the clerk in a government tax department who reduces the tax burden of a business executive through deliberate miscalculation in return for some kickbacks, the magistrate or judge who perverts the course of justice in favor of an individual who offers him a bribe: all these public officials would be committing acts of political corruption. Thus, political corruption generally involves reciprocities between the public official and the other beneficiary of the corrupt act. Political corruption can reach astronomical and scandalous proportions particularly when top government officials are involved in it. The pervasiveness and frequent incidence of the phenomenon of political corruption across the various levels of officialdom generates not only wonder and scandal but also the ire and resentment of the wider public. The pervasiveness of the phenomenon requires explanation.

There must surely be conditions or factors that explain the widespread incidence of political corruption. Most social scientists tend to explain the phenomenon in terms of the nature of a political or social system, economic conditions, and the inadequacies of legal and institutional frameworks. In Herbert Werlin's view, "rising corruption is a sign of fundamental political disorder."[1] James Scott sees political corruption "as a political event."[2] The central thesis of his book is that "patterns of corruption can be related to the character of the political system and to the nature and rate of socioeconomic change."[3] It may be said that the way a political system operates can give rise to political corruption. In a system of politics in which accession to political office depends very much on the goodwill and financial contributions of some individuals to the electoral campaigns of a candidate for a political office, there is some kind of "understanding" that the successful candidate will reciprocate those contributions with appropriate rewards of various kinds. In consequence, the candidate elected to a public office may feel indebted to those who have in various ways helped him to win that office, while they, on their part, also expect favors from him in return for their contributions and other kinds of assistance given to him in his quest for a public office. In his desire to redeem promises he may have made in the course of his bid for a public office and to do what in his opinion will help insure his re-election the next time around, the elected official awards jobs, contracts, and other favors to his benefactors, among whom would be ill-qualified cronies, fellow members of his ethnic groups, and relatives. The decision to reward his electoral benefactors and others is likely to involve him in political corruption. Thus the political system can corrupt an elected public official.

Political corruption can flourish under weak political leadership. For political leaders or top public officials who are weak can hardly be expected to control subordinate officers tempted by bribes and other forms of political corruption, either because, being weak leaders, they do not have the nerve or courage to exert control, or, perhaps, being dishonest themselves, they have compromised their own integrity and moral authority and so cannot discipline others. Political leaders of this ilk would either ignore or minimize reports of corruption, or perhaps procrastinate before acting on the reports. In this way, the firmness and resoluteness required to deal with political corruption are not displayed by those leaders. The inability or, perhaps better, the reluctance to deal firmly with corrupt public officials—especially top officials—may stem from the political process that ties the hands of a leader whose accession to power was made possible through the support—including financial support—of people who later find themselves in his government. Also, political leaders who want to give the impression that their subordinate officers are men and women of probity may hush reports of corruption because they do not want to air their dirty linen in public, so to speak. Such attitudes or responses to political corruption will only allow it to infect other members of officialdom.

A certain perception of the institution of government will breed corruption. In postcolonial states in particular, governments are generally perceived as distant or objective entities whose activities have little bearing on the welfare and the daily lives of the citizens, and to whose activities the citizens, in consequence, have very little ideological and emotional attachment. In Chinua Achebe's novel *No Longer at Ease*, the hero, Obi, is asked, "Have they given you a job yet?" The narrator immediately comments: "In Nigeria the government was 'they'. It had nothing to do with you or me. It was an alien institution and people's business was to get as much from it as they could without getting into trouble."[4] The perception of the colonial system of government as an alien institution must have characterized attitudes toward government adopted by most colonized peoples in Africa (see chapter 4, section 4) and perhaps elsewhere. These attitudes toward government have probably not changed much even in the postcolonial setting. It can hardly be denied that such a perception of government can engender negative attitudes and mentalities that may lead public officials to treat governmental or public property or interests with unconscionable and disdainful insouciance. Such careless attitudes toward the institution of government and its property can easily skew moral orientations, especially those of public officials, and thus give rise to political corruption. Moreover, to refer to the government with the vague pronoun "they" points up a weakness or incomprehensibility of, or confusion surrounding, the idea of national or common interest. Political corruption will thrive more in an atmosphere in which commitment to the national or public or common interest is weak and is constantly being subverted by other, nonpublic loyalties or obligations.

A social system may be an explanatory factor in the frequent incidence of political corruption. I said in introducing this chapter that the phenomenon of political corruption is common to all human societies, even though the frequency and prevalence of its incidence may differ among societies. This suggests that political corruption infects human societies irrespective of the social systems evolved by those societies. Even so, it can be said that some social systems influence the incidence or perpetration of political corruption more than others. In this connection, it might be supposed that a society characterized by the individualist ethos will, because of its emphasis on, and obsession for, individual interests, be more greatly infected by political corruption than a society characterized by the communitarian ethos with its emphasis on community or public interests. But this supposition is clearly false. For empirical evidence shows that African societies whose social structures are more communitarian than individualist are nevertheless riddled with more frequent and scandalous levels of political corruption than most non-African individualist societies. This is because some features of the communitarian social structures, such as have been evolved by African societies, tend to lead, or put pressure on, individuals holding public office to involve themselves in acts of political corruption. I shall mention a few of such social features or practices.

In the extended family system of African societies, an individual, as I explain in chapter 9, section 3.1.3, bears a dual responsibility: for himself and for the members of the group. These responsibilities are naturally onerous. To be able to shoulder them successfully requires an adequate personal economic position. An individual public official who has access to public resources may, in the process of striving to achieve that adequate economic position, take advantage of his official status and commit acts of official corruption. Second, the extended family system with its web of relatives— far and near—gives rise to patronage: the public official is expected to find jobs for some members of the extended family either in his own organization or elsewhere. This often leads to nepotism, which is an act of political corruption. Nepotism is likely to be a characteristic more of the extended family system than the nuclear family system, for in the former there are hordes of people whose needs are to be attended to. The causal factors or circumstances of political corruption, to be sure, are legion; but the pressures on an individual holding some public office to meet, or show sensitivity to, the demands of the members of the extended family must certainly be among the outstanding. Third, in a communitarian social system, social relations are generally supported and maintained through the exchange of gifts among members of the community as well as through the offering of gifts to elders, some of whom may hold official positions in the community.

It would be correct to say that among the ordinary members of the society gifts are given as an expression of love, friendship, sympathy, and compassion or, similarly, to reciprocate an act of kindness or goodwill. No intentions of suborning or corrupting the recipient are implied here. But, it would also be correct that gifts to elders holding official positions are offered most probably for different reasons: as a sign of respect for or courtesy to the office, or in appreciation for an act of kindness by the recipient to the giver, or in anticipation of some reciprocities from the recipient (i.e., the public official) in the form of favors. Gifts offered to public officials can be described as bribes intended immediately to ingratiate the giver to a public official, and, subsequently, to ask him or her for some favors. Gifts can thus insidiously corrupt a public official. It may therefore be said that the traditional practice of giving gifts to elders, or to public officials and "big men" and "big women" in government in the modern political setup is a causal factor in political corruption.

The poor economic circumstances of a country may also be noted as a causal factor in the incidence of political corruption. Such economic circumstances may lead to inflation and the erosion of salaries and may in turn depress the material or financial circumstances of public officials (as well as others), making it impossible to make ends meet and to make ordinary life bearable. Political corruption occurs also of course in wealthy nations; but the relative poverty of some nations makes the incidence of political corruption much more prevalent, even less shameful. The truth of the matter, however, is that in both poor and rich nations political corruption occurs throughout the various echelons of officialdom, infecting officials at all levels. It would be easy to put down political corruption among lower-level officials to their economic situations; but this kind of causal explanation gains less plausibility when we consider the fact that financially well-off top public officials also involve themselves in political corruption. It can be said that in general the economic circumstances of public officials may not be significantly different from, that is, significantly worse than, those of many of their compatriots. One would have to conclude, then, that, as far as economic circumstances are concerned, the phenomenon of political corruption may more realistically be put down to graft, greed, avarice, and the desire for an ostentatious style of life insupportable by one's legitimate means.

The lack of an adequate legal and institutional framework or controls may also explain the widespread incidence of political corruption. Inadequate laws governing corrupt behavior, inadequate institutional checks, ineffective law enforcement agencies, inadequate legal sanctions against culprits, weak civil service regulations that make it difficult to remove corrupt officials: these factors may explain the proliferation of political corruption, since they seem to make it possible for some public officials to feel that they can commit corrupt acts with impunity. The assumption here is that, if the appropriate sanctions and controls are instituted and the powers and activities of the law enforcement agencies are expanded, political corruption will be considerably reduced, if not eradicated. This assumption, however, may be only partially true, as I point out below.

Now, the question I wish to explore at this point is, does the prevalence and the politically infectious nature of political corruption consequent upon the legal, social, economic, political, and other circumstances of a society mean that we can sensibly and correctly refer to "the culture of political corruption"? There is no denying that the prevalent and persistent nature of the phenomenon of political corruption does give the impression that politically corrupt practices have (almost) acquired the status of a system, a norm—"the thing to do"—and that political corruption may be said thus to have insinuated itself into the culture of a people. The impression leads a political scientist, Victor Le Vine, writing specifically about the situation in Ghana, to assert that "by the end of the 1960s Ghana had developed what we term a culture of political corruption."[5] He adduces facts (some of which are based on personal interviews) and arguments to substantiate his view. Even though it is undeniable that Ghana suffered from political corruption during the period Le Vine mentions, and has indeed suffered from this political disease since then, and even before then, I think nonetheless that the term "culture of political corruption" he employs to characterize the phenomenon is inappropriate. Moreover, some of the statements he makes or quotes from the people he interviewed (in Ghana) are inconsistent with the notion of a culture of political corruption. While I do not disagree with Le Vine over the widespread existence of political corruption in Ghana, I think that the concept he presents of a *culture* of political corruption is incoherent. Note that my worry here is conceptual rather than empirical and thus has nothing to do with the specific circumstances of a particular society.

Culture is the way of life of a people. It is a public phenomenon, a product consciously and purposively created by a people or a society. Most, if not all, members of the society share and participate in the cultural products of their society. A cultural product has a positive meaning for the life of a people as a whole. To talk of a culture of political corruption, then, is to imply that political corruption is a cultural product of a people to whose lives it has some positive meaning and value, that political corruption is a public phenomenon undertaken or committed in the glare of publicity, that the members of a society as a whole participate in the enjoyment of political corruption, and that political corruption is a culturally determined practice or involvement.

It would not be correct, however, to speak of a culture of political corruption for several reasons. First, political corruption is not a purposively created cultural product having a value for the people of a society as a whole, and hence the attempts by successive governments to eradicate it by means of the law. Second, political corruption cannot be undertaken publicly; an act of political corruption is always a furtive act, a clandestine operation. No one boasts of being politically corrupt. This feature of political corruption is entirely different from a genuine product of a culture. With regard to bribes, an outstanding form of political corruption, John Noonan makes the following apt observation: "In no country do bribetakers speak publicly of their bribes, or bribegivers announce the bribes they pay. No newspaper lists them. No one advertises that he can arrange a bribe. No one is honored precisely because he is a big briber or a big bribee. No one writes an autobiography in which he recalls the bribes he has taken or the bribes he has paid."[6] Third, political corruption is not a culturally determined practice or norm, for not all the people—not even all public officials—who grow up in a culture come to internalize it, subsequently valuing and involving themselves in it. Finally—and this is purely a point of logic: if the concept of a culture of political corruption were a coherent concept, it would mean that the phenomenon of political corruption is a culturally *sanctioned* practice. And if this were true, it would make nonsense, at least in part, of Le Vine's definition of political corruption as "the *unsanctioned*, unscheduled use of public political resources and/or goods for private, that is, nonpublic ends."[7]

For the foregoing reasons I find the concept of a culture of political corruption incoherent. A people or a society does not create, develop, and espouse a "culture" of political corruption, even if many of its public officials are involved in it. And I think it would be more appropriate to put political corruption in the same category of such moral evils as lies, theft, fraud, greed, and others, all of which, like political corruption, are prevalent in

human societies. And, those individual public officials who involve themselves in political corruption, like thieves, are of course members of the
human society.

Let us now turn to some of the statements made by Le Vine or his interviewees about what he calls "the culture of political corruption." Even
though Le Vine says that "it appears that the documentary evidence on the
extent, operation, and growth of political corruption permits the conclusion
that at least on the level of visible official behavior, a case has been established for the existence of an incipient Ghanaian culture of political corruption," [8] he asserts elsewhere that "in Ghana it is still thought reprehensible
for a chief or any other man in public office to use the political goods
entrusted him for private, unsanctioned purposes." [9] (The word "still" is, I
suppose, a reference to what obtained in previous periods, in the traditional
setting.) The last statement of Le Vine's is inconsistent with the notion or
existence of a culture of political corruption. He also makes the following
logically bizarre and unhelpful statements:

> What we have called the "culture of political corruption" may have predis-
> posed most Ghanaians to tolerate a certain amount of corruption, *but that
> toleration may have been more a function of resignation than of acquiescence,*
> and in any case the fact that all post-independence Ghanaian governments—
> including Nkrumah's—have evinced much *concern* about the problem shows
> they have perceived limits to the public's tolerance. Further, if our assessment
> of the traditional contexts of corruption is correct, the Ghanaian norms for
> judging corruption must have *retarded the growth of public tolerance.*[10]

How, one may ask, can a society that merely tolerates—thus not fully accepting—political corruption but sees it rather as a *problem* be said to nurture a culture of political corruption? One of Le Vine's interviewees asserts,
"During the old regime there were reports of embezzlement of state funds
. . . and sorts of dubious deeds leading to the loss of public funds. All these
evils are prevalent in our society today and they have to be *eradicated;* else
the progress we talk so much about will never come to pass." [11]

The desire to eradicate acts of political corruption from society suggests
the conviction that these corrupt acts are not such as can willingly and
purposively be developed as part of the culture of a people. The desire to
eradicate political corruption and so to make progress "come to pass" is
indeed the reason for the numerous commissions of inquiry—about sixty in
a decade and a half[12]—set up by successive governments in Ghana during a
period when, according to Le Vine, a culture of political corruption was
being developed. The civil service regulations enacted in those days mention
certain deeds as acts of misconduct: these include "fraud, dishonesty, stealing, giving and receiving of presents and gifts, engaging in any activity outside [a civil servant's] official duties which are likely to . . . lead to his
taking improper advantage of his position in the Civil Service." [13] Two of the
regulations say: "No Civil servant shall receive presents in any form in the
course of his duties which may have the effect of influencing his decision,

nor may he receive any compensation or reward for the performance of any official duties except as approved by government. A Civil servant shall not give presents to other Civil servants which may influence them in matters in which he is interested." [14]

Thus, attempts are persistently made in Ghana to stave off political corruption from the body politic. As Le Vine himself notes, "Political corruption . . . has few defenders." [15] The attempts may have some success in some societies; but they may fail in others. The failure is not to be translated by any means, however, as implying a conscious and explicit desire by most people to elevate political corruption to a status of moral acceptability in their culture. According to Le Vine, a large number of political scientists "all agree that the key component of a political culture is the body of orientations, attitudes, and values that yield criteria for determining what is politically legitimate and what is not." [16] The statements of both Le Vine and the people he interviewed indicate, implicitly and explicitly, the desirability of sloughing off certain orientations and attitudes that were becoming part of their political experience. It is clear that they do not regard political corruption as a legitimate behavior by a public official and do not desire to allow it to insinuate itself into their political culture, even if its incidence in the society, as they were aware, was prevalent.

There is thus a clear need to make a distinction between culture and society. Because of the prevalence and persistence of certain undesirable acts, such as violence and child abuse, that occur frequently in human societies, one may speak of "the culture of violence" or "the culture of child abuse." But this surely is a metaphorical use of the term "culture," a use that does not suggest, implicitly or explicitly, the real existence of a *culture* of child abuse or violence. Thus certain undesirable acts may be rampant *in* a society without their having to be considered as part of the society's culture or as being consciously and purposively nurtured into that society's culture as such.

It is very puzzling that in most attempts to provide a causal explanation for the incidence of rampant political corruption, the *moral* circumstances are generally ignored or are mentioned only in passing and are thus regarded as peripheral to the phenomenon. Thus Scott observes: "Recurring acts of . . . corruption are thus more successfully analyzed as normal channels of political activity than as cases of deviant pathology requiring incarceration and/or moral instruction for the perpetrator(s)." [17] Patrick Dobel, however, does give attention to morality as an important factor in the causal explanations of the phenomenon of political corruption. "In a limited sense," he notes, "most corruption requires individual moral choices and depends upon the human capacity for avarice and evil." [18] Political corruption, on his showing—and I would certainly agree with him—stems from the moral incapacity to make the appropriate or desirable moral choice required by a situation in favor of the common welfare.

Dobel's analysis seems to me to be impaired, however, by his overemphasis on sociopolitical economic causes. He observes that "there is a unanimous agreement among the theorists that the source of systematic corruption lies in certain patterns of inequality. . . . [and that] the corruption of a state results from the consequences of individual human nature interacting with systematic and enduring inequality in wealth, power and status."[19] (Among the theorists he refers to are Thucydides, Plato, Aristotle, Machiavelli, and Rousseau. In fact, Dobel draws on the views of these people in his analysis.) To Dobel, "inequality dominates the causes of systematic corruption," but, he adds, "human nature must also be addressed."[20] The presumption here is that the eradication of inequality among the citizens of a state will in turn help eradicate corruption from the state. But this presumption is flawed on two grounds. First, the eradication of inequality—and the consequent installation of equality—will hardly affect the nature of the individual human being in such a profound or significant way as to remove all proclivities toward corruption. It is certainly not true that social, economic, and political equality will eradicate the human tendency toward avarice and evil. Second, Dobel's emphasis on inequality as the dominant cause of corruption seems to imply that in any society it is the victims of inequality who are the greatest culprits of political corruption. But this, surely, cannot be true, for the victims of inequality, having little access to the centers of political power or the resources of the state and generally marginalized politically, do not have the greatest opportunity to cheat and plunder the state. Unless it can successfully be argued—and I doubt that it can—that the removal of inequality from society will considerably elevate the moral status of the individual human being—that is, both the beneficiary and the victim of inequality—and deposit her on the path of moral virtue, the dominant place given to inequality in the causal explanations of political corruption is an exaggeration and will not be true in the long run.

I think that political corruption is crucially a *moral* problem and should be grappled with from that standpoint. To see it as such is to take the bull by the horns. I shall take up a discussion of the moral circumstances of the problem of political corruption in due course, after having looked at its incidence on the political scene of Africa in the traditional setting.

2. Political Corruption in the Politics of Traditional Africa

Political corruption is a feature not only of colonial and postcolonial but also of traditional (indigenous) African polity. It can be said, however, that its growth was undoubtedly fostered by the colonial and postcolonial political systems with their more elaborate bureaucracies and complicated ways of achieving their goals, which gave rise to fresh opportunities for illegitimate and immoral gains. The traditional polity, operating within a less complex society, generally evolved simple bureaucracies, with small numbers of officials: officialdom consisted mainly of the chief (and some members of the royal family), his councillors (or elders), and a few other lieutenants. Even so, it cannot at all be denied that political corruption in the form of receiving and giving bribes or misusing or misappropriating public or communal or lineage goods and resources does exist in the traditional systems of politics and administration in Africa. There is a great deal of evidence to indicate that corruption was—and is—rife among the traditional officialdom, and that involvement in corrupt practices is certainly one of the causes of the deposition of chiefs in traditional African societies. Thus, Sarbah notes that if "the family find he [i.e., the chief] is misappropriating, wasting or squandering the ancestral fund, it is to their interest to remove him at once and appoint another in his stead."[21] And J. B. Danquah also observes: "Unwarranted disposal of stool property, including land, is another great cause for deposition."[22] Also, if a chief "squandered" a substantial part of the public revenue "in unimportant matters,"[23] he would be removed. And what applies to the chief applies also to the head of a lineage (i.e., a councillor) inasmuch as he too is a trustee of the property of the lineage. As regards the councillor, Sarbah observes that "a councillor holds his office for life, but, should he be guilty of treason or *receiving bribes to pervert justice*, he can be suspended or dismissed."[24]

As in the electoral systems of modern democracies, the election of the chief presents an occasion for prospective candidates to distribute gifts and bribes to the electors, who are also members of the royal lineage (see chapter 4, section 2.1.1). Bribes are also distributed by prospective candidates to the electors to remove an allegedly incompetent or irresponsible chief. Thus, both election (or, "enstoolment," enthronement) and deposition (or, "destoolment") of the chief are occasions for political corruption. The prospective candidates, if they succeeded in becoming chiefs, would shower favors on their benefactors. The consequences of corruption involved in the election of the chief are considered so socially and politically disruptive that the Confederacy Council of Asante, one of the best organized and administered states in precolonial Africa, adopted a committee recommendation to the effect that "Any member of Royal Family who contests, offers, or accepts any bribe in any form in any enstoolment case shall be guilty of an offence and shall be struck off the roll of the Royal family and shall forfeit his right of succession to the Stool."[25]

The institution of sanctions is not the only attempt that has been made to check the growth of political corruption. A practice of the precolonial political system was that the chief was not, as noted in chapter 4, section 3, allowed to own personal property; nor could he "engage in trade to enrich himself."[26] Even though this practice started undergoing some changes at the beginning of the twentieth century,[27] the rationale behind the denial of private property to the chief was to preempt conflict of interest, conflict between his managing his own private property and his managing the property of the state, between his taking care of his private interests and his taking care of the interests of the public, a conflict that often lies at the root of political corruption. The practice was thus intended to stave off corruption. But whether or not the intentions of the practice could be achieved would depend not only on what an incumbent chief would regard as sufficient resources for the maintenance of his regal office but also on his moral virtues and lifestyle.

In the traditional African society the offer of gifts to people in authority or in some respectable position in society—social, political, or religious—is a common feature. It can hardly be denied that at least some of these gifts, as mentioned in the preceding section, would be bribes given personally to public officials in anticipation of a reciprocal favor, direct or indirect, immediate or subsequent.

The traditional African society is thus not free from political corruption. But corruption by public officials incurs the displeasure of the people, for it is regarded as morally wrong. Those who commit it are removed from office or made to suffer some form of public disgrace.

3. The Moral Circumstances of Political Corruption

Now, having shown in section 1 that the political system of a state, certain features of its social structures, its economic circumstances, the inadequacies of the law and its enforcement may all be considered factors or conditions that can lead a public official to involve himself in political corruption, I wish to assert that political corruption is essentially or fundamentally a *moral* problem; it is a moral pollution of officialdom as well as of the wider society. In the event of the public discovery of scandalous acts of official corruption, people talk, in anguish and disbelief, about both the decline of societal morals and the low status (or lack) of moral virtue, integrity, and character of our public officials; thus, people generally do not rationalize the incidence of political corruption by referring to the political system of their society as such, or the economic circumstances of the accused or convicted public official. They would rather rail against the moral character of the public official. The moral posture or response of the general public in the event of the discovery of acts of political corruption, in my view, has justification.

Political corruption is so called because it is a kind of corruption that infects (some) individuals holding political or public office, while the victims are *public* fortunes, resources, or interests. But it should more realistically be seen within the context of such concepts as moral weakness, moral responsibility, and virtue (or, good character). The political system or process may be improved, its weaknesses removed; economic situations may improve and the salaries of public officials may be increased; legal institutions may be improved, the powers and activities of law enforcement officers augmented and punishments for convicts of politically corrupt acts increased: yet none of these attempts at dealing with the problem of political corruption will eradicate it or considerably minimize it. That this is so is a matter of common knowledge. In most states governments tinker with the problem of political corruption: some officials indicate, often with inflated rhetoric, that they are decidedly against such corrupt political practices and promise to do something about them and thus to clean the Augean stable. But inevitably before long some—perhaps most—other officials and members of the government also fall victim to those morally unacceptable patterns of public behavior. Greed, avarice, and an inordinate desire for ostentatious living have been allowed to run berserk, blunting the moral visions of people inside and outside the government.

Because moral circumstances do not come to the fore in the causal explanations of the incidence of political corruption, the factor of morality does not feature prominently, either, in the attempts to deal with the problem; how to deal with the moral character of the offending public official has not often formed part of the arsenal of techniques advocated for fighting political corruption. Dobel, however, rightly—in my opinion—sees the need for the cultivation of "civic virtue" and for "moral education."[28] But, as I have said before, it is the political and institutional factors, not the moral, that are almost invariably noted, particularly in the writings of social scientists. Werlin, for instance, thinks that "political reform is the answer to corruption."[29] But, if attempts intended to deal with the problem of political corruption by such measures as changes in the political structure, the institution of fraud detection squads within the public service, the tightening and enforcement of legal sanctions against public officials who commit politically corrupt acts mostly fail to reduce the incidence of political corruption in a significant way, then it makes sense to say that a more serious approach to dealing with the problem must lie somewhere else. That "somewhere else" is, in my opinion, the moral character of the individual public official and his motives for seeking elected public office. I was once told by a fairly senior public official who was seeking election to parliament in a country in Africa: "If I get elected, I would seek an appointment as secretary of trade. If I get it, *man will live well.*" This prospective member of parliament was obviously motivated by nothing but self-interest, a motivation that can be said to reflect his moral character. It must be noted that the economic circumstances of this particular public office seeker were comparatively better than those of many of his compatriots. Armed with this kind of determination to enrich himself and indulge in ostentatious living at the expense of public resources, he would not be stopped by reforms in the political order.

Also, such features as patronage, communal relationships, and kinship and extended family obligations and loyalties, which characterize societies in Africa and elsewhere, could, I have said, give rise to political corruption. There is no guarantee that if these features of a social order are removed, the incidence of political corruption will be reduced. The reason is that some social systems that have not evolved these politically corruptive features also have serious experiences of political corruption. This clearly shows that, even though the roles of legal, social, and political structures are relevant to the causal explanation of the rampant incidence of political corruption, there is nevertheless a more fundamental cause of political corruption. This more fundamental cause is the moral character of the public official as well as of the member of the public who seeks a favor from him or her.

Now, having shown that political corruption is fundamentally a moral problem, the next question is to determine a satisfactory approach to dealing with it. Because of the fundamental and resilient character of the problem, a most satisfactory approach will have to be equally radical: it will require radical or profound changes in the moral beliefs, behavior, and attitudes of both public officials and other members of the wider society. In this connection, many people see the need for an "ethical revolution" as the most satisfactory way to grapple with the problem of political corruption. A former Nigerian president, Shehu Shagari, is said to have launched Nigeria's "ethical revolution" in 1982 and to have set up an "Ethical Revolution Committee."[30] I find this notion of moral (ethical) revolution interesting and important, and would like to provide an elaborate philosophical analysis of it.

3.1 The Concept of Moral Revolution

There are two essential features of a revolution. These essential or characteristic features relate to the *fundamental* (radical) nature of the changes involved in a revolution and the *newness* of the situations or states of affairs that emerge therefrom. It can correctly be said that these two features adequately define the concept of revolution. It must be noted, however, that in the definition of revolution, the idea of the new is relevant only when that which is supposed to be new is contrasted with, or seen against the background of, the old, that is, against the background of the previously existing situation, order, paradigm, vision. In other words, it is not every use of the word "new" that implies the occurrence of revolution. For instance, in "new school," "new film," "new invention," where "new" means, according to the *Concise Oxford Dictionary,* "introduced for the first time," "of recent origin," the sense of new is different from the sense relevant and applicable to the meaning of revolution. The idea of an *old* order giving way to a new one is crucial to the concept of revolution, including of course moral revolution, a species of it.

Moral revolution is a revolution in morals. But this statement does not say much and requires considerable conceptual unpacking. The attempt to unpack it requires that a distinction be made between two uses or senses of the term "morals" or "morality."

Morality is a set of social rules, values, and norms that guide the conduct of people in a society. It is concerned with people's beliefs about right and wrong conduct and good and bad character. In this definition, two basic approaches or ways of viewing morality can be distinguished. Morality is seen, on one hand, as a system of moral beliefs, values, and ideals. But it is also seen, on the other hand, as involving behavior, attitude, or orientation, that is, the manner of responding to the existing and accepted moral beliefs and rules. Thus, we speak not only of moral rules and prescriptions but also of moral behavior or attitude, meaning a behavior that is in conformity with the accepted moral beliefs and rules; thus, the moral person is one whose attitude or response to moral rules is satisfactory and commendable. These two uses of morality—that is, morality as a system of moral beliefs and rules and morality as consisting of moral attitudes and responses to moral rules—must be kept distinct. (Of course there are other senses of "morality," but I have fastened onto these two senses because my analysis of the concept of moral revolution is structured on them.) The distinction is in fact a distinction between moral *belief* and moral *commitment.* The former, inasmuch as it involves moral facts, is a basis for the latter and prior to it, though it does not determine it; for mere moral knowledge or awareness of moral rules does not, contrary to what the Greek moral philosophers thought, necessarily insure the right and expected moral response or moral behavior.

3.1.1 Substantive Moral Revolution. Now, the two senses of morality logically lead to two conceptions of moral revolution, which can thus be defined as fundamental changes either in the moral beliefs, values, and ideals of a society or in the attitudes and responses of individuals in a society to that society's moral beliefs and values. The first kind of moral revolution, which I call "substantive" moral revolution or moral revolution in the substantive sense, involves fundamental shifts in the existing moral paradigms or moral conceptual schemes and the adoption of new ones. This kind of moral revolution insists that the old moral order or scheme radically change and yield place to a new order.

Moral revolution of this kind is a facet of moral change. This is not to say of course that every kind of moral change constitutes moral revolution in the substantive sense. A moral change may be superficial, skimming over but not profoundly affecting the existing basic moral structure. On the other hand, a far-reaching moral change that affects the existing moral structure in a fundamental way can appropriately be described as moral revolution. A moral revolution in the substantive sense, then, involves fundamental changes in the moral beliefs, values, and ideals of a people. But not only that: it also involves the inauguration of new moral paradigms and, consequently, the replacement of the old.

Within this definitional framework, it is pretty clear that the morality that Jesus Christ sought to introduce in the New Testament was revolutionary. The old morality of "An eye for an eye, and a tooth for a tooth" was to be replaced by that of turning the other cheek; the old morality of "loving your friends while hating your enemies" was to be replaced by that of loving your enemies and praying even for those who persecute you; the old morality of doing good to someone in expectation of a good turn was to be replaced by a new morality of doing good for its own sake, that is, of performing generous acts without expecting a good turn. Within the socioethical context in which Jesus was presenting or issuing his moral prescriptions and ideals, one would notice that he was striking a new moral chord. In that context the moral values of universal love, mercy, forgiveness, long-suffering, doing good for its own sake, and others were new and constituted fundamental changes to the old Judaic values of vengeance, retribution, expressions of hatred and cruelty toward one's enemies, and limited demonstration of love. Thus, in that context, the morality of Jesus was revolutionary.

As it was with Jesus and the Judaic morality, so it was with Muhammad, founder of the Islamic religion, and the old nomadic Arab morality. For there is a great deal of evidence that in the Quran Muhammad was preaching a new morality, generally subversive of the old pre-Islamic moral values or practices. This new morality is of course a dimension of the corpus of commands and religious truths said to have been revealed to him by God. The moral virtues of generosity and hospitality were, to be sure, in existence in pre-Islamic Arabia; but they were narrowly conceived, for the practical demonstration and application of them did not extend beyond the confines of the tribe, beyond, that is, the ties of kinship.[31] Thus the tribe, rather than the individual—that is, any individual—was thought of as the locus of human values. Muhammad, however, perhaps as part of his religious teachings, insisted that the practice of such values be extended to all people irrespective of their tribal affiliations. In so doing, Muhammad can be said to have introduced fundamental changes in the conception of the moral law hitherto held by the Arabs. He introduced to his contemporary Arabs the concept of a universal moral law. This was something new on their moral horizon; it was a new moral ideal. Muhammad also introduced far-reaching changes in the moral rules regarding sex and marriage. He eliminated vengeance and retaliation, which were outstanding ingredients in the moral sauce of the pre-Islamic Arabs, and replaced them with the morality of forgiveness and compassion. The prohibition against gambling, drinking wine, and taking interest (that is, on loans) constituted, in the words of a foremost scholar of Islamic law, "the clearest *break* with ancient Arabian standards of behavior."[32]

Thus, because Jesus and Muhammad brought about fundamental shifts in the existing moral paradigms of their times, both can be said to have effected substantive moral revolution. The new moral orders they instituted or tried to institute may be said to be offshoots of the religious revolutions in which they were involved; but perhaps it may be more correct to regard these new moral orders as inevitable concomitants of the religious revolution: the creation of a new religious world would unavoidably require a new morality adequate to it.

But substantive moral revolution may be enmeshed not only in radical changes in the religious weltanschauung but even more markedly in radical changes in sociopolitical revolution, in the basic transformation of the existing sociopolitical structure. The reason is that every sociopolitical revolution is basically a *moral* issue (even though a moral revolution need not be a sociopolitical issue). The ultimate impulse to a sociopolitical revolution can generally—perhaps invariably—be said to be moral: concern for human interests and welfare. Among the motivating factors of a sociopolitical revolution the moral generally stand out: sociopolitical revolutionaries vehemently protest against widespread official corruption, the self-aggrandizement of rulers and public officials, the glaring social injustices and economic inequalities, the concentration of the wealth of the nation in the hands of a few to the detriment of the well-being of the broad masses of the population, and so on. Such undesirable patterns of behavior can insinuate themselves into the morals of a society, in the sense that those who believe and practice them do not see anything wrong with them. It is surely the avowed aim of sociopolitical revolutionaries to demolish such moral beliefs and practices and to establish new ones, supposedly adequate to the realities of the new social world intended to be created.

Substantive moral revolution may be a genuine response to the inadequacies of the existing moral beliefs and values. Such a response may be a conscious one, when it is authored or produced by an individual or a group of individuals disillusioned and disenchanted with the conventional morality produced by the sociopolitical system to which they belong because they consider it inadequate to new social realities. A radically new morality may form part of the corpus of revealed religious beliefs that are themselves revolutionary; it may be a concomitant of a sociopolitical revolutionary process.

But a substantive moral revolution may be an unconscious process, produced not by an individual or a group of individuals at a specific time as such but may result from far-reaching changes in socioeconomic circumstances. An individualist ethic, for instance, may be fostered in the wake of the growth of mercantilism and the transition from, say, nomadic to settled life or agrarian to industrial life, to replace a previously existing social or communal ethic. It may be supposed that under the impact of socioeconomic factors such as urbanization, the growth and development of commercial and capitalist economy, and the problems of providing for basic needs in a modern world, there can be a gradual, unconscious drift toward some form of individualism in societies that were hitherto communal and practiced a social morality. The pursuit of self-advancement and the fulfillment of basic needs may now tend to come first, while the pursuit of the conditions to satisfy the needs of the wider clan and society may come second. Earlier, it was the other way round. A new social world appears, and with it the emergence of some form of individualist ethic to replace the old social morality. The remarkable thing here is that all such changes that fundamentally affect the existing moral values and ideals take place without the generality of the population being conscious of them. But they do occur because the existing moral visions tend no longer to be adequate to the new social realities. The old moral imperatives lose their resilience and consequently fail to assert their grip on the moral consciousness of the people. Thus, a substantive moral revolution may be consciously undertaken; but it may also occur gradually without people being conscious of it.

There are some features of the traditional African system of values that would, in the interest of the progress and success of the politics of the new African nation-state (a heterogeneous state), need to undergo profound changes by way of substantive moral revolution. An entirely new morality with respect to attitudes toward government and public property and resources, and hence toward public office, will need to be created. People will have to be morally weaned from the influences of communocultural loyalties that obscure and subvert devotion and commitment to the national political community. A new national political morality that considers it totally morally unacceptable to use one's official position to obtain jobs for members of the extended family will need to be put in place. In other words, a new conception of loyalty to the state, fashioned and underpinned by new moral values, will need to be created.

3.1.2 Commitmental Moral Revolution. Now, moral revolution can be conceived also in terms of fundamental changes in the attitudes and responses of individual members of a society toward that society's moral beliefs, values, and principles. It involves the adoption of new attitudinal or orientational paradigms with respect to the existing morals; it involves making a new and positive commitment to known and accepted moral rules and principles. Because, in my view, political corruption is invariably the result of the inability of the public official to carry out the moral rules of which he is certainly aware, this kind of revolution is more germane to the problem of political corruption.

When we say a man has weak morals, we are not at all referring to that man's moral values and principles, for it would be quite senseless to describe these as "weak." But what we do mean is that his response to them, that is, his attempts to bring himself to follow those values and principles in particular situations, are feeble. Similarly, when we say a man is without morals, we do not mean that he does not at all entertain or believe in any principles of right and wrong. What we mean is that he utterly fails, sometimes or frequently, to act in conformity with moral principles; he does not live up to them. Again, when the head of a state or some responsible citizen speaks of the "decline in morals" or "decline in moral standards," his utterance shows him as decrying or bemoaning the low level of commitment of his compatriots to the existing moral values and principles of the society. All this indicates, to repeat, the ambiguity in the word "moral," which is used either in the sense of moral beliefs and principles or in the sense of moral attitude. The assumption, in the instance of failure to conform to moral rules, is that the person knows and has accepted the existing moral rules and principles as adequate guides to his conduct. He is therefore expected to behave in conformity with them. It is when he fails to conform that we speak of his having weak morals or being without morals. But what the person would really be experiencing is *moral failure.* Thus, if any fundamental changes are to be made in his morals, they are such changes in his orientation or attitude to the existing moral beliefs and principles as would dispose him to a new and unrelenting *commitment* to them. For this reason, I call this kind of moral revolution "commitmental" moral revolution. Implicit in the foregoing statements is the distinction between moral belief and moral commitment.

The logic of what I have said so far in my analysis is this: while from the perspective of substantive moral revolution the existing moral beliefs and values are explicitly held as inadequate to a particular social reality, they are from the perspective of commitmental moral revolution implicitly considered adequate. From the latter perspective, however, what are, or should be, considered inadequate or unsatisfactory are our *practical responses and attitudes to the existing moral values and principles.*

One of the central problems of our moral life is the problem of moral weakness, that is, the problem of knowing the right thing and yet doing the wrong thing, of acting against our better judgment: for example, accepting or giving a bribe when we know it is wrong, the problem of our failing to bring ourselves to do something we know or strongly believe to be right. We are all familiar indeed with the phenomenon of moral conflict, the conflict between moral belief and moral commitment, the difficulty in carrying out a moral decision. The ancient Greek philosophers called this problem of moral conflict *akrasia:* moral weakness, weakness of will, incontinence.

Philosophical investigation into the phenomenon of moral conflict or the relation between moral knowledge and action in the experience of the West may be said to have been broached by Socrates twenty-four hundred years ago, when he argued that knowledge is a necessary and sufficient condition for attaining virtue and hence for doing the right thing. Knowledge, for Socrates, is an insurance against wrong-doing; so that if a person knows that X is wrong he would refrain from doing X. For the ancient Greek philosophers all wrong-doing is due to ignorance; there is no psychological or mental state to be described as *akrasia,* "knowing the good and yet doing the evil." What is thought to be an acratic (that is, weak-willed) act, then, according to Socrates, is explainable in terms of ignorance of what is right, and of evaluative illusion. Both Plato and Aristotle followed Socrates in maintaining that moral knowledge is the final and irresistible determinant of action. Thus, the Greek philosophers constructed a bridge between moral knowledge and action that appeared to them easily crossable. Human experience, however, shows that getting across the bridge is not easy at all.

Within the framework of the arguments of the ancient Greek philosophers regarding moral weakness, commitmental moral revolution can be effected either by augmenting the amount of moral knowledge we possess or by giving our moral knowledge a more precise and coherent formulation (as Aristotle in fact does), or most probably by both. But this would not do. Moral knowledge consists either in the knowledge of the definitions of moral concepts or in the awareness of universal moral rules and principles. But neither sense of moral knowledge bears within itself the power to carry out the *practical* implications of the consciousness of moral rules. This is because in a particular moral situation what is required is the application or the obeying of a moral rule, not the mere awareness of it. A man may know and may even accept a universal moral rule such as that it is wrong to collect bribes in the course of the performance of his official duties. But he may fail to apply this universal rule to a particular moral situation he is confronted with: he is thus not able to effect the transition from knowledge to action. Thus, the supposedly easily crossable bridge constructed by the ancient Greek philosophers between knowledge (or, belief) and action has indeed turned out to be an equally easily collapsible bridge. A commitmental moral revolution, then, can be effected neither by augmenting the compendium of our moral knowledge nor by making most acute our awareness of universal moral rules. The reason is that commitment to action is definitely not a concomitant of moral knowledge or consciousness of moral rules, even though knowledge of moral rules is of course very important in moral behavior.

That commitmental moral revolution cannot be accomplished within the structure of ancient Greek moral thought is due very largely to the fact that its heightened intellectualistic (or, rationalistic) character attributes to the intellect functions that really belong to other faculties. For it places a higher premium on the intellect at the expense of the will, ignoring at the same time such concepts as assent, deciding, intending, conviction, and effort of will—all of which are relevant antecedents of action and are extremely useful in explaining failures to act. Even though all these concepts are relevant antecedents of action, I do not imply by any means that each of them is operative (or, present) in every action. In a particular action situation, some of these concepts may be passed by. But what can never be passed by, I maintain, is the concept of the will. This concept, then, is central and stands out as the most brilliant in the constellation of concepts involved in a belief-action situation. In commitmental moral revolution, the concept of the will is crucial and useful inasmuch as it is most relevant in the whole enterprise of translating our moral convictions, intentions, and decisions into actions.

Yet many philosophers find the concept of the will bizarre, even incoherent, mainly because of the substantive or entitative character supposedly attributed to it by those who believe in its reality and intelligibility.[33] I think that it is possible to deny the will as an entity but *not* as a capacity or ability with which our decisions and intentions are translated into actions. This will enable us appropriately, and without any inconsistency, to use such locutions as "strong-willed," "weak-willed," "strength of will," "weakness of will," "effort of will." When we are faced with obstacles or temptations to do or not to do something, we exercise an effort of will, a certain tenacity of purpose. The exercise, if it is strong enough, may enable us to overcome temptations. One does not have to interpret the will in entitative terms for it to have meaning. It would be enough, it seems to me, to regard the will as some kind of inner motive force, crucially relevant in the attempt to translate our moral intention and decision into action. If the experience of commitmental moral revolution involves, as it does, the ability to carry out our moral decisions with action and to succeed in doing what we know is right and refrain from doing what we know is wrong, then, due recognition must be given to the will as some inner force or capacity indispensable to our decisions and intentions to do something or to refrain from doing something. The failure of a commitmental moral revolution is in fact a failure of the will. Public officials who involve themselves in acts of political corruption do not sufficiently exercise their moral capacities or effort of will.

Now, I have defined revolution, of any kind, in terms of fundamental changes and the adoption or emergence of new paradigms. But with commitmental moral revolution, it will not make sense of course to talk of making fundamental changes in the human will or replacing a will with a new one. So, as regards commitmental moral revolution we would have to talk about the will in different terms. Even though the will cannot be changed as such, it nevertheless can be exercised; its "condition" can be strengthened through sufficient effort to enable it effectively to fulfill its role in commitmental moral revolution. I have defined commitmental moral revolution in terms of fundamental changes in one's attitudes and responses to accepted moral beliefs and rules in the positive direction, and this in turn involves, or rather requires, making the greatest effort of will. It involves, that is, exercising sufficient strength of will or will-power that will dispose one to follow a moral belief or rule with action, with practical commitment; it involves, consequently, replacing an undisciplined response to moral rules with a disciplined response, replacing easy succumbing to temptations to do the wrong thing with gaining mastery over oneself and so overcoming temptation.

Now, having made a distinction between substantive and commitmental moral revolution, I would like, first, to examine the relation, if any, there is between these two kinds or conceptions of moral revolution and, second, to inquire whether the two are of equal importance or status in the world of morality, in our moral practice.

To take the first. It can be said at once that whatever relation there may exist between substantive and commitmental moral revolution, it cannot be said to be a logical one. For fundamental changes in moral beliefs and values do not logically (necessarily) imply fundamental changes in moral attitudes and responses; nor do the latter logically imply the former. Thus, there is no logical connection between the two. But, could there be a causal relation? Does substantive moral revolution have a causal effect on commitmental moral revolution in the sense of bringing it about, and vice versa? It is worth noting that the concern for commitmental moral revolution is predicated on the assumption that the existing moral beliefs and values are adequate, but that what are inadequate and wanting are the appropriate and expectable attitudes and responses to these moral beliefs and values. This being so, the question of commitmental moral revolution causally affecting substantive moral revolution would not arise.

Substantive moral revolution would not necessarily guarantee the creation of new moral attitudes and responses to new moral prescriptions and rules. The law, as I said in section 1, is most likely to be used as an instrument for forging new moral attitudes. While such institutional arrangements could be of some use in getting people to obey the moral law, it is most unlikely that the expectable maximum result will be *permanently* achieved. We know for a fact that the existence of the law with its phalanx of punishments and other kinds of sanctions does not by itself make a person moral. Even though it is not my intention to deny the effectiveness of the law in our responses and attitudes toward moral rules and principles, I wonder how lasting this could be. Experience seems to indicate, without doubt, that the use of the law to enforce morality does not produce lasting results: it seems merely to scotch the snake, without killing it.

Yet Sir Patrick Devlin has argued persuasively for the legal enforcement of morals.[34] But one must be hesitant to endorse such a course, because it can hardly achieve any lasting success. A point that was succinctly made by some African chiefs in a family dispute is worth noting: "We have the power to make you divide the crops, for this is our law and we will see this is done. *But we have not power to make you behave like an upright man.*"[35] That is, when it comes to the field of morality, the field of human conduct, when it comes to actually making a man "behave like an upright man," the law becomes virtually powerless. The reason is that, after it has been decreed that doing X is against the law and is punishable by a heavy fine and a long-term imprisonment, it is up to the individual, now in the know of the demands of the law and the consequences of its violation, to take up a definite stand with respect to action X, whether he should do it or not. And here, in the obeying of the law, the exercise of the will is the most relevant factor. In the exercise of the will the law is ineffectual, otherwise we would be involved in a vicious circle. In the final analysis, it would be correct to say that submission to any regulation—be it positive (that is, man-made) law, divine law, moral law, or school rules—requires the active exercise of the human will. Morality in the sense of moral rules and prescriptions can be legislated (some parts of it are already embodied in the positive law); but morality in the sense of moral attitudes or responses can hardly be so legislated. We enact a law; we do not enact the will to obey the law. Thus, whatever the relationship is between law and morality—and there certainly is some relationship between them, for after all it is a fact that certain spheres of morality and the law overlap and that their demands quite often coincide—that relationship is not such as can be made the basis for the use of the law as an instrument for enforcing moral behavior. I realize, however, that this is a controversial point.

But it must be borne in mind that the successful operation of the socio-legal institutions of a society requires the demonstration of very high moral standards in those men and women who run them. If those who are to run our public institutions, if those public officials who are to enforce the prescriptions of the law, are themselves corrupt to the core, how can the law itself be enforced? If the answer to this question is that we should bring sanctions against those guilty public officials, one may retort by further asking, how can this be effectively done when the officials who are to impose those sanctions are themselves equally corrupt? Do you, then, recruit a new set of officials? And, how can the probity and virtuous character of the new recruits be assured or guaranteed? *At every turn, then, the ultimacy of the moral is clear and insistent.* Thus, it seems to me that there is no real guarantee that substantive moral revolution will lead to, or open the way for, commitmental moral revolution. The causal relation between the two kinds of moral revolution, which, if it exists at all, goes from the direction of substantive to commitmental moral revolution, appears, then, to be tenuous and fragile.

The significance of the role of the will that has been underlined in the preceding discussion is germane to the second inquiry I wish to undertake as I come to the end of the chapter. That inquiry concerns the relative importance of the two kinds of moral revolution. It seems to me that in our moral life and practice commitmental moral revolution is more important and overriding. It is most likely that rational human beings, who know their basic wants and desires and the conditions for the satisfaction of these wants, will choose to establish a social system that will conduce to the realization of those conditions. One outstanding condition is the evolving of the appropriate set of moral values and principles. Not only do some of the adopted moral values and ideals impinge upon and underpin the laws made by society from time to time but, because of the fundamental force they do exert on human relationships, they also find their way into the texture of the constitution—the basic law of the governance of society.

The point I am at pains to make is that rational beings, even though they sometimes think and act irrationally, will nevertheless produce a moral system that will accord with their conceptions of the good life and the good society. Yet, granted that moral values, ideals, and principles, having been fashioned on the anvil of rationality, have been adopted by the rational society as reasonable and adequate as a guide to the conduct of the members of the society; granted that the rational society knows its needs and desires and the conditions under which these can be met; and granted that these values, or some of them, have been enshrined in the preambles of political constitutions; granted all this: it does not at all follow that the rational ethics so produced and adopted will necessarily generate practical commitment. Rationality can produce a system of rationally acceptable moral beliefs, values, and principles; but it cannot, just on that score, also create the strength or effort of will that is indispensable in the practical observance of moral beliefs and principles. The reason is that being rational is conceptually distinct from being moral—in the sense of acting in conformity with moral rules. Thus, even when it is granted that rational beings will choose or evolve a coherent and viable system of moral principles and rules, the problem of following these beliefs and principles with practical commitment will still stare us in the face.

It should be clear, then, that while substantive moral revolution will not be necessary—will not have to be undertaken—if the existing moral beliefs and values are held, or should be held, as adequate, commitmental moral revolution, as a means of counteracting people's moral weaknesses, will be necessary, since for most people the gap between moral beliefs and moral commitment is a yawning gap. It seems that the most adequate means of bridging the gap and ceasing to pay lip service to our moral beliefs and principles is to recognize the need to adopt completely new attitudes and responses, in the positive direction, to those moral principles.

All this seems to suggest that even though the commitmental and substantive are both species of moral revolution, commitmental moral revolution nevertheless appears *more* fundamental than substantive moral revolution inasmuch as moral life is an enterprise more of *practice* than theory or mere knowledge of moral beliefs or rules. Thus, however or in whatever manner our moral beliefs, principles, ideals, and standards come about, the basic, real, and most pressing problem is how to succeed in conducting our lives in conformity with the accepted moral principles and standards.

Conclusion

I have pointed out in this chapter that political corruption—the misuse of one's political or official position for personal ends in violation of accepted moral or legal norms—is a common feature of the functioning of governments in all human societies. Corruption is a universal phenomenon despite the fact that it is universally abhorred. There is obviously a need to look for an adequate explanation for this phenomenon. Most social scientists, I said, seem to think that political corruption arises from the weaknesses and shortcomings of the political and legal systems as well as from the economic situations of people. They put little, if any, stress on the moral circumstances of corruption, though morality clearly lies at the core of the phenomenon of political corruption. Thus, for me, political corruption is fundamentally a moral problem. Even though it can be said that improvements in the political system and in the enforcement of the law against corruption may result in the reduction of the incidence of politically corrupt acts, the effects would be limited; and it is unlikely anyway that all the weaknesses or imperfections in human institutions can be removed. The morally weak-willed public officials and others would take advantage of the loopholes in the legal and political institutions. The therapies prescribed by most social scientists, therefore, appear to be mere nostrums. For after all, people cannot be compelled to be honest. I have argued therefore that the effective enforcement of the law will ultimately depend on the probity or moral uprightness of the law enforcement agents who, as individual persons, are expected to display high standards of moral character and behavior. This fact indicates the ultimacy of the *moral* not only in the understanding or explanation of the phenomenon of political corruption but also in the attempt to deal with it realistically. A realistic approach to dealing with the problem of corruption is radically to change the attitudes and responses of people, including public officials, to accepted moral (and legal) rules and prescriptions: this radical change in moral responses is what I call commitmental moral revolution.

The public official who indulges in acts of political corruption knows that what he is doing (or, intends to do) is wrong, both legally and morally. This is the reason why he pursues those corrupt acts in a clandestine manner. In a situation where he is tempted to commit a politically corrupt act, he faces a moral conflict: whether to fulfill his personal interest by indulging in an act of political corruption or to refrain from doing that and in this way fulfill his public responsibilities. It is true, of course, that not every one who has the opportunity for corrupt advantages seizes it; but some do succumb to the temptation occasioned by the opportunity. Political corruption, then, is—or results from—the moral incapacity not only of public officials but also of other members of the society to commit themselves to behavior that will not harm the public or common welfare. Thus, if we are really serious about reducing political corruption considerably, to minimal and negligible levels, we would need more than the devices of the law, improvements in people's economic situations, and reforms in political structures. We would need to come to grips with matters of personal integrity, character, and honesty with respect to public officials who happen to be in the position where they can involve themselves in politically corrupt acts as well as to members of the general public who, in seeking favors from public officials, tempt them and make (some of) them succumb to temptation. Both public and nonpublic persons would need to steel their moral wills to avoid involving themselves in acts of political corruption.

8

Tradition and Modernity

It may be said that from the point of view of a deep and fundamental conception of tradition, every society in our modern world is "traditional" inasmuch as it maintains and cherishes values, practices, outlooks, and institutions bequeathed to it by previous generations and all or much of which on normative grounds it takes pride in, boasts of, and builds on. The truth of the assertion that every society in the modern world inherits ancestral cultural values implies that modernity is not always a rejection of the past, but it also casts serious doubts on the appropriateness of perceiving tradition and modernity as polar opposites. The polarity derives from a different sense given to the notion of the traditional—depicted by sociologists and anthropologists as rural, agrarian, prescientific, resistent to change and innovation, and bound by the perception of its past. By contrast, the modern is characterized as scientific, innovative, future oriented, culturally dynamic, and industrial and urbanized. It is the alleged contrast that grounds the polarity between the traditional and the modern—between tradition and modernity.

The contrast, however, is based on some false assumptions. Historical inquiries would show that even though the society characterized as "traditional" has a large proportion of beliefs and practices inherited from the past, it nevertheless does experience varieties of changes over time. It is undoubtedly true that the rate at which changes take place in one human society is slower, perhaps much slower, than that in another society. But this does not mean that the society with a much slower rate of development or change is static or unchanging or resistant to change or resiliently tradition-bound. A less rapid rate of change is still a change. No human culture is absolutely unchanging, totally refusing to take advantage of possible benefits that often accompany encounters between cultures. Absolute changelessness is therefore impossible and cannot be considered a necessary condition of any human society. In other words, the traditionality of the tradition-centered society is, to my mind, often overstated. Urbanization is an offshoot of the process of societal growth. In the final analysis, then, it all appears to be a matter of degree of change or development. But it is undeniable that societies that are called "modern" also do recognize traditions (at any rate, some of them) as relevant, not as obstacles, to their development. The enduring elements of the traditions of modern societies can, at least in some forms, be traced far back into their past. The history of modern Europe reveals that, although Western (or, European) modernity had by the nineteenth century reached some advanced level, it nevertheless even at that time contained medieval elements.[1] This supports the conviction that "traditional" elements are not necessarily at variance with "modern" elements (see section 5).

It is interesting to note that, because of the tradition/modernity polarity that has influenced the thinking and analysis of some scholars, when a society seems to be sloughing off some of the elements of its past cultural life in the process of its change and development, this phenomenon is described as "the passing of traditional society."[2] Yet the traditional society that is said to be passing or to have passed would, nevertheless, retain many of its traditions intact or unscathed, despite the palpable changes that may have taken place within it. This should suggest that the central, fundamental, and persistent meaning of "traditional" is that which comes down or is inherited from the past and becomes an enduring element in the cultural life of a people. All the other depictions or characterizations of the traditional I refer to are themselves adventitious and tentative. What I consider the deeper and fundamental meaning of "traditional" inspires much of the discussion of this chapter.

I begin by grappling with the following questions: What is tradition? Is tradition distinguishable from culture? How does an idea or a particular cultural practice or value become or ossify into a tradition? How do ideas and values, previously considered alien by a people, find their way into the texture of their culture and thus become part of their tradition? What lies at the basis of different attitudes toward a cultural past? Having grappled with such questions, I then undertake a close normative examination of the traditional ideas, values, practices, and institutions of Africa (drawing examples from the Ghanaian cultural experience) in terms of their relevance to the modern cultural setting. I follow this examination with a look at the meaning of modernity and a discussion of whether modernity is a relative concept and how we judge whether the legacy of the past is worth being given some attention or place within the scheme of things or practices of a present.

1. On the Notion of Tradition

The British philosopher H. B. Acton defines tradition as "a belief or practice transmitted from one generation to another and accepted as authoritative, or deferred to, without argument."[3] The erudite American sociologist Edward Shils also defines it as "anything which is transmitted or handed down from the past to the present."[4] And, in a most recent publication, Samuel Fleischacker defines tradition as "a set of customs passed down over the generations, and a set of beliefs and values endorsing those customs."[5] Ignoring, for the moment, the second part of Acton's definition, which I comment on in due course, we can see that the (roughly similar) definitions provided by these three scholars reflect what is generally considered the meaning of tradition, a meaning that derives from the Latin etymology of the word *traditum:* that which is handed down from the past. The "past" here does not mean the recent past. It refers rather to previous generations, to the times of our forebears or ancestors: thus, a tradition is anything that has endured through generations.

What is not easy to decide, however, is *how long* a practice or belief must last for it to mature or be regarded as a tradition. In the view of Shils, it must last "over at least three generations."[6] I agree. We invariably associate traditions with the hallowed ways, beliefs, and practices of our forebears, and this association suggests a very long span of time. We would not regard a practice or institution that has lasted a mere three decades or so as a tradition. A horizontal line representing the career or fate of cultural products as they pass from generation to generation will help to illustrate some important points about tradition.

G_1 (cv 1–10)	G_2 (cv 2–9)	G_3 (cv 3–9)	G_4 (cv 3–8)	G_5 (cv 3–7; 11–13)	
a	b	c	d	e	e_1

Let "G" stand for "generation," "cv" for "cultural value" (i.e., for any cultural product of a society), while the numbers represent the various cultural values created or accepted and maintained by the various generations. I must point out that G_1 is introduced merely for the purpose of clarifying the issues, for we cannot, strictly speaking, identify any generation of an ongoing society as G_1.

Now, what does this horizontal line tell us? G_1, the "first generation" of a society, created some cultural values, a set of ten of such values (let us use the letter a to represent this set: thus, G_1 created a). The set a does not of course constitute a tradition. We notice that two of the values created by the first generation were discarded by the second generation. But the set of values that remains—let us call it b—would not constitute a tradition either; nor would the set of values that persists through the third generation, that is, c. At G_4, however, the set of cultural values that remains (i.e., 3–8—let us call this set d) could constitute a tradition, having lasted over what can be regarded as a long span of time; so also would the set of values (cv 3–7, to be called set e) handed down to, and preserved at, G_5, having endured through four generations. It must be noted that at G_5 a new set of values (namely, cv 11–13, to be called e_1) is also created. But e_1 cannot form itself into a tradition just yet, not having yet lasted over several generations. If it persisted over generations, it could ossify into a tradition. (A new set of values could of course have been created also at G_2 or G_3 or G_4, but that set will, like e_1, not have the status of a tradition.) It must be noted that, in view of the fact that the rate of change or development differs from one human society to another, the number of practices or products of a culture that are dropped or created in the course of the cultural life of people in different societies will greatly differ. Thus, in a society with a slow rate of change, it might be possible to see the whole set of a at G_2 or even at G_3. But this fact does not affect the conceptual intentions represented by the line.

Several propositions may be inferred from the analysis of the line. One relates to the conceptual or semantic relation between culture and tradition. There is an intimate relationship between the two notions, resulting, perhaps, from the fact that both tradition and culture are socially inherited beliefs and practices that profoundly affect the texture of our lives. Consequently, the two terms are often used interchangeably. Thus, Fleischacker defines culture as "a set of practices and beliefs that persists over several generations."[7] This sounds like his own definition of tradition as "practices—rituals, customs, superstitions—that are passed down . . . from generation to generation."[8] He also says that cultures "can be identified as authoritative traditions."[9] It is clearly indicated by the line, however, that among the cultural products that are created by a society some may not evolve into a tradition, thus losing their alleged or apparent "authoritativeness."

The line may perhaps help to clarify the relation between the two notions and the appropriateness of the interchangeable use of the two terms. It is clear from the line that a (i.e., the set of *cultural* values at G_1) does not constitute a tradition; nor does b. This means that the term "culture" and the term "tradition" do not—or may not—refer to the same thing and may therefore not be used interchangeably. Although each generation of people creates cultural values, whether any of those values will evolve into a tradition is a function of time. A dance form created and enjoyed by the present generation, for example, may or, despite its aesthetic appeal, may not outlive its creators, that is, the present generation; thus there is no knowing whether this particular cultural product will ossify into a tradition. And as long as we do not know whether a cultural product will evolve into a tradition, culture may be said to be distinguishable from tradition. But we notice also that at G_4 and G_5, d and e would have evolved into traditions. At these stages, then, the traditions of a people can be said to be (the same as) the culture, or much of the culture, of the people. At these stages culture and tradition mesh, and the expressions "traditional culture" and "cultural tradition" would make sense. Strictly speaking, however, it would be more correct to say that culture constitutes the content of tradition, that tradition consists of—is the bearer of—those cultural products that have persisted over generations of people.

Even more important, the analysis of the line suggests that we take another look at the definition of the notion of tradition. In the definitions of tradition provided by Acton, Shils, and Fleischacker the expressions "handed down," "passed down," and "transmitted" feature crucially. To say that a belief or practice is handed down to a generation is to say that it is bequeathed to the generation, passed on to it. But what this really means is that the belief or practice is placed at the disposal of the new generation in the expectation that that generation would preserve it. But the preservation of it, in part or in whole, would depend very much on the attitude the new generation adopts toward it and would not necessarily be automatic, as the word "transmit" would suggest. If we look back across the line, we find that some of the cultural values created at G_1 are dropped by subsequent generations, or they simply sink into oblivion—winnowed away by time. Those values were, for one reason or another, not accepted, maintained, or preserved by subsequent generations. This means that the continuity and survival of a pristine cultural product depends on the normative considerations that will be brought to bear on it by a subsequent generation. The forebears—the previous generations—do not "transmit" their cultural creations as such; what they do, rather, is to place them at the disposal of subsequent generations of people. But the subsequent generations may, on normative or other rational grounds, either accept, refine, and preserve them or spurn, depreciate and, then, abandon them. The desire or intention of a subsequent generation to preserve or abandon inherited cultural products often results from some kind of evaluation of those cultural products and the tradition they lead to. Such critical evaluations are essential for the growth and revitalization of cultural tradition. But, remember, the evaluation of tradition, which takes place from time to time, would surely be otiose, meaningless, and irrelevant *if* tradition were *merely transmitted*.

Since that which is placed at the disposal of subsequent generations can be abandoned or rejected and thus can, in consequence, fail to evolve into a tradition, the generally accepted definition of tradition as that which is "handed down" or "passed down" or "transmitted" from generation to generation requires some amendment. A new definition I propose is this: a tradition is any cultural product that was created or pursued by past generations and that, having been accepted and preserved, in whole or in part, by successive generations, has been maintained to the present. (Note that "present" here means a certain, a particular present time, not necessarily *our* present, contemporary world.)

Who, then, are the makers of a tradition? Inasmuch as a tradition consists of cultural products, we could say initially that the makers of a tradition are the creators of those cultural products. But, except with a feeling of hubris, they could not realistically say at the time of their cultural creations that they were establishing a tradition, since it is possible for their creations not to last more than a generation, not to outlive their generation. But to the extent that it may be the desire of subsequent generations that inherit cultural products to preserve, nurture, and make them available for other generations, we could also say that these subsequent generations are to be counted among the makers of a tradition. In the making of a tradition—in fostering the values of a culture to mature into a tradition—then, the role of the latter appears equally, if not more, important than that of the former. For, without the desire of subsequent generations to foster received cultural values—if subsequent generations thought it fit to abandon received cultural values and practices—there would be no tradition.

The role of a subsequent generation in fostering a tradition is not merely to preserve as much of what it has inherited as it considers worthwhile in terms of the ethos and aspirations of a present; it should surely be more than that. The reason is that if the role of fostering is to be most effective, it must be critical; the content of the tradition must be given a critical look from time to time. The critical examination of a tradition is not necessarily intended off-handedly to subvert it root and branch—that would be impossible to do. The purpose of this critical attitude is, rather, to refine the inherited tradition, from the normative perspective of a present generation, in order to make that tradition more presentable to a contemporary cultural palate. A tradition often controls, conditions, or influences the life of a people, and it is appropriate that, for this function of tradition to have the expected salutary effect on the life of the people, it be revitalized: a present generation will have to convince itself that it is satisfied with the entire tradition it has inherited and that the tradition it has inherited constitutes a viable cultural framework for its functioning. This conviction does not of course foreclose the possibility of its adding novel features to the inherited tradition.

Now, the refinement or abandonment of a tradition and the need to revitalize it by adding on new elements are the consequences of two main factors: internal criticism of the tradition undertaken from time to time, and the adoption of worthwhile or appropriate nonindigenous (or, alien) ideas, values, and practices. The causal factors of cultural change (or, transformation of tradition) are, thus, internally—and externally—induced. It would be a safe assumption to make that those cultural values and practices that evolve into tradition were, at the time of their creation, grounded in some historical circumstances, certain conceptions of human society, social relations, certain metaphysical ideas, and other kinds of ideas, beliefs, or presuppositions. That is to say, the beliefs, values, practices, or institutions of a tradition are almost invariably grounded in some conceptions. But the conceptions themselves may not, from the perspective of subsequent generations, have been adequately rationally grounded. Consequently, subsequent generations may discover them to be simply false, inconsistent, morally unacceptable, or inadequate to the realities of their times.

There is no denying, I think, that the inadequacies, shortcomings, or imperfections of a tradition are to be attributed to the limitations of the human intelligence, foresight, and experience. These limitations make it impossible for a generation to see far into the future and so be able to create values, practices, and beliefs all of which will be absolutely free from defects or imperfections and continuously hold the attraction of future generations.

Yet, despite their imperfections, certain features of an inherited tradition persist for generations. It may be that the reason for the persistence of certain features of a received tradition that are considered inelegant is that most people, either out of an irrational deference to pristine values and patterns— out of a desire not to rock the traditional cultural boat that has been kept afloat by time—or out of an intellectual or moral inertia that prevents their conceiving new ways of doing things, would rather conveniently settle in the inherited cultural milieu and be molded by it than to mold it. In the course of time, however, some self-assertive individual moralists, idealists, visionaries, intellectuals, or social reformers, more independent of mind, may emerge, seething with verve and intense desire to deal with the shortcomings of the inherited traditions. These individuals would embark on criticisms of their traditions and might succeed in getting their compatriots to realize the need to get rid of the encumbrances discovered in the received tradition.

The grounds of the criticisms may be several. Some critics may see a tradition (i.e., an element or feature of tradition) as a drag on the kind of progress they envisage for their societies: thus, they see it as dysfunctional; others may see it as discordant with the ethos of a new set of cultural values that a new generation is bent on establishing; others may see it as simply morally unacceptable and argue for its expulsion from the moral or intellectual life of the people; others may see it as not cohering with other parts of the whole tradition; while still others may see the metaphysical foundations of a tradition of beliefs and practices as false or implausible, no longer convincing or credible. The aims of the criticisms may vary, reflecting the attitude of a particular critic to the tradition. Criticisms may be aimed at either refining or modifying a received tradition to bring it more into harmony with the contemporary cultural trends, or at abandoning a tradition altogether because it is seen as good for nothing or as totally out of tune with the contemporary cultural ethos. It must be borne in mind, however, that such critical attitudes will be inspired by a particular critic's perception of the quality or relevance of her own inherited tradition; that is to say, the critical attitudes result from the experience of functioning within the framework of the inherited tradition. Thus, cultural changes that take place in the wake of internal criticisms can—and often do—originate from within the tradition itself. But it must be noted that the criticisms are not aimed at renouncing the entire complex of inherited tradition, only some features of it. The reason is that it is unlikely that the whole legacy of a past can be disavowed—all in one sweep and at one time.

If the criticisms were aimed at renouncing the entire system of a cultural tradition—at the entire legacy of the past (i.e., at the elimination of *d* or *e* of the line)—that would result in a "cultural revolution," a concept I find unintelligible. For, within the framework of a comprehensive (not a truncated) conception of culture—a conception that sees culture as encompassing the *total* way of life of a people—it would hardly make sense to argue for the elimination of that way of life in its entirety, which is what cultural revolution means or should mean. There can surely be radical changes—revolutions, if you like—in some specific aspects of the cultural traditions of a people. Thus, there can be agricultural, moral, industrial, politicolegal revolution; there can of course also be mental revolution, involving radical changes in the mental habits or outlooks of a people. Cultural revolution is none of these, even though that concept, I suspect, is most probably used to refer to radical changes in the mental outlooks of people, that is, as the equivalent of mental revolution. To establish equivalence between cultural and mental revolution, however, is to identify a genus with its species, and that would be a logical error. There are indeed endogenous factors that can give rise to refinement, reform, or total abandonment of *some specific*—certainly not all—features of an entire cultural tradition.

Changes—some of them fundamental—and refinements in the cultural traditions of a people may be brought about also by exogenous (i.e., alien, nonindigenous) causal factors. These factors come into play in the wake of encounters between an indigenous cultural tradition and an alien tradition. It is true that no cultural tradition can claim to be a pure tradition, in the sense of having evolved or developed on its own terms, in total isolation from alien cultural influences. In one way, elements of an alien cultural tradition can be voluntarily assimilated through adaptation by an indigenous tradition; in another, alien cultural elements may be regarded as having been foisted on an indigenous tradition. In the history of the growth and evolution of cultures, the former (i.e., voluntary assimilation) has been a more common and more effective mode of cultural diffusion than the latter. The outstanding character of the former mode of cultural diffusion is its voluntary feature: it allows an indigenous tradition to select such elements from the encountered alien tradition as it considers worthwhile and conducive to the smooth course of its own cultural development. The indigenous tradition would obviously have to consider the alien tradition—some elements of it at any rate—as having something that it does not itself have but that it would consider worth having, even though it is possible for some elements of an alien tradition to turn out to be harmful rather than worthwhile. But in order for the adopted elements of the alien tradition to be most beneficial to an indigenous tradition, the latter will have to shape, assimilate, and appropriate them not only to suit its ideals, purposes, and aspirations but also to function effectively and with success.

The success in appropriating and molding the elements of an alien cultural tradition is determined by the adaptive capacity of the indigenous tradition. It is the exercise of this capacity that will make the adopted elements of the alien tradition meaningful and understandable to the practitioners of the indigenous tradition, establish a real basis for genuine commitment and attachment to the appropriated elements of the alien tradition, and, consequently, enable the users of the indigenous tradition to build on, and thus to contribute to the advancement of, the received elements of the alien tradition. In the absence of an adaptive capacity, the indigenous tradition may absorb the alien tradition without fully appreciating the real implications of the absorption. The consequences will be that the users of the indigenous tradition may not be able to function well in the alien tradition or to participate fully and intelligently in the nuances of the alien cultural tradition and contribute to its advancement. Cultural change based on the adaptation of the appropriated elements of an alien cultural tradition would appear to be more enduring than that resulting from some external imposition, for it would be based on some commitment and on an understanding and appreciation of value.

An indigenous cultural tradition, however, can also come into possession of elements of an alien tradition by having them foisted upon it by the external practitioners of the alien tradition. The imposition immediately deprives the indigenous tradition of the opportunity to appraise and select such elements of the encountered tradition as it would consider worth appropriating. This mode of the acquisition of the elements of an alien cultural tradition is certainly not the most suitable, for a variety of reasons. First, the imposition of an alien cultural tradition will have a damaging effect on the self-perceptions and self-understandings of the recipients of that tradition. Second, the circumstances of the acquisition of the values and practices of an alien cultural tradition would be such that it cannot be predicted for how long the tradition will endure in its new (i.e., the indigenous) cultural environment, since the people upon whom the alien cultural tradition is foisted may not easily or fully appreciate it and may therefore have little, if any, commitment to it. Third, and following from the second, in the forced, nonvoluntary circumstances in which the elements of an alien tradition are introduced to an indigenous tradition, the users of the latter will find themselves absorbed merely in the outward frills of the alien tradition; but not only that: they will also find themselves confused in the pursuit of the practices and institutions of the imposed tradition.

Having said all this, however, it can hardly be denied that any encounter between cultural traditions will result in one tradition borrowing elements from another, whether the appropriation is by voluntary selection and choice or through forcible imposition of some sort.

The phenomenon of cultural borrowing or appropriation has interesting implications for our understanding of the nature of culture and of humankind itself. From the fact that people of a different cultural tradition can appreciate the worth of another cultural tradition and would desire to appropriate at least some elements of it, it seems to follow that there are certain cultural values that human beings, irrespective of their cultural backgrounds, can be said to share in common; for example, technology. Culture is of course an enactment of a human community. And, even though it can be said that it is an enactment initially and immediately for the people who belong to a particular cultural environment, it can be said also that, given our common humanity, it is a creation potentially for humankind as such.

This is the whole basis of the appreciation or borrowing of cultures created by other peoples, even though I do not imply by any means that all peoples will necessarily have to adopt the products of a particular culture. But what this means is that such cultural products are there for the taking by those who may consider it worthwhile to adopt them. A particular cultural creation will thus have two faces: a particular face—when the appreciation of the cultural creation is confined to its local origin—and a potentially universal face—when that appreciation transcends the borders of the environment that created it. The appreciation may be passive—when no attempt is made to appropriate the cultural creation, notwithstanding one's enjoyment of it—or it may be active—when some attempt is made to appropriate the particular cultural creation and allow it to shape life and thought.

Now, what is meant by appropriating an element of a cultural tradition, say, an idea, belief, value, practice or institution? It means accepting it, taking possession of it, and making it one's own. A once alien idea or value that has been accepted by a different tradition as its own is one that will in time be meshed with the endogenous elements of that cultural tradition. This means: what was originally an alien cultural value will, along with the old (i.e., existing) elements of the indigenous tradition, now shape and influence the life and thought of the users of the indigenous cultural tradition; that what was originally an alien cultural value will assume a new character utterly or almost utterly different from that which it may have had at the time of its adoption; and, in consequence, that it will lose its "alienness" from the point of view of its recipients as it enters the indigenous cultural stream and blends with it. By this time it would be irrelevant for the practitioners of the indigenous tradition to ask *whence* that idea or value or practice entered the (i.e., their) tradition and *when*.

Within the framework of the analysis I have made of the notion of tradition and the role cultural borrowing plays in the emergence of a people's tradition, I find it difficult to endorse Appiah's skepticisms about the possibility of identifying some precolonial system of ideas or values of a particular African people as (part of) *their* tradition. Appiah writes: "But the Fanti live on the coast of modern Ghana, and this case allows us to focus on the question whether, in cultures that have exchanged goods, people, and ideas with each other and with Europe (or, in East Africa, with Middle and Far East) for many centuries, it makes sense to insist on the possibility of identifying some precolonial system of ideas as *the* Fanti tradition."[10] I think I have said enough to bring home the point that, because of the historical encounters between different peoples of the world and the cultural borrowing (or, "exchange") that results from those encounters, the tradition (or, cultural heritage) of any people consists of some elements that must have been appropriated from other cultures or traditions but that having been adopted, developed, maintained, modified or refined, and cherished by the recipients (i.e., the borrowers) can be said to have become part of *their* tradition.

To identify an idea or value as part of the cultural tradition of a people is not by any means to imply that that idea or value was necessarily originated by those people; nor is it to imply that a particular set of ideas or values is necessarily distinctive of a people, that it *uniquely* belongs to the tradition of that people. The use of the definite article ("the"), as in the phrase "*the* Fanti tradition," does not necessarily imply that the elements of a people's tradition are all autochthonous in their genesis. As I point out above, originally alien cultural elements that are appropriated and maintained by a people over several generations or centuries can be said by this later time to have become a part of their own tradition: hence the justifiability of such utterances as "*the* Chinese tradition," "*the* European tradition," and so forth. In all such utterances the definite article implies no uniqueness or distinctiveness; nor does it always imply a specifically identifiable origin.[11] Thus, Shils is right, in my view, when he speaks of "the *tradition* of European painting and sculpture" despite the historically acknowledged appropriation of African works of art.[12]

None of the world's great religions sprouted originally out of the metaphysical soil of the West. Christianity—the major religion of the West—was imported there, having originated in the Near East. Accepted by the Western people—who in the Middle Ages became its crusaders and in modern times its missionaries—it took root in their religious culture and became not only the main religion of the West but the foundation of much of its metaphysics, morals, and law. Thus, today it is appropriate, and makes sense, to speak of "*the* Western *Christian* tradition."

If cultural "exchanges" (or, as I prefer to say, cultural borrowing) resulted in the impossibility of identifying a tradition as the tradition of a particular people as such, then, no group of people on earth (save perhaps the first generations of the ancestors of a particular cultural community) could ever be said to have fashioned a tradition that was purely theirs. The phenomenon of cultural exchange or borrowing makes clear that traditions have widespread roots.

Thus, given our knowledge of the historical phenomenon of cultural borrowing and its effect on the development or emergence of some of the elements of the tradition of a people, it would make sense to identify some precolonial ideas as belonging to, as having become part of, the tradition of some African people, *if* those ideas are known to have gained root in the life and thought of those people. This kind of interpretation could redeem the intelligibility as well as the consistency of Appiah's reference to "our own traditions"[13] (even though I am not sure which traditions he has in mind by his use of "our": Asante, Akan, Ghanaian, or African).

Now, as I come to the end of the analysis of the notion of tradition, I wish to make some remarks about two conceptions that have been held about tradition: one is about "the authority of tradition" and the other about the "invention of tradition." The conception of the authority of tradition derives, it seems, from the reverence sometimes—or even often—shown to tradition by its adherents. The reverence manifests itself in the form of appeals or references to the ideas, ideals, beliefs, principles, sayings, achievements, and the general ways of life and patterns of behavior of the forebears who created them. The fact of the appeals and references to tradition, the fact that a present generation, finding it difficult to depart from an inherited tradition, may prefer to yield to its influences, use it as a basis for thought and action, and build on it: all this suggests that tradition has "authority." This is perhaps the reason why Acton regards tradition also as that which is "accepted as authoritative, or deferred to, without argument." He goes on from the definition quoted above to say in fact that a practice or belief becomes a tradition when "it is not questioned by its adherents nor thought by them to need justification." [14] He considers the "authoritativeness" of a tradition to be "clearly the most important feature." [15] Fleischacker also thinks that tradition refers to "the practices and standards of conduct that we accept *unquestioningly when presented to us by our society.*" [16] He says that "traditions are first and foremost the sum total of what is *not* argued in the transmission of knowledge and practice from parents to their children." [17]

Even though we can, I think, admit that traditions are not mere data for rational critique and that they are often experienced as normatively obliga- tory—as exerting an authoritative force—it nevertheless would not be en- tirely correct to say that a tradition is received unquestioningly. A new gen- eration that receives a tradition may—and often will—have to rationally reground it by deploying fresh reasons or arguments, if it considers that tradition worthwhile and so wants to maintain it. Contemporary Western intellectuals, for instance, from time to time are having to justify and ratio- nally defend the democratic or liberal tradition. Their arguments, which may include criticisms of some aspects of the received tradition, help revital- ize the tradition by providing it with new intellectual and ideological moor- ings. A new and serious look by intellectuals of a new generation is surely an important factor in the growth of cultural traditions. So that it is not absolutely true that a tradition needs no justification; nor is it true, as Acton says, that "there is a certain opposition between tradition and reason, just as there is between authority and criticism." [18] My thesis is that tradition can be *rationally* examined from within, by the adherents of the tradition them- selves, even though some of the criticisms that will result from the examina- tion of a particular visionary critic may not be appreciated by her contem- poraries. A critical look at culture is an important factor in preventing cultural sterility. If tradition were absolutely authoritative and not at all sub- ject to questioning or argument, the development of human culture would cease. The development of human culture has reached its present state— whether palatable or unpalatable—because successive or intervening genera- tions have often consciously and purposively argued and maintained ways that have flown in the face of inherited tradition.

Perhaps religion is the most outstanding example of an area of our thoughts, outlooks, feelings, and practices where the authoritative and resil- ient force of tradition can best be felt. Yet, the existence of atheism, agnosti- cism, disavowals of religious beliefs, conversions from one religious tradition to another, sporadic—and sometimes fairly constant—attacks made on a religious tradition even by those supposedly brought up within that tradition: all these phenomena are clear examples of erosion into the authority of inherited religious tradition and make the notion of the "authority" of tradition manifestly suspect.

I would, thus, like to point out that to the extent that a tradition can be rejected or dropped by a present, that is, a later, generation, that therefore the continuity or survival of a tradition depends on the normative weight it can carry with that generation, the influence or power of a tradition is indeed a function of this normativity. In other words, it is a present generation that invests an inherited tradition with (much of its) "authority," out of respect for or conviction of its quality or out of ignorance or out of its inability to produce any better alternative. Thus, tradition does not have an automatic objective authority, one that is self-determined or internal to itself or a feature of itself, standing as an eternal monolith to which successive generations bow in reverent obeisance. Much of the authority an inherited tradition is said to have derives from the evaluative activities of a recipient generation.

We may say that tradition is evaluated from time to time as human beings seek to improve their conditions or situations—moral, social, political, intellectual—for the desire to improve their conditions will often involve having to take a critical look at what has been inherited from the past. We may not *always* be aware that in undertaking certain actions we are in fact subjecting a received tradition to some questioning or that we are assessing it in some fashion. Yet, it would be right to say that whenever we introduce some amendments to the age-old constitution, the political system, the judicial system, or the inheritance system (as was done in Ghana a little over a decade ago to its age-old, and terribly unfair inheritance system), our action will involve evaluation or questioning of tradition. Thus, the fact that tradition can be—and has now and then in the past been—evaluated clearly subverts any absolute authority it is alleged to possess simply by virtue of itself.

Now, on the notion of an "invented tradition." In their book *The Invention of Tradition*, Eric Hobsbawn and Terence Ranger have collected historical essays in which the authors argue that some of the modern cultural symbols, supposed to belong to ancient national traditions, are not ancient at all. In the introduction to the volume, Hobsbawn says: " 'Traditions' which appear or claim to be old are often quite recent in origin and sometimes invented."[19] The term "invented tradition," he explains, "includes both 'traditions' actually invented, constructed and formally instituted and those emerging in a less easily traceable manner within a brief and dateable period—a matter of a few years perhaps—and establishing themselves with great rapidity. The royal Christmas broadcast in Britain (instituted in 1932) is an example of the first; the appearance and development of the practices associated with the Cup Final in British Association Football, of the second."[20] An invented tradition is contrasted with "real"[21] or "genuine"[22] tradition. It is one to which antiquity is ascribed, even though in historical reality it is largely of recent origin. In Ranger's view, "the most far-reaching invention of tradition in colonial Africa took place when the Europeans believed themselves to be respecting age-old African custom. What were called customary law, customary land-rights, customary political structure and so on, were in fact *all* invented by colonial codification." [23]

Now, within the framework of my analysis of the notion of tradition, the concept of an invented or constructed tradition, strictly speaking, is not intelligible. If a cultural value, practice, or institution—one of an endogenous origin—is not old enough to have spanned, or to have been inherited by, several generations, then it cannot, in terms of the illustrative analysis of the line, be characterized as a *tradition*. The status of such a cultural value, practice, or institution will be analogous to e_1 (at G_5) on the line: it is not yet hallowed by time and so cannot qualify as a tradition. Thus, to take Hobsbawn's example, if the royal Christmas broadcast in Britain, instituted in 1932, is not regarded as of long enough duration, then it is not yet a tradition, even though it could become one if it continued to be made. To call it an "invented tradition" is to imply that some people refer to it as a tradition or as their tradition. But such people would simply be mistaken: for, they would be saying that that practice has been around for a considerable length of time, long enough to become a tradition when it has in reality not been so. What I am saying here with regard to the royal Christmas broadcast in Britain will apply also to an African customary law or customary political structure referred to in the quotation from Ranger. Similarly, unless a cultural value, practice, or institution of an exogenous origin has been appropriated and assimilated into another cultural tradition for a very long time, it cannot correctly be described as a tradition of that culture, even though it could become one if it continued to be cherished by that culture.

Invented traditions are thus based on false—because fabricated—claims about the longevity of cultural practices. It is possible for a people to make false or dubious claims about their past; such claims would not constitute real traditions: real traditions are lived, practiced, and held over a very long period of time.

Having said all this, however, I must note, by way of a rider, that a cultural practice, value, or belief, which may be regarded by the historian as "invented" because, according to his inquiries, it has not been around for long enough and is thus of recent emergence, may in fact be a new form of an old practice, value, or belief. A tradition can be transformed, but its central or essential features may persist over many generations and constitute the basis for its identity and recognition. In this connection, the traditions of democratic thought and practice and ideas or beliefs about natural (human) rights are cases in point.

The concept of natural rights, which in this century has taken on the new label of human rights, can be said to have made its debut in Athens in the sixth century B.C. when thinkers of the time came under the conviction that the source of all law was divine or human nature, the latter itself a creation of the divine. The notion of the divine as the source of the law must have been a very old notion; but it received an unambiguous intellectual articulation at the hands of the Greek thinkers of the sixth century B.C. The pre-Socratic philosopher Heraclitus (fl. 510 B.C.) is said to have asserted that "human laws are sustained by the one divine law."[24] Sophocle's *Antigone* (fifth century B.C.) stresses the conception of the law as that which is derived from eternal moral principles, universally valid and, by reason of their divine origin, superior to positive (or man-made) law. In the fifth century B.C., however, the divine status of the laws of the state was called into question. Because of the naturalist and humanist intellectual orientation of a number of the thinkers of the time, especially the Sophists with their rejection of absolute and universal values, a distinction came to be made between *phusis* (nature) and *nomos* (convention, custom, law), between what was rooted in divine or natural process and what was enacted by humans. The distinction implied, of course, that positive laws were not part of the eternal or immutable order of things. Laws *(nomoi)* came to be considered a matter of human agreement, "covenants made by the citizens," as the Sophists Antiphon and Hippias called them.[25] The idea of an absolute moral law constituted the foundation of the ethics of Socrates and Plato. And Aristotle, in his discussion of ethics, draws a distinction between justice "by nature" *(phusikon)* and justice "by convention" *(nomikon)*. Natural justice, he says, "has the same force everywhere and does not depend on what we regard or do not regard as just."[26] The requirements of natural justice would not, it is implied, differ from society to society but would be common to all codes of law. Aristotle's distinction between justice by nature and justice by convention, together with the Stoic philosophers' doctrine of natural law as the universal decrees of the divine reason that are the same for all men, adumbrated the natural law doctrine enthusiastically and relentlessly espoused by medieval European philosophers and theologians such as Aquinas.

Conceptions of natural law or natural justice in time spawned theories of natural rights, which in the seventeenth century held that human beings are endowed with certain eternal and unalienable rights. After the eighteenth century, however, the concept of natural rights fell on evil days precisely because of its source in, or link with, natural law, an idea that had by then become controversial. The skeptical attitudes toward natural law and, consequently, to natural rights stemmed from what was considered a doubtful metaphysic of the divine, or of human nature. But despite the chequered history of the notion of natural rights, it is pretty much the same notion now called human rights, an influential notion that constitutes an important plank in the political or constitutional platform of many nations in our contemporary world.

Like the concept of natural law or natural rights, the political concept and practice of democracy in the West goes far back to ancient Greek tradition and achieved its apotheosis also in the fifth century B.C. in the Funeral Oration of Pericles, the famous Athenian statesman and democrat. "Our constitution is called a democracy," said Pericles, as reported by Thucydides, "because power is in the hands not of a minority but of the whole people. No one . . . is kept in political obscurity because of poverty."[27] In the following century, Plato launched a scathing attack on democracy and defended authoritarian rule. Aristotle also held a low opinion of democracy, describing it as a system in which the poor rule and use their power to oppress the rich. Even though he did not roundly excoriate the political concept of democracy to the extent Plato did, he did not extol it like Pericles either. Yet, despite the enormous intellectual influence wielded by both Plato and Aristotle in their day, their criticisms or negative attitudes toward democracy failed to stop the development of the idea, most probably, I think, because of the virtues and potential of the idea. There have of course been many amendments or refinements of the original idea of democracy down the ages: for instance, while the form of democracy that was practiced in ancient Athens was direct or participatory, indirect or representative democracy is being practiced today. Yet, it is essentially the same idea that has been given different translations, formulations, or articulations since the dawn of what is called the modern world.

The moral and political ideas of human (natural) rights and democracy have gone through some transformation, through some refinements and adaptations in the course of their careers, often with the deployment of different arguments on their behalf. But because their ancestries are clearly known, they cannot be said to be inventions of the twentieth century. What is true of human or natural rights and democracy may be true also of some other values, ideas, or practices. Yet, where there is no awareness of the transformative process that a tradition may have gone through, that tradition may erroneously be thought of as invented and therefore as inauthentic or not genuine. But it may not have been "invented."

Traditions, *if* they are traditions, cannot be invented, for they are not arbitrarily created, referring, as they do, to practices actually *lived,* or ideas and beliefs known to have been actually held, for a very long time. If certain practices that are not traditions are nevertheless, out of ignorance or arrogance, called traditions (and are thus invented), they still are not traditions; statements saying that they are, are simply false. In other words, "invented traditions" are *not* traditions. Strictly speaking, then, that is, in terms of the meaning of the notion of tradition, there will be no such thing as an "invented tradition."

2. Attitudes toward a Cultural Past

The African predicament I mention earlier in this book—the besetting crisis of development in practically all aspects of the African life—generates wonder. Wonder can give rise to philosophical contemplation. But it can also engender attitudes that are not particularly philosophical or rational. For, in times of wonder, in times when situations do not seem to be immediately comprehensible or explicable rationally, human beings sometimes tend to ask all kinds of questions and to look for all kinds of answers or causal explanations. In such situations, some people tend to ground causal explanations in supernaturalism or fantastic metaphysics. Thus, an article in a Ghanaian newspaper in which the late Ghanaian scholar Paul Ansah seeks to reflect on the African predicament is titled, "Is Africa Accursed or Bewitched?" [28] He says no. And that answer, to me, is appropriate. For there is no need or justification to take refuge in supernatural or fatalistic metaphysical causal explanations for phenomena, such as the African predicament, that can be causally explained in rational terms, that is, by exploring the underlying reasons. The reasons or causes of the African predicament may be legion, but here I would like to focus on one main reason, regarded by many people as the root cause of all of Africa's woes: the (alleged) neglect or denigration or subversion of the traditional cultural values of African societies in matters of development and the creation of African modernity. This, to some people, stands out most brilliantly in the galaxy of causes leading to the African predicament in the postcolonial era. And, to arrest further decline in the African life, they would advocate a return to the cultural past of Africa. Thus, N. K. Dzobo urges a return to Africa's cultural past: "Sankofa is therefore a necessary journey into the past of our indigenous culture, so that we can march into the future with confidence and with a sense of commitment to our cultural heritage." [29] *Sankofa,* meaning to return for it, to go back for it (in the Akan language of Ghana), is thus a philosophy of cultural revivalism or cultural renaissance. Dzobo's statement expresses what to my mind is an extreme position.

Now, the consciousness of a people of their cultural past, that is, of the cultural values, practices, institutions, and achievements of their forebears, evokes diverse, even opposing, sentiments among them. For, while some of them, with nostalgic sentiments, would, as we have seen, argue for and urge the revival of the indigenous cultural past, others may evince totally negative attitudes—attitudes almost disdainful and condemnatory of most, if not all, of the inherited ancestral cultural values and practices. The negative attitudes may tend to be iconoclastic: bent on advocating the abandonment of the entire ancestral cultural values, beliefs, practices, and institutions.

The cultural revivalists and the cultural antirevivalists both of course deploy arguments—provide reasons—to bolster their positions. The arguments of the revivalists would include the following five elements.

First, the revival of a sense of commitment to a people's cultural heritage is called for because, it is argued, this will serve as the basis of the search for cultural identity and cultural pride. The intention is to emphasize that the cultural products of the past (i.e., their art forms, their values, institutions, and social, ethical and political beliefs) are as worthwhile as those of other cultures, and that these can—and should—constitute the cultural context within which an individual member of the society must function. The cultural identity of a people, to be achieved, it is hoped, through cultural revivalism, is the basis of their unity as a people. It is also the basis of their effort or vision to create authentic values for the future, their perception of reality, their understanding of themselves, and their shared apprehension and interpretation of societal experiences. Furthermore, there is the assumption that the revival and development of the cultural heritage of a people will be a springboard for making original contribution to global civilization by developing the possibilities of one's own culture.

Second, the revival of a people's cultural heritage, it is argued, will lead to mental liberation. The most enduring effect of the subjection of a people to colonial rule is most probably on the thinking patterns of the subjected (colonized) people. Colonial rule makes the subjected people intellectually servile to the system of ideas and values introduced to them by the colonial rulers, making them think, almost invariably, in terms of the conceptual systems of the colonial rulers that they have come to know and absorb. It places the subjected people on an intellectual or ideological leash from which they are unable, or do not, for some reason, see the need, to release themselves. In the process, so argues the revivalist, colonial rule infects the subjected people with a certain mental outlook, a certain pattern of thinking. This pattern of thinking has come to be dubbed "colonial mentality" and to be regarded as a negative intellectual attribute. For the mentality of the person infected by this kind of thinking is supposed to have been skewed under the influence of the colonial thought categories, resulting in the tendency to regard foreign cultural products as of much greater worth than those of the indigenous culture. The indigenous cultural products are in fact spurned by the individuals with colonial mentality; some individuals even, unashamedly, show aversion to speaking the local languages. The defenders of the philosophy of cultural revivalism are concerned with effecting the release of the mind from the cultural or intellectual leash and the concomitant casting away of the self-demeaning garb of colonial mentality along with the reorientation of the mind in the direction of positive, or at least unbiased, evaluation of the indigenous cultural products.

Third, cultural revivalism may also be seen as a critique of the present forms of life of the erstwhile colonized people that are considered degenerate and hollow, having resulted, the revivalist would say, from both the wholesale, cavalier acceptance of alien cultural values and the neglect of the indigenous, traditional values. There is a conviction that the regeneration of the present can come only through the evocation of the past indigenous cultural values and institutions.

Fourth, there is a conviction on the part of the revivalist that the failures and frustrations in the attempts to make progress in efforts at development are attributable to the neglect of the values of the African people and, consequently, their having to operate alien systems to which they have no intellectual, ideological, or emotional attachments. This fact has generated the desire to explore an alternative model of development, one that is animated by the ethos of the traditional system of values, and to try to fashion the future in terms of the spirit of the past. The arguments of the cultural revivalists here are, in the main, that the African culture should be the basis of development in the modern world, that modernization should proceed by building on Africa's cultural traditions, that the resources of tradition should be harnessed to the modern goals, methods, and processes of development, and that the traditional can be integrated with the modern.

Fifth, it is the conviction of the cultural revivalist that the development of the cultural traditions of the component communocultural groups of a new independent nation-state will contribute to national integration and thus to nation-building. The basis of the conviction is that it would be more appropriate and fruitful to find ways of integrating the common elements in the cultural products of the various cultural groups and elevating them to the status of the national, notwithstanding the "ethnic" origins of those products. In this way, some basis of national cultural understanding and unity would emerge.

These arguments of the cultural revivalist are legitimate, powerful, arguments that I will examine critically in the course of the chapter.

The arguments of the antirevivalist are, simply, that traditional cultural values cannot be accommodated by the ethos of the modern scientific culture and so cannot be reconciled with it, and that, if Africans are to "catch up" with the advanced, industrialized countries of the world, they must abandon a great part, if not the whole, of their cultural heritage, which is prescientific and can boast only of primitive or simple technology. Let me here refer to the views of two African philosophers, Marcien Towa from Cameroun, and Paulin Hountondji from Benin, both of whom denounce any appeal to the past.

For Towa, any attempt to resuscitate the cultural values of the African past would be irrelevant to the present goals and concerns of the African people. Thus, he writes: "An original African philosophy torn from the dark night of the past could not be, if it ever existed, but the expression of a situation that was itself in the past."[30] A past situation should not, in his view, be resuscitated. Furthermore, he says:

> The desire to be one's self immediately leads to the proud reappropriation of one's past, because the essence of self is no more than the culmination of its past; however, when the past is examined and scrutinized lucidly, dispassionately, it reveals that contemporary subjugation can be explained by reference to the origins of the essence of the self, that is to say, in the past of the self and nowhere else.[31]

Towa implies here that the African cultural past would (or, should) have (ideally, normally) constituted the basis of the African identity in the modern world but for the fact that the "essence" of that past was such as could easily be subjugated (that is, through the European colonial conquest). The foundations of a culture that would so easily be overpowered by an invading culture must, he would say, be weak indeed. Given such historical circumstance, what, Towa might ask, would be the point in resuscitating the values of such a culture? Any attempt to do so will not be worth our while. What will be worth our while to pursue, in his opinion, is the cultivation of European science and technology—themselves the result of the pursuit of rationality—that made the subjugation and domination of Africa by Europe very easy. Of course no one will disagree with the recommendation to cultivate science and to practice rationality. (But, one may ask, does the cultivation of science and technology definitely require an unrelenting renunciation of the entire cultural past of a people? Most people, I think, will say no. Military and political weakness or failure may demand or even mandate changes or improvements in aspects of a culture, but not necessarily the renunciation of all aspects of the culture.)

Yet, in a later work, Towa realizes that there was within the African past itself a rational ethos attested to not only in ancient Egyptian thought (appropriately considered African by him) but also in the African traditional folktale, which he regards as embodying the critical spirit. He acknowledges that a modern philosophical enterprise in Africa, for instance, can be established on such a tradition of critical thought.[32] This means surely that something worthwhile can be salvaged from the African cultural past. Thus Towa evinces an attitude of ambivalence, if not straightforward inconsistency, in his perception of the relevance of the values of the inherited tradition of Africa for fashioning an African modernity.

The Beninois philosopher Paulin Hountondji exhibits similar ambivalence and confusion in his perception of the status of the African cultural tradition in the modern circumstances of the African people. Denying the existence of philosophy in the African tradition, he says of those who want to argue its existence, the African ethnophilosophers:

> They have not seen that African philosophy, . . . like African culture in general, is before us, not behind us, and must be created today by decisive action. Nobody would deny that this creation will not be effected *ex nihilo*, that it will necessarily embrace the heritage of the past and will therefore rather be a recreation. But this and simple withdrawal into the past are worlds apart.[33]

These words are as bizarre and incomprehensible as they are incompatible.[34] Hountondji does not explain in what sense African culture "is before us," yet to be created—an enterprise that will have to involve "the heritage of the past." It is not clear whose "heritage of the past" he has in mind. The context seems to indicate that the heritage of the past is a reference to African culture. But if this is so, how can it be said—and does it make sense to say—that African culture "is before us"? And, does it make sense to recreate that which is in the future, that which is before us? On the other hand, if recreation—an enterprise he says will not be effected ex nihilo—makes sense and can therefore be undertaken, then it would mean surely that African culture is indeed *not* before us. Moreover, the fact that recreation will not be effected ex nihilo implies that it will (have to) be effected from elements of some existent culture; and it makes sense to assume that this existent culture is what Hountondji means by "the heritage of the past," a reference, I take it, to the African cultural past.

Later in his book, Hountondji, surprisingly, speaks of "our cultural renaissance." He goes on to say: "African culture must *return* to itself, to its internal pluralism and to its essential openness. We must therefore, as individuals, liberate ourselves psychologically and develop a free relationship . . . with African *cultural tradition*."[35] It is strange, to say the least, for one who maintains that African culture "is before us" to advocate an African cultural *renaissance*—in effect, a return to itself!

And so it is that the perception of the normative status of the values of the cultural past in the (modern) contemporary scheme of things in Africa has led to a thicket of tensions, confusions, unclarities, ambivalences, controversies, and inconsistencies. It behooves us to enter the thicket and employ rationality or analysis in a more serious and dispassionate fashion in order to cut away the controversies and confusions surrounding the perceptions of the relevance or otherwise of the African cultural heritage to the pursuit of a modern cultural life.

It seems to me that those confusions and inconsistencies and ambivalences stem from the failure to delineate or distinguish between what may be regarded as positive and negative features of the African culture. (Every human culture has both positive and negative elements.) It is this failure that leads the revivalists to collapse the two features of the culture into something entirely positive—valuable, while leading the antirevivalists to collapse them into something entirely negative—worthless. It must be noted that while the revivalists, defenders of tradition, are adulatory of the values of the cultural past and think that the postcolonial predicament of Africa must be put down to the neglect of those values in designing both colonial and postcolonial political institutions, they are critical of many of the values, ideas, and practices—mostly of alien origin, they would say—that exert a great deal of influence on the contemporary cultural life of the African people. The antirevivalists, opponents of tradition, on their part, are adulatory of both modern science and technology and the values and institutions that go with them, and they think that the creation of African modernity depends heavily on the cultivation of those kinds of intellectual equipment and their accompanying institutions, while they are very critical of those values of the African cultural past of which the revivalists are enamored.

I think that neither the revivalists nor the antirevivalists are entirely correct in all of their arguments and criticisms. At this point, however, I wish to make a distinction between the extreme or unrestricted revivalist position and the extreme or unrestricted antirevivalist position. An extreme revivalist position is one that entertains nostalgic sentiments about the cultural products of the past and would perhaps not countenance any criticisms of them: for him or her the heritage of the past is perfect (or, near perfect) and can constitute a viable context for a modern life. An extreme antirevivalist position is one that considers the heritage of the past as good for nothing in terms of the ethos, purposes, and aspirations of life in the modern world. Therefore, there is no real justification for reviving such things of the past as are dead or are on the verge of dying or are not of much worth for

modern life. I find the positions of both the extreme revivalist and antirevivalist mistaken, implausible, and unjustifiable because they appear unnecessarily to overstate their case. I will critically examine both positions. To take
the antirevivalist position first.

The antirevivalist position, based on an evaluation of the value of the
inherited tradition, is at once a rejection of all products of an entire cultural
past. The position implies that despite the comprehensive nature of culture
as an embodiment of the total way of the life of a people, nothing worthwhile can be derived from the values, beliefs, and practices of the cultural
past for purposes of life in the present. There is, therefore, no justification,
according to antirevivalists, for the present to celebrate the past: tradition
and modernity are for them polar concepts that cannot be integrated.

It seems to me, however, that the position of the antirevivalist is at least
empirically aberrant, for anthropologists and other scholars are unhesitant
about speaking of some virtues or great qualities they perceive in the traditions of peoples whose cultures are the subject of their investigations. Dugald Campbell, the Briton whose views on the cultural practices of the people of central Africa in the nineteenth century I discuss in chapters 4 and 5,
makes the following observations: "The social status of equality observed by
the primitive peoples of mankind is now the aim and ambition of the most
highly civilized communities; and in central Africa we have a complete object lesson before us of the result of life under conditions of equality." [36]
Campbell is here extolling an aspect of the socioethical thought and practice
of the people of central Africa, who, even though they are described as "the
primitive peoples of mankind," had created some system or practice sought
by "the most highly civilized communities." R. S. Rattray, the British anthropologist who spent over two decades in the Gold Coast (now Ghana) to
study the culture of the Asante [Ashanti] and whose views I refer to in
chapters 4 and 5 of this book, also speaks of the value of equality: "Here
then we have a far more real equality than any which our [British] laws
confer upon us. To the Ashanti our equality would seem a fictitious fellowship." [37] Rattray was also "astonished at the words of wisdom" contained in
Ashanti (Asante) proverbs, an astonishment that might make the prejudiced
reader "refuse to credit that a 'savage' or 'primitive' people could possibly
have possessed the rude philosophers, theologians, moralists, naturalists and
even, it will be seen, philologists which many of these proverbs prove them
to have had among them." [38] Rattray is extolling the profundity of the Asante
intellect that created the proverbs or maxims.

There is reason to believe that anthropological accounts of different cultures are replete with some kinds of positive assessment of some aspect or
other of those cultures. This suggests that it is possible to identify as worthwhile—not as exotic—some product from the cultural past of a people that
would not necessarily be out of harmony with the present scheme of things,
notwithstanding the fact that it may need to be refined or pruned. But the
refinement and pruning would hardly result in the total effacement of that
product of the cultural past. It is thus implausible, in my view, to argue

the rejection of the whole complex of creations of the cultural past of a people. An indiscriminate rejection of an entire cultural past would be an absurdity.

Extreme cultural antirevivalism has no historical warrant; in fact it flies in the face of historical evidence. For there surely are cultural values, ideas, practices, and institutions that, for some reasons, have never been allowed completely to sink into oblivion or have undergone some refinement over generations or have consciously been revived where they seem to have been forgotten or ignored by some intervening generations. The phenomenon known in European history as the Renaissance, which began in the fourteenth century of our era and included a rebirth or revival of the Greek philosophical and scientific ideas, immediately comes to mind.

The revival—whether immediately or mediately, whether in whole or in part—of some ancestral cultural values and practices indicates that vestiges of ideas or values such as democracy and human (natural) rights that are prominent in the contemporary world can surely be detected on the cultural terrains of a very distant past. And this means that an idea or value or practice or institution of a (distant) cultural past can be revived or adapted by later generations, if the latter consider it worth their while to do so. Thus, an extreme or unrestricted antirevivalism with respect to the values of a cultural past will not stand up to a historical analysis. Extreme antirevivalism, whose rejection of the worth of the entire products of a cultural past is irrational, would only lead to the loss of much in the past that, on rational or normative grounds, could be exploited for the benefit of a present generation. The extreme antirevivalist's view seems to make modernity a total rejection of the past, a view that can hardly stand up to historical or empirical analysis, for, as I say in my introductory remarks of this chapter (see also section 5), modernity contains many elements of the cultural past.

To reject or excoriate the position of the extreme, unrestricted antirevivalist, however, is not by any means to sing a paean to a cultural past *in its entirety* and thus to embrace the position of the revivalist. The reason is simple: not every aspect of a cultural past—not every cultural product of the past—ought to be revived or given a place in the scheme of things of the present. Thus it would be impossible for me to support the position of the revivalist if that position were to advocate the resuscitation of the whole corpus of the pristine cultural products of the past.

One aspect of the African postcolonial experience where the revivalist position would do more harm than good is the aspect of development. Part of the argument of the revivalist is that the failure of the "experts" of development to give adequate consideration to the cultural values of developing societies has stunted their development. The basis or framework of development, it is argued, ought to be the culture of the people. This argument has often been invoked, particularly with respect to the development efforts of developing societies, the underlying assumption being that the natural or historical process of development of such societies was disrupted (for instance, by colonial rule, or some other kind of foreign imposition) in the course of their histories in a way, most people agree, that did great violence to their cultural systems. Realistic, meaningful, enduring, and self-sustaining development, it is argued, can take place only with the resuscitation of the atavistic cultural values of such societies. Hence the call for returning to the cultural roots of those societies.[39] This view of culture as a basis for development is so widely held that it can in fact be called a commonplace.

The cultural-basis view of development is intuitively attractive because of the following facts: the development of a human society does not take place in a cultural vacuum; it is within a culture that a human being finds his or her identity and can be what he or she is or wants to be; all human activity springs from a cultural base and takes on, or derives, its significance from the context of that culture; and the cultural model of development is a totalistic (not segmented) model—encompassing, as it must, all aspects of human life and thought and thus effectively accommodating the complex nature of the human being and of human society. If the development activity is to come to grips with the problems of human society, then it can do so only within the culture of a society. For these and perhaps other reasons, the cultural model of development is compelling.

All this said, however, it would not follow that for purposes of development the entire corpus of a cultural past must be revived, as the revivalists think. The reason is that the view that the viable framework of development is culture is only generally and abstractly true. We know for a fact, of course, that every society has a culture, but not every society is developed. This implies, surely, that not every culture is a viable framework for development. That view will be true only in certain conditions, a fact that suggests a conditionality or qualification of the view itself. The conditionality is that the elements of the culture must be such as can function adequately and successfully and conduce to the attainment of the goals of development, which, in ultimate terms, mean the satisfaction of basic human needs. If, therefore, the cultural substrate of development, or some aspects of it, should be found to be an impediment to the development effort, then it would be necessary to take a critical look at that cultural substrate and do something about it. In consequence of the conditionality, if a culture spawns and nurtures attitudes, practices, mental outlooks, and behavioral patterns that can be shown to frustrate efforts at development, then it can be said that that culture, as it exists, cannot constitute itself into a viable framework for development. The viability of a development framework with respect to a culture is determined by, or contingent upon, the characteristics of that culture. The revivalists seem to assume that all the characteristics of a culture can constitute themselves into a viable framework for development. In this assumption they are wrong, in my opinion.

The conditionality implies that in analyzing problems of development we should critically examine the cultural setting of that development. This examination is of course intended to identify such aspects of the culture as can be said to hinder development: to identify those beliefs, attitudes or habits, behavioral patterns, social practices, and institutions of a society that can or do hinder its satisfactory or effective functioning and, so, generate besetting problems of development for that society. There will be a need for a profound and critical reappraisal of the relevance and effect of those cultural values and practices on efforts at development. This is, to me, the only way to brace up an otherwise inadequate or weak cultural framework for the arduous task of development.[40] By advocating a return to and maintenance of the entire corpus of the cultural past and thus not showing any awareness of the negative features of the culture that are deleterious to the course of development, the revivalists have taken a position that is misguided and counterproductive in matters of the development and progress of their societies.

Thus, in my view, the positions of both the extreme, unrestricted cultural revivalist and the extreme, unrestricted antirevivalist must be rejected on the grounds that both positions are infected by an unnecessary hyperbole. The rejection follows from the logic of my view that not all the products of a cultural past can be said to be valuable or worthless in terms of the ethos of a present, or of a later epoch.

I think that the position of the extreme cultural revivalist and the position of the extreme antirevalist are both bedeviled by sweeping, hasty, premature, and lopsided judgments about the positive or negative features of the cultures of Africa. The fact, for me, is that the traditional conceptions of things have not yet been given adequate philosophical analysis and interpretation for use as a sure basis for deciding on their normative weight and status in the modern (contemporary) scheme of things. This being so, any judgment about the total relevance or irrelevance of a traditional cultural value or practice to the contemporary cultural setting is bound not only to be premature but also to be a distortion of the truth. A view that represents a wholesale condemnation or exaltation of the culture of a people would not be realistic and could easily be falsified if serious normative investigations into the complexities of that culture resulted in one's rejection or appreciation of some features of it. In my view, a realistic normative assessment of the cultural past or cultural traditions of a people must proceed by examining the experiences of the practice of *specific* aspects or areas of those traditions.

This specific-aspect or specific-problem approach would not only be more appropriate and fruitful but it would also fulfill the demands of the open-minded stance that should characterize any objective evaluation or scientific inquiry, while avoiding the unforeseen errors that often ensue from generalizations. The methodology I am suggesting is intended, therefore, to avoid the Scylla of wholesale, nostalgic acceptance or apotheosis of tradition and the Charybdis of wholesale, indiscriminate, cavalier rejection of it. To bring clarity into the confused and perplexing perception of the normative status of the values of the African cultural past in the cultural lives of the African people in the modern world, I make a distinction between the positive and negative features of the African culture and discuss them in some detail in the next section.

3. Normative Consideration of Our African Cultural Products

In this section I consider what may be regarded as disvalues or negative features as well as the values or positive features of the cultural traditions of Africa. In this way, we will be able, realistically, to determine where revivalism makes normative sense and where it would be senseless to pursue it. The negative features of a culture are either those features that may be considered dysfunctional because they are seen as impeding the march toward progress (that is, the kind of progress a present generation would like to embark on) or those features that may be considered dissonant with the moral and aesthetic intuitions or perceptions of a present generation. The analysis of the notion of tradition undertaken in the previous section makes it clear that every human culture, because of the limitations of the human intelligence and foresight, has its imperfections and hence would have negative features. Yet, the civilization and progress of humankind require that the imperfections—those negatives—be dealt with and, as fast as possible, removed. The considerations I wish to undertake cannot of course claim to be exhaustive of what might be described as the positive or negative features of our African cultural traditions. The positivity or negativity of those cultural features is to be perceived in terms of the attempt to revitalize the inherited cultural tradition, build a modern African society, create institutions that will adequately serve the purposes of life in the modern setting, and equip contemporary African people and their descendants with the scientific, intellectual, and technological wherewithall to function satisfactorily in an interdependent world that is increasingly and speedily becoming technological and innovative. A tradition that does not accommodate itself to changed circumstances in ways that will allow it to function satisfactorily in the new circumstances will atrophy sooner than later. I begin by looking at some of what I would consider negative features of the African cultural traditions.

3.1 Negative Features of Our African Cultures

3.1.1 Science and Our Cultures. Even though culture is manifested most patently and forthrightly in the arts of a people, in their material way of life, in their dress, in their institutions, I shall nevertheless start off by looking at what may be considered the mental aspects of culture, that is, the attitudes of the users of a culture toward the things of the mind, such as science and knowledge and the cognitive attitude toward life in general.

In another publication I point out—indeed I stress—the empirical orientation of African thought, maintaining that African proverbs, for instance, many of which bear some philosophical content, address—or result from reflections on—specific events, situations, or experiences in the lives of the people, and that even such a metaphysical concept as destiny (or, fate) is reached inductively, experience being the basis of the reasoning that led to it.[41] Observation and experience constitute a great part of the sources of knowledge in African cultures.[42] The empirical basis of knowledge does have immediate practical results in such areas as agriculture and herbal medicine: our ancestors, whose main occupation was farming, knew of the system of rotation of crops; they knew when to allow a piece of land to lie fallow for a while; they had some knowledge of the technology of food processing and preservation; and long before the introduction of Western medicine, they knew about the medicinal potencies of herbs and other plants—their main natural sources of healing. (Even today, there are countless testimonies of people who have received cures from "traditional" healers where the application of Western therapeutics were ineffective.)

Several scholars have asserted that African life in the traditional setting is intensely religious or spiritual. John Mbiti, for example, says that "Africans are notoriously religious, and each people has its own religious system with a set of beliefs and practices. Religion permeates into all the departments of life so fully that it is not easy or possible to isolate it."[43] And furthermore, "in traditional life there are no atheists."[44] Kofi Busia says that Africa's cultural heritage "is intensely and pervasively religious," and that "in traditional African communities, it was not possible to distinguish between religious and nonreligious areas of life. All life was religious."[45] Many colonial administrators in Africa used to refer to Africans, according to Geoffrey Parrinder, as "this incurably religious people."[46] Yet despite the intense religiosity of the African cultural heritage, the empirical orientation or approach to most of their enterprises was very much to the fore. I strongly suspect that even the African knowledge of God in the traditional setting was, in the context of a nonrevealed religion of traditional Africa, empirically reached. The well-known Akan proverb, "No one teaches God to a child" or, as I would like to translate it, "No one shows God to a child" (obi nkyere abofra Nyame), a proverb that has been taken by W. E. Abraham[47] and B. E. Oguah[48] as indicative of an intuitive or rationalist (i.e., nonempirical) approach to knowledge, is in fact a piece of empirical knowledge. For the child, lying on his back, *sees* the sky, which is believed to be the abode of God. From this experience, God's existence is inferred. Taken in its broad sense, this proverb indicates that it is on the basis of their experience of the world that the African people came to a knowledge or conviction of the existence of a supreme being.

Now, one would think that such a characteristically empirical epistemic outlook would naturally lead the African people to a profound and extensive interest in science as a theory, an interest, that is, in the acquisition of theoretical knowledge of nature, beyond the practical knowledge that they seem to have had of it, albeit not in a highly developed form, and that they have utilized to their benefit. But, surprisingly, there is no evidence that such an empirical orientation of thought in the traditional African cultures led to the creation of the scientific outlook or a deep scientific understanding of nature. It is possible, arguably, to credit people who practice crafts and pursue such activities as food preservation, food fermentation, and herbal therapeutics (see next section) with some amount of scientific knowledge; after all, the traditional technologies, one would assume, must have had some basis in science. Yet it does not appear that the African people's practical knowledge of crafts or forms of technologies led to any deep scientific understanding or analysis of the enterprises they were engaged in. Their observations may have led to interesting facts about the workings of nature; but those facts never received the elaborate and coherent theoretical explanations. Science requires explanations that are generalizable, facts that are disciplined by experiments, and experiments that are repeatable and verifiable elsewhere. But the inability (or is it lack of interest?) of the users of our African cultures to engage in sustained investigations and to provide intelligible scientific explanations or analyses of their own observations and experiences stunted the growth of science.

Science begins not only in sustained observations and investigations into natural phenomena but also in the ascription of causal explanations or analyses to those phenomena. The notion of causality is of course crucial to the pursuit of science. African cultures appreciated that notion very well. But, for a reason that must be linked to the (alleged) intense religiosity of the cultures, causality is generally understood in terms of spirit, of mystical power. The consequence of this is that purely scientific or empirical causal explanations, of which the users of our African cultures are also aware, are often not regarded as profound enough to offer complete satisfaction. This leads them to give up, but too soon, on the search for empirical causal explanations, even for causal relations between natural phenomena or events, and resort to supernatural causation.

Empirical causation, which asks what—and how—questions too quickly give way to agentive causation, which asks who—and why—questions. Agentive causation leads to the postulation of spirits or mystical powers as causal agents; thus, a particular metaphysic is at the basis of this conception of causation. According to Mbiti, "The physical and spiritual are but two dimensions of one and the same universe. These dimensions dove-tail into each other to the extent that at times and in places one is apparently more real than, but not exclusive of, the other"[49] (see also the second quotation from Busia above). It is the lack of distinction between the purely material (natural) and the immaterial (supernatural, spiritual) that leads to the postulation of agentive causation in all matters. For in a conception of a hierarchy of causes, it is easy to identify the spiritual as the agent that causes changes in relations even among empirical phenomena. In view of the critical importance of causality to the development of science, a culture that is obsessed with supernatural or mystical causal explanations would hardly develop the scientific attitude in the users of that culture and consequently would not attain knowledge of the external world that can empirically be ascertained by others, including future generations.

Yet the (alleged) intense religiosity of the African cultural heritage need not have hindered interest in science, that is, in scientific investigations both for their own sake and as sure foundations for the development of technology. Religion and science, even though they perceive reality differently, need not be incompatible. Thus, it is possible for religious persons to acquire a scientific knowledge and outlook. But to be able to do so most satisfactorily, one should be able to separate the two, based on the conviction that purely scientific knowledge and understanding of the external world would not detract from one's faith in an ultimate being. A culture may be a religious culture, even an intensely religious culture at that; but, in view of the tremendous importance of science for the progress of many other aspects of the culture, it should be able to render unto Caesar what is Caesar's and unto God what is God's ("Caesar" here referring to the pursuit of the knowledge of the natural world). The inability of the traditional African cultures to separate religion from science, as well as the African conception of nature as essentially animated or spirit-filled (leading to the belief that natural objects contain mystical powers to be feared or kept at bay or, when convenient, to be exploited for the human being's immediate material benefit), is the ground of the agentive causal explanations favored by the users of our cultures in the traditional setting. Science, as already stated, is based on a profound understanding and exploitation of the important notion of causality, that is, on a deep appreciation of the causal interactions between natural phenomena. But where this is enmeshed with—made inextricable from—supernaturalistic molds and orientations, as a purely empirical pursuit, it hardly makes progress.

Also, religion, even if it is pursued by a whole society or generation, is still a highly subjective cognitive activity, in that its postulates and conclusions are not immediately accessible to the objective scrutiny or verification by others outside it. Science, on the contrary, is manifestly an objective, impartial enterprise whose conclusions are open to scrutiny by others at any time or place, a scrutiny that may lead to the rejection or amendment or confirmation of those conclusions. Now, the mesh in which both religion and science (or, rather the pursuit of science) find themselves in traditional African cultures makes the relevant objective approach to scientific investigations into nature well-nigh impossible. Moreover, in consequence of this mesh, what can become scientific knowledge accessible to all others will become an esoteric knowledge, a specialized knowledge, accessible only to initiates probably under an oath of secrecy administered by priests (male and female), traditionally acknowledged as the custodians of the verities and secrets of nature. These custodians, who are believed to "know," are often consulted on the causes of frequent low crop-yield, lack of adequate rainfall over a long period, the occurrence of bush fires, and so on. Knowledge about the operations of nature becomes not only esoteric but also, for that reason, personal rather than exoteric and impersonal. This preempts the participative nature of the search for deep and extensive knowledge of the natural world; for others would not have access to, let alone participate in, the type of knowledge that is regarded as personal and arcane.

Knowledge of the potencies of herbs and other medicinal plants is in the traditional setting probably the most secretive of all. Even if the claims made by African medicine men and women of having discovered cures for deadly diseases can be substantiated scientifically, those claims cannot be pursued for verification since that knowledge is esoteric and personal. The desire to make knowledge of the external world personal has been the characteristic attitude of traditional African healers who claim to possess knowledge of medicinal plants, claims at least some of which can be scientifically investigated. In the past, all such possibly credible claims to knowledge of medicinal plants just evaporated on the death of the traditional healer or priest. And science, including the science of medicine, stagnated.

I think that the personalization of the knowledge of the external world is attributable to the mode of acquiring that knowledge: quite simply, that mode is not based on experiment. And, in the circumstance, the only way one can come by knowledge of, say, herbal therapeutics, is through mystical or magical means, a means not subject to public or objective scrutiny and analysis.

The lack of the appropriate attitude toward sustained scientific probing, required for both vertical and horizontal advancement of knowledge, appears to have been a characteristic of the African cultural past. One need not have to put this want of the appropriate scientific attitude down to the lack of the capacity for science. And I, on my part, would like to make a distinction here: between the intellectual capacity on one hand, and the proclivity or impulse to exercise that capacity long enough to yield appreciable results on the other hand. The impulse for sustained scientific or intellectual probing does not appear to have been nurtured and promoted by our traditional cultures.

It appears in fact that the traditional cultures throttled the impulse toward sustained and profound inquiry for reasons that are not fully known or intelligible. One reason, however, may be extracted from the Akan proverb, literally translated: "If you insist on probing deeply into the eye sockets of a dead person, you see a ghost."[50] Curiosity or deep probing, the proverb says, may lead to dreadful consequences. The proverb, as Ebenezer Laing also sees, stunts the "development of the spirit of inquiry, exploration and adventure." The attitude sanctioned by the proverb would, he points out, be "inimical to science."[51] Not only to science, I might add, but to all kinds of human knowledge. My colleague Kofi Asare Opoku,[52] however, explained to me in a conversation that the intention of the proverb is to put an end to a protracted dispute that might tear a family or lineage apart: a dispute that has been settled, in other words, should not be resuscitated, for the consequences of the resuscitation would not be good for the solidarity of the family. Thus, Opoku would deny that this proverb is to be interpreted as damaging to intellectual or scientific probing. In response to Opoku's interpretation, I would like to raise the following questions: why should further evidence not be looked for if it would indeed help settle the matter more satisfactorily? Why should further investigation be stopped if it would unravel fresh evidence and lead to what was not previously known? To end a dispute prematurely for the sake of family solidarity to the dissatisfaction of some members of the family certainly destroys the pursuit of moral or legal knowledge or appreciation. So, whether in the area of legal, moral, or scientific knowledge, it seems to me that the proverb destroys the impulse or proclivity to deep probing, to the pursuit of further knowledge.

The general attitude of the users of the traditional African cultures expressed in such oft-used statements as "This is what the ancestors said," and "This is what the ancestors did" may be put down to the inexplicable reluctance—or lack of the impulse—to pursue sustained inquiries into the pristine ideas and values of the culture. It is this mentality, one might add, that often makes the elderly people even in contemporary African societies try to hush and stop children with inquisitive minds from persistently asking certain kinds of questions and, thus, from pursuing intellectual exploration. (I provide evidence in due course to show that our forebears did not expect later generations to regard their modes of thought and action as sacrosanct and unalterable, and to think and act in the same way they did. So that, if later generations—their descendants—failed to make changes, amendments, or refinements such as may be required by their own times and situations, that must be put down to the intellectual indolence or shallowness of the descendants—later generations.)

The pursuit of science—the cultivation of rational or theoretical knowledge of the natural world—seems to presuppose an intense desire, at least initially, for knowledge for its own sake, not for the sake of some immediate practical results. It appears that the traditional African cultures have very little if any conception of knowledge for its own sake. They had a conception of knowledge that is practical. Such an epistemic conception seems to have had a parallel in the African conception of art. For it has been said by several scholars[53] that art is conceived in the African traditional setting in functional or utilitarian terms, and that the African aesthetic sense does not find the concept of "art for art's sake" hospitable. Even though I think that the purely aesthetic element of art is not discounted in traditional art appreciation and judgment and is equally valued—as I say elsewhere[54]—the functional features of art more often come to the fore. This practical or functional orientation of art must somehow have dwarfed a conception of art for art's sake, consequently infecting the African conception of knowledge, which in turn resulted in the lack of interest in the acquisition of knowledge, including scientific knowledge, *for its own sake.*

Traditional African cultures, then, do not have a commitment, however spasmodic, to the advancement of the scientific knowledge of the natural world; they make no attempts, however feeble, to investigate the scientific theories underpinning the technologies they develop; they do not foster any disposition to pursue sustained inquiries into many areas of the life and thought of the people; and the successive generations of the participants in the culture could not, as a consequence, augment the compendium of knowledge that they had inherited from their forebears. Instead they were satisfied to give it a hallowed status as the basis of their own thought and action. In our contemporary world, where sustainable development—much of which is concerned with the enhancement of the material well-being of human beings—depends on the intelligent and efficient exploitation of the resources of nature, an exploitation that can be effected only through science and its progeny technology, the need to cultivate the appropriate scientific attitudes is imperative.

For this reason, contemporary African cultures will have to come to terms with the contemporary scientific attitudes and, in the wake of contact with the Western cultural tradition, adopt more pro-scientific approaches to looking at things in Africa's own environment. The postcolonial governments of African nations have for decades been insisting on the cultivation of science in the schools and universities as an unavoidable basis for technological, and hence industrial, advancement. More places and facilities are made available for those students who are interested in the pursuit of science. Yet, surprisingly, very many more students register for courses in the humanities and the social sciences than in the mathematical and natural sciences. Have the traditional cultures anything to do with this lack of real or adequate or sustained interest in the natural sciences?

3.1.2 Technology and Our Cultures.   Like science, technology—the application of knowledge or discovery to practical use—is also a feature or product of culture. It develops in a cultural milieu and its career or future is also determined by the characteristics of that culture. Technology is an enterprise that can be said to be common to all human cultures; it can certainly be regarded as among the earliest creations of any human society. This is because the material existence and survival of human society depend on the ability of humans to make at least simple tools and equipment and to develop techniques essential for the production of basic human needs such as food, clothing, shelter, and security. The concern for such needs is naturally more immediate than the pursuit and acquisition of the systematic knowledge of nature, that is, science. Thus, in all human cultures and societies the creation of simple forms of technology antedates science—the rational and systematic pursuit of knowledge and understanding of the natural world, of the processes of nature, based on observation and experiment. Technology antedates science even in the cultures of Western societies, historically the sources of advanced and sophisticated technology. From antiquity through the Middle Ages into the modern European world, innovative technology showed no traces of the application of consciously scientific principles.[55] Science-based technology was not developed until about the middle of the nineteenth century.[56] Thus, technology was for centuries based entirely on empirical knowledge.

The pursuit of empirical knowledge underpins much of the intellectual enterprise of the traditional African setting. (Note that philosophical knowledge is also thought to have a practical orientation.) And so, as in other cultures of the world, practical knowledge and the pursuit of sheer material well-being and survival led the cultures of Africa to develop the simple techniques and technologies that characterize any premodern society. Basic craftsmanship emerged: the blacksmith made farming implements such as the cutlass and the hoe and ax; the goldsmith produced the bracelet, necklace, and rings (including the earring), and further: "African coppersmiths have for centuries produced wire to make bracelets and ornaments—archaeologists have found the draw-plates and other wire-making tools."[57] There were potters, carpenters, wood carvers, and cloth weavers, all of whom evolved specialized techniques. Food production, processing, and preservation techniques were developed; and so were techniques for extracting medicinal potencies from plants, herbs, and roots. In time many of these technical activities burgeoned into industries.

There was a great respect and appreciation for technology because of the products it could offer. The need for, and the appreciation of, technology should have translated into real desire for innovation and improvement on existing technological techniques and products. But there is little evidence to support the view that there were attempts to innovate technologies and refine techniques received from previous generations. There were no doubts whatsoever about the potencies of traditional medicines extracted from plants and herbs. Yet there were—and are—enormous problems involving both diagnosis and dosage, problems that do not seem to have been grappled with. Diagnosis requires systematic analysis of cause and effect, an approach that would not be fully exploited in a system, like the one evolved by the traditional African cultures, where the causes of illness, like many other natural occurrences, are often explained in agentive (i.e., supernatural, mystical) terms. Such a causal approach to coping with disease would hardly dispose a people toward the search for effective diagnostic technologies.

Traditional healers are often capable of prescribing efficacious therapies. But their methods here generate two problems: the preparation of the medicine to be administered to a patient, and the quantity of the medicine for a specific illness. The herbal healer, having convinced himself of the appropriate therapeutic for a particular disease, a therapeutic that would often consist of a concoction, must next decide on the quantity of each herbal ingredient for the concoction. Then he must determine the appropriate and effective dosage for a particular illness. Both steps obviously require exact measurement of quantity. Failure to provide exact measurement would affect the efficacy of the concoction as well as the therapeutic effect of the dosage. With the latter, there is the possibility of underdoing or overdoing. Yet, the need for exact measurement does not seem to have been pursued by our African cultures, and this cultural defect is in fact still taking its toll also in the maintenance of machines. Kwasi Wiredu mentions the case of a Ghanaian mechanic who, in working on engine maintenance, resorts to the use of his sense of sight rather than of a feeler gauge in adjusting the contact breaker point in an automobile distributor.[58] The mechanic, by refusing to use a feeler gauge and other technical aids, of course fails to achieve the required precision measurement. Because the habit or attitude of the mechanic is not peculiar to him but is a habit that has generally grown upon a number of mechanics in the African environments, it can be said that the development of that habit is a function of the culture. If one considers that precision measurement is basic not only to the proper maintenance of machines but also to the quality of manufactured products of all kinds, one can appreciate the seriousness of the damage to the growth of technology caused by the failure of our African cultures to promote the practice of precision measurement.

Even though it is correct to say that technology was for centuries applied without resort to scientific principles, it is also conceivable that this slowed down the advancement of technology, depriving technology of a necessary scientific base. The making of simple tools and equipment may not require or rest on the knowledge of scientific principles; but not so the pursuit of most other technological enterprises and methods. It cannot at all be doubted that the preparation of medicinal concoctions by traditional African herbal healers and their prescriptive dosages, for instance, must have been greatly hampered by the failure to attend to the appropriate scientific testing of the potencies of the various herbs and the amounts of each (herb or plant) required in a particular concoction. Theoretical knowledge should have been pursued to complement their practical knowledge.

Food technology, practiced in the traditional setting mainly by African women, is a vibrant activity, even though the scientific aspect of it is not attended to. According to Samuel Sefa-Dede, who has done an enormous amount of research in traditional food technology in Ghana, "The scientific principles behind the various unit operations may be the same as found in modern food technologies, but the mode of application may be different." [59] The techniques traditionally deployed in food preservation undoubtedly involve the application of principles of science: physics, chemistry, and biology, which the users of those techniques may not have been aware of. The techniques of preserving food all over Africa include drying, smoking, salting, and fermenting. The drying technique is aimed at killing bacteria and other decay-causing micro-organisms and thus preserving food for a long time; smoking serves as a chemical preservative; and so does salting, which draws moisture and micro-organisms from foods; fermentation of food causes considerable reduction of acidity levels and so creates conditions that prevent microbial multiplication. [60] It is thus clear that there are scientific principles underlying these methods.

Let us look at the specific example of a woman in the central region of Ghana, underlying whose practice of food technology is clearly a knowledge of some principles of physics, chemistry, and metallurgy. [61] The woman is a processor of "fante kenkey," a cereal dumpling made from maize dough that has fermented for two to four days. A portion of the dough is made into a slurry and cooked into a stiff paste. This is mixed with the remaining portion through a process called aflatization to produce aflata, which is wrapped in dried banana leaves and boiled for three to four hours. To the amazement of the modern scientific research team studying traditional food technology, this woman is able to solve a problem arising from the technique she uses in processing fante kenkey. She challenged the research team to figure out how they could solve this very practical problem, which can arise when one is boiling fante kenkey in a forty-four-gallon drum.

> Imagine that you have loaded a forty-four-gallon barrel with uncooked fante kenkey. You set the system up on the traditional cooking stove, which uses firewood. The fire is lit and the boiling process starts. In the middle of the boiling process, you notice that the barrel has developed a leak at its bottom. The boiling water is gushing into the fire and gradually putting out the fire. What will you do to save the situation?

The possible solutions suggested by the research team were found to be impractical. The first was to transfer the product from the leaking barrel into a new one. The problems with this solution were that the kenkey will be very hot and difficult to unpack, the process will also be time-consuming, and furthermore another barrel may not be available.

The woman then provided the solution: adjust the firewood in the stove to allow increased burning; then collect two or three handfuls of dry palm kernels and throw them into the fire—this will heat up and turn red hot; finally, collect coarse table salt and throw it unto the hot kernels. The result will be that the salt will explode and in the process seal the leak at the bottom of the barrel.

According to Sefa-Dede, the solution provided by the woman is based on the sublimation of the salt with the associated explosion. The explosion carries with it particles of salt that fill the opening. It is possible that there is interaction between the sodium chloride in the salt and the iron and other cations forming the structure of the barrel. A few questions may arise as one attempts to understand the source of knowledge of the traditional practitioners: Why were dry palm kernels used as heat exchange medium? What is peculiar about table salt in this process? In the case under discussion, it can certainly be said that the woman has some knowledge about the thermal properties of palm kernels. (It is possible that there is traditional knowledge about the excellent heat properties of palm kernels. For traditional metal smelters, blacksmiths, and goldsmiths are known to use palm kernels for heating and melting various metals.) The woman, it can also be said, has added knowledge of some chemistry and metallurgy. Even though it is clear that the ideas and solutions she was able to come up with are rooted in basic and applied scientific principles, she cannot, like most other traditional technology practitioners, explain and articulate those principles. But not only that: they must have thought that the whys and hows did not matter; it was enough to have found practical ways to solve practical problems of human survival.

Thus, the pursuit of scientific principles would not have been of great interest to the users of traditional technologies, concerned as they were with reaping immediate practical results from their activities. The result was that there was no real understanding of the scientific processes involved in the technologies they found so useful. Yet the concern for investigating and understanding those principles would most probably have led to innovation and improvement of the technologies. It can therefore be said that the weak scientific base of the traditional technology stunted its growth and accounts for the maintenance and continual practice of the same old techniques. The understanding of the principles involved would probably have generated extensive innovative practices and the application of those principles to other yet-unknown technological possibilities. Once some technique or equipment was known to be working, there was no desire or effort on the part of its creators or users to innovate and improve on its quality, to make it work better or more efficiently, to build other—and more—efficient tools. Is this complacency or the feeling of having come to the end of one's intellectual or technological tether a reflection on the levels of capability that could be attained by our African cultures?

There are, however, some positive features in the organization of technology in the traditional setting that I discuss in the next chapter.

3.1.3 Social and Moral Features of Our Cultures. I turn now to a discussion of the social and moral fallout of the social practices of our societies, beginning with the communitarian ethos of African cultures. Aristotle proclaimed centuries ago that the human being is by nature a social (political) animal, and that it is impossible for him to function as human outside society. Our traditional cultures also maintain the idea that community or social life is a necessary condition for human existence and natural to humankind (see chapter 2). Human sociality is thus seen as intrinsic to our basic human nature. It is quite appropriate therefore to institute a social arrangement that will translate the notion of natural human sociality into concrete and practical terms. Hence, the institution of community life as part of the African cultural values. Communitarian social arrangement makes for the development and practice of such socioethical values as mutual aid, solidarity, interdependence, collective action, and reciprocal obligation. It enjoins upon the individual member of the group the obligation to think and act for the welfare and survival of the group as a whole. The communitarian structure would seem to be an ideal social arrangement, which reflects, and seems mandated by, our basic conception of human nature, if it is given the appropriate, prudent, and guarded translation in the real world of human activity and goals.

The communitarian social arrangement, as established and practiced in African cultures, has, however, spawned some features that have thrown the worthwhileness and continuity of the arrangement in its old form into question. Among the features I have in mind, let me first mention the inheritance systems, beginning with a quotation from Julius Nyerere: "The inheritance systems were such that in almost all places death led to the dispersal of, for example, a large herd of cattle, among a large number of people."[62] The inheritance systems of many communocultural groups in most African societies are such as raise the expectations of a number of the members of a lineage (or, extended family) to inherit, or at least have a claim to, the property left by a deceased wealthy member of the family. The wills of business or propertied persons are quite often contested in the courts either by their children or by other members of the extended family—nephews, nieces, and cousins—on the grounds that they "have reason" to believe that the original will of the deceased has been tampered with by some interested party or parties. Interminable legal wrangles would invariably ensue. The case becomes even worse when a business person dies intestate. The most probable consequence would be the apportionment of the man's properties, including his business capital, which, thus, eventually becomes dissipated. His previously flourishing business enterprises, now parceled out to several individuals, could well suffer from capital hemorrhage and dwindle into nonexistence. The names of the business enterprises also disappear. Thus, the inheritance systems featured or evolved by the communitarian society—of the type structured by the African cultures—have often worked against the development, proper maintenance, smooth management, and continuous survival of business enterprises.

This feature of the communitarian social arrangement is surely one of the constraints that have impeded the emergence on the African commercial scene of famous, giant family businesses like Macy's, Singer, Alexander's, Jordan Mash, Marks and Spencer, and many others in cities of Western countries whose beginnings can be traced to the work of a business patriarch a century or half a century ago. In the late twentieth century, when the idea of free market capitalism is pervading and influencing most economies of the world, there is a need not only to create private enterprises but also to maintain them beyond the life spans of the individuals who created them; indeed, beyond generations. There is very little evidence in the history of the economic activities of many an African nation of the existence of transgenerational business enterprises. This situation, in my view, is to be put down to the African cultures.

There are two features of the inheritance system that are particularly morally disturbing, especially among the Akan communities in Ghana—and perhaps in other matrilineal systems elsewhere. One is the automatic claim and takeover by members of the extended family of the property of a man who dies intestate, almost to the total neglect of the inheritance rights or interests of the deceased's wife and children. This is true especially with the matrilineal system of kinship. The other is the automatic deprivation of the inheritance rights of children born of a man from a matrilineal system and a woman from a patrilineal system in the event of the death intestate of the man. The reason is that in the matrilineal system the man's relatives, according to custom, inherit his property. Such inheritance systems that deprive offspring of rights are simply morally reprehensible; they are also *unjust* in view of the contributions that would have been made by the woman and her children to the properties of the deceased.

The individual in a communitarian social context is expected to contribute to the welfare of the group (or, clan) and to bear at least part of the burden of the unfortunate members of the group. The individual's sense of responsibility is measured by his responsiveness to the needs and demands of the group. The status and respect he commands derive from the extent to which he is able to demonstrate sensitivity to the needs particularly of the unfortunate members of the group. At the same time, however, this individual has to take care of his own interests. The responsibility the communitarian social arrangement evolved by our cultures imposes on the individual may not be easy to bear successfully unless one is a wealthy person. And so the individual must necessarily become wealthy: he should strive to be in such a social or economic position as would enable him to help the unfortunate kinsmen and kinswomen. In the process, he may become corrupt. The causes of corruption, to be sure, are legion; but the pressures on an individual holding some official position to meet the demands of members of the extended family must certainly be one of the outstanding causes (see chapter 7, section 1).

One way of helping members of the extended family, apart from doling money and other specific material things to them, is to help them find jobs. There is on that account a great deal of pressure on those in employment to find jobs for members of their extended family or group. The communitarian social structure, an outstanding and famous feature of the African cultures, has thus come to nurture patronage. But efforts to assist members of the family by finding jobs for them, or by favoring them for promotion, often leave offices and institutions staffed with unqualified and incompetent personnel. Family pressure for the employment of more members of the family also promotes overstaffing, inefficiency, and laziness. Patronage destroys incentive, just as it drives away well-qualified and competent people. For if appointment and promotion depend on one's relationship with people in authority, one feels little need to work in such a way as to merit a particular position or promotion. Thus patronage also destroys the system of hiring and promoting on merit, just as it throttles the desire to exercise one's talents and endowments: it leads to the shrugging of the shoulders of the individual to be advantaged by patronage (for he knows that however he performs, he will get the job or will be promoted), or of the individual to be disadvantaged by it (for he also knows that however he performs, he will not get the job or promotion). A culture that nurtures such a system will never attain the high levels of efficiency and productivity necessary for the realization of development goals.

Thus, a successful man—particularly a businessman—in African societies would have a burdensome responsibility with so many dependents from the extended family to look after. The expenses to be incurred in support of the many dependents would certainly constitute a heavy drain on the profits that should be saved and reinvested to expand the business. Before long, the financial sources of the growth of the business enterprise would dry up. Thus the success of the business enterprise would become its undoing: a paradox of business success! And this is to be put down to the type of social arrangement evolved by our African cultures. The notion of savings or thrift certainly exists in traditional African cultures (see chapter 5 section 2), but its practical application is thwarted in a social context in which profits and other resources have to be consumed in the furnace of largess distribution.

A concept that never evolved out of the African cultures is that of the illegitimate child. Every child, whether born in or out of wedlock, whether his or her father is identified or not, is considered a human being—a being of moral worth—who should be received into the human family. From one point of view, this is certainly a great principle, fashioned out of a great sense of humanity: a great expression of human love and care that ought to be admired and cherished. Yet the principle seems to have given free rein to irresponsible young, unmarried couples to produce children. Sometimes a young woman cannot identify her child's father; sometimes the father will run away, never acknowledging the child. Always there is the assumption that the mother's extended family will look after the child. Indeed, the care of such a child invariably does become the responsibility of the supposedly fortunate or successful members of the extended family, increasing the amount these successful members have to distribute as largess and thus compounding their personal financial problems. Thus, because of the problems unleashed upon the extended family and upon the wider society generally, this principle has gone sour and has engendered disenchantment.

Let me say, parenthetically, that I am not implying by any means that other cultures or societies do not have social problems. But we have to distinguish emergent social problems, such as homelessness, drug addiction, and unemployment, from problems that obviously stem from persistent features of a cultural structure, problems that are thus culture related or, perhaps better, culture sanctioned. Culture-structured problems are more difficult to deal with and take more time to solve or dissolve.

The ethnically plural character of the African nation-state in the modern world has given rise to a plurality of cultures that in turn have given rise to group loyalties. The evils caused by the pursuit of ethnic or communocultural loyalties are legion: in inter-ethnic (or better, intercultural) relations it has clouded the moral vision of members of the various communocultural groups. It is common knowledge that unethical acts committed by a member of one cultural group are condoned, if not positively accepted, when done against members of another group. That is to say, transethnic unethical conduct is often allowed to pass as ethical. Thus, the knowledge of theft of things belonging to members of another cultural group, for instance, would quite often be hushed by members of the group to which the thief belongs. The thief, if he is able to escape detection or arrest, would hardly be given up by the members of his group, even though the principles of morality require that he be given up. In terms of objective moral principles, this attitude in itself is of course wrong; but not only that: it is destructive of harmony in the relations between the various communocultural components of a modern nation-state. A variant of this moral attitude is the unflinching ethnic loyalty and support enjoyed by politicians or persons seeking political office who are known to be morally corrupt and unsuitable for the offices of state they are seeking.

It may be assumed that group loyalties are a general characteristic of "ethnicity;" but it is certainly wrong to use them as a basis for constructing a behavior pattern toward others outside an ethnic group. It may be supposed, incidentally, that transethnic moral behavior results from a belief in the doctrine of ethical relativism, the doctrine that a particular action may be considered right by one culture or society but wrong by another. I do not think, however, that an unacceptable transethnic moral attitude is simply a matter of ethical relativism. The reason is that, even though an unethical act, such as stealing things belonging to members of a different group, may be condoned, it would be correct to say that the condoning ethnic group will not accept or condone it if that act were to be committed against members of its own group: in that case, it would be regarded as absolutely wrong. So, it is more a matter of moral ambivalence or double standards than one of ethical relativism. Nevertheless, it can be said, surely, that a culture that fosters behavioral patterns that interfere with the interests of others simply because these others belong to another culture and that systematically fly in the face of universally accepted principles of moral behavior cannot be considered an enlightened culture, wherever it is practiced.

Our African cultures appear to foster attitudes toward public or government matters that militate against the application of one's greatest effort and induce apathy and carelessness in the service to the public. In Ghana, this attitude is expressed, or rather sanctioned, by a proverb that says: "We do not carry the government on our heads; we drag it on the floor" (aban womfa nsoa, wotwe no daadzie). The proverb has negative implications and consequences: it could whittle down the commitment of public officials to matters of state or matters of public concern; it is a mandate for regarding public or governmental matters as inconsequential, as matters not worthy of great care or attention or respect; it is a sure recipe for political and administrative indolence, corruption, and irresponsibility. The proverb has an affiliate in the concept denoted by the words *aban adwuma*, an Akan expression that means "government work" or "government undertaking"; but it may also be rendered as "public enterprise." The meaning of the expression usually is clear from the context. It is usually used when someone wants to contrast a private enterprise, the entire profit from which will accrue to the private owner, and hence requires his full attention and commitment, with a public enterprise (or, government undertaking or project) the failure or success of which he cares less about because the profit or gain from it accrues to someone else or to others—that is, the government. The two sayings can generate an attitude that treats governmental matters or public enterprises with unconscionable insouciance. The logical implications of these attitudes toward government or public enterprise seem to conflict with what Rattray says in the extensive quotation referred to in chapter 4, section 3, in which he speaks of the eagerness of the citizens (of Asante) to participate in the business of government. It must be noted, however, that Rattray is describing features of the system of traditional politics or government. It appears from the two sayings that the atavistic political values or attitudes may have changed with the emergence of a central government fashioned by the colonial rulers. But it may also be mentioned that it is one thing to be interested or concerned about the efficient way in which the business of government must be done; it is quite another to be honest in one's involvement in that business.

The traditional state is to all intents and purposes a social welfare state (see chapter 5) in which great attention, albeit excessive, is officially given to the enhancement of the welfare of each individual, a conduct that would involve a great state expenditure. The goals of the welfare state generate a paradox: on one hand, the state naturally desires to accumulate capital in order to pursue its plans; on the other hand, the capital that is being accumulated is consumed in the furnace of the dispensation of official largess, an act sanctioned by custom. The consequence of the paradox is that it would be difficult to accumulate capital for saving and reinvestment. From the moral point of view, the welfare state has much to commend it; but the efficient management of the economy requires tightening the purse strings by limiting how much should go into cushioning an individual's economic welfare. There is clearly a need for control here if the economy is to stay buoyant. In the absence of control, it would have been difficult for the traditional economy to move ahead because of the lack of savings.

3.1.4 Ancestorship. The African people, like others, value their traditions. Ancestorship—reverence of the ancestors—is one of their traditions. It is appropriate for a people to celebrate the memory of their ancestors or forbears and to show appreciation for their achievements through statues, plaques, remembrance days, names given to children, and other forms of memorial. But the African people, in my opinion, pay unnecessarily excessive and incessant attention to their ancestors. The ancestors are ever present in their consciousness. One reason for the excessive veneration of the ancestors is the belief that, having gained a spiritual status that presumably is invested with power that human beings do not possess but that they can exploit to enhance their mundane interests and welfare, the ancestors are believed to be in a position to bestow honors on their living descendants.

This excessive attention has resulted in their considering the modes of thought and action of the ancestors as embalmed, unalterable, and ever venerable, incapacitating most people from seeing beyond such utterances as "This is what the ancestors said," or "This is what the ancestors did." This mentality is an impediment to the cultivation of the innovative spirit or outlook required for making progress in the various spheres of human existence and the transition to modernity.

As for the resilient belief that the ancestors can bestow favors on their descendants and provide succor to them, there is no shred of evidence to justify it. The struggles, failures, and frustrations that the postcolonial African people have been experiencing in grappling with the enormous problems of development and nation-building clearly show that the ancestors— even if they are alive and well—cannot be helpful. Excessive and undue attention to the ancestors constraints people from giving the necessary attention to the future dimension of their mundane existence. One will be justified, then, in regarding the almost-worshipful attention to the ancestors as a negative feature of the African cultures.

These, then, are some of the features of our traditional African cultures that I consider negative from the point of view of the trends, demands, and development of a modern African society. It will be to our own moral, social, political, and intellectual chagrin to argue for the revival or maintenance and continuity of such negative features. On the contrary, a way forward in the pursuit of progress and modernity requires that the problems unleashed by those features of the cultures be grappled with most assiduously and realistically—unhampered by nostalgia, unfettered by atavism.

3.2 On the Positive Features of Our Cultures

The foregoing discussion of some of what may be regarded as disvalues or negative features of African cultures that need to be radically modified or simply abandoned in the attempt to revitalize the cultures for purposes of life in both the modern world and the future is of course not meant to exhaust all the negative things that can be said of the cultures. But I turn now to a discussion of what may be regarded as the positive features of the cultures that ought to be revived or maintained, even if refinements or amendments, as may be required by the ethos of the contemporary culture or by the circumstances of the multicultural statehood, may be needed. I must state that in attempting to point out what, in my opinion, are the values or positive features of the culture, I do not mean to apotheosize those features, for, as human institutions, they can lay no claim to perfection. I merely mean to point up the normative weight, and hence the relevance, of those features: that they are worthwhile and ought to be maintained and pursued even in the circumstances of the modern world. In this section, however, I limit my attention to a discussion of the humanist strand in African life and thought and postpone other matters of similar positive character to chapter 9.

In chapter 5, section 3, I point out that the concept of humanism is pervasive and fundamental in African social and moral thought and practice, that it even inspires religious faith and practice, and that it is that concept that the advocates of the so-called African socialism really had in mind in their arguments for the choice of socialism. What I want to do now is to indicate how the concept features or is understood in African thought and to point up its fundamental importance and relevance.

The well-known Akan proverb, "It is the human being that counts; I call upon gold, it answers not; I call upon cloth, it answers not; it is the human being that counts" expresses the idea that a human being is of a higher worth than gold or riches, and therefore it is he or she that counts or matters. This means that the worth of the human being ought to be given the ultimate consideration. The thought here finds expression in another proverb, similar in content: "The human being is more beautiful than gold." Before explicating the latter proverb, let me make some observations about how Akan aesthetics impinges on its morality. It seems to be true that in Akan conceptions, the aesthetic is not perceived merely in works of art and in events and scenes that temporally hold the attentive eye and ear of a person, arousing her interest and affording her enjoyment as she looks and listens. Akan aesthetics considers the beautiful to include more in the life of the human being, setting up standards of value for appraising, not just works of art, but other aspects of human life and culture as well. Thus, beauty is seen in the works of art and in the human figure as well as in the ethical behavior of people. Thus, in the Akan language of Ghana, for example, aesthetic terms are employed in evaluating ethical behavior as well: an individual's character may be described as ugly or as beautiful, or as becoming or unbecoming; an action may be described as "agreeable to the eye" or tasteful—referring to conduct or action that is agreeable to the moral palate. The terms "ugly," "beautiful," "becoming," "unbecoming," "agreeable to the eye," "tasteful," are all aesthetic terms, essentially.

Now, in the proverb "The human being is more beautiful than gold," the aesthetic strand in the perception of the worth of the human being, indicated by the word "beautiful," suggests undoubtedly that a human being is to be enjoyed for his or her own sake, not for the sake of anything else; for, that which is beautiful is of course enjoyable for its own sake.

It seems that the enjoyment of the human being—which is involved in the meaning of humanism—is an outstanding feature of the African cultures. In the view of Kenneth Kaunda, "To a certain extent, we in Africa have always had a gift for enjoying Man for himself. It is the heart of our traditional culture."[63] But, then, what is it to enjoy a human being?

To enjoy a human being certainly means several things: it is to appreciate her value as a human being and to express that appreciation in some concrete fashion such as demonstrating in her favor the virtues of compassion, generosity, hospitality, and so on; it is to be open to the interests and welfare of others, and to feel it a moral duty to offer some help where it is needed; it is, furthermore, to recognize the other person as a fellow human being, which, in turn, means to acknowledge that her worth as a human being is equal to our own and that there are some basic values, ideals, and sentiments (such as hopes and fears) that we all share by virtue of our common membership in the human species. To enjoy and appreciate the human being also means, at the public policy level, that the basic rights, which intrinsically belong to an individual by virtue of her being human, ought not to be interfered with, subverted, or set at nought. Thus, even though the proverb is an aesthetic expression, the thrust of its intended meaning is surely ethical: to point up the worth of a human being and the respect that ought to be accorded to her because of her humanity.

The humanist basis of African morality has been noted.[64] This conception of the origin and nature of morality rejects supernaturalist notions of morality. It sees morality as anchored in human experiences in living together, in the existential conditions of human beings. A humanist conception of morality is most likely to eliminate controversies surrounding the foundations of moral value. Also, a morality whose central focus is the concern for human well-being would expectably be a social—not individualistic—morality, having altruistic thrust. In our contemporary world, in which most people hanker after wealth, often at the expense of others, the moral principle embedded in the proverb "The human being is more beautiful than gold" is most important: it is indeed a moral—a categorical—imperative.

The humanist moral outlook fostered by African cultures is something that, I think, is worth being cherished in our modern world, for its goal is, from the moral point of view, fundamental. It seems to me that the most adequate morality is one that is humanly, socially, and altruistically grounded. This kind of morality should not be thrown overboard even in a technological world. For technology does not in any way mandate that the humanist essence of a culture should be subverted or abandoned. The value of concern for human well-being is intrinsic and should be maintained, not sacrificed on the altar of technology.

4. The Legacy of the Past in the Present

Now, the fairly elaborate discussion of what may be regarded as the positive and negative features of African traditional cultures in the foregoing two sections indicates, on one hand, that the culture of a people, embracive as it is of their total way of life, is a complex phenomenon, that an off-handed, wholesale rejection or acceptance of a cultural past in its entirety would be an oversimplification, and that, therefore, the positions of both the extreme revivalist and the extreme antirevivalist are untenable. The discussion indicates, on the other hand, that something of value can be found in the cultural past of a people, and that, if one were to examine the ancestral system of values objectively, one would find some values that would be considered relevant to the modern circumstances of Africa.

But here lies the all-important question: By what criteria are we to accept or reject traditional values, ideas, attitudes, and institutions? How, that is, do we judge that the legacy of a past is or is not worth being given some attention or place within the scheme of things of a present? An inkling of the answer to these questions was given in some concluding statements about the positive or negative features of the African traditional cultures. We may now elaborate on that answer.

There are, I think, at least two important criteria for judging the relevance of values, ideas, and institutions of a past to the circumstances of a present. These are the fundamental nature of a set of pristine values and attitudes and the functionality of past ideas and institutions in the setting of the present.

There surely are values that can be held as so fundamental to human existence that they can, for that reason, be said to transcend particular generations or epochs. Such fundamental and abiding values must be related to, or generated by, considerations of basic, sedimented human desires, wants, hopes, ideals, and sentiments. I am aware of course that a statement about the fundamental or abiding values is at variance with the view of the moral relativist who would have no use for a conception of fundamental or abiding or lasting values. Yet, it can hardly be seriously doubted that the possibility of human society is grounded on the reality of a core of fundamental human values the pursuit of which makes for the continuous existence, stability, and smooth functioning of society. A society without some shared values cannot exist *as* a society; the notion of shared values is basic to society. A present age must ask whether it can abandon such basic human values and continue to exist as a human society. An age or generation that does not pursue, for instance, the ethic of respect for human life and where wanton killings of human beings are the order of the day cannot survive as a human *society* for any length of time. Similarly, if sociality is natural to humans, as was proclaimed by Aristotle and others including some African traditional sages, then community life, a nonatomistic relational life, ought to be regarded as a fundamental human value. Thus, it is the basic, abiding character of certain values cherished and pursued by a tradition that makes those values relevant and brings that tradition into the normative embrace of a later age. Such fundamental human values provide a credible normative framework for human fulfillment.

The relevance of ideas and institutions of a past to a present would be determined also by their functionality, that is, whether or not they can play any meaningful or effective roles in the present scheme of things and so conduce to the attainment of the goals and vision of that present. Ideas and institutions that have survived many generations and proved their worth can be considered suitable for the purposes of a present moment; otherwise, they must be regarded as obsolete, consequently to be jettisoned and replaced by new ones. It is the profound appreciation of the worth of some values, ideas, and practices of a past and the resilience and acknowledged efficacy of those values that recommend them to a present age and underpin the significance of such utterances as "our *traditions* of democracy," "our *traditions* of hospitality," "our *traditions* of humanism," and "our *traditions* of liberal thought." Such intellectually or morally satisfying utterances are most probably an insinuation of a firm belief in some basic human values that, perhaps in different forms and shapes, transcend particular generations in the trajectory of a cultural tradition. All such traditions, as depicted in those utterances, are of course not a sudden emergence, as our analysis of the notion of tradition in section 1 clearly indicates; they are the ideas and values that have been hallowed not only by time but also by function, notwithstanding the possibility or likelihood of their having undergone some transformation in the course of their history.

That traditions, or traditional values, are not a sudden emergence is a conceptual truth, involved in the meaning of tradition. What are considered today the traditions of a society have, if they are indeed traditions, a long history behind them. The ideas of natural (human) rights and democracy in the cultural traditions of Western societies, which I briefly discussed earlier, are examples. Just as in a family lineage descendants tend to be forgetful (or, sometimes totally ignorant) of their forebears, so are we all sometimes oblivious of the origins of some of our present ideas, practices, or institutions. One outstanding reason for this is that the ancient or past cultural values or institutions would have gone through processes, sometimes profound processes, of refinement prior to arriving at their present status or character. The profound nature of the changes or refinements those ideas, practices, and institutions may have gone through can mislead a present generation into supposing that they are of recent origin. The refinements and pruning are of course consciously and purposively undertaken by the users of a culture who see those atavistic values and institutions as worthwhile, but who, nevertheless, also see the need to refine them in order to make them most relevant to the circumstances and ethos of their age. The reasons for refining, amending, or abandoning ideas, practices, and institutions received from previous generations are not far to seek. One reason is that certain features or aspects of the traditional conceptions of things may be disharmonious with the situations of later generations, those received conceptions having been fashioned in conditions entirely different from those of later generations. Another reason is that the institutions and practices may, in the forms in which they are received, be considered dysfunctional by later generations. This reason clearly indicates that refinements and amendments to traditional cultural values and institutions, as well as rejections of them, may have to be undertaken for the sole purpose of *revitalizing* the received cultural tradition, not abandoning it root and branch.

At this point I wish to follow up on my promise to provide evidence to indicate that the ancestors of the African people assumed that later generations, that is, their descendants, would make changes in the practices and institutions bequeathed to them. The traditional sages maintain, according to an Akan proverb, that "times change" (mmere di adannan). "Times" here refers to generations, histories, and, therefore, events, circumstances, situations. The sages also say, according to another Akan proverb, "the resting place of the ancients [i.e., ancestors], we no longer rest there."[65] There is, I think, a logical connection between the two sayings of the traditional sages: the latter saying can be seen as the consequent of the former. If times change, then, some of the ancestral customs or practices or modes of thought and action need not, in fact should not, be tenaciously adhered to if later (including the present) generations have good reasons not to hold on to them. The reason is, simply, that the ancestral "resting place"—a reference to old or inherited customs and practices—may no longer be convenient or appropriate; a better one may have to be created.

There is indeed a very significant Akan proverb that forthrightly states the need to evaluate a cultural past. This is expressed in the proverb, "A person cutting a path does not know that the part that he has cleared behind him is crooked."[66] The point here is that it is the person or persons who come after who realize that the path is crooked. The path refers to the whole corpus of the cultural values and practices pursued by the forebears and inherited by subsequent generations; it is a reference, in short, to the entire legacy of the past. The proverb implies that later generations (including present generations) are expected to take a critical look at their cultural heritage with a view to eliminating or amending the "crooked" or inelegant aspects of that heritage. It implies, further, that explanations of thought and action of a present age in terms of off-handed references to what the ancestors are supposed to have said or to have done that may not have been given adequate critical reappraisal by a present generation would have no rational warrant even within the indigenous thought system itself. The proverb, in a nutshell, enjoins a critical evaluation of a cultural heritage. It suggests the conviction in fact that the expression "new wine in old wine bottles" must be inverted to become "old wine in new wine bottles." The inverted form of the expression points to the need for a reinterpretation and reevaluation by later generations of their cultural traditions—the "old wine"—if they are to unburden themselves of the encumbrances inherent or discoverable in the received tradition. Later generations should take a critical look at the ingredients or elements of the old wine.

The growth of a human culture, its capacity to avoid decadence and dysfunction and to adapt itself to new situations and demands, its capacity to constitute itself into a credible and viable framework for human fulfillment—all this is due, surely, to the reinterpretation and critical reevaluation of a cultural tradition as it moves through history. This critical reevaluation of a received cultural tradition will not only suggest refinement or appropriate amendment that, in the name of renewal and revitalization, ought to be made to it but also direct attention to the aspects of it that, in the name of progress and success, ought to be expunged from the cultural life and thought of a people. It is, remember, this critical reinterpretation and reevaluation that will also lead to the euphoric affirmation of the abiding worth of what can truly be acknowledged as positive features of the values of a cultural tradition.

5. On the Notion of Modernity

I devote the final section of this chapter to a discussion of modernity, a very important notion indeed. The notion of modernity, like the notion of development, has been very significant for the peoples of the world for more than a century. It has in fact assumed or rather gained a normative status, in that all societies in the world without exception aspire to become modern, to exhibit in their social, cultural, and political lives features said to characterize modernity—whatever this notion means or those features are. By virtue of the overwhelming and resilient importance of the notion, Western societies generally, from which the notion is said to have emerged, have become the quintessence of modernity, the mecca to which peoples from non-Western societies go for inspiration and knowledge as to models of thought and action in pursuit of the development of their societies and transition to modernity.

Yet it has not been easy for both Western and non-Western intellectuals to define modernity, to explicate what its essential features are or ought to be. This is, I think, due to the complex and controversial or contested nature of the notion. The complexity seems to spring from, among other things, the fact that modernity is essentially a cultural phenomenon, culture itself being a complex and an all-engulfing concept: it is obviously not all features of a particular culture that will be attractive to others outside that culture; some features of a culture may in fact be scoffed at by people who do not belong to it. The controversial nature of the notion of modernity stems, I think, from the fact that it spews out some moral prescriptions—an inevitable concomitant of a cultural system that modernity is. Many may not be attracted by the ethic of individualism, for instance, which is an essential feature of modernity as pursued in Western societies. Much has been written about modernity, mostly by Western intellectuals; my brief discussion will, I hope, illuminate some of the highlights.

Modernity can be defined as the ideas, principles, and ideals covering a whole range of human activities that have underpinned Western life and thought since the seventeenth century. The constitution of modernity makes it a philosophical doctrine and, as such, it is essentially linked to Western cultures; it was, and is, culture dependent, even though this fact does not in any way confine the appreciation of the notion, and the exploitation of its practical implications and consequences, to the West. But it cannot be denied that those characteristics that cohered into what is called modernity evolved endogenously in societies of Europe, even though it cannot be denied either that some non-European cultural inventions or institutions may have been appropriated or exploited by Europe, but uniquely developed by it.

Among the factors that provided the impetus to the development of modernity, the intellectual currents of the premodern era, especially of the medieval period, cannot be underrated. Lynn White is most probably right in saying that "without medieval technology . . . what we call the modern world would not have come into being."[67] Yet, in accounts of the emergence of modernity, attention is often focused on the scientific developments and achievements of seventeenth-century Europe, the technology and industrial revolution of the eighteenth century, the sweeping social and economic changes associated with the practice of capitalism in and after the seventeenth century, and the Reformation and Counter-Reformation that gave rise to what is called the Protestant ethic with its emphasis on individual responsibility. But it can be said, with considerable certainty, I think, that not all of these important antecedents or makings of modernity were inventions or creations—bolts from the blue, as it were—of the centuries between the sixteenth and the eighteenth. The truth is that the intellectual impulse or ferment of at least several of the factors that gave rise to modernity can be traced to the Middle Ages, specifically to some features and consequences of the Renaissance movement, which was an intellectual movement.

Humanism, the fundamental principle and the intellectual, perhaps also ideological, engine of modernity, placed the ultimate value in individual humans and in their rationality. It placed a premium on the creative capacities of the human being and on the concern for her leading an abundant life in this mundane world. Humanism can certainly be regarded as the foundation of the doctrines of individual rights, individual freedom, the need to allow the exercise of individual capabilities and endowments and other features of the value of individuality, and the cult of reason—all of which constituted the intellectual background of modernity. The achievements of modern science, of Western economic systems, and of democracy and civil liberties, and the diversity of modern intellectual and artistic culture would be inconceivable without the pervasiveness of humanism in modern Western culture.[68]

But, it must be remembered that humanism, as a doctrine, can be traced to ancient Greek thought and was an outstanding feature of the Renaissance movement; it was not a creation of modernity; modernity exploited it. It would not be false to assert that conceptual elements of modernity, such as humanism and secularism, and the Copernican system of science—a system that can be considered a cornerstone of modernity,[69] predate modernity. According to Leo Strauss, "liberal democracy, in contradistinction to communism and fascism, derives powerful support from a way of thinking which cannot be called modern at all: the premodern thought of our western tradition."[70] George Lodge asserts that the American founding fathers "following the Lockean ideology, rejected the authoritarianism of the eighteenth century Europe, preferring the decentralization, dispersion, division of power characteristic of *an earlier period.*"[71] (By the "earlier period," Lodge is referring to the medieval period.) It would be correct to say, then, that in many instances modernity is either a logical fleshing out, or a representation of advanced forms, of conceptual elements of the thought systems of preceding European cultures. Conceptual elements such as representative democracy and the nation-state and phenomena such as industrial technology, however, can be said to have made their debut after the seventeenth century. Even so, modernity can in many ways be regarded as a *stage*—an advanced or sophisticated or enlightened stage—of European (or Western) civilization, some features of which will continue to become more sophisticated in response to new ideas about human progress. It is certainly not a completed thing, despite the talk of "postmodernity" by some Western intellectuals.

Let me digress here somewhat in order to make some observations on the concept of postmodernity. The concept becomes intelligible, to my mind, only if there is evidence to show beyond doubt that some new conceptual systems, social practices, institutions, habits, and outlooks make a complete break with their modern moorings, that they represent completely new paradigms radically different from those maintained in the modern times, and that they, thus, eclipse the modern scheme of things. This means that if what are regarded as new conceptual systems, situations, or features are just new forms or refinements of the modern schemes—the result therefore of transformative processes, then, the new situations cannot appropriately be described as postmodern. There does not seem to be much evidence of an entirely new mental outlook or a radically new metaphysic—new perception of reality—to fully justify the description of some phenomena as postmodern.

"Postmodernity" is essentially a reaction to the problems of modernity, a critical response to what has been characterized by some Western intellectuals as a "crisis of modernity." Stirrings of postmodernity seem to spring from skepticism about (some) modern institutions and forms of life. The critiques and skepticisms may lead to revisions and amendments to modernity. One outstanding feature of Western modernity is the ascendancy of reason, whose apotheosis may be said to have begun with the philosophical works of the French philosopher Descartes in the seventeenth century. An attack has been launched by some Western intellectuals over the last few decades on the "special status" accorded to reason in the Western intellectual culture since the dawn of modernity. And the attack is called a postmodern critique of reason. But the attack is surely *not* intended to debase the place of reason in human life and to replace it with something else. As I understand it, the attack on reason seeks, on one hand, merely to raise questions and doubts about its ascendant or privileged status in the activity of human life and its fulfillment, and, on the other hand, to give recognition to other, perhaps equally important, features of human nature, such as feeling. I do not think it is the intention of the critiques of reason to privilege feeling over reason as such. Yet, the recognition of the element of feeling in human life would not, to my mind, be a postmodern discovery. For it cannot be said that that element was never part of the Western conception of human nature, even if it was—or may have been—suppressed or sublimated in the behavior of individual persons in Western societies. Thus, what may be characterized as a postmodern perception or outlook may in fact not be radically or entirely new to Western culture examined in its *historical* dimensions.

For instance, if the Communitarian movement (or, agenda) initiated in 1990 by Amitai Etzioni and others that is "committed to creating a new moral, social, and public order based on *restored* communities"[72] became influential, gained currency in the social and moral thought and practice of the wider American society, succeeded in making people aware—as before, and long ago—of their commitment to the community and appreciate their responsibilities to other members of the community (just as they are ever aware of their individual rights), the new community ethos that might be engendered by the movement could be characterized as postmodern. There might be some justification in the characterization in view of the fact that individualism has been an outstanding feature of Western modernity. Yet, on the basis of our knowledge of the characteristics of medieval European society, which was a communal society[73] and whose culture forms part of the American cultural heritage—historically speaking—one would be justified in saying that what would be regarded as postmodern was in many ways *premodern:* it would be the resuscitation of a premodern—a medieval—social and moral value and practice. The Communitarian movement is aimed at satisfying what Leroy Rouner refers to as "our nostalgia for *premodern* times when natural bonds to kith and kin were unshakable."[74]

This is not to imply, by any means, that in the future dimensions of human history there will be no postmodern social order. So long as human beings exercise their intellects and their inventive and innovative spirits, new discoveries, inventions, ideas, and systems will be evolved that will be of such a nature as to herald a transition to a postmodern world. The transition to a postmodern world will thus result from positive and profoundly new contributions to society or to human progress, not just from mere negative reactions to modernity's problems or (some of) its characteristics. Unless criticisms and skepticisms yield positive constructions, they will hardly constitute a harbinger for a postmodern world. Postmodernity will have to affirm or generate new phenomena or systems or outlooks.

For instance, if there is overwhelming evidence that an individualist structure of society that had for centuries in the modern world been maintained by a cultural tradition is giving (or has in fact given) way to, say, a communitarian structure; or if an antisupernaturalistic metaphysics adhered to by a cultural tradition for centuries in the modern world is found to be giving (or in fact to have given) way to a supernaturalistic metaphysics or a kind of metaphysics that clearly demonstrates that the old, that is, modern, metaphysics has completely petered out or sunk into oblivion, so that what we see in both situations are clear discontinuities: then, the communitarian structure in regard to the first example and the new (supernaturalistic) metaphysics in regard to the second can appropriately be described as postmodern. Also, suppose a communitarian culture or tradition that has been evolved and adhered to by a society for centuries in the modern era atrophies and gives way to an individualist culture—an individualist culture that has been maintained for centuries by other societies in the modern world: it can be said that for the former (communitarian) culture the new individualist cultural outlook would be a postmodern experience; but not so, as far as the latter (individualist) culture is concerned. In other words, what would be a postmodern idea or structure or formation for one cultural tradition may not be postmodern at all for another cultural tradition. This seems to suggest the relative or contestable or incommensurable character of a concept of postmodernity.

Let us now get back to our attempt to understand the notion of modernity. Modernity is etymologically linked to the Latin *modernus,* a word that the medieval scholars derived from *modo,* meaning "just now," "recently,"[75] also "present" (*tempus modernum:* present, modern times). The terms *modernus* ("man of today") and *modernitas* ("modern times") were used in medieval Latin throughout Europe from the fifth century A.D. and more frequently after the tenth century.[76] *Modernus* was used as the opposite of *antiquus, vetus,* and *priscus,* meaning "old," "ancient."

We learn that Cassiodorus (c. A.D. 485–580), a scholar and statesman, for the first time distinguished between the "ancients" *(antiqui)*, the masters of the ancient classical culture, and the "moderns" *(moderni)*, their present heirs. Cassiodorus conceived modernity in terms of the revival of the classical heritage, a heritage he considered superior.[77] His conception of modernity was influential for many centuries until after the twelfth century when it was challenged, and then it divided medieval scholars into two groups, with the "ancients" advocating the superiority of antiquity to modernity and the "moderns" upholding the superiority of modernity.[78] What we should note, for the moment, is that the perception of the social and intellectual formation of some era in European history as "modern" *predated* the seventeenth century. This really introduces an element of confusion—perhaps complexity—into the notion of modernity as it has been understood and used since the seventeenth-century Europe.

Now, the interesting question is, does the reference to, say, the ideas and values of the Greeks as "ancient" involve qualitative attribution? Will the distinction made by a medieval writer between *vita moderna* (life of today, modern life) and *vita antiqua* (ancient life), or one made by a nineteenth-century writer between medieval European life and European life of the nineteenth century, be a qualitative distinction? The answers to these questions are yes, as the late medieval dispute over the superiority or inferiority of the ancient Greek culture seems to suggest. But it must be borne in mind, I think, that the qualitative distinction will not necessarily be in favor of the nineteenth-century life, a much later form of the cultural life of the (European) tradition. It depends, in my view, on the spheres or specific ways of life that are being compared. If the comparison is being made in the areas of science, technology, and political and economic progress, one would have to come down on the side of the nineteenth-century European life. If the comparison is being made, however, in the areas of social and moral life, the decision may not be as simple and straightforward. I think it can be said that the way of life within later forms of a culture may not necessarily be superior in *all* ways to the way of life practiced within previous forms of that culture. From the historical fact of the decline or demise of civilizations, it cannot be asserted that later forms or stages of a culture are in their entirety necessarily superior to earlier forms of it, for the decline or demise is a clear reflection—a sure evidence—of the degenerate state into which some aspects of the later forms of the culture may have fallen. Thus the qualitative distinction between different forms or stages of a culture may not always (have to) be made in favor of the later forms or stages of the culture in their entirety.

It would be correct to say, I think, that the latest generations of a trajectory of a particular cultural tradition would claim the status of being "modern," not just in the medieval European sense of "people of today" or "people of now" *(moderni)*, but in the sense that they see their times culturally different in contrast to earlier or "ancient" times. Thus the medieval Arabic philosophers who had been cultivating the Greek-Hellenistic intellectual culture for centuries referred to the Greek philosophers as "the ancients" (in Arabic, *qudamā'*; literally, "predecessors").[79] They certainly saw themselves as "modern" *(muta'akhirūn,* "the people of now, the latter-day thinkers"); so did some of the medieval Latin scholars. In characterizing themselves or their times as modern, both the Arabic and Latin scholars were expressing their sense of cultural difference from the ancients *(qudamā', antiqui)*. But not only that: they must surely have considered their own times as advanced (or, more advanced) in most, if not all, spheres of human endeavor. The social and economic changes and the scientific and technological achievements of the post-seventeenth-century European generations provided the basis of their claim to the status of being modern. They must also have regarded their sociocultural traits and achievements as in many ways discontinuous with those of previous European societies and cultures. There is reason to believe, however—even though I am not attempting to prophesy— that two or three centuries from now greater, more sophisticated achievements will probably have been made by the generations of those times in most spheres of the human enterprise that would justify their claim to "modernity" or "late modernity." When they look back on our *present* world, they will most probably consider it as "less modern," if not "premodern."

I remarked a while ago on the complexity of the notion of modernity. I wish now to make further remarks on the complex nature of this notion. The notion gives the impression that its elements are wholly or essentially modern, having occurred since the sixteenth century, and that, because of its European origin and development, those elements are also wholly European. This impression is false. For, first, modernity inevitably contains elements that are clearly traditional, inherited, and appropriated from previous generations of the European civilizational trajectory. Second, modernity, in its evolution, must have appropriated elements from other non-European cultural traditions: this fact follows from the logic of the widely accepted view (explicated and amplified in my analysis of the notion of tradition in section 1) that no cultural tradition has historically been devoid of elements from other, that is, alien, cultural traditions. For instance, according to Shils, "The laying open of Africa to explorers and colonizers was followed by the bringing back to Europe of works of African art which were assimilated into and changed greatly the tradition of European painting and sculpture."[80] Much of Europe's borrowing and assimilation of African art probably took place after the middle of the eighteenth century, that is, during the modern era. It can thus be said that, despite its origin in Europe, modernity took on elements from other, non-European (non-Western) sources. But not only that: the fact that modernity, based in Europe, thought it appropriate to take on and assimilate elements from non-European sources seems to suggest that the non-European elements were themselves modern, or at least bore the tinge of modernity. That would have been the reason why those elements were given a place in the scheme of things of European modernity. But this means generally that there are elements of the traditional thought of "traditional societies" not entirely dissimilar to, or incompatible with, those of

European (Western) modernity—at least early modernity. Thus, Benjamin Schwartz says, "There may indeed be elements of Chinese traditional thought which are similar to or compatible with elements of modern Western thought."[81]

All this not only makes modernity a complex notion but also implies that the view of modernity as of European origin is true only in reference to certain specific features or achievements of the cultural traditions of Europe, or perhaps better, to certain aspects of the human enterprise. Modernity, then, in the way it has developed in Western societies, cannot claim or be proven to be superior in all of its manifestations to other cultural traditions, despite the fact that a number of its ideas, values, and institutions have assumed the status of a model for other non-Western cultures.

It would be correct to say, however, that the approach taken by non-Western cultures to (Western) modernity as a model will be selective, and this for at least two reasons. One is that non-Western cultures may not feel enamored of all the manifestations of modernity that have been pursued in Western societies: no cultural tradition has commended itself in its entirety to others outside that tradition. Another—and surely related to the first—is the desire on the part of non-Western societies to preserve those of their cultural values that they consider not only worthwhile but also preferable to their Western equivalents. One of Western modernity's principles or basic ideas is individualism; another is antisupernaturalism, which, in the Western conception, is closely linked with humanism. These principles would hardly find embrace in the bosom of the cultures that resiliently value community life and consider the religious life intrinsic to—inseparable from—their total way of life. But while these cultures may not be enamored of such social and metaphysical principles as individualism and antisupernaturalistic humanism, they would be impressed by the material progress that is undoubtedly the hallmark of Western modernity. It may be said in fact that material progress—progress based on economic prosperity—is the real essence of modernity in the way the notion has been conceived and pursued in Western societies. But the engines of material progress of Western modernity are science and technology on one hand and the capitalist mode of economic activity on the other. Science and technology have led to advanced forms of industrialism that have, in turn, greatly enhanced economic production and material abundance in industrialized nations.

In view of the need and desire of the human society—whether it is a type oriented to supernaturalism (religiosity) and anti-individualism or not—to enhance its material existence, it would be expected that the economic arrangement evolved by Western modernity will serve as a model for (most) non-Western societies. But the important question is, is it possible to assume Western models of science and technology and the capitalist economic system without taking on other cultural values of Western modernity in tandem? This question may be answered both yes and no. There is a very close link, for instance, between capitalism on one hand and democracy, individual freedom (distinguished from unbridled individualism), and human rights on the other, though identifying this link is not to imply that it is a logical one. There is no such link, however, between capitalism and anti-supernaturalistic metaphysic, or between capitalism and individualistic ethic. (I distinguish individualistic ethic from individual initiative or enterprise; while the latter is certainly part of the idea and practice of capitalism, the former is not.) The possibility of this delinking provides the basis for the selective approach to the ideas, principles, or paradigms evolved by (Western) modernity that may be undertaken by the adherents of non-Western cultures.

6. Conclusion

In this long but crucial chapter I have attempted to provide some clarification of the notions of tradition and modernity. I argue that tradition be defined rather as that which is inherited, accepted, and preserved from previous generations than as that which is merely handed down or transmitted from previous generations. The amendment I am suggesting is based on the fact that cultural values, beliefs, and institutions received from, or bequeathed by, the past can be rejected or disavowed by a present, that is, a subsequent generation. Thus, a present generation, to the extent that it preserves and nurtures what it has inherited from the past and places it at the disposal of succeeding generations is more appropriately regarded as a maker of tradition than is the original generation that created values and practices that eventually evolved into a tradition. Within this definitional framework, the idea of the authority of tradition becomes nearly implausible: a tradition has no real authority, if by authority it is meant that tradition can influence or control the lives of its adherents *without* the adherents themselves being prepared, and seeing the need, to submit to it. Similarly, the notion of the invention of tradition also becomes unacceptable: real traditions are not invented.

The conception of modernity may give the impression that modernity represents a break with tradition and is thus irreconcilable with it; such an impression would clearly be false. For one thing, every society in the *modern* world has many traditional elements inherited and accepted from previous, that is, "premodern," generations; for another, if in *modern* times we can talk sensibly about "our *traditions* of so-and-so" (for instance, our traditions of humanist ethic), then traditions are not irreconcilable with modernity. Thus the modernity of tradition would be an intelligible concept, just as would the tradition of modernity—inasmuch as modern culture itself has become a tradition. The intelligibility of the concept of the modernity of tradition not only logically eliminates the alleged antithesis between tradition and modernity but also makes implausible the distinction between reason (or rationality) and tradition that has been made especially by social scientists since—and under the influence of—Max Weber. It cannot at all be denied that in the development of human culture some features of the cultural tradition of a people have, through the activity of *reason*, been abandoned, modified, or refined.

Modernity, which is essentially the intellectual basis of life in the Western world but has mutatis mutandis become a common heritage of humankind, can only be said to be a *new* stage in cultural development, a surrogate, if you like, for advanced forms of human knowledge, techniques, and socio-economic structures. But it can also be said that some features of modernity make it a relative notion, inasmuch as not all features of it are attractive to non-Western cultures, whose approach to embracing it would therefore be selective. The aspects of modernity, however, that cannot really be rejected or compromised on, where great improvements in material conditions are hoped for, are technology and the economic system that has come to be known as the free enterprise (or market) system.

It is worth noting that the use and deep appreciation of such expression as "our *tradition* of democratic politics," "our tradition of humanist ethic," and so on, are probable references to what may be regarded as abiding or sedimented practices, outlooks, and beliefs that, though perhaps in different shapes and forms, transcend particular generations in the trajectory of a cultural tradition. These practices and beliefs probably relate to the texture of human desires, goals, ideals, and aspirations as conceived and cherished by a particular cultural tradition. What is of interest about tradition is that those who originally established its contents (or elements) as well as those who inherited, preserved, and placed it at the disposal of later generations were human beings who were attempting to grapple with problems some of which, perhaps basic to human life as such, may not be entirely dissimilar to those of later generations, including a present generation. This is the reason why much of the Funeral Oration of Pericles extolling the virtues of democracy in fifth century B.C. Athens (almost twenty-five hundred years ago) can be appreciated and embraced by generations of the eighteenth as well as the twentieth centuries of our modern era.

I have given reasons why the positive, nostalgic attitude of acceptance of the entire cultural past of a people on one hand, and the casual rejection of it in its entirety on the other hand, are both wrong-headed approaches to an objective, normative assessment of a cultural past. I have also pointed up what I consider the positive and negative features of African cultures (dwelling a great part of the time on the Ghanaian experience), features that, on normative grounds, may be regarded as either symphonic or discordant with the ethos of modern cultural life.

9

Epilogue

Which Modernity? Whose Tradition?

In the preceding chapters, I have made such observations as the following: that modernity is not entirely antithetical to, or irreconcilable with, tradition, inasmuch as modernity contains many of the elements of previous cultural traditions; that in the light of our common humanity and the essentialism that this seems to involve, there is some justification for believing in a core of common or universal ideas and values—a distinction, is made, however, between essential and contingent (or functional) universality; that, even though a cultural product has a specific cultural or social origin, given our common humanity, it can nevertheless be said to be a creation generally for humankind as such; that, in consequence of the very last observation, values and products of what might be regarded as alien cultures are appreciated, borrowed, and appropriated by other cultures; that, even though modernity developed from Western cultures, its products have become the common heritage of humanity as such; and that, despite the important characteristics of Western modernity, not all aspects of it are necessarily attractive to non-Western cultures. These observations and others related to them constitute the background and framework for the discussion of the phenomenon of modernization in Africa—of what should constitute the important features of African modernity.

In this concluding chapter, I deal with the question, what is modernization—or, what is it to be or become modern? But the important cluster of specific questions I discuss include the following: Are there alternative forms of modernity? Does it make sense to forge creatively a (new) modernity appropriate to particular cultural traditions? And how can this creative modernity be undertaken? The answers of these questions provide some answers to the main question that heads this epilogue, "Which Modernity? Whose Tradition?"

Being modern or becoming modern must somehow be related to modernization: becoming modern is perhaps the outcome of the process of modernization; to be modern is to have successfully gone through the process of modernization. In consequence, "being modern" and (becoming) "modernized" would, in the final analysis, be considered co-extensive terms. The co-extensive character or the logical equivalence of the two concepts appears to be subverted, however, by the meaning that has been given to the concept of modernization. Modernization, according to many scholars, means "Westernization"—taking on the values, ideas, and institutions (political, economic, technological, etc.) of the West. The late Sir Hamilton Gibb, a foremost scholar of Near Eastern cultures, said it succinctly: "The plain truth of the matter is that 'modernization' means 'Westernization'."[1] Since the feature of Westernization that has palpably been most outstanding and ascendant is industrialization, with its concomitant of phenomenal economic growth, modernization has come to be equated with industrialization: a modern or modernized society is one that is a technologically advanced industrial society.

But the assertion that there is a link between modernization and Westernization, which Gibb's language, for instance, suggests is a conceptual (logical) link, is not well founded. The link cannot be conceptual; it can only be empirical. For it is possible for a nation or society to become Westernized without becoming modernized; just as it is possible for a nation or society to be modernized without fully becoming Westernized. African nations, through their long contacts with Westernism, have, whether voluntarily or involuntarily, acquired Western values and institutions without becoming modernized, that is, industrialized, in any real sense; Japan is a modernized nation, but it is not wholly Westernized, having preserved many of its own traditional cultural values and institutions. Thus the link between modernization and Westernization can only be empirical, not conceptual. This logically implies that modernization cannot be defined in terms of Westernization. And, because Western nations are industrialized nations, modernization has come to be defined in terms also of industrialization. But such a definition is mistaken. It must be noted that we can talk of modernization in reference to practically all spheres of the human enterprise: in reference to architectural style, commercial practices, scientific outlook and beliefs, the political or social or educational system, and so on.

If an African political leader or social worker says, "We need to modernize our inheritance system," he would not mean that they should simply replace their traditional system of inheritance with the system practiced in Western cultures. He would mean that they should amend or refine their inheritance system by getting rid of those features of it that are considered inelegant or inappropriate from the point of view of their experiences and goals in the modern world, or that they should abandon it root and branch and replace it entirely with a new system that is not necessarily a Western type but a new type that is either endogenously produced or has aspects borrowed from some other cultures, Western or non-Western. What I am at pains to dispute is the (logical) equivalence some people want to establish between modernization and Westernization. Similarly, if a traditional food technologist says, "We need to modernize our traditional food industries," she certainly would not mean that they should "industrialize" their traditional industries. For that would be senseless. Thus, modernization does not simply mean Westernization or industrialization.

One can—and should—understand the basis of the (conceptual) link that has been assumed by some people between modernization on one hand and Westernization and industrialization on the other hand. Modernity emerged and developed in Western European cultures and societies that also became industrialized in the course of time. But even though the technological and the industrial may be said to have become its most outstanding characteristics Western modernity nevertheless evolved other important features. Besides the advanced forms of science and technology developed by Western modernity, urbanism, individualism, the ascendancy of reason, the emergence of the nation-state secularism and the relegation of religion to the private sphere of life—these, and others related to them, are among the central characteristics of Western modernity. Thus, if the process of modernization is intended to mean taking on the characteristics of Western modernity and in this way becoming "modern," then modernization, to repeat, cannot simply mean industrialization or becoming technologically advanced; it must, in principle, mean *more* than that.

Perhaps it should be noted in passing that some of these features of Western modernity are being questioned by Western intellectuals themselves who see inadequacies in them that have negative consequences for both public and private spheres of human life: technology and industrialism, undisciplined and unguided by other values, are resulting in environmental and ecological degradation; individualism, which in its extreme form appears to be antithetical to natural human sociality, is causing an atomization of human society, a weakening of social ties, and a fragmentation of social and moral values. One Western philosopher speaks of the unbearable 'loneliness' attendedant upon individualism.[2] For these reasons, some Western intellectuals are advocating a stronger sense of community or some kind of balance between individuality and sociality; secularism, which manifests itself in the separation of church and state, does not seem to have been celebrated by all sections of Western societies: there have from time to time been efforts, for instance, to restore the religious act of prayer in public schools;[3] there has been an attack by Western intellectuals on the ascendancy of reason stemming from the realization in recent modernity that the human being is not a purely and wholly rational animal and that she is of a complex nature. And so on. Unless the consequences or problems unleashed by Western modernity are seriously and effectively tackled, they will, in the opinion of such Western intellectuals, in time negate the gains or the original intentions of (Western) modernity and impede the achievement of the long-term goals of human flourishing and fulfillment, thus bringing modernity itself to grief.

Urbanism—the culture of city dwelling—has become a feature of Western modernity, even though this does not mean that rural and small-town life has disappeared. Urbanism developed out of a population growth in urban centers or large cities. The extensive application of advanced technologies in Western societies led to industrialization, which in turn resulted in the creation of jobs in specific centers, drawing large portions of the hitherto rural populations to these centers. The concentration of huge numbers of people in some specific centers and the concentration of civic, political, and professional activities required to run a modern state created a tide of urbanism that cannot be stemmed. Thus the creation of modernity in Africa can hardly avoid an urban culture. But modernity will be more desirable, in my opinion, if the urban culture that will necessarily emerge with it in modern Africa does not result in the fragmentation of community life and the cultivation of outlooks and attitudes so individualistic and careless about interpersonal relationships that such congregations of people become "lonely crowds."

The description of large populations in urban centers as lonely crowds is an oxymoron. Yet that description would take on significant meaning in modern Africa if urbanism were allowed to result in fragmenting community life and making each person think in terms only of his or her own interests without any commitment to a shared social life that characterizes the traditional society. The consequence of this will be that one individual will come to be suspicious and fearful of the other and will keep to himself or herself. Leading a lonely life will thus become a preferable (or a preferred) way of life. This need not be so if we have a clear and deep understanding of the value of community life for our individual lives. On normative grounds, the idea or value of community life—greatly appreciated and practiced in premodern and "traditional" societies of the world—should not be allowed to be swept away by modernity. Because of the importance of this value for human life, a way must be found to reincarnate it even in modern urban settings.

The premodern social life in Western societies was largely communal.[4] This communal social fabric appears to have been torn apart by transition to modernity in the West (even though, as I point out below, there is evidence that individualism in Western societies developed independently of such features of Western modernity as industrialization and urbanization). Does this mean, first, that there is a necessary (logical) link between modernity and the fragmentation of communal life, and second, that urbanization is a sufficient condition for individualism? Some people, I believe, will deny any such necessary link, even though they will admit the possibility of the erosion of some features of community ties of the type experienced in previously rural settings. And to say that urbanization is a sufficient condition for individualism is in a sense to imply that urbanization is absolutely incompatible with communality—with the pursuit of community life or communal values—that urbanism and communitarianism (communalism) cannot at all coexist, that urbanism will have to lead to individualism. But any alleged sufficiency of that condition is patently and deeply undercut by the nostalgic sentiments expressed by people whose societies have been largely urbanized, people who now dwell in urban settings. Here, I am referring specifically to communitarian thinkers of the West whose cultures are of course urban but who, nevertheless, are advocating the restoration of communal values, of a robust sense of community.

Some American academics and intellectuals concerned about the need for a new community ethos in their society have put forward what they call the Communitarian Agenda (see p. 266). The effect, in the words of one American political scientist, is that "community, its nature, and its desirability are now a part of the conversation of many political intellectuals in the United States; *it has become a watchword of the age.*"[5]

And so it is that in the last two decades many publications authored by Western scholars have come out extolling the virtues of—and emphasizing the need for—community but pointing up also the weaknesses of an unbridled individualism. Their intention is not, to be sure, to sweep away the individualist outlooks or mentalities of their compatriots but to find some kind of balance between individuality and communality: to moderate the two systems. The putative concern for the community and the barrage of procommunity literature indicate that people do not consider urbanization a necessary or sufficient condition for the fragmentation of communal values and the concomitant inauguration of individualism. If urbanization were recognized as a sufficient condition for individualism, it would be senseless, on logical grounds, and futile, on pragmatic grounds, to talk of amending or tinkering with its consequence, which is individualism. It may also be inferred from the expression of concern that modernity or urbanization was not necessarily expected to result in the fragmentation of community life. The concern for a robust sense of community is indeed an appropriate reflection of, and response to, our natural human sociality.

In saying all this, however, I am not implying at all that urbanization will leave the claims of the community unscathed, without any disruption of the pristine kinship or communal ties and sensibilities. The emergence of an urban culture and the concomitant transformation of social life can be expected to affect pristine social attitudes, concerns, and obligations. The reason is that people who emigrate from different towns and villages to cities and other urban centers do so more as individuals than as groups. There would, in many instances, be no kinship ties between such individual urban dwellers, who, in the relations among themselves, may not be spontaneously moved by the sanctions of the solidarity and caring system of the traditional community life. They would be in the urban centers to seek better lives for themselves, unsupported by any benefits or anticipations of assistance that might have been available to them as members of a lineage group in the villages. Developing communal relationships—especially of the type based on kinship bonds—may have no salient part in the urban dweller's attitude toward such "strange" individuals in his urban environment. It is most probable that, in all his thought and action, he would give consideration primarily to his own individual (egoistic) welfare: thus, generating the rumblings of the individualistic outlook.

The most important question, however, relates to the *extent* to which the individualistic outlook will take over from the ethos of the communal way of life evolved by African cultures. Can it be expected that the individualistic ethos will cut into the pristine communal orientation sufficiently deeply to numb or vitiate the sentiments of a shared, communal life that characterize pre-urban life? Will the ethos of individualism, in the wake of urbanization, make demolitionary inroads into the traditional communal values? Well, maybe; and perhaps to some extent.

I have pointed out in previous publications[6] that individuality—in the sense of individual initiative and responsibility for oneself (for one's own interests)—does exist in the traditional cultural setting, but this individuality does not give rise to moral egoism. Instead the system that obtains is that of dual responsibility—responsibility to oneself as an individual as well as responsibility to the group. In the preceding chapter (section 3.1.3) I list what I consider to be negative features of the communitarian system as is practiced in the traditional setting of Africa. By pointing up those negative features I do not imply, given the fundamental importance of the value of the community for human life, that the African communitarian social or moral practice should be totally abandoned, that communitarian values should give way to extreme individualism—the type that tends to ride roughshod over the claims of the community. I mean to suggest instead that the practice would need to be re-evaluated and the necessary refinements made to it.

There is evidence that urban or city life has not vitiated communal sensibilities and outlooks among most African people. African scholars, including Kwesi Dickson and John Mbiti, have noted that the practice whereby two people who did not know one another before try to establish as closely as possible the kinship ties that may exist between them is encountered in villages and small towns;[7] the practice, to my knowledge, goes on also in large cities, including cities overseas. In fact the practice takes on greater significance when it is encountered in large cities, since it can be assumed that in villages and small towns most people already know their relatives. It is a well-known practice—and here I am drawing on my knowledge solely of the Ghanaian experience—that city dwellers from the same town or district, whether related by kinship ties or not, form associations to foster and strengthen social bonds between them and to help one another in times of need or crisis. It is known that such associations are also formed by compatriots from African countries who live in large cities in countries overseas for the same purposes. In Ghana, many city dwellers frequently return to their villages and small towns in order to fulfill social as well as moral obligations.

Evidence suggests that the individualistic outlook that may develop in an African urban setting may be limited or moderate, a type that may not necessarily subvert an urban dweller's relations to his relatives in the village or the values of solidarity with, and sensitivity to, the needs of other members of the kinship group. Urban life that comes in the wake of industrialization need not—should not—itself necessarily disrupt or sever social and moral connections between the urban dweller and his relatives in the village or among urban dwellers themselves. The urban dweller does not have to be oblivious to the obligations and responsibilities to his relatives or other urban dwellers.

The statement "Urbanization generates individualism" is an empirical, not an a priori, statement and would require empirical evidence to establish its truth or falsity. Whether urbanization will generate full-fledged individualism to replace the ethos of traditional communal values in Africa is a matter that is in the womb of time. But it must be noted that in the West the trend towards individualism was a function of a synergy of factors, not just of the factor of urbanism.

It must be noted also that the community is essentially a normative—a moral—concept, not spatial (or geographic)—confined to village or small towns, or demographic—confined to small populations. Community is a concept that can be applied to all human societies, irrespective of their sizes; it is a moral value that ought to be cherished and practiced in all human societies, small and large, traditional and modern, developing and developed, "primitive" and "advanced." The arguments for its restoration in modern Western societies underline its phoenixlike character, its resiliency. To denigrate it is, indeed, to put down a human value that is basic to humanity's well-being.

Now, even though Western modernity has in many ways become a paradigm for non-Western cultures, the latter are not necessarily enamored of all of its features, and the approach to appropriating it will therefore be selective. Two questions immediately come up: can a non-Western society that appropriates only *some* characteristics of Western modernity be said to be or to have become modern? If the answer to this question is yes, what significance does this have for the conception of modernity? I think it is possible for a non-Western society that rejects some features of Western modernity to become modern or be said to be modern *if* it can be said to have achieved at least some of the basic goals of modernity: developed economy, technological and industrial advancement, the installation of democratic politics; in fine, when that society can be said to be developed, in the comprehensive sense of its having the capability of providing adequate responses to the entire existential conditions in which, or through which, human beings function.[8] But remember that the goals of modernity are common *human* goals and not particularly Western. But if a non-Western society (like some of the societies in East Asia), can—without having donned the entire regalia of Western values and institutions—be said to be modern, then, it means that it is possible, perhaps desirable, to creatively forge a new modernity appropriate to a particular cultural tradition. It follows also that it would be wrong to define modernization in terms of Westernization.

But if modernization means neither industrialization nor Westernization *simpliciter*, what would it mean? To repeat, "becoming modern" and "being modernized" must of course be conceptually affiliated, if "being modernized" is not interpreted as "being Westernized," even though "being modernized" would include having successfully appropriated some of Western science and technology. But what, really, is it to be or become modern or modernized? This question is not easy to answer in a direct and satisfactory way that will be acceptable to practitioners of all cultures, in view of certain differences of values and goals held by different societies. Secularism, for instance, which is said to be a feature of modernity as developed in the West, cannot be accepted by deeply religious societies (why should a society become secular in order to be modern?); individualism, a characteristic feature of Western modernity, can hardly be endorsed by societies and cultures that are sensitive to community life; some aspects of Western technology do not hold much attraction to some other societies. Such differences in cultural values would make a monolithic conception of modernity not only difficult but also highly contestable. Modernity, denoting a (global) cultural phenomenon, is indeed a complex notion.

But even if modernity cannot be defined by a monolithic set of cultural values, it nevertheless can be broadly conceived in terms of an *ethos:* in terms, that is, of the innovative ethos—of the commitment to innovation aimed at bringing about the kinds of progressive changes in the entire aspects of human culture necessary for the enhancement and fulfillment of human life. The cultivation of the innovative spirit or outlook is the most outstanding feature of the notion of modernity: it can be said to define modernity. But the foresight to perceive which aspects of the cultural life of a people should be brought within the purview of the innovative enterprise is equally important. Thus, to be or become modern is to demonstrate commitment to bringing about, through pruning and refinement or recreation, required changes in the values, practices, and institutions inherited from the past to a level of sophistication that will augment their functionality and relevance to modern (contemporary) life; and to have the capability of spawning ideas or adapting ideas and practices appropriated from other cultures and employing them sufficiently effectively to enhance a society's innovative capacities and goals. (Innovation, however, does not necessarily mean a rejection of the entire past.) In traditional or premodern life, commitment to the innovative ethos was not very much in evidence.

Now, the foregoing discussion constitutes a conceptual and ideological framework for evolving a conception of modernity in Africa. What follows from the discussion is that African modernity can creatively be forged from the furnace of the African cultural experience, an experience that, as noted earlier, is many-sided, having sprung from the encounters with alien cultures and religions and from problems internal to the practice of the indigenous cultural ideas and values themselves. The African cultural experience is not demeaned by being many-sided, even though many-sidedness generates and compounds problems of cultural identity, just as it complicates the task of making a definite cultural sense out of the total. But making such a cultural sense depends on the ingenuity of the practitioners of the culture. The creation of modernity out of the cultural experience of a people will ensure that the institutions that are fashioned and the values that are established are those to which the people will have emotional, ideological, and intellectual, attachments. Modernity emerging in this way will not only endure but have real meaning for the people and shape their lives in a more positive direction.

Modernity, whatever else it involves, certainly involves a transition to a new era: the transition is borne partly on the wings of the elegant or worthwhile features of a cultural tradition, and partly through the production of new ideas and the invention of new techniques of far-reaching consequences. The latter may involve whatever can usefully and suitably be appropriated and adapted from outside a given culture in addition to what can be acquired from within the culture itself by way of the exercise of the indigenous intellectual, evaluative, and adaptive capacities. The former will require the abandonment of what I call the negative features of a culture as well as the maintenance—albeit through refinement—of what I call the positive features. The creation of modernity in Africa will be a function of both methods of transition.

Let me start with science and technology, which have historically been among the central supports—as well as the engines—of modernity. In the creation of modernity in Africa adequate and sustained attention must be paid to science and technology. For it cannot be denied that the modern world is becoming an increasingly technological world: technology is, by all indications, going to become the distinguishing feature of global culture in the coming decades. Africa will have to participate significantly in the cultivation and promotion of this aspect of human culture if it is to benefit from it fully and make significant contributions to it. But the extensive and sustained understanding and acquisition of modern technology insistently require adequate cultivation of science and the scientific outlook. To acquire a scientific and technological outlook the African people will need to adopt a new mental orientation, a new and sustained interest in science to provide a firm base for technology, and a new intellectual attitude toward the external world uncluttered by mysticism, superstition, and the "personalization" of knowledge. The alleged spirituality of the African world—which in the traditional setting is in many ways allowed to impede sustained inquiries into the world of nature—will have to come to terms with materiality, that is, with the physical world of science. Knowledge of medicinal plants, for instance, clearly a form of scientific knowledge, must be rescued from the quagmire of mysticism and brought to the glare of publicity, its language made exoteric and accessible to many others.

A sustained interest in science is important for at least two reasons. It would provide an enduring base for a real technological takeoff at a time in the history of the world when the dynamic connections between science and technology have increasingly been recognized and made the basis of equal attention to both: technology has become science-based, while science has become technology-directed. The second reason, a corollary to the first, is that the application of science to technology will help improve traditional technologies.

Ideally, technology, as a cultural product, should take its rise from the culture of a people if it is to be directly accessible to a large section of the population and its nuances fully appreciated by them. For this reason, one approach to creating modern technology in Africa, as elsewhere, is to upgrade or improve existing traditional technologies whose development seems to have been stunted in the traditional setting because of their very weak scientific base. Let us recall the food technologist referred to in the preceding chapter (section 3.1.2). She was able to find practical ways of solving problems by resorting to ideas and solutions rooted in basic science but without the benefit of knowledge of physics, chemistry, engineering, or metallurgy. Her use of technology would raise the following questions: why were dry palm kernels used as heat exchange medium? What is peculiar about table salt (sodium chloride) in this process? Yet for most traditional technology practitioners the whys and hows do not often matter, as long as some concrete results can be achieved through the use of a particular existing technology. But the why and how questions of course matter very much. Improving traditional technologies will require not only looking for answers to such questions but also searching for areas or activities to which the application of existing technologies (having been improved) can be extended.

Traditional technologies have certain characteristics that could—and must—be featured in the approach to developing modern technology in Africa. Traditional technologies are usually simple, not highly specialized technologies: this means that large numbers of the people can participate in the application or use of the technologies, as well as contribute to their development; but it also promotes indigenous technological awareness. The materials that are used are locally available (palm kernels and table salt, for example, are readily available household items) and the processes are effective. Traditional technologies are developed to meet material or economic needs: to deal with specific problems of material survival. They can thus immediately be seen as having direct connections with societal problems and as being appropriate to meeting certain basic or specific needs. If the technologies that will be created by a developing nation in Africa feature some of the characteristics of the traditional technologies, they will have greater relevance and impact on the social and economic life of the people.

The improvement of traditional technologies is contingent on at least two factors. One is the existence or availability of autonomous, indigenous technological capacities. These capacities would need to be considerably developed. The development of capacities in this connection is not simply a matter of acquiring skills or techniques but, perhaps more important, of understanding and being able to apply the relevant scientific principles. It might be assumed that the ability to acquire skills presupposes the appreciation of scientific principles; such an assumption, however, would be false.

One could acquire skills without understanding the relevant underlying scientific principles. The food technologist is a good example. The lack of understanding of the relevant scientific principles will impede the improvement exercise itself. The other factor relates to the need for change in certain cultural habits and attitudes on the part of artisans, technicians, and other practitioners of traditional technologies. Practitioners of traditional technologies will have to be weaned from certain traditional attitudes and be prepared to learn and apply new or improved techniques and practices. Some old, traditional habits, such as the habit referred to in chapter 8 of using the senses in matters of precision measurements, will have to be abandoned; adaptation to new—and generally more effective—ways of practicing technology, such as resorting to technical aids in precision measurements, will need to be pursued. The cultivation of appropriate attitudes toward improved or modern technology and the development of an indigenous technological capacity will provide the suitable cultural and intellectual receptacle for the modern technologies that may be transferred from the technologically advanced industrial countries of the world to African countries.

Now, the transfer of technology from the technologically developed world is a vital approach to bringing sophisticated technology to Africa. It could also be an important basis for developing, in time, an indigenous technological capacity and the generation of fairly advanced indigenous technologies. But all this will depend on how the whole complex matter of technology transfer is tackled. If the idea is not well executed it may lead to complacency and passivity on the part of the recipients, reduce them to permanent technological dependency, and involve them in technological pursuits that may not be immediately appropriate to their goals of social and economic development. On the other hand, an adroit approach to technology transfer by its recipients will, as I said, be a sure basis for a real technological takeoff for the recipient country.

Transfer of technology involves the transfer of some techniques and practices developed in some technologically advanced country to some developing country. The assumption or anticipation is that the local people, that is, the technicians or technologists in the developing country, will be able to acquire the techniques transferred to them. Acquiring techniques theoretically means being able to learn, understand, analyze, and explain the whys and hows of those techniques and thus, finally, be able to replicate and design them through the efforts of the local technologist. It is also anticipated that the local technologist, who is the beneficiary of the transferred technology, will be able to adapt the received technology to suit the needs and circumstances of the developing country, to build on it, and, if the creative capacity is available, to use it as an inspiration to create new technologies appropriate to the development requirements and objectives of the developing country.

The assumptions and anticipations underlying the transfer of technology of course presuppose the existence, locally, of an autonomous technological capacity that can competently deal with, the intricacies of the transferred technology. In the event of the nonexistence of an adequate indigenous technological capacity, the intentions in transferring technology cannot be achieved. There is a paradox here: autonomous, indigenous technological capacities are expected to be developed *through* dealing with transferred technologies (this is certainly the ultimate goal of technology transfer); yet the ability to deal effectively with transferred technologies requires or presupposes the existence of indigenous technological capacities adequate for the purpose. The paradox can be resolved, however, if we assume that there will be indigenous technological capacities, albeit of a minimum kind, that would therefore need to be nurtured, developed, and augmented to some level of sophistication required in operating a modern technology. The assumptions also presuppose that the transferred technology, developed in a specific cultural milieu different in many ways from that of a developing country, is easily adaptable to the social and cultural environment of the developing country. This presupposition may not be wholly true. But despite the problems that may be said to be attendant on the transfer of technology, technology transfer is, as I said, an important medium for generating a more efficient modern technology in a developing country.

Now, technology is of course developed within a culture; it is thus an aspect—a product—of culture. Technology transfer, then, is certainly an aspect of the whole phenomenon of cultural borrowing or appropriation that follows on the encounters between cultures. There appears, however, to be a difference between transfer of technology to a developing country and the normal appropriation by a culture of an alien cultural product. The difference arises because of the way the notion of technology transfer is conceived and executed. It can be admitted that what is anticipated in technology transfer is primarily *knowledge* of techniques, methods, and materials all of which are relevant to matters of industrial production. But knowledge is acquired through the active participation of the recipient; it is not transferred on to a passive agent or receptacle. In the absence of adequate and extensive knowledge and understanding of the relevant scientific principles, the attitudes of the recipients of transferred technology will be only passive, not responsive in any significant way to the niceties of the new cultural products being introduced to them. In the circumstance, that which is transferred will most probably remain a thin veneer, hardly affecting the scientific or technological outlook and orientation of the recipient. Machines and equipment can be transferred to passive recipients who may be able to use them for a while; but the acquisition of knowledge (or understanding) of techniques—which is surely involved in the proper meaning of technology—has to be prosecuted *actively*, that is, through the active exercise of the intellects of the recipients.

In an ideal situation of cultural borrowing, an element or product of the cultural tradition of one people is accepted and taken possession of by another people. The alien cultural product is not simply "transferred" to the recipients. Instead, goaded by their own appreciation of the significance of the product, they would seek it, acquire it, and appropriate it, that is, make it their own; this means that they would participate actively and purposefully in the acquisition of the product. To the extent that what is called technology transfer is an aspect of the phenomenon of cultural borrowing, and that the people to whom some technology is transferred are thus expected to understand and take possession of it through active and purposeful participation in its acquisition, "transfer of technology" is, in my view, a misnomer. For, what is transferred may not be acquired, appropriated, or assimilated.

For the same reasons, Ali Mazrui's biological metaphor of "technology transplant" will not do either. In Mazrui's view, "there has been a considerable amount of technology transfer to the Third World in the last thirty years—but very little technology transplant. Especially in Africa very little of what has been transferred has in fact been successfully transplanted."[9] To the extent that this biological or medical metaphor clearly involves passivism on the part of the recipient (metaphorically, the transplant patient) who thus has no choice in actively deciding on the "quality" of the foreign body to be sewn into his body, and that there is no knowing whether the physical constitution of the recipient will accept or reject the new body tissue, the biological perception of acquiring the technological products of other cultures is very misleading. The biological metaphor also will not do on a further ground: the body into which a foreign body tissue is to be transplanted is in a diseased condition, which makes it impossible for it to react in a wholly positive manner to its new "addition" and to take advantage of it. Even if we assume, analogically, that the society that is badly in need of the technological products of other cultures is technologically or epistemically "diseased," the fact would still remain that, in human society, the members of the society would, guided by their needs and goals, be in a position not only to decide on which technological products of foreign origin they would want to acquire but also to participate actively and positively in the appropriation of those products.

Thus, neither technology transfer nor technology transplant is a useful concept for describing the acquisition of technology from other cultures; neither has been a real feature or method in the phenomenon of cultural borrowing. Our historical knowledge of how the results of cultural encounters occur seems to suggest that what is needed is, not the transfer or transplant of technology, but the *appropriation* of technology—a perception or method that features the active, adroit, and purposeful initiative and participation of the recipients in the pursuit and acquisition of a technology of foreign production.

It must also be noted that just as in cultural borrowing there are principles or criteria that guide the borrowers in their selection of products from the alien—that is, the encountered—culture, so, in the appropriation of technology some principles or criteria would need to be established to guide the choice of the products of technology created in one cultural environment for use in a different environment. Technology can transform human society in numerous ways. For this reason, a developing society will have to consider technology rather as an instrument for the realization of *basic* human needs than as an end—as merely a way of demonstrating human power or ingenuity. The word "basic" is important here and is used to point up the need for technology to be concerned fundamentally and essentially with such human needs as food, shelter, clothing, and good health. The pursuit and satisfaction of these basic needs should guide the choice and appropriation of technology. Thus, what ought to be chosen is the technology that will be applied to water, health, housing, industry, food and agriculture, roads and transportation, and other most relevant activities that make ordinary life bearable. On this showing, advanced technologies such as those involved in military and space exploration may not be needed by a developing country in Africa. But as a developing society comes to be increasingly shaped by technology, certain aspects will become a specialized knowledge; it may then become necessary to create a leaven of experts to deal with the highly specialized aspects of those technologies. The adaptability of technological products to local circumstances and objectives must be an important criterion in the appropriation and development of technology.

Finally, the fundamental, most cherished values of a culture will also constitute a criterion in the choice of technology. Technology can transform human society. This social transformation will involve changes not only in our ways and patterns of living but also in our values. But we human beings will have to decide whether the (new) values spewed out by technology are the kinds of values we need and would want to cherish. Technology emerges in, and is fashioned by, a culture; thus, right from the outset, technology is driven or directed by human purposes, values, and goals. And, if this historical relation between technology and values is maintained, what will be produced for us by technology will have to be in consonance with those purposes, values, and goals.

Just as traditional attitudes toward science and technology will have to be swept away or radically changed in the transition to a *self-created modernity,* so will other attitudes, outlooks, practices, and institutions. I can mention only some of these. Even though the communitarian social arrangement appears to be a social ideal that reflects our basic conception of human nature, in the traditional African environment, it nevertheless bristles with several excesses that would need to be pruned away in the setting of our modern world. The inheritance systems of most African societies (see chapter 8, section 3.1.3) are disruptive of the growth of private business enterprise and hence of economic development; but they are disruptive also of social peace and harmony because of the incessant feuds and legal wrangles that often follow the death of a wealthy business person in the extended family, feuds that do not serve the course of solidarity promised by the communitarian arrangement. These systems of inheritance will need to be amended to allow continued growth of established private business enterprises. The communitarian social order also has a tendency to nurture patronage and, in consequence, corruption and irresponsibility; just as it can whittle away opportunities for savings and profit accumulation because of the extensive contributions a burgeoning business person is called upon to make toward the welfare of other "less fortunate" members of the family.

In pointing up some of the problems or excesses of the communitarian social order, I am not, to repeat, suggesting that that order be totally abandoned and replaced with an individualist order; I am saying only that some features of it would need to be amended or refined or abandoned. To make the notion of nation-state viable in Africa, loyalties that are traditionally given to communocultural groups (otherwise called "ethnic" groups) constituting the new nation-state will have to be transferred to the latter. A revolution is certainly required in this area of the African political life: the old conception that held the multinational state as a complex of "ethnic" groups will need to be swept away in its entirety, to be replaced with a new conception of the state that will reject the primary group as the focus of trust and loyalty and also command what in chapter 3 I call "metanational" loyalties and identities. In section 3 of that chapter I propose steps that can bolster the pursuit of nationhood. Attitudes toward funerals, childlessness (infertility), polygamy, and the joy of having many children entertained in traditional African cultures will have to radically change.

These, then, are some of the old ways in the traditional African culture life that, in my view, will need to be radically changed or simply abandoned in the attempt and desire to create African modernity. The basic premise is this: in the transition to a new—a modern era—some of the elements of the past cultural life will simply have to be left behind; these would be the debris and the encumbrances of the passing era, elements that, on normative or functional grounds, cannot be borne over the bridge to the new era.

Modernity, which involves a transition to a new era characterized by advanced forms of knowledge, techniques, and economic and political institutions as well as by radical departures from some inherited traditions, includes features of a cultural tradition that would be considered symphonic with forms of life in the new era. These will include the positive features of a cultural tradition, for these tend to abide on grounds of their considerable normativity and functionality. They may invariably have to go through processes of modification and refinement to bring them more in line with the demands of the times, or to enable them play their traditional roles better in a new setting. I want now to continue in more elaborate detail what I characterize as the "positive features" of African cultures, beginning with some further comments on the relation between humanism and communitarian thought and life and the (possible) effect of technology (or industrialism) on humanist thought and behavior.

Humanism (see chapter 5, section 3; chapter 8, section 3.2) the doctrine that relates crucially to the mundane interests and well-being of humans, is fundamental and pervasive in African social and moral thought and behavior. The relation of humanism to communitarian way of life is, I believe, one of cause and effect: the latter an offshoot of the former.[10] To say this, however, is not to imply by any means that the causal relation is a necessary one. For, if the relation were necessary, we would expect the doctrine of humanism, wherever and whenever it is held, to lead to a communitarian social thought and practice. But this is not so. As I say in my analysis of the notion of modernity (chapter 8, section 5), early Western modernity espoused the humanist doctrine, but the espousal led to the installation, not of a communitarian way of life, but to individualism. Thus, the aim of the apostles of individualism in Western modernity, captained by John Locke, was to sweep away what Robert Nisbet refers to as "the *communal* debris of the Middle Ages."[11] It may be said that in the premodern era of Western cultural development, humanism and communitarianism were philosophical or ideological allies; in the modern era, however, one of them was dropped, to be replaced by a different doctrine, individualism. The replacement implies that individualism and communitarianism were held by Locke and others as incompatible doctrines (a position still maintained by some, but by no means all, Western liberal thinkers of today).

But it is clear that there are no logical tensions in interpreting humanism as implying either individualism or communitarianism, for the two are, in my view, not incompatible. But it seems that in matters of insuring the mundane interests and well-being of every member of society, the communitarian social arrangement—because of its basic thrust and declared focus on the well-being of all the members of the community—may be said to have an edge over the individualist framework. A consideration of the intrinsic moral worth, capacities, talents, and the general conditions of self-development of the individual human being, however, would suggest that it will be more appropriate to give both the individual and the community equal moral consideration and standing if the maximum fulfillment of the life of the human person is to be achieved. The proper and adequate functioning or realization of one of the values requires deep links with the other. In creating African modernity, then, a social and political theory should be evolved such as will integrate the values of individuality and community.

Within the framework of Western modernity, one gets the impression that industrialism and urbanism, both of which are the concomitants of technology, are conceived as subversive of the communitarian ethos, disruptive of social ideals, and, consequently, destructive of the concern for the interests of others, to be replaced by the pursuit of individual and egoistic interests. The impression, in other words, is that industrialism and urbanism will (have to) result in the breakdown of communitarian values, on one hand, and the inauguration of unbridled forms of individualism, on the other hand. Even though it may be said that Western modernity recognizes technology, industrialism, urbanism, and individualism as ideological allies, it cannot be said, nonetheless, that individualism is a necessary consequence of the conjunction of the other three factors. For, early forms of individualism seem not to have been causally related to them but to have developed independently. After all, by the middle of the nineteenth century when industrialization was at its height in the West and generating the growth of urbanism, individualism had long settled down in the social and moral thought and life of people in Western societies: the humanist thought of the medieval and postmedieval period stressed the talents, capacity, initiative, and responsibility of the individual; the Protestant religion that emerged in the sixteenth century celebrated the individual's relation to God; political individualism was born of the democratic ferment of the premodern period (particularly in England); Locke was advocating the individualist ideology in the second half of the seventeenth century. All this makes it patently clear not only that the individualist ethos had been cultivated by Europeans long before their societies were open to the floodgates of industrialism and urbanism but that it was the result of a synergy of factors or circumstances. It could be said, in fact, that the individualist ethos was more a causal factor in the emergence of those economic and social phenomena than an effect. It may have to be admitted, though, that industrialism and urbanism were allowed, in turn, to augment the drift toward individualism. This need not have occurred.

Technology, then, with its concomitants of industrialism and urbanism, does not have to lead to individualism or the total breakdown of communitarian values. The relation of the triad technology, industrialism, and urbanism to individualism is not one of causal determinism. It is appropriate, from the normative point of view, that communitarian values should not succumb to technological or industrial changes or the growth of urbanism to the extent of their near extinction. For, after all, technology is made for humans, and not humans for technology. This means that human beings should be at the center or focus of the technological enterprise. Technology and humanism (i.e., concern for human welfare) are not—and should not be considered—antithetical concepts; technology and industrialism should be able to coexist with the concern for the interests and welfare of the people in the technological society, otherwise they will jettison their own relevance and raison d'être. So, it should be possible for the African people to embark on the "technologicalization" of their societies without losing the humanist essence of their cultures. The value of concern for human well-being is a intrinsic, fundamental, and self-justifying value that should, on that score, be cordoned off against any technological subversion of it. In this connection, the words of Kenneth Kaunda are apposite:

> I am deeply concerned that this high valuation of Man and respect for human dignity which is a legacy of our [African] tradition should not be lost in the new Africa. However "modern" and "advanced" in a Western sense the nations of Africa may become, we are fiercely determined that this humanism will not be obscured. African society has always been Man-centered. We intend that it will remain so.[12]

I support the view that the humanist essence of the African cultures—an essence that is basically moral—ought to be maintained and cherished in creating African modernity. It must be borne in mind that technology alone cannot solve all the deep-rooted social problems such as poverty, oppression, exploitation, and economic inequalities in human societies *unless* it is underpinned and guided by some basic moral values; in the absence of the strict application of those values, technology will in fact create other problems, including environmental problems. Social transformation, which is an outstanding goal of the comprehensive use of technology, cannot be achieved unless technology moves along under the aegis of basic human values. Technology is a human value, of course. And, because it is basic to the fulfillment of the material welfare of human beings, there is a tendency to privilege it over other human values. But to do so would be a mistake. The reason is that technology is obviously an instrumental value, not an intrinsic value to be pursued for its own sake. As an instrument in the whole quest for human material fulfillment, its use ought to be guided by other—perhaps intrinsic and ultimate—human values, in order to realize its maximum relevance to humanity.

In considering technology's aim of fulfilling the material needs of humans, the pursuit of the humanist and social ethic of the traditional African society can be of considerable relevance because of the impact this ethic can have on the distributive patterns in respect of the economic goods that will result from the application of technology: in this way, extensive and genuine social—and in the sequel, political—transformation of the African society can be insured, and the maximum impact of technology on society achieved.

Related to the doctrine of ethical humanism is the African appreciation of the twin values of humanity and brotherhood (i.e., unity of the humankind). The value attached to humanity in African moral thought derives from the belief that humanity is a creation of God. This belief is expressed in the Akan proverb, "All human beings are children of God; no one is a child of the earth." The moral significance of this proverb—its relevance to a conception of the human being as of intrinsic value, worthy of dignity and respect—is pointed up in chapter 2, section 4. The human being is held as possessing a speck of God in him or her. This is what is called the soul. This theomorphic perception of humanity constitutes all human beings into one universal family of humankind—a family that, however, is fragmented into a multiplicity of peoples and cultures. The common membership of one universal human family should, it is held, constitute a legitimate basis for the idea of universal human brotherhood (or unity). Thus, part of the African view of humanity is to recognize all persons, irrespective of their racial or ethnic background, as brothers. This is the reason why in African cultures the word "brother" is used to cover various and complex family relationships linked by blood ties. But the word is also used, significantly, by persons between whom there are no blood ties at all.

The African idea of human brotherhood is stated also in the proverb, "Man's brother *is* man." This is to say that a human being can be related *only* to another human being, not to a beast. The comprehensive meaning given to the word "brother" in African cultures is intended, indeed, to lift people up from the purely biologically determined blood-relation level onto the human level, the level where the essence of humanity is held as transcending the contingencies of human biology, race, ethnicity, or culture.

This perception of humanity is expressed in the Akan proverb, "Humanity has no boundary." The meaning of the proverb is that, while there is a limit—a boundary—to the area of cultivation of land, there is no such limit in the cultivation of the friendship and fellowship of human beings; the boundaries of that form of cultivation are limitless. For, humanity is of one kind; all humankind is one species. This is most probably the reason why in almost all African languages there is really no word for "race." There are, instead, the words "person," "human being," and "people." So that, where others would say, "the black race," or "the white race," Africans would say, "black people," "white people," and so on. And, instead of "people of mixed race," they would say, "people of mixed blood." The latter expression, however, is somewhat vague, since "people of mixed blood" also describes people of dual ethnic parentage in African societies. But, in terms of the African perception of humanity, the important point is that the offspring of any "blood mixing" is a human being—a child of God—and therefore belongs to the one human race of which we are all a part.

The recognition in the African cultural tradition of all human beings as brothers by reason of our common humanity is a lofty ideal that must be cherished and made a vital feature of African modernity. It is a bulwark against developing bigoted attitudes toward peoples of different cultures or skin colors who are also members of the one human race.

In Chapter 8 section 3.1.3, I attend to what I regard as negative features of the way the economy was managed in the traditional setting. There are, however, some features of the conception of economics or economic management held in the traditional culture that can be said to be positive and can therefore be given a place in the economic practices of the modern world. One feature may be said to be linked to, or derived from, statements made by people in times of economic hardship. Here, as in a few other places in this book, I refer only to the Akan language of Ghana. There is, to my knowledge, no word in the Akan language that directly translates economy or economics, itself derived from the Greek *oikonomia*, meaning household management. (Comments from colleagues from most other African language groups, in response to my inquiries, reveal that in some African languages the word for "trade" is used for economics, while in others the word that means "frugality" or "thrift" is used. But, clearly, neither word is a good translation for "economics"). The Akan word *asetena*, however, may adequately do the job. According to a well-known dictionary of the Akan language, *asetena* means "life, livelihood, condition or circumstances of life." [13] When the Akan wants to say: "Living conditions are hard" or "The economic situation is hard" or "The economic situation is bad" or simply "Livelihood is hard," he would almost invariably say, *asetena mu aye den* ("Circumstances of life are hard"), or *asetena mu nnye* ("Circumstances of life are not good"). Language, a vehicle of concepts, not only embodies but also influences a philosophical point of view. If *asetena* can be used for economy, as I claim it can, it will imply a certain conception of economy or economics. The Akan word is clearly more comprehensive than the English,

since the idea of "circumstances of life" surely means more than purely economic; but the Akan word incudes the economic.

Implicit in the Akan word, then, is at least an adumbration of a conception that regards the economy not as a separate sphere of existence dominated by the profit motive but a sphere in the social order interrelated with
law, politics, and morality; it is a conception of economy that does not
regard the goal of economic activity in terms merely of the production of
material goods. A person's livelihood depends to a large extent on how the
economy of her society is managed. But, inasmuch as the management of
the economy is greatly influenced by public policy and by considerations of
human well-being, it cannot be isolated from the society's politics or law or
socioethical values. Economic activity is thus not conceived as divorced from
the social and political order; the development of the human society is not
to be conceived exclusively in economic terms but to be conceived as an
integrated enterprise. This idea, embedded in the traditional culture, of not
separating the economy from other aspects of life but seeing it as enmeshed
with politics, morality, and the law is, in the light of the complexities of the
human being and society, a remarkable idea. The idea indicates that there is
a normative dimension to economic activity: economics should be about
how the state or the community can properly use economic means to enhance general welfare, the good life of each member of the society. This
normative view of economics must be linked with the humanist and communitarian morality of African cultures. The integrative and normative conception of economics is a conception that, I think, can—indeed ought to—
be maintained in the modern schemes of economic activity.

There are other ideas of economic management held in traditional African cultures that can positively feature in a modern economic setting. Ideas
of private ownership exist in the traditional economic thought and practice
side by side with public ownership (see chapter 5). In the traditional cultural
setting, people do not look to the chief and his council members (i.e., the
government) for their material welfare, even though the chief is often prepared to help individuals in distress; nor is the process of economic development controlled by the government. Individuals and families take responsibility for themselves and function in many ways independently of the
government. The acquisition of wealth is highly commended, while ideas of
individual savings, frugality, capital accumulation, and efficient management
of money are valued, even though the practical translation of these ideas in
real life appears impeded by the particular social arrangement evolved by
the African communitarian society. And, if we conceive the purpose of economic management to be not only to produce wealth but also to see to the
horizontal distribution of the wealth created, we would appreciate that the
social morality—the morality of concern for others practiced in our traditional society—would be relevant to the distribution of resources and services.

One outstanding cultural value of the traditional African society that is a
feature of the ever-present consciousness of ties of kinship is the emphasis

on the importance of the family—the extended family. The family is recognized in African cultures, as in other cultures, as a fundamental and most valuable institution. It is the model of communal life and thought as well as the immediate context or medium for the concrete and spontaneous expression of communal values such as love, caring, cohesion, solidarity, interdependence, and mutual sympathy, responsibility, or helpfulness. It is also the crucible for character formation, an effective instrument for moral education and the development and inculcation of moral values, and constitutes the root of our pristine identities and community lives. I consider the traditional African perception of the family a positive feature of the African culture. Because of its status as a fundamental human value, and given that family ties are important for human fellowship and togetherness, the family is an institution that ought to be firmly maintained in creating African modernity. For the maintenance of the family is not only an insurance against the fragmentation of communal values cherished in traditional African societies but a necessary and sufficient condition for creating a greater sense of community. A strong sense of the community presupposes—and must be built on—a strong sense of the family.

Since a human community is a complex of families, any talk of strengthening the community will be meaningless if it does not emphasize the need to strengthen family ties. The reason is that the fragmentation of the community has its origin in the fragmentation of the family: if an individual has no ties—or has only loose ties—with his or her family, he or she can hardly be expected to have any strong ties to the community. As an Akan proverb states, "The decline and fall of a nation begins in its homes." When the character of individuals degenerates as a result of the fragmentation of family—and consequently communal—bonds, the ultimate victim is the integrity of the nation. The creation of modernity—of African modernity—should not lead to the disintegration of the family or community life. That will spell the moral as well as the social doom of the modern African nation-state.

It seems to me that the positive features of the traditional African sociopolitical thought and practice suggest that an appropriate guide for a sociopolitical order in modern Africa would be an ideology of a social, or better communal, democracy or a welfare (humanist) capitalism, an ideology that will allow the practice of a free or private enterprise system but that will also demonstrate commitment and sensitivity to the needs and welfare of the disadvantaged or worse-off members of the society. The communitarian ethos of the traditional African social life that disposes people generally to do things together as a team should inspire and undergird a communal democracy. In the opinion of the American philosopher John Dewey, democracy "is the idea of community life itself. . . . The clear consciousness of a communal life, in all its implications, constitutes the idea of democracy." [14] The communal conception of democracy sees democracy as a government, not of or for the majority, but of and for the people as a whole, and considers each citizen of equal worth, concern, and respect in the enterprise of government. Thus, guided by the ideology of communal democracy, a modern African government will have to demonstrate responsibility for communal well-being in its thought and action (not the kind of irresponsibility for aggrandizing people in government and their coterie of power seekers that has been demonstrated in most African states of the postcolonial era).

Traditional African political cultures feature positive ideas and values that can—and ought to be—given adequate consideration in the effort to create a modern democratic political system. I will highlight some of these. In the traditional political practice, individuals and families take responsibility for themselves rather than looking to the government (the chief) for their welfare; members of a family bear each other up. Thus, in times of personal or familial crises, there is no need for government intervention; little demand is made on the government. The traditional system of government thus could be characterized as a "limited government," a term usually applied to Western political systems since Locke. Thus, a communitarian political and moral theory would give rise to a system of government in which people will look inwardly, to themselves and their extended families, rather than outwardly, to their government. The basis of traditional political authority is contractual: this implies the trusteeship principle of political power, a government that is not only open but is based on the wishes of the people and on the accountability of the ruler (the chief) to the governed. The traditional system of rule is participatory, the citizens being allowed to take active part in running the affairs of the state or the community; government is considered a matter of public concern. Inspired perhaps by the communitarian ethos, traditional politics is consensual rather than majoritarian, a politics of inclusion, compromise, and reconciliation.

Civic responsibility is expressed by sentiments of personal commitment to the affairs of the state. Thus civic republican possibilities are embedded in the traditional African ways of running the affairs of the state, possibilities that seem to have faded with the institution of a central government that was referred to as "they" or "them" because it was considered alien—having been established by a colonial power. (By "republican," I am referring to the idea of government as of everyone's business, a view of government in which everyone is involved.)[15] These, in a nutshell, are important ideas and values of politics generally developed by the traditional African cultures that can—and ought to—make a transition to modernity. Consensus and the politics of local self-government of the traditional system could help avoid or at least reduce conflicts that characterize (or are likely to characterize) the political life of the modern communoculturally plural African nation-state.

Having said all this regarding what I consider to be positive features of the traditional African political cultures, however, I do not mean to imply that they are exhaustive of the features of a democratic political order; only that they should be considered part of the threads in the democratic tapestry to be woven by modernity in Africa. Even so, there would be a need not only to adapt and refine them to suit the demands and circumstances of the communoculturally heterogeneous postcolonial nation-state in Africa but also to create appropriate institutions to give them concrete expression in the setting of the modern world.

The final feature of the traditional African cultures I consider positive and worth pursuing for African modernity is practical wisdom. Wisdom is conceived in the traditional African society as having both a practical and a theoretical dimension; but theoretical wisdom must have direct relevance to practical problems of life, to dealing with concrete human problems. The basis of wisdom, much of which is embedded in African proverbs (or maxims) is in human experience. Most African proverbs about wisdom deal with the practical wisdom that is indispensable in grappling with concrete problems that arise in concrete situations. Practical wisdom is of course important for all of our life situations; it is of utmost importance in matters of reconstructing the modern African society of the postcolonial era.

I have considered some features of the traditional African cultures positive, others negative—all from the perspective of the social, economic, political, and technological circumstances and demands of the changing world of Africa in modern times. The features I have delineated, which are by no means exhaustive of the spheres of the African moral, social, intellectual, and political life that could be examined critically and normatively for purposes of life in our modern world, apply mutatis mutandis to most African societies or cultures. But it must be recognized that those ideas and values considered positive operated in less complex societies and may not, in their unadulterated or unrefined forms, be harmonious with the ethos of the contemporary sociopolitical setting of the communoculturally heterogeneous postcolonial African nation-state. In the circumstance, what is required is the cultivation of a mind-set that is disposed to refining, improving, innovating, re-evaluating, and critically examining the many-sided cultural heritage of Africa in the attempt to forge creatively an African modernity appropriate to African cultural traditions.

The characterization of certain features of the traditional African cultures as positive suggests that something worthwhile can be mined from the African cultural ore that can then be hammered out on the anvil of the African goals, experiences, and aspirations in the modern world. Ways may have to be found for translating the positive traditional values and institutions into the functional idiom of modern circumstances. Modernity—successful modernization—in Africa will have to develop from some elements within the traditional setting—a setting that is already culturally complex—and from the mature, nuanced, and successful responses to the exogenous cultural forces that have affected the African society. Thus an authentic African modernity would not be merely a transplantation of external—in this instance—mostly Western traits. It would, to my mind, be worthwhile to adopt a view of modernity that does not regard all the values of the African tradition as something to be spurned and cavalierly jettisoned but instead regards some of those values as something that can be a positive leaven in the enrichment and fulfillment of human life.

The many-sided nature of the African cultural heritage is of course not peculiar to the African experience: it is an aspect of the historical phenomenon of cultural borrowing that follows encounters between different cultures. As long as peoples of different cultures come into contact, appreciate what is good in other cultures, and know what will be relevant and conducive to the fulfillment of their own goals and aspirations, cultural borrowing will continue to be an important feature of the human cultural experience as well as a lever of human progress. But practical wisdom dictates that what is borrowed or taken or received from alien cultures be such as will enrich the lives of the recipients, rather than confuse and deracinate them culturally. In this connection, it is imperative that wisdom and adaptive capacity be profoundly exercised in pursuit of modernity, a pursuit that requires and proceeds on an innovative ethos. African modernity must be a self-created modernity if it is to be realistic and meaningful, sensitive, enduring, self-sustaining.

There is no denying that in the development of the human being and society, the cultural factor cannot be ignored or denigrated. The reason is that any meaningful human development takes place in a cultural milieu and is in fact conditioned or influenced by it. The cultural milieu, even though it cannot be said to be a windowless monad and would have received or adopted a good many elements from other cultures, must nevertheless stay self-identical or internally cohesive in its essentials for a reasonably long time for a meaningful and recognizable development to take place. This is in fact a necessary condition for the development of a human society in all its complexities. In the absence of this condition, development becomes distorted, uneven, and without sure foundations.

Africa is trying feverishly to develop and become modern; but it is trying to develop in a cultural setting with which, for many reasons, it has not fully and satisfactorily come to terms. Since, to repeat, no human culture can be said to be a windowless monad, impervious to influences from outside and developing on its own original terms, what will need to be done in Africa is thoughtfully, ingeniously, and purposively to mold what can be (or, has been) received from outside to suit our own situations, visions, and aspirations and thus ultimately to mesh it with the positive and worthwhile aspects of the indigenous cultures. This cultural mesh, having been woven of our experiences, common sense, imagination, creative spirit, and sense of history would be vitalized and, thus, braced up for the gargantuan task of making a transition to the complex life of the modern world.

Let me say, finally: a transition to modernity—as a transition to any new era—involves costs, and it is necessary to recognize and appreciate the costs that will be incurred by African societies in their desire to modernize, to make desirable changes required by the attempt to function in the modern setting of our world. With this said, however, I wish quickly to add that our values as human beings are created within the crucible of the existential conditions in which we live, move, and have our being, and that those values are often—and should be—formed by our conceptions of what we want to be or what we think we ought to be. Modernity is a stage—a significant stage at that—in the civilizational trajectory of humankind. It behooves humankind, while it is inebriated by its sophisticated achievements—especially in its scientific and technological endeavors made possible by modernity—to create and maintain values consistent with its conceptions of what human beings, and their societies, ought to be. Modernity is created for humanity, and not humanity for modernity. Inebriation with modernity—or the great desire to make a transition to modernity—should therefore not be allowed to lead to the subversion or fragmentation of basic human values, to humanity's own chagrin. The essence of our humanity—of which our natural sociality is an intrinsic part—cannot, should not, be jettisoned—or left behind—as an encumbrance in the transition to modernity. The decision whether to repudiate or maintain our basic human values cannot be determined simply—and inevitably—by such societal forces as technology and urbanism, to the exclusion of any human involvement. For in the final analysis, the pursuit of those values is indeed always a matter of rational or moral choice that human beings are free to make; that choice is not a determined or imposed choice. The costs—and there will be costs—of modernization must be negotiated, but, yes and always, to the advantage of basic human values.

Notes

Chapter 1

1. Thus, in the wake of cuts in financial grants to universities in Britain by the Margaret Thatcher government in the mid-1980s, philosophy departments in some half dozen British universities were closed down.

2. A. R. Lacey, *A Dictionary of Philosophy* (London: Routledge and Kegan Paul, 1976), p. 159.

3. W. V. O. Quine, "Two Dogmas of Empiricism," in *From a Logical Point of View* (Cambridge, Mass.: Harvard University Press, 1953), ch. 2.

4. Ludwig Wittgenstein, *Tractatus Logico-Philosophicus*, trans. David F. Pears and B. F. McGuinness (London: Routledge and Kegan Paul, 1961), p. 4.112.

5. Brenda Almond, *Philosophy or Sophia: A Philosophical Odyssey* (Harmondsworth, England: Penguin Books, 1988), p. 12.

6. Gilbert Ryle, *Plato's Progress* (Cambridge: Cambridge University Press, 1966), p. 9.

7. Ibid, p. 20.

8. Ibid, p. 17.

9. W. V. O. Quine, *The Time of My Life: An Autobiography* (Cambridge, Mass.: MIT Press, 1985), e.g. pp. 342, 398, 432, 434, 462.

10. Ibid., p. 406.

11. Ibid., p. 477; my emphasis.

12. Antony Flew, *An Introduction to Western Philosophy: Ideas and Arguments from Plato to Sartre* (London: Thames and Hudson, 1971), p. 60.

13. Joseph Owens, *A History of Ancient Western Philosophy* (New York: Appleton Century Crofts, 1959), p. 395.

14. A. H. Armstrong, "Plotinus," ch. 12 of A. H. Armstrong, ed., *The Cambridge History of Later Greek and Early Medieval Philosophy* (Cambridge: Cambridge University Press, 1967), p. 195.

15. Plato, *Apology,* 38b.

16. Aristotle, *Nicomaechean Ethics,* 1103b; emphasis mine.
17. Corliss Lamont, *The Philosophy of Humanism* (New York: Frederick Ungar, 1965), pp. 12–14.
18. Ludwig Wittgenstein, *Zettel,* ed. G. E. M. Anscombe and G. H. von Wright, trans. G. E. M. Anscombe (Berkeley and Los Angeles: University of California Press, 1967), no. 455.
19. Michael Walzer, "Philosophy and Democracy," *Political Theory* 9, no. 3 (August 1981): 379–99.
20. For a detailed account of the allegory of the cave, see Plato's *Republic,* 514a–521b. Quotations from the *Republic* are from F. M. Cornford's translation (London: Oxford University Press, 1945).
21. Plato, *Republic,* 519c–d.
22. Plato, *Republic,* 520b–c; emphasis mine.
23. Plato, *Republic,* 519e–520a; emphasis mine.
24. Plato, *Republic,* 520a.
25. Plato, *Republic,* 539e–540a; emphasis mine.
26. G. C. Field, *Plato and His Contemporaries* (London: Methuen, 1967), p. 131.
27. Ibid., p. 91.
28. Plato, *Republic,* 473d; see also 501e.
29. Plato, *Republic,* 494a.
30. Aristotle, *Nicomaechean Ethics,* 1095a.
31. W. F. R. Hardie, *Aristotle's Ethical Theory* (Oxford: Clarendon Press, 1968), p. 119.
32. Ibid., p. 120.
33. W. D. Ross, *Aristotle* (London: Methuen, 1923), p. 202.
34. Hardie, *Aristotle's Ethical Theory,* p. 123.
35. Bertrand Russell, *A History of Western Philosophy,* (New York: Simon and Schuster, 1945), p. 174.
36. Qtd. in Karen I. Vaughn, *John Locke, Economist and Social Scientist* (Chicago: University of Chicago Press, 1980), p. 115.
37. Ibid., p. xi.
38. Ibid.
39. Joseph A. Schumpeter, *A History of Economic Analysis* (New York: Oxford University Press, 1954), pp. 116–18.
40. Robert L. Heilbroner, *The Worldly Philosophers: The Lives, Times, and Ideas of the Great Economic Thinkers,* 6th ed. (New York: Simon and Schuster, 1986), p. 42.
41. Karl Marx, *Eleven Theses on Feuerbach* (1845).
42. John Rawls, *A Theory of Justice* (Cambridge, Mass.: Harvard University Press, 1971).
43. Norman Daniels, ed., *Reading Rawls* (New York: Basic Books, 1975), p. xiii; Kai Nielsen, "On Finding One's Feet in Philosophy: From Wittgenstein to Marx," *Metaphilosophy* 16, no. 1 (January 1985): 5.
44. G. W. F. Hegel, *Philosophy of Right,* trans. T. M. Knox (Oxford, Clarendon Press, 1942), p. 11; emphasis mine.
45. John Rawls, "Kantian Constructivism in Moral Theory," *Journal of Philosophy* 77, no. 9 (September 1980): 518, for example.
46. John Rawls, "Justice As Fairness: Political Not Metaphysical," *Philosophy and Public Affairs* 14, no. 3 (summer 1985): 224.
47. Joseph Raz, "Principles of Equality," *Mind* 87 (July 1978): 321.
48. K. C. Anyanwu, "The Idea of Art in African Thought," in Guttorm Floistad,

ed., *Contemporary Philosophy: A New Survey,* vol. 5, *African Philosophy* (Dordrecht, Netherlands: Martinus Nijhoff, 1987), p. 237.

49. H. Odera Oruka, "African Philosophy: A Brief Personal History and Current Debate," in Floistad, Contemporary African Philosophy, p. 56; emphasis is in original

50. Ibid., p. 66; emphasis in original.

51. Brian R. Wilson, ed., *Rationality* (Oxford: Basil Blackwell, 1974); see, for instance, Peter Winch, "Understanding a Primitive Society," pp. 78–111, and Steven Lukes, "Some Problems About Rationality," pp. 194–213.

52. Robin Horton, in fact, thinks that African thought in the traditional setting was of "eminently rational and logical character." "African Traditional Thought and Western Science," in Wilson, *Rationality,* p. 160.

53. P. O. Bodunrin, "The Question of African Philosophy," in Richard A. Wright, ed., *African Philosophy: An Introduction,* 3d ed. (Lanham, Md.: University Press of America, 1984), p. 2.

54. Rawls, "Justice As Fairness," p. 225.

Chapter 2

1. Kwame Gyekye, *An Essay on African Philosophical Thought: The Akan Conceptual Scheme,* rev. ed. (Philadelphia: Temple University Press, 1995), ch. 10.

2. Kwesi A. Dickson, *Aspects of Religion and Life in Africa* (Accra: Ghana Academy of Arts and Sciences, 1977), p. 4.

3. Jomo Kenyatta, *Facing Mount Kenya* (New York: Vintage Books, 1965), p. 297.

4. Ibid., p. 188.

5. John S. Mbiti, *African Religions and Philosophy* (New York: Doubleday, 1970), p. 141; emphasis mine.

6. Ifeanyi A. Menkiti, "Person and Community in African Traditional Thought," in Richard A. Wright, ed., *African Philosophy: An Introduction,* 3d ed. (Lanham, Md.: University Press of America, 1984), pp. 171 and 180.

7. Ibid., p. 172.

8. Ibid., p. 174; also pp. 178 and 179.

9. Ibid., p. 173.

10. Kwame Nkrumah, *Consciencism: Philosophy and Ideology for Decolonization and Development with Particular Reference to the African Revolution* (London: Heinemann, 1964), p. 73.

11. Leopold S. Senghor, *On African Socialism,* trans. Mercer Cook (New York: Praeger, 1964), p. 49.

12. Ibid., pp. 93–94; emphasis mine.

13. Jeremy Bentham, *An Introduction to the Principles of Morals and Legislation* (1823; Oxford: Basil Blackwell, 1948), p. 126.

14. Will Kymlicka, *Contemporary Political Philosophy: An Introduction* (Oxford: Clarendon Press, 1990), p. 206.

15. Menkiti, "Person and Community in African Traditional Thought," p. 176; emphasis mine.

16. Ibid., p. 172.

17. Ibid., p. 174.

18. Ibid., p. 173; emphasis mine.

19. Ibid.

20. Ibid., p. 172.

21. Ahene-Affoh, *Twi Kasakoa ne Kasatome Ahorow Bi* (in the Akan language) (Accra: Ghana Publishing Corporation, 1976), p. 51.

22. Menkiti (in "Person and Community in African Traditional Thought," p. 174) argues that the relative absence of ritualized grief over the death of a child in African societies, in contrast to the elaborate burial ceremony and ritualized grief in the event of the death of an older person, supports his point about the definition of personhood by the community. It is not true, however, that every older person who dies in an African community is given an elaborate burial. The type of burial and extent of the grief expressed over the death of an adult depends on the community's evaluation of the deceased's moral life. Attitudes toward the death of children mostly spring from superstitious beliefs and are irrelevant to conceptions of personhood.

23. Eliot Deutsch, in *Personhood, Creativity, and Freedom* (Honolulu: University of Hawaii Press, 1982), ch. 1, argues that personhood is an achievement. It is not clear to me, however, that he has moral achievement in mind. In a later publication, however, which incorporates some of the chapters of this book, he says: "Personhood, we have argued, is an achievement concept. A human being is a person to the degree to which he or she becomes an integrated, creative, and freely acting social and *moral being*" (*Creative Being: The Crafting of Person and World* [Honolulu: University of Hawaii Press, 1992], p. 195; emphasis mine; also pp. 179–80).

24. Menkiti, "Person and Community in African Traditional Thought," p. 179; emphasis mine.

25. Ibid.

26. Joseph Raz, *The Morality of Freedom* (Oxford: Clarendon Press, 1986), p. 381; emphasis mine.

27. Ibid., pp. 378–79; emphasis mine.

28. Ibid., p. 369.

29. Ibid., p. 247.

30. Ibid., pp. 312–13.

31. Michael J. Sandel, *Liberalism and the Limits of Justice* (Cambridge: Cambridge University Press, 1982), p. 179.

32. Alasdair MacIntyre, *After Virtue: A Study in Moral Theory* (Notre Dame, Ind.: University of Notre Dame Press, 1984), p. 221.

33. Ibid., p. 220; emphasis mine.

34. Menkiti, "Person and Community in African Traditional Thought," p. 180.

35. Sandel, *Liberalism and the Limits of Justice*, p. 33.

36. Charles Taylor, "Atomism," in his *Philosophy and the Human Sciences: Philosophical Papers*, vol. 2 (Cambridge: Cambridge University Press, 1985), p. 189.

37. Ibid., p. 190.

38. MacIntyre, *After Virtue*, p. 69.

39. Ibid., p. 70.

40. Immanuel Kant, *Groundwork of the Metaphysic of Morals*, trans. H. J. Paton (London: Hutchinson University Library, 1965), p. 95.

41. Ibid., p. 96.

42. Raz, *Morality of Freedom*, p. 170.

43. Ibid., p. 183.

44. For the standard characterization of the act of supererogation, see, for instance, David Heyd, *Supererogation: Its Status in Ethical Theory* (Cambridge: Cambridge University Press, 1982), p. 115; John Rawls, *A Theory of Justice* (Cambridge, Mass.: Harvard University Press, 1971), p. 117; Raz, *Morality of Freedom*, p. 196.

45. J. O. Urmson, "Saints and Heroes," in A. I. Melden, ed., *Essays in Moral Philosophy* (Seattle: University of Washington Press, 1958), pp. 214–15.

46. Ibid., pp. 205, 211, 213, 215.

47. Heyd, *Supererogation*, p. 166.

48. Rawls, *Theory of Justice*, p. 117.

49. Heyd, *Supererogation*, p. 119; emphasis in the original.

50. Urmson, "Saints and Heroes," p. 213.

51. Ibid., p. 210.

52. Ibid., pp. 209, 211, 215.

53. Heyd, *Supererogation*, p. 181.

Chapter 3

1. G. W. Herder, "Ideas for a Philosophy of History" in F. M. Barnard, ed., *Herder's Social and Political Thought* Oxford: Oxford University Press, 1965, p. 324; emphasis mine.

2. J. G. Fichte, *Addresses to the German Nation,* trans. R. F. Jones and G. H. Turnbull Westport, Conn.: Greenwood Press, 1979, p. 215; emphasis mine.

3. Friedrich von Schlegel, quoted in Christopher J. Berry, "Nations and Norms," *Review of Politics* 43, no. 1 (January 1981): 84.

4. Ibid., p. 84.

5. Ludwig von Mises, *Nation, State, and Economy: Contributions to the Politics and History of Our Time,* trans. and with an introduction by Leland B. Yeager (New York: New York University Press, 1983), p. 12.

6. L. T. Hobhouse, *Social Evolution and Political Theory* (New York: Columbia University Press, 1928), p. 146.

7. *Washington Post,* April 28, 1994, p. 1; emphasis mine. Nelson Mandela made this remarkable statement on the occasion of the historic multiracial elections in South Africa held April 26–29, 1994. The second part of the quotation, "We are starting a new era of hope, reconciliation and nation building" appears also in *Newsweek,* May 9, 1994, pp. 32–33.

8. Walker Connor, "Nation-Building or Nation-Destroying?" *World Politics* 24 (1972): 336; reprinted in his *Ethnonationalism: The Quest for Understanding* (Princeton, N.J.: Princeton University Press, 1994), p. 42.

9. Basil Davidson, *The Black Man's Burden: Africa and the Curse of the Nation-State* (New York: Random House, Times Books, 1992); emphasis mine.

10. Ibid., pp. 58–59; emphasis mine.

11. My view about the divisive or disintegrative effect of the misuse of political power or its concentration in *one* ethnocultural group in a multinational (multiethnic) state resonates in an interview given by the distinguished French political scientist René Lemarchand. In response to a question, Lemarchand said: "The central argument that you hear from the Tutsi in Burundi is that ethnicity is a myth of the colonizer—the Belgians—and that there is no fundamental difference between Hutu and Tutsi. And in a sense they are right. They speak the same language, they have the same customs, they owe allegiance to the same political institutions—nonetheless, *power gravitated to the Tutsis and because of this, their identity is seen by the Hutus as separate from that of the Hutu themselves.*" "Myth Making and Ethnic Identity in Burundi: An Interview with René Lemarchand." *The Woodrow Wilson Center Report* 7, no. 3 (November 1995): 9; emphasis mine.

12. We know that immediately after regaining political independence in December 1961, Tanzania (then known as Tanganyika) declared Kiswahili as the national language of the new nation-state. Writing, almost three decades (i.e., about a generation) later, Maria G. Kente made the following remarkable observation: "Kiswahili has united the many different ethnic groups of Tanzania (about 120 different vernaculars) and played an important role in the people's efforts to liberate themselves. . . . Although it will take years and many resources in order to cater for all the needs, *there is no doubt that Kiswahili has made an important contribution to the development of a national identity in Tanzania.*" Maria G. Kente, "The Role of a National Language in Tanzania," in Jude J. Ongong'a and Kenneth R. Gray, eds., *Bottlenecks to National Identity: Ethnic Co-operation Towards Nation Building*, Proceedings of the Third Professors World Peace Academy of Kenya Conference, Mombasa, Kenya, September 15–18, 1988 (Nairobi: Professors World Peace Academy of Kenya, 1989), p. 38; emphasis mine.

13. Max Weber, *Economy and Society*, vol. 1, ed. Gunther Roth and Claus Wittich (New York: Bedminster Press, 1968), p. 389.

14. David Miller, *Market, State, and Community* (Oxford: Clarendon Press, 1989), p. 279; also his "The Ethical Significance of Nationality," *Ethics* 98, (July 1988): 658.

15. David Miller, *On Nationality* (Oxford: Clarendon Press, 1995), p. 19.

16. E. K. Francis, "The Ethnic Factor in Nation Building," *Social Forces* 46 (1968): 341.

17. George de Vos and Lola Romanucci-Ross, eds., *Ethnic Identity: Cultural Continuities and Change* (Mountain View, Calif.: Mayfield Publishing Company, 1975), p. 9; see also p. 19.

18. Henry George Liddle and Robert Scott, *A Greek-English Lexicon* (Oxford: Clarendon Press, 1968), p. 480.

19. Anthony D. Smith, *The Ethnic Origins of Nations* (Oxford: Basil Blackwell, 1986), p. 22.

20. Ibid.

21. Liddle and Scott, *Greek-English Lexicon*, pp. 342b–44b.

22. Walker Connor, "A nation is a nation, is a state, is an ethnic group, is a . . ." *Ethnic and Racial Studies*, 1, no. 4 (October 1978): 386; reprinted in his *Ethnonationalism*, p. 100.

23. Anthony D. Smith, *State and Nation in the Third World* (New York: St. Martin's Press, 1983), p. 63.

24. Donald L. Horowitz, "Ethnic Identity," in Nathan Glazer and Daniel P. Moynihan, eds., *Ethnicity: Theory and Experience* (Cambridge, Mass.: Harvard University Press, 1975), pp. 116–18.

25. Ibid. p. 121; emphasis mine.

26. Igor Kopytoff, ed. *The African Frontier: The Reproduction of Traditional African Societies* (Bloomington: Indiana University Press, 1987), p. 31.

27. Talcott Parsons, "Some Theoretical Considerations on the Nature and Trends of Change of Ethnicity," in Glazer and Moynihan, *Ethnicity*, p. 53.

28. Ibid., p. 56. Parsons says (ibid., p. 57): "There are many cases of the marriage of members of different ethnic groups. The question therefore of the ethnic adherence of a married couple can become indefinite and the same is of course true for their children and for their further descendants. Indeed in such cases there may be a certain optional rather than ascriptive character to ethnic identity"

29. Harold R. Isaacs, "Basic Group Identity: The Idols of the Tribe," in Glazer and Moynihan, *Ethnicity*, pp. 29–30.

30. See my *An Essay on African Philosophical Thought* (Philadelphia, Pa.: Temple University Press, 1995), pp. 191–95.

31. See chapter 8, section 1.

32. I owe the distinction between public and private culture to Miller, *On Nationality,* p. 26.

Chapter 4

1. *Findings,* (Washington, D.C.) Special issue, Africa Regional Studies Program, World Bank, September 1993, p. 1.

2. Adolphe L. Cureau, *Savage Man in Central Africa: A Study of Primitive Races in the French Congo,* trans. E. Andrews (London: T. Fisher Unwin, 1915), p. 279.

3. Dugald Campbell, *In the Heart of Bantuland: A Record of Twenty-nine Years' Pioneering in Central Africa Among the Bantu Peoples* (London: Seeley, Service, 1922), p. 42, emphasis mine.

4. Meyer Fortes and E. E. Evans-Pritchard, *African Political Systems* (Oxford: Oxford University Press, 1940), p. 12.

5. Jack Donnelly, "Cultural Relativism and Universal Human Rights," *Human Rights Quarterly* 6, no. 4 (November 1984): 413–14.

6. Ibid., p. 414.

7. Daryll Forde, ed., *African Worlds* (Oxford: Oxford University Press, 1954), p. 78.

8. Ndabaningi Sithole, *African Nationalism* (Cape Town, 1959), pp. 96–97.

9. Hilda Kuper, *An African Aristocracy: Rank Among the Swazi* (Oxford: Oxford University Press, 1961), p. 63; Isaac Schapera, *Handbook of Tswana Law and Custom* (Oxford: Oxford University Press, 1955), p. 84.

10. Sithole, *African Nationalism,* p. 95.

11. Ibid., p. 98.

12. Ibid., p. 86.

13. Julius K. Nyerere, "Democracy and the Party System," in Rupert Emerson and Martin Kilson, eds., *The Political Awakening of Africa* (Englewood Cliffs, N.J.: Prentice-Hall, 1965), pp. 122–23.

14. Julius K. Nyerere, "One Party Rule," in Paul E. Sigmund, ed., *The Ideologies of the Developing Nations* (New York: Praeger, 1963), p. 197.

15. "African Socialism and Its Application to Planning in Kenya" Kenya Government Sessional Paper No. 10, (Nairobi, Kenya: Ministry of Information, 1965), section 9; emphasis mine.

16. V. G. Simiyu, "The Democratic Myth in the African Traditional Societies," in W. O. Oyugi and A. Gitonga, eds., *Democratic Theory and Practice in Africa* (Nairobi: Heinemann Kenya, 1987), p. 55.

17. Ibid., p. 69.

18. Ibid., p. 64.

19. Ibid. (also p. 68).

20. Ibid., p. 69.

21. Ibid., p. 66.

22. Ibid., p. 55.

23. Ibid., p. 65.

24. Ibid., p. 69.

25. Ibid., p. 55; emphasis mine.

26. Ibid., p. 68; emphasis mine.

27. Dankwart A. Rustow, "Democracy: A Global Revolution?" *Foreign Affairs,* fall 1990, p. 85.

28. The present tense is used to indicate that the system is still maintained in most parts of Africa.

29. Fortes and Evans-Pritchard, *African Political Systems,* p. 1; emphasis mine.

30. J. B. Danquah, *Akan Laws and Customs* (London: Frank Cass, 1928), p. 13.

31. R. S. Rattray, *Ashanti Law and Constitution* (Oxford: Clarendon Press, 1929), p. 82. A few of the injunctions have been left out, and some changes have also been made in Rattray's translations from the Akan language.

32. Ibid.; Danquah, *Akan Laws and Customs,* p. 116.

33. John Mensah Sarbah, *Fanti National Constitution* (1897; London: Frank Cass, 1968), p. 11.

34. Rattray, *Ashanti Law and Constitution,* p. 407, n. 1: "Their very expression for a market and a meeting-place in council was the same, i.e., *adwabo,* surely an extraordinarily significant fact."

35. Danquah, *Akan Laws and Customs,* p. 119. "Enstool" and "destool" are technical terms for "enthrone" and "dethrone."

36. Rattray, *Ashanti Law and Constitution,* p. 87.

37. Brodie Cruickshank, *Eighteen Years on the Gold Coast of Africa,* 1 (London, 1854), p. 236; emphasis mine.

38. Ibid., p. 251.

39. Rattray, *Ashanti Law and Constitution,* pp. 406–7; emphasis mine.

40. G. C. Field, *Plato and His Contemporaries* (London: Methuen, 1967), p. 81.

41. John Mensah Sarbah, *Fanti Customary Laws* (London: William Clowes and Sons, 1897), p. 78.

42. Danquah, *Akan Laws and Customs,* p. 115.

43. Ibid., p. 117.

44. Rattray, *Ashanti Law and Constitution,* p. 405.

45. Consensus, as a feature of the decision-making procedure, appears to have been common to African communities. The following description of the practice in traditional Buganda society in Uganda exemplifies the practice elsewhere in Africa: "The monarch ruled through a council of heads of clans and there were many councils of heads, sub-heads and chiefs at the various levels of society. After every debate a consensus had to be reached or sought. Consensus was very central to the operation of democracy and justice in traditional Buganda society and of African societies generally. If after deliberations the heads of clans reached a consensus it would be taboo on the part of the monarch to reject or oppose what the clan leaders had agreed upon. That would spell disaster. . . . It should be pointed out that the king rarely took part in the deliberations himself, the rationale being that the monarch should not prejudice the proceedings of the debate. Democracy demanded that the king execute what had been arrived at without his contribution. If the king had anything to contribute he would get it across through one of his closest councilors, who would then pass it on for discussion and eventual consensus formation. We need to note that consensus formation was carried on at the highest level, as well as at the various levels in the structure of society down to the extended family. . . . What is important about equality in traditional Buganda society is that, regardless of class, every citizen of the tribe was free to contribute to consensus formation. Consensus formation was not an exclusive right of clan heads and chiefs. The people of lower classes were always conscious of their civil rights and always attempted to exercise them." E. Wamala, "The Socio-Political Philosophy of Traditional Buganda

Society: Breaks and Continuity into the Present", in A. T. Dalfovo et al., *The Foundations of Social Life: Ugandan Philosophical Studies*, 1 (Washington, D.C.: Council for Research in Values and Philosophy, 1992), pp. 40 and 46–47.

46. Dennis Austin, "African and Democracy: Reflections on African politics: Prospero, Ariel, and Caliban," *International Affairs* (London), 69, no. 2 (April 1993): 204.

47. Ibid., p. 212; emphasis mine.

48. Ibid., p. 204.

49. Ibid.

Chapter 5

1. "African Socialism and Its Application to Planning in Kenya," Kenya Government Sessional Paper No. 10 (Nairobi, Kenya: Ministry of Information, 1965), p. 2; emphasis mine.

2. Bede Onuoha, *The Elements of African Socialism* (London: Andre Deutsch, 1965), p. 30; emphasis mine.

3. Léopold S. Senghor, *On African Socialism*, trans. and with an introduction by Mercer Cook (New York: Praeger, 1964), p. xi.

4. Andrew Shonfield, *Socialism for Africa* (Moscow: Novosti Press Agency Publishing House, 1965), p. 13.

5. Senghor, *On African Socialism*, p. 49; emphasis mine.

6. Julius K. Nyerere, *Ujamaa: Essays on Socialism* (Dar es Salaam: Oxford University Press, 1968), p. 12.

7. Ibid., p. 8.

8. Kwame Nkrumah, *Consciencism: Philosophy and Ideology for Decolonization and Development with Particular Reference to the African Revolution* (London: Heinemann, 1964), p. 73. The second quoted statement reappears in Kwame Nkrumah, "African Socialism Revisited," *African Forum: A Quarterly Journal of Contemporary Affairs* 1, no. 3 (winter 1966): p. 8; on p. 9 Nkrumah states: "Socialism, therefore, can be, and is, the defense of the principles of communalism in a modern setting."

9. Quoted in N. A. Ollennu, *Principles of Customary Land Law in Ghana* (London: Sweet and Maxwell, 1962), p. 4.

10. Nyerere, *Ujamaa*, p. 7.

11. Jomo Kenyatta, *Facing Mount Kenya* (New York: Vintage Books, 1965), p. 299.

12. Dugald Campbell, *In the Heart of Bantuland: A Record of Twenty-nine years' Pioneering in Central Africa Among the Bantu Peoples* (London: Seeley, Service, 1922), pp. 47–48.

13. J. B. Danquah, *Akan Laws and Customs* (London: Frank Cass, 1928), p. 201.

14. Nkrumah, *Consciencism*, p. 74; emphasis mine.

15. Ibid.

16. R. S. Rattray, *Ashanti* (Oxford: Oxford University Press, 1923), p. 226; also p. 230.

17. Danquah, *Akan Laws and Customs*, p. 197.

18. John Mensah Sarbah, *Fanti Customary Laws* (London: William Clowes and Sons, 1897), p. 89.

19. M. J. Field, *Akim-Kotoku: An Oman of the Gold Coast* (London: Crown Agents for the Colonies, 1948), p. 57.

20. S. M. Molema, *The Bantu: Past and Present* (Edinburgh: W. Green and Son, 1920), p. 115

21. Max Gluckman, *Politics, Law, and Ritual in Tribal Society* (Oxford: Oxford University Press, 1965), pp. 36 ff.; emphasis mine.

22. Kenneth D. Kaunda, "Humanism in Zambia," in Bastiaan de Gaay Fortman, ed., *After Mulungushi: The Economics of Zambian Humanism,* (Nairobi: East African Publishing House, 1969), p. 21.

23. Rattray, *Ashanti,* p. 221.

24. Ray A. Kea, *Settlements, Trade, and Politics in the 17th Century Gold Coast* (Baltimore, Md.: Johns Hopkins University Press, 1982), p. 99.

25. Field, *Akim-Kotoku,* p. 73.

26. Kea, *Settlements, Trade, and Politics,* p. 6

27. Nyerere, *Ujamaa,* pp. 5, 7.

28. Sarbah, *Fanti Customary Laws,* p. 60; also p. 89.

29. Ibid., p. 57.

30. Danquah, *Akan Laws and Customs,* p. 206.

31. Sarbah, *Fanti Customary Laws,* p. 89.

32. Danquah, *Akan Laws and Customs,* p. 210.

33. S. K. B. Asante, *Property Law and Social Goals in Ghana, 1844–1966* (Accra: Ghana Universities Press, 1975), p. 24.

34. Ibid., p. 13.

35. The attempt to uncover the values, thoughts, attitudes, and feelings of people with a preliterate culture cannot, at least initially, avoid references to maxims or proverbs and other methods of expressing those values, etc.

36. R. S. Rattray, *Ashanti Proverbs* (Oxford: Oxford University Press, 1916).

37. Rhoda Howard, "Evaluating Human Rights in Africa: Some Problems of Implicit Comparisons," *Human Rights Quarterly* 6, no. 2 (May 1984): 174.

38. Ivor Wilks, *Asante in the Nineteenth Century: The Structure and Evolution of a Political Order* (Cambridge: Cambridge University Press, 1975), p. 430.

39. Rattray, *Ashanti Proverbs,* no. 654; C. A. Akrofi, *Twi Proverbs* (Accra: Waterville Publishing House, n.d.), no. 877.

40. Akrofi, *Twi Proverbs,* p. 146.

41. Kofi A. Busia, "The Ashanti of the Gold Coast," in Daryll Forde, ed., *African Worlds* (Oxford: Oxford University Press, 1954), p. 205.

42. John S. Mbiti, *African Religions and Philosophy* (New York: Doubleday, Anchor Books, 1970), p. 84.

43. E. Bolaji Idowu, *Olodumare: God in Yoruba Belief* (London: Longmans, 1962), p. 116.

44. John Iliffe, *The Emergence of African Capitalism* (Minneapolis: University of Minnesota Press, 1983), pp. 4–8.

45. Kea, *Settlements, Trade, and Politics,* p. 2.

46. Iliffe, *The Emergence of African Capitalism,* p. 45; emphasis mine.

47. Nkrumah, *Consciencism,* p. 74.

48. Iliffe, *The Emergence of African Capitalism,* p. 37.

49. Ibid., emphasis mine.

50. Ibid., pp. 31–36 and pp. 69ff.

51. For example: Kwame Gyekye, *An Essay on African Philosophical Thought: The Akan Conceptual Scheme,* rev. ed. (Philadelphia: Temple University Press, 1995), esp. pp. 143–46; Kwasi Wiredu, *Philosophy and an African Culture* (Cambridge: Cambridge University Press, 1980), p. 6 and passim; and "Moral Foundations of an African Culture," in Kwesi Wiredu and Kwame Gyekye, *Person and Community: Ghanaian Philosophical Studies,* (Washington, D.C.: Council for Research in Values and

Philosophy, 1992), pp. 193–206; Kwesi A. Dickson, *Aspects of Religion and Life in Africa* (Accra: Ghana Academy of Arts and Sciences, 1977), ch. 1

52. Kenneth Kaunda, *A Humanist in Africa* (London: Longmans, 1966), p. 32.

53. Nkrumah, "African Socialism Revisited," p. 3; Nkrumah, *Consciencism*, p. 77; emphasis mine.

54. Nyerere, *Ujamaa*, pp. 6–7.

55. Ibid., p. 12.

56. Ibid., pp. 3–4; emphasis in original.

57. Ibid., p. 4.

58. Ibid., pp. 1–12.

59. Ibid., p. 1.

60. Kenneth Kaunda, *Take Up the Challenge* (Lusaka, Zambia: Government Printer, 1970), p. 50.

61. Kaunda, "Humanism in Zambia," p. 12.

62. Ibid., p. 20; emphasis mine.

63. Charles Njonjo in a speech in Kenya's parliament in May 1981; reported in *Weekly Review,* May 15, 1981, pp. 11–13; quoted in Iliffe, *The Emergence of African Capitalism*, p. 3.

64. Gyekye, *An Essay on African Philosophical Thought*, pp. 154–55.

65. On the origin of the term "ideology," see Emmet Kennedy, *A Philosophe in the Age of Revolution: Destutt de Tracy and the Origins of 'Ideology'* (Philadelphia: American Philosophical Society, 1970); also his "Ideology from Destutt de Tracy to Marx," *Journal of the History of Ideas*, 40, no. 3 (July–September 1979): 353–68.

66. Kennedy, *A Philosophe in the Age of Revolution*, p. 47.

67. Thucydides, *History of the Peloponnesian War*, trans. Rex Warner (Harmondsworth, U.K.: Penguin Books, 1954), bk. 2, chs. 37 and 40.

68. George C. Lodge, "The Connection Between Ethics and Ideology," *Journal of Business Ethics* 1 (1982): 87. Also, his *The New American Ideology* (New York: Alfred A. Knopf, 1975), pp. 9–11.

Chapter 6

1. David Beetham, *The Legitimation of Power* (London: Macmillan, 1991), p. 16.

2. Ibid., p. 4.

3. Rulers in postcolonial African states, military and civilian, who have organized free and fair elections while they were in power are very few indeed; those who have lost power through elections were for three decades (i.e., until 1991) nonexistent.

4. Beetham, *The Legitimation of Power*, p. 94; emphasis mine.

5. Ibid.

6. The statement was made in a speech by Kwame Nkrumah in the course of a debate in the Ghana parliament on February 1, 1966. See *Official Debate of Parliament*, 2d Parl., 2d sess., February 1, 1966, vol. 43; emphasis mine.

7. Thus, following the nationwide elections held in Senegal in 1989, which were alleged not to have been fair, the leader of one of the opposition parties, Abdoulaye Wade, made the following statement: "It is not a question of a local election but a referendum, of a problem of legitimacy; we are asking the Senegalese people, 'is [President Diouf] legitimate?' If not, we must have new presidential and legislative elections." Charles Lane, "Dilemma of Democracy", *West Africa*, December 17–23, 1990, p. 3043.

8. Beetham, *The Legitimation of Power*, p. 13.

Chapter 7

1. Herbert H. Werlin, "The Roots of Corruption: The Ghanaian Enquiry," *Journal of Modern African Studies* 10, no. 2 (1972): 250.
2. James C. Scott, *Comparative Political Corruption* (Englewood Cliffs, N.J.: Prentice-Hall, 1972), p. 2.
3. Ibid., p. 3.
4. Chinua Achebe, *No Longer at Ease* (New York: Fawcett Premier, 1969), p. 38.
5. Victor T. Le Vine, *Political Corruption: The Ghana Case* (Stanford, Calif.: Hoover Institution Press, 1975), p. 12
6. John T. Noonan, *Bribes* (New York: Macmillan, 1984), p. 702.
7. Le Vine, *Political Corruption*, p. 2; emphasis mine.
8. Ibid., p. 37.
9. Ibid., p. 85.
10. Ibid., p. 99; emphasis mine.
11. Ibid., p. 50; emphasis mine.
12. Ibid., pp. 115–20.
13. Ibid., p. 122.
14. Ibid.
15. Ibid., p. 111.
16. Ibid., p. 8.
17. Scott, *Comparative Political Corruption*, p. viii.
18. Patrick J. Dobel, "The Corruption of a State," *American Political Science Review* 72, no. 3 (September 1978): 961.
19. Ibid.
20. Ibid., p. 970.
21. John Mensah Sarbah, *Fanti Customary Law* (London: Frank Cass, 1897), p. 78.
22. J. B. Danquah, *Akan Laws and Customs* (London: Frank Cass, 1928), p. 115.
23. Ibid., p. 117.
24. John Mensah Sarbah, *Fanti National Constitution* (London: William Clowes and Sons, 1906), p. 32; emphasis mine.
25. K. A. Busia, *The Position of the Chief in the Modern Political System of Ashanti* (London: Frank Cass, 1968), pp. 211–12. The meeting under reference, according to Busia, was held in 1938.
26. Ibid., p. 199; also pp. 50–51.
27. Ibid., pp. 200 and 202.
28. Dobel, "Corruption of a State," p. 972.
29. Werlin, "Roots of Corruption," pp. 250–51.
30. *West Africa*, January 24, 1983, p. 192, and February 21, 1983, pp. 495–96. I might also mention that the military officers who overthrew a military regime in Ghana in June 1979 did, in the few months following, stress the need for what they called "moral revolution."
31. W. Montgomery Watt, *Muhammad at Medina* (Oxford: Clarendon Press, 1956), p. 327; Tor Andrae, *Muhammad, The Man and His Faith* (New York: Harper and Brothers, 1960), p. 75.
32. Joseph Schacht, *An Introduction to Islamic Law* (Oxford: Clarendon Press, 1964), p. 13; emphasis mine.
33. In the wake of the attacks on the Cartesian conception of the mental contained in the influential book *The Concept of Mind* (London: Hutchinson, 1949), by

the late Oxford philosopher Gilbert Ryle, the concept of the will seems to have fallen on evil days. In the Cartesian metaphysics, the will was held as being a part of the mind, itself considered a nonphysical *entity*. Having denied that there is a nonphysical entity called Mind with a separate and distinct nature and existence from the body, it was only logical for Ryle and his followers to deny that there is an entity called Will, which, in the words of Ryle, "stands behind a person to make him do what he does or wants to do" (ibid., p. 63). It is clear, however, from the statements of Ryle that what he is really worried about are the facultative (or, entitative) over-tones supposedly or possibly embedded in the talk about the Will. Thus, he is concerned to deny the will as an entity but *not* as capacity with which our intentions are translated into action. This enables him appropriately, and without any inconsistency, to use such locutions as "strong-willed," "weak-willed," "strength of will," "weakness of will," effort of will." An effort of will, Ryle says, means "a particular exercise of tenacity of purpose occurring when the obstacles are notably great, or the counter temptations notably strong" (ibid. p. 73).

34. Sir Patrick Devlin, *The Legal Enforcement of Morals* (Oxford: Oxford University Press, 1965).

35. Max Gluckman, *The Judicial Process Among the Barotse of Northern Rhodesia* (Manchester, England: University of Manchester Press, 1955), p. 172; emphasis mine.

Chapter 8

1. According to Nisbet, "Neither the fifteenth nor the sixteenth century ended medieval society if, by medieval, we have reference to types of kinship, property, education, religion, and class. . . . For, measured in institutional terms, large sections of European society remained medieval until the nineteenth century." Robert A. Nisbet, *The Quest for Community* (New York: Oxford University Press, 1953), p. 85.

2. Daniel Lerner, *The Passing of the Traditional Society* (New York: Glencoe, 1958).

3. H. B. Acton, "Tradition and Some Other Forms of Order," *Proceedings of the Aristotelian Society*, n.s., vol. 53 (1952–53): 2.

4. Edward Shils, *Tradition* (London: Faber and Faber, 1981), p. 12.

5. Samuel Fleischacker, *The Ethics of Culture* (Ithaca: Cornell University Press, 1994), p. 45.

6. Ibid., p. 15.

7. Ibid., p. 71.

8. Ibid., p. 70.

9. Ibid., p. 21 (also, p. 145).

10. Kwame Anthony Appiah, *In My Father's House: Africa in the Philosophy of Culture* (New York: Oxford University Press, 1992), p. 99; emphasis in the original.

11. On this, see my *Essay on African Philosophical Thought: The Akan Conceptual Scheme*, rev. ed. (Philadelphia: Temple University Press, 1995), p. xxix.

12. See p. 269.

13. Appiah, *In My Father's House*, p. 103.

14. Acton, "Tradition," p. 3.

15. Ibid., p. 5.

16. Fleischacker, *The Ethics of Culture*, p. 21; emphasis mine.

17. Ibid., p. 70; emphasis mine.

18. H. B. Acton, "Tradition," p. 5.

19. Eric Hobsbawm and Terence Ranger, eds., *The Invention of Tradition* (Cambridge: Cambridge University Press, 1983), p. 1.

20. Ibid., p. 1.

21. Ibid., p. 2.

22. Ibid., p. 8.

23. Ibid., p. 250.

24. W. K. C. Guthrie, *A History of Greek Philosophy,* vol. 3 (Cambridge: Cambridge University Press, 1969), p. 55; also p. 129.

25. Ibid., p. 38; also pp. 70 and 108.

26. Aristotle, *Nicomachean Ethics,* 1134b18.

27. This part of Pericles' *Funeral Oration* is also referred to at p. 164.

28. Paul A. V. Ansah, "Is Africa Accursed or Bewitched?" *The Independent* (Accra, Ghana), February 17–24, 1993, p. 4.

29. N. K. Dzobo, "Sankofaism: A Philosophy of Africa's Mental Liberation," *Sankofa: Ghana's Illustrated Arts and Cultures* 5, no. 1 (January–June 1981): 35.

30. See Abiola Irele, "Contemporary Thought in French-Speaking Africa," in Albert G. Mosley, ed., *African Philosophy: Selected Readings* (Englewood Cliffs, N.J.: Prentice-Hall, 1995), p. 281.

31. Ibid., p. 282.

32. Ibid., p. 284.

33. Paulin J. Hountondji, *African Philosophy: Myth and Reality* (Bloomington: Indiana University Press, 1983), p. 53.

34. For a further critique of Hountondji, see Gyekye, *An Essay on African Philosophical Thought,* pp. 8–9.

35. Hountondji, *African Philosophy,* p. 166; emphasis mine.

36. Dugald Campbell, *In the Heart of Bantuland: A Record of Twenty-nine Years' Pioneering in Central Africa Among the Bantu Peoples* (London: Seeley, Service, 1922), p. 44.

37. R. S. Rattray, *Ashanti Law and Constitution* (Oxford: Oxford University Press, 1929), p. 407.

38. R. S. Rattray, *Ashanti Proverbs* (Oxford: Oxford University Press, 1916), pp. 11–12.

39. See, for example, Henryk Skolimowski, "The Cultural Model of Development: Alternative to Faustian Technology," *Alternatives: A Journal of World Policy* 5, no. 4 (January 1980); K. Twum-Barima, *The Cultural Basis of Our National Development,* J. B. Danquah Memorial Lectures, 25th Series, February 1982 (Accra: Ghana Academy of Arts and Sciences, 1985); and Thierry G. Verhelst, *No Life Without Roots: Culture and Development,* trans. Bob Cumming (Atlantic Highlands, N.J.: Zed Books, 1987).

40. On the concept of development, see my "Taking Development Seriously," *Journal of Applied Philosophy* 11, no. 1 (1994): 45–56.

41. Gyekye, *An Essay on African Philosophical Thought,* pp. 16–18 and 106–7.

42. It is instructive to note that the Ewe word for "knowledge" is *nunya,* a word that actually means "thing observed." This clearly means that observation or experience was regarded as the source of knowledge in Ewe thought: see N. K. Dzobo, "Knowledge and Truth: Ewe and Akan Conceptions," in Kwasi Wiredu and Kwame Gyekye, eds., *Person and Community: Ghanaian Philosophical Studies,* pp. 73–84. It is most probably appropriate to characterize African thought generally as empirical.

43. John S. Mbiti, *African Religions and Philosophy* (New York: Doubleday, Anchor Books, 1970), p. 1.

44. Ibid., p. 38.

45. Kofi A. Busia, *Africa in Search of Democracy* (New York: Praeger, 1967), pp. 1, 7.

46. Geoffrey Parrinder, *African Traditional Religion* (New York: Harper and Row, 1962), p. 9.

47. W. E. Abraham, *The Mind of Africa* (Chicago: University of Chicago Press, 1962), p. 55. I have thus changed the position I took in my *An Essay on African Philosophical Thought*, p. 202, on the interpretation of this proverb.

48. B. E. Oguah, "African and Western Philosophy: A Comparative Study," in Richard A. Wright, ed., *African Philosophy: An Introduction*, 3d ed. (Lanham, Md.: University Press of America, 1984), p. 219.

49. Mbiti, *African Religions and Philosophy*, p. 74.

50. The Akan version is, "wo feefee efun n'aniwa ase a, wohu saman."

51. Ebenezer Laing, *Science and Society in Ghana*, J. B. Danquah Memorial Lectures, 20th series, March 1987 (Accra: Ghana Academy of Arts and Sciences, 1990), p. 21.

52. Kofi Asare Opoku of the Institute of African Studies, University of Ghana, Legon.

53. Robert W. July, for example, says: "Art for art's sake had no place in traditional African society" and that it was "essentially functional." See his *An African Voice: The Role of the Humanities in African Independence* (Durham: Duke University Press, 1987), p. 49; also Claude Wauthier, *The Literature and Thought of Modern Africa* (London: Heinemann, 1978), pp. 173–74.

54. See Kwame Gyekye, *African Cultural Values: An Introduction* (Philadelphia, Pa.: Sankofa Publishing Company, 1996), ch. 8.

55. Lynn White, *Medieval Religion and Technology: Collected Essays* (Berkeley: University of California Press, 1978), p. 127.

56. Lord Todd, *Problems of the Technological Society*, Aggrey-Fraser-Guggisberg Memorial Lectures (Accra: Ghana Publishing Corporation, for the University of Ghana, 1973), p. 8.

57. Arnold Pacey, *The Culture of Technology* (Oxford: Basil Blackwell, 1983), p. 145.

58. Kwasi Wiredu, *Philosophy and an African Culture* (Cambridge: Cambridge University Press, 1980), 9.15.

59. Samuel Sefa-Dede, "Traditional Food Technology," in Robert Macrae, Richard K. Robinson, and Michele Sadler, eds., *Encyclopedia of Food Science, Food Technology and Nutrition* (New York: Academy Press, 1993), p. 4,600.

60. Sefa-Dede, ibid.; also, "Harnessing Food Technology for Development," in Samuel Sefa-Dede and Richard Orraca-Tetteh, eds., *Harnessing Traditional Food Technology for Development* (Legon: Department of Nutrition and Food Science, University of Ghana, 1989); Esi Colecraft, "Traditional Food Preservation: An Overview," *African Technology Forum* 6, no. 1 (February–March 1993): 15–17.

61. The encounter was between this traditional food technologist and research scientists and students from the Department of Nutrition and Food Science of the University of Ghana, headed by Samuel Sefa-Dede. The description of the encounter presented here was given to me by Sefa-Dede both orally and in writing, and I am most grateful to him.

62. Julius K. Nyerere, *Ujamaa: Essays on Socialism*, (Dar es Salaam: Oxford University Press, 1968), p. 108.

63. Kenneth D. Kaunda, *A Humanist in Africa* (London: Longmans, 1966), p. 22.

64. See, e.g., Kwasi Wiredu, *Philosophy and an African Culture* (Cambridge: Cambridge University Press, 1980), pp. 5–6, in Kwasi Wiredu and Kwame Gyekye, eds., *Person and Community: Ghanaian Philosophical Studies*, 1 (Washington, D.C.: Council for Research in Values and Philosophy, 1992), pp. 194–95; Gyekye, *An Essay on African on Philosophical Thought*, pp. 143–46.

65. The Akan version of this maxim reads: "Tete asoe, wonsoe ho bio."

66. The Akan version of the maxim reads: "Nea oretwa kwan nnim se n'akyi akyea."

67. White, *Medieval Religion and Technology*, p. xxiv.

68. Lawrence E. Cahoone, *The Dilemma of Modernity: Philosophy, Culture, and Anti-Culture* (Albany: State University Press of New York, 1988), p. 269.

69. Ibid., p. 1.

70. Hilail Gildin, *Political Philosophy: Six Essays by Leo Strauss* (New York: Bobbs-Merrill, 1975), p. 98.

71. George C. Lodge, *The New American Ideology*, (New York: Alfred Knopf, 1975), p. 74; emphasis mine.

72. Amitai Etzioni, *The Spirit of Community: The Reinvention of American Society* (New York: Simon and Schuster, a Touchstone Book, 1993), p. 2; emphasis mine.

73. Thus, Nisbet writes that "in general, the philosophy of community was dominant in medieval thought. . . . The group was primary; it was the irreducible unit of the social system at large." Robert A. Nisbet, *The Quest for Community* (New York: Oxford University Press, 1953), p. 81.

74. Leroy S. Rouner, ed., *On Community* (Notre Dame, Ind.: University of Notre Dame Press, 1992), p. 2; emphasis mine.

75. Matei Calinescu, *Five Faces of Modernity* (Durham, N.C.: Duke University Press, 1987), p. 13.

76. Ibid., p. 14.

77. Tilo Schabert, "A Note on Modernity," *Political Theory* 7, no. 1 (February 1979): 125.

78. Ibid.

79. See, for instance, Kwame Gyekye, *Arabic Logic: Ibn al-Tayyib on Porphyry's Eisagoge* (Albany: State University of New York Press, 1979), p. 38, section 45; al-Qifti, *Tarikh al-Hukama*, p. 256.

80. Shils, *Tradition*, p. 260.

81. Benjamin I. Schwartz, "The Limits of 'Tradition Versus Modernity' as Categories of Explanation: The Case of the Chinese Intellectuals," *Daedalus* 101, no. 2 (spring 1972): 82.

Chapter 9

1. Sir Hamilton A. R. Gibb, *Studies on the Civilization of Islam*, ed. Stanford J. Shaw and William R. Polk (Boston: Beacon Press, 1962), p. 331.

2. Leroy S. Rouner, ed., *On Community* (Notre Dame, Ind.: University of Notre Dame Press, 1992), p. 2: "the loneliness which attended this individualism finally seemed more than we could bear."

3. It may be mentioned that since its emergence, Western modernity has not succeeded in fully and permanently removing religion from public life and banishing it to the realm of the private, entirely rejected as a factor in the determination of public life. The American Declaration of Independence made reference to the *divine* origin of the individual's inalienable rights; the Bible, in particular, is used for swear-

ing in courts of judicature in Western countries; God is often invoked in public ceremonies: "So help me, God" is often the concluding utterance recited by persons being sworn into public office in Western countries; the United States Congress has Christian chaplains who offer prayers before the start of the day's deliberations (this may also be the true in parliaments and legislative bodies in other Western countries); and the fact that controversies have raged interminably over the religious act of prayer in public schools indicates that some people are not satisfied with the idea of withdrawing religion from public life. The (almost) incessant occurrence of the controversies surrounding the place of religion in public life contrasts very sharply with the universal, popular, and incontrovertible acceptance of the place of science, technology, and industrialism in public life: all this indicates that, contrary to the declared intentions of Western modernity, the influence of religion over public life has not entirely declined or been banished.

4. See the quoted view of Robert A. Nisbet, chapter 8, n. 1. In his recent book, Derek Phillips denies that earlier societies, such as those of ancient Greece and medieval Europe, were communal, as Western communitarian thinkers would have us believe. He writes: "Communitarians emphasize the peace and harmony of earlier times and places, while I see even more domination, subordination, exploitation, and human suffering than surrounds us today" (*Looking Backward: A Critical Appraisal of Communitarian Thought* [Princeton, N.J.: Princeton University Press, 1993], p. 195). I cannot deal with the details of Phillips's arguments here. But it is clear from the quoted statement, which comes at the end of his book, that he characterizes the communitarian society in ways all of which may not be implicit or explicit in the characterizations provided in the writings of Western communitarian thinkers. I doubt very much whether egalitarianism—implied in the statement—has been asserted as a feature of the communitarian society; or is the absolute absence of human suffering. On the other hand, Phillips does not indicate whether these earlier societies were individualistic. He says that "throughout history most people have spent more time in family contexts than in any other social context, and family interests, priorities, and loyalties generally have cut deeper than any other attachments" (*ibid.*, p. 226, n. 67). Surely most people will agree that the family is the archtype of the community or the communal life. Communitarians do not hesitate to point up the importance and relevance of the family to the concept of the community.

5. Robert A. Fowler, *The Dance with Community: The Contemporary Debate in American Political Thought* (Lawrence: University of Kansas Press, 1991), p. 3; emphasis mine.

6. For my comments on individuality in the traditional cultural setting, see Kwame Gyekye, *An Essay on African Philosophical Thought: The Akan Conceptual Scheme*, rev. ed. (Philadelphia, Pa.: Temple University Press, 1995), pp. 154–62; "Communitarian Features of African Socio-Political Thought," *The Responsive Community*, forthcoming; *African Cultural Values: An Introduction* (Philadelphia, Pa.: Sankofa Publishing Company, 1996), pp. 47–51; and the volume edited with Kwasi Wiredu, *Person and Community*, Ghanaian Philosophical Studies, 1 (Washington, D.C.: Council for Research in Values and Philosophy, 1992), pp. 193–206.

7. Kwesi A. Dickson, *Aspects of Religion and Life in Africa* (Accra: Ghana Academy of Arts and Sciences, 1977), p. 4; John S. Mbiti, *African Religions and Philosophy* (New York: Doubleday, Anchor Books, 1970), p. 136.

8. See Kwame Gyekye, "Taking Development Seriously," *Journal of Applied Philosophy* 11, no. 1 (1994): 48 and 56.

9. Ali A. Mazrui, "Africa Between Ideology and Technology: Two Frustrated Forces of Change," in Gwendolen M. Carter and Patrick O'Meara, eds., *African Independence: The First Twenty-five Years* (Bloomington: Indiana University Press, 1985), pp. 281–82.

10. Gyekye, *An Essay on African Philosophical Thought*, pp. 154–55.

11. Robert A. Nisbet, *The Sociological Tradition* (New York: Basic Books, 1969), p. 51; emphasis mine.

12. Kenneth Kaunda, *A Humanist in Africa* (London: Longmans, 1966), p. 28.

13. J. G. Christaller, *Dictionary of the Asante and Fante Language Called Twi (Tshi)*, 2d ed., revised and enlarged (Basel: Basel Evangelical Missionary Society, 1933).

14. John Dewey, *The Public and Its Problems* (New York: Holt, 1927), p. 148–49.

15. Thus, I am using "republican" in the original sense that derives from its Latin etymology—*res publica:* a public affair, a matter of public concern. To show republican spirit or outlook is, thus, to demonstrate interest and commitment to matters of public concern; it is to cultivate civic virtue or to acquire civic responsibility.

Bibliography

Abraham, W. E. *The Mind of Africa.* Chicago: University of Chicago Press, 1962.

Achebe, Chinua. *No Longer at Ease.* New York: Fawcett Premier, 1969.

Acton, H. B. "Tradition and Some Other Forms of Order." *Proceedings of the Aristotelian Society,* N.S., 53 (1952–53): 1–28.

"African Socialism and Its Application to Planning in Kenya." Kenya Government Sessional Paper No. 10. Nairobi, Kenya: Ministry of Information, 1965.

Ahene-Affoh. *Twi Kasakoa ne Kasatome Ahorow Bi* (in the Akan language). Accra: Ghana Publishing Corporation, 1976.

Akrofi, C. A. *Twi Proverbs.* Accra: Waterville Publishing House, n.d.

Akyeampong, Daniel A. *The Two Cultures Revisited: Interactions of Science and Culture.* J. B. Danquah Memorial Lectures, 25th series, February 1992. Accra: Ghana Academy of Arts and Sciences, 1993.

Almond, Brenda. *Philosophy or Sophia: A Philosophical Odyssey.* Harmondsworth, England: Penguin Books, 1988.

Andrae, Tor. *Muhammad, the Man and His Faith.* New York: Harper and Brothers, 1960.

Ansah, Paul A. V. "Is Africa Accursed or Bewitched?" *The Independent* (Accra, Ghana), February 17–24, 1993.

Anyanwu, K. C. "The Idea of Art in African Thought." In Guttorm Floistad, ed., *Contemporary Philosophy: A New Survey,* vol. 5, *African Philosophy.* Dordrecht, Netherlands: Nijhoff, 1987.

Appiah, Kwame Anthony. *In My Father's House: Africa in the Philosophy of Culture.* New York: Oxford University Press, 1992.

Aristotle. *Metaphysics.*

———. *Nicomachean Ethics.*

Armstrong, A. H., ed. *The Cambridge History of Later Greek and Early Medieval Philosophy.* Cambridge: Cambridge University Press, 1967.

Asante, S. K. B. *Property Law and Social Goals in Ghana, 1844–1966.* Accra: Ghana Universities Press, 1975.

Austin, Dennis. "Africa and Democracy: Reflections on African Politics: Prospero, Ariel, and Caliban." *International Affairs* (London), 69, no. 2 (April 1993): 203–21.

Avineri, Shlomo, and Avner de-Shalit, eds. *Communitarianism and Individualism.* Oxford: Oxford University Press, 1992.

Beetham, David. *The Legitimation of Power.* London: Macmillan, 1991.

Bentham, Jeremy. *An Introduction to the Principles of Morals and Legislation.* 1823; Oxford: Basil Blackwell, 1948.

Berry, Christopher J. "Nations and Norms." *Review of Politics* 43, no. 1 (January 1981): 75–87.

Bodunrin, P. O. "The Question of African Philosophy." In Richard A. Wright, ed., *African Philosophy: An Introduction,* 3d ed. Lanham, Md.: University Press of America, 1984.

Busia, Kofi A. *Africa in Search of Democracy.* New York: Praeger, 1967.

———. "The Ashanti of the Gold Coast." In Daryll Forde, ed., *African Worlds.* Oxford: Oxford University Press, 1954.

———. *The Position of the Chief in the Modern Political System of Ashanti.* London: Frank Cass, 1968.

Cahoone, Lawrence E. *The Dilemma of Modernity: Philosophy, Culture, and Anti-Culture.* Albany: State University of New York Press, 1988.

Calinescu, Matei. *Five Faces of Modernity.* Durham, N.C.: Duke University Press, 1987.

Campbell, Dugald. *In the Heart of Bantuland: A Record of Twenty-nine Years' Pioneering in Central Africa Among the Bantu Peoples.* London: Seeley, Service, 1922.

Carter, Gwendolen M., and Patrick O'Meara, eds. *African Independence: The First Twenty-five Years.* Bloomington: Indiana University Press, 1985.

Christaller, J. G. *Dictionary of the Asante and Fante Language Called Twi (Tshi).* 2d ed. revised and enlarged. Basel: Basel Evangelical Missionary Society, 1933.

Colecraft, Esi. "Traditional Food Preservation: An Overview." *African Technology Forum* 6, no. 1 (February–March, 1993): 15–17.

Connor, Walker. *Ethnonationalism: The Quest for Understanding.* Princeton, N.J.: Princeton University Press, 1994.

———. "Nation-Building or Nation-Destroying?" *World Politics* 24 (1972): 319–55.

———. "A nation is a nation, is a state, is an ethnic group, is a . . ." *Ethnic and Racial Studies* 1, no. 4 (October 1978): 377–400.

Cruickshank, Brodie. *Eighteen Years on the Gold Coast of Africa.* Vol. 1. London, 1854.

Cureau, Adolphe L. *Savage Man in Central Africa: A Study of Primitive Races in the French Congo.* Trans. E. Andrews London: T. Fisher Unwin, 1915.

Dalfovo, A. T., et al. *The Foundations of Social Life: Ugandan Philosophical Studies.* Vol. 1. Washington, D.C.: Council for Research in Values and Philosophy, 1992.

Daniels, Norman, ed. *Reading Rawls.* New York: Basic Books, 1975.

Danquah, J. B. *Akan Laws and Customs.* London: Frank Cass, 1928.

Davidson, Basil. *The Black Man's Burden: Africa and the Curse of the Nation-State.* New York: Random House, Times Books, 1992.

de Vos, George, and Lola Romanucci-Ross, eds. *Ethnic Identity: Cultural Continuities and Change.* Mountain View, Calif.: Mayfield Publishing Company, 1975.

Deutsch, Eliot. *Creative Being: The Crafting of Person and World.* Honolulu: University of Hawaii Press, 1992.

———. *Personhood, Creativity, and Freedom.* Honolulu: University of Hawaii Press, 1982.

———, ed. *Culture and Modernity: East-West Philosophic Perspectives.* Honolulu: University of Hawaii Press, 1991.

Devlin, Sir Patrick. *The Legal Enforcement of Morals.* Oxford: Oxford University Press, 1965.

Dewey, John. *The Public and Its Problems.* New York: Holt, 1927.

Dickson, Kwesi A. *Aspects of Religion and Life in Africa.* Accra: Ghana Academy of Arts and Sciences, 1977.

Dobel, Patrick J. "The Corruption of a State." *American Political Science Review,* 72, no. 3 (September 1978): 958–73.

Dodds, E. R. *The Greeks and the Irrational.* Berkeley: University of California Press, 1951.

Donnelly, Jack. "Cultural Relativism and Universal Human Rights." *Human Rights Quarterly,* 6, no. 4 (November 1984): 400–419.

Dzobo, N. K. "Knowledge and Truth: Ewe and Akan Conceptions." In Kwasi Wiredu and Kwame Gyekye, eds., *Person and Community: Ghanaian Philosophical Studies,* 1. Washington, D.C.: Council for Research in Values and Philosophy, 1992.

——— "Sankofaism: A Philosophy of Africa's Mental Liberation." *Sankofa: Ghana's Illustrated Arts and Cultures* 5, no. 1 (January–June 1981): 32–35.

Eccleshall, Robert, et al. *Political Ideologies: An Introduction.* London: Hutchinson, 1984.

Eisenstadt, S. N. *Tradition, Change, and Modernity.* New York: John Wiley and Sons, 1973.

Etzioni, Amitai. *The Spirit of Community: The Reinvention of American Society.* New York: Simon and Schuster, a Touchstone Book, 1993.

Fichte, J. G. *Addresses to the German Nation,* trans. R. F. Jones and G. H. Turnbull. Westport, Conn.: Greenwood Press, 1979.

Field, G. C. *Plato and His Contemporaries.* London: Methuen, 1967.

Field, M. J. *Akim-Kotoku: An Oman of the Gold Coast.* London: The Crown Agents for the Colonies, 1948.

Findings (Washington, D.C.). Special issue. Africa Regional Studies Program, World Bank, September 1993.

Fleischacker, Samuel. *The Ethics of Culture.* Ithaca: Cornell University Press, 1994.

Fleishman, Joel L., et al. *Public Duties: The Moral Obligations of Government Officials.* Cambridge, Mass.: Harvard University Press, 1981.

Flew, Antony. *An Introduction to Western Philosophy: Ideas and Arguments from Plato to Sartre.* London: Thames and Hudson, 1971.

Floistad, Guttorm, ed. *Contemporary Philosophy: A New Survey.* Vol. 5, *African Philosophy.* Dordrecht, Netherlands: Martinus Nijhoff, 1987.

Forde, Daryll, ed. *African Worlds.* Oxford: Oxford University Press, 1954.

Fortes, Meyer, and Evans-Pritchard, E. E. *African Political Systems.* Oxford: Oxford University Press, 1940.

Fortman, Bastiaan de Gaay, ed. *After Mulungushi: The Economics of Zambian Humanism.* Nairobi: East African Publishing House, 1969.

Fowler, Robert A. *The Dance with Community: The Contemporary Debate in American Political Thought.* Lawrence: University of Kansas Press, 1991.

Francis, E. K. "The Ethnic Factor in Nation Building." *Social Forces* 46 (1968): 338–46.

Gibb, Sir Hamilton A. R. *Studies on the Civilization of Islam.* Ed. Sanford J. Shaw and William R. Polk. Boston: Beacon Press, 1962.

Gildin, Hilail. *Political Philosophy: Six Essays by Leo Strauss.* New York: Bobbs-Merrill, 1975.

Gluckman, Max. *The Judicial Process Among the Barotse of Northern Rhodesia.* Manchester, England: University of Manchester Press, 1955.

———. *Politics, Law, and Ritual in Tribal Society.* Oxford: Oxford University Press, 1965.

Guthrie, W. K. C. *A History of Greek Philosophy.* Vol. 3. Cambridge: Cambridge University Press, 1969.

Gyekye, Kwame. *African Cultural Values: An Introduction.* Philadelphia, Pa.: Sankofa Publishing Company, 1996.

———. *Arabic Logic: Ibn al-Tayyib on Porphyry's Eisagoge* Albany: State University of New York Press, 1979.

———. *An Essay on African Philosophical Thought: The Akan Conceptual Scheme.* Rev. ed. Philadelphia, Pa.: Temple University Press, 1995.

———. "Man as a Moral Subject: The Perspective of an African Philosophical Anthropology." In Joris Van Nispen and Douwe Tiemersma, eds., *The Quest for Man: The Topicality of Philosophical Anthropology.* Assen/Maastricht, Netherlands: Van Gorcum, 1991.

———. "Taking Development Seriously." *Journal of Applied Philosophy* 11, no. 1 (1994): 45–56.

———. *The Unexamined Life: Philosophy and the African Experience.* Inaugural lecture delivered before the University of Ghana, May 7, 1987. Accra: Ghana Universities Press, 1988.

Hardie, W. F. R. *Aristotle's Ethical Theory.* Oxford: Clarendon Press, 1968.

Hegel, G. W. F. *Philosophy of Right.* Trans. T. M. Knox. Oxford: Clarendon Press, 1942.

Heidenheimer, Arnold J., ed. *Political Corruption: Readings in Comparative Analysis.* New York: Holt, Rinehart and Winston, 1970.

Heilbroner, Robert L. *The Worldly Philosophers: The Lives, Times, and Ideas of the Great Economic Thinkers.* 6th ed. New York: Simon and Schuster, 1986.

Herder, G. W. "Ideas for a Philosophy of History." In F. M. Barnard, ed., *Herder's Social and Political Thought.* Oxford: Oxford University Press, 1965.

Heyd, David. *Supererogation: Its Status in Ethical Theory.* Cambridge: Cambridge University Press, 1982.

Hobhouse, L. T. *Social Evolution and Political Theory.* New York: Columbia University Press, 1928.

Hobsbawm, Eric, and Terence Ranger, eds. *The Invention of Tradition.* Cambridge: Cambridge University Press, 1983.

Horowitz, Donald L. "Ethnic Identity." In Nathan Glazer and Daniel P. Moynihan, eds., *Ethnicity: Theory and Experience.* Cambridge, Mass.: Harvard University Press, 1975.

Horton, Robin. "African Traditional Thought and Western Science." In Brian R. Wilson, ed., *Rationality.* Oxford: Basil Blackwell, 1974.

Hountondji, Paulin J. *African Philosophy: Myth and Reality.* Bloomington: Indiana University Press, 1983.

Howard, Rhoda. "Evaluating Human Rights in Africa: Some Problems of Implicit Comparisons." *Human Rights Quarterly* 6, no. 2 (May 1984): 160–79.

Idowu, Bolaji E. *Olodumare: God in Yoruba Belief.* London: Longmans, 1962.

Iliffe, John. *The Emergence of African Capitalism.* Minneapolis: University of Minnesota Press, 1983.

Independent Journal of Philosophy, vol. 4 1983: *Modernity* (1).

"Intellectuals and Tradition." *Daedalus* 101, no. 2 (spring 1972).

Irele, Abiola. "Contemporary Thought in French Speaking Africa." In Albert G. Mosley, ed., *African Philosophy: Selected Readings.* Englewood Cliffs, N.J.: Prentice-Hall, 1995.

Isaacs, Harold R. "Basic Group Identity: The Idols of the Tribe." In Nathan Glazer and Daniel P. Moynihan, eds., *Ethnicity, Theory, and Experience.* Cambridge, Mass.: Harvard University Press, 1975.

July, Robert W. *An African Voice: The Role of the Humanities in African Independence.* Durham: Duke University Press, 1987.

Kant, Immanuel. *Groundwork of the Metaphysic of Morals.* Trans. H. J. Paton. London: Hutchinson University Library, 1965.

Kaunda, Kenneth D. *A Humanist in Africa.* London: Longmans, 1966.

———. "Humanism in Zambia." In Basiaan de Gaay Fortman, ed., *After Mulungushi: The Economics of Zambian Humanism.* Nairobi: East African Publishing House, 1969.

———. *Take Up the Challenge.* Lusaka, Zambia: Government Printer, 1970.

Kea, Ray A. *Settlements, Trade, and Politics in the Seventeenth-Century Gold Coast.* Baltimore, Md.: Johns Hopkins University Press, 1982.

Kennedy, Emmet. "Ideology from Destutt de Tracy to Marx." *Journal of the History of Ideas* 40, no. 3 (July–September 1979): 353–68.

———. *A Philosophe in the Age of Revolution: Destutt de Tracy and the Origins of 'Ideology'.* Philadelphia, Pa.: American Philosophical Society, 1970.

Kente, Maria G. "The Role of a National Language in Tanzania." In Jude J. Ongong'a and Kenneth R. Gray, eds., *Bottlenecks to National Identity: Ethnic Cooperation Towards Nation Building.* Nairobi: Professors World Peace Academy of Kenya, 1989.

Kenyatta, Jomo. *Facing Mount Kenya.* New York: Vintage Books, 1965.

Kopytoff, Igor, ed. *The African Frontier: The Reproduction of Traditional African Societies.* Bloomington: Indiana University Press, 1987.

Kuper, Hilda. *An African Aristocracy: Rank Among the Swazi.* Oxford: Oxford University Press, 1961.

Kymlicka, Will. *Contemporary Political Philosophy: An Introduction.* Oxford: Clarendon Press, 1990.

———. *Liberalism, Community, and Culture.* Oxford: Clarendon Press, 1989.

Lacey, A. R. *A Dictionary of Philosophy.* London: Routledge and Kegan Paul, 1976.

Laing, Ebenezer. *Science and Society in Ghana.* J. B. Danquah Memorial Lectures, 20th series, March 1987. Accra: Ghana Academy of Arts and Sciences, 1990.

Lamont, Corliss. *The Philosophy of Humanism.* New York: Frederick Ungar, 1965.

Lane, Charles. "Dilemma of Democracy." *West Africa,* 17–23 December 1990.

Le Vine, Victor T. *Political Corruption: The Ghana Case.* Stanford, Calif.: Hoover Institution Press, 1975.

Lerner, Daniel. *The Passing of the Traditional Society.* New York: Glencoe, 1958.

Liddle, Henry George, and Robert Scott. *A Greek-English Lexicon.* Oxford: Clarendon Press, 1968.

Lodge, George C. "The Connection Between Ethics and Ideology." *Journal of Business Ethics* 1 (1982): 85–98.

———. *The New American Ideology.* New York: Alfred Knopf, 1975.

Lukes, Steven. "Some Problems About Rationality." In Brian R. Wilson, ed., *Rationality.* Oxford: Basil Blackwell, 1974.

MacIntyre, Alasdair. *After Virtue: A Study in Moral Theory.* Notre Dame, Ind.: University of Notre Dame Press, 1984.

Marx, Karl. *Eleven Theses on Feuerbach.* 1845.

Mbiti, John S. *African Religions and Philosophy.* New York: Doubleday, Anchor Books, 1970.

Menkiti, Ifeanyi A. "Person and Community in African Traditional Thought." In Richard A. Wright, ed., *African Philosophy: An Introduction.* 3d ed. Lanham, Md.: University Press of America, 1984.

Metz, Steven. "In Lieu of Orthodoxy: The Socialist Theories of Nkrumah and Nyerere." *Journal of Modern African Studies* 20, no. 3 (1982): 377–92.

Miller, David. "The Ethical Significance of Nationality." *Ethics* 98 (July 1988): 647–62.

———. *Market, State, and Community.* Oxford: Clarendon Press, 1989.

———. *On Nationality.* Oxford: Clarendon Press, 1995.

Mises, von Ludwig. *Nation, State, and Economy: Contributions to the Politics and History of Our Time.* Trans. and with an introduction by Leland B. Yeager. New York: New York University Press, 1983.

Molema, S. M. *The Bantu: Past and Present.* Edinburgh: W. Green & Son, 1920.

Morehouse, Ward, ed. *Science, Technology, and the Social Order.* New Brunswick, N.J.: Transaction Books, 1979.

Mulhall, Stephen, and Adam Swift. *Liberals and Communitarians.* Oxford: Blackwell, 1992.

Nielsen, Kai. "On Finding One's Feet in Philosophy: From Wittgenstein to Marx." *Metaphilosophy* 16, no. 1 (January 1985).

Nisbet, Robert A. *The Quest for Community.* New York: Oxford University Press, 1953.

———. *The Sociological Tradition.* New York: Basic Books, 1969.

Nkrumah, Kwame. "African Socialism Revisited." *African Forum: A Quarterly Journal of Contemporary Affairs* 1, no. 3 (winter 1966): 3–9.

———. *Consciencism: Philosophy and Ideology for Decolonization and Development with Particular Reference to the African Revolution.* London: Heinemann, 1964.

Noonan, John T. *Bribes.* New York: Macmillan, 1984.

Nyerere, Julius K. "Democracy and the Party System." In Rupert Emerson and Martin Kilson, eds., *The Political Awakening of Africa.* Englewood Cliffs, N.J.: Prentice-Hall, 1965.

———. "One Party Rule." In Paul E. Sigmund, ed., *The Ideologies of the Developing Nations.* New York: Praeger, 1963.

———. *Ujamaa: Essays on Socialism.* Dar es Salaam: Oxford University Press, 1968.

Oguah, B. E. "African and Western Philosophy: A Comparative Study." In Richard A. Wright, ed., *African Philosophy: An Introduction,* 3d ed. Lanham, Md.: University Press of America, 1984.

Ollennu, N. A. *Principles of Customary Land Law in Ghana.* London: Sweet and Maxwell, 1962.

Onuoha, Bede. *The Elements of African Socialism.* London: Andre Deutsch, 1965.

Oruka, H. Odera. "African Philosophy: A Brief Personal History and Current Debate." In Guttorm Floistad, ed., *Contemporary African Philosophy: A New Survey,* vol. 5, *African Philosophy.* Dordrecht, Netherlands: Martinus Nijhoff, 1987.

Outlaw, Lucius. "African Philosophy: Deconstructive and Reconstructive Challenges." In Guttorm Floistad, ed., *Contemporary African Philosophy: A New Survey,* vol. 5, *African Philosophy.* Dordrecht, Netherlands: Martinus Nijhoff, 1987.

Owens, Joseph. *A History of Ancient Western Philosophy.* New York: Appleton Century Crofts, 1959.

Pacey, Arnold. *The Culture of Technology.* Oxford: Basil Blackwell, 1983.

Parrinder, Geoffrey. *African Traditional Religion.* New York: Harper and Row, 1962.

Parsons, Talcott. "Some Theoretical Considerations on the Nature and Trends of Change of Ethnicity." In Nathan Glazer and Daniel P. Moynihan, eds., *Ethnicity: Theory and Experience.* Cambridge, Mass.: Harvard University Press, 1975.

Pfaff, William. *The Wrath of Nations: Civilizations and the Furies of Nationalism.* New York: Simon and Schuster, 1993.

Phillips, Derek L. *Looking Backward: A Critical Appraisal of Communitarian Thought.* Princeton, N.J.: Princeton University Press, 1993.

Plato. *Apology.*

———. *Republic.* Trans. F. M. Cornford. London: Oxford University Press, 1945.

al-Qifti. *Tarikh al-Hukama.*

Quine, W. V. O. *The Time of My Life: An Autobiography.* Cambridge, Mass.: MIT Press, 1985.

———. "Two Dogmas of Empiricism." In *From a Logical Point of View.* Cambridge, Mass.: Harvard University Press, 1953.

Rattray, R. S. *Ashanti.* Oxford: Clarendon Press, 1923.

———. *Ashanti Law and Constitution.* Oxford: Oxford University Press, 1929.

———. *Ashanti Proverbs.* Oxford: Oxford University Press, 1916.

Rawls, John. "Justice As Fairness: Political Not Metaphysical." *Philosophy and Public Affairs* 14, no. 3 (summer 1985): 223–51.

———. "Kantian Constructivism in Moral Theory." *Journal of Philosophy* 77, no. 9 (September 1980): 515–72.

———. *A Theory of Justice.* Cambridge, Mass.: Harvard University Press, 1971.

Raz, Joseph. *The Morality of Freedom.* Oxford: Clarendon Press, 1986.

———. "Principles of Equality." *Mind* 87 (July 1978): 321–42.

"Reconstructing Nations and States." *Daedalus* 122, no. 3 (summer 1993).

Ross, W. D. *Aristotle.* London: Methuen, 1923.

Rouner, Leroy S., ed. *On Community.* Notre Dame, Ind.: University of Notre Dame Press, 1992.

Rudolph, Lloyd I., and Susanne Hoeber Rudolph. *The Modernity of Tradition: Political Development in India.* Chicago: University of Chicago Press, 1967.

Rustow, Dankwart A. "Democracy: A Global Revolution?" *Foreign Affairs,* fall 1990, pp. 75–91.

Russell, Bertrand. *A History of Western Philosophy.* New York: Simon and Schuster, 1945.

Ryle, Gilbert. *The Concept of Mind.* London: Hutchinson, 1949.

———. *Plato's Progress.* Cambridge: Cambridge University Press, 1966.

Sandel, Michael J. *Liberalism and the Limits of Justice.* Cambridge: Cambridge University Press, 1982.

Sarbah, John Mensah. *Fanti Customary Laws.* London: William Clowes and Sons, 1897.

———. *Fanti National Constitution.* London: William Clowes and Sons, 1906.

Schabert, Tilo. "A Note on Modernity." *Political Theory* 7, no. 1 (February 1979): 123–37.

Schacht, Joseph. *An Introduction to Islamic Law.* Oxford: Clarendon Press, 1964.

Schapera, Isaac. *Handbook of Tswana Law and Custom.* Oxford: Oxford University Press, 1955.

Schumpeter, Joseph A. *A History of Economic Analysis*. New York: Oxford University Press, 1954.

Schwartz, Benjamin I. "The Limits of 'Tradition Versus Modernity' as Categories of Explanation: The Case of the Chinese Intellectuals." *Daedalus* 101, no. 2 (spring 1972): 71–88.

Scott, James C. *Comparative Political Corruption*. Englewood Cliffs, N.J.: Prentice-Hall, 1972.

Sefa-Dede, Samuel. "Harnessing Food Technology for Development." In Samuel Sefa-Dede and Richard Orraca-Tetteh, eds., *Harnessing Traditional Food Technology for Development*. Legon: Department of Nutrition and Food Science, University of Ghana, 1989.

———. "Traditional Food Technology." In Robert Macrae, Richard K. Robinson, and Michele J. Sadler, eds., *Encyclopedia of Food Science, Food Technology, and Nutrition*. New York: Academic Press, 1993, 4600–6.

Selznick, Philip. *The Moral Commonwealth: Social Theory and the Promise of Community*. Berkeley and Los Angeles: University of California Press, 1992.

Senghor, Léopold S. *On African Socialism*. Trans. and with an introduction by Mercer Cook. New York: Praeger, 1964.

Shils, Edward. *Tradition*. London: Faber and Faber, 1981.

Shonfield, Andrew. *Socialism for Africa*. Moscow: Novosti Press Agency Publishing House, 1965.

Simiyu, V. G. "The Democratic Myth in the African Traditional Societies." In W. O. Oyugi and A. Gitonga, eds., *Democratic Theory and Practice in Africa*. Nairobi: Heinemann, Kenya, 1987.

Singer, Peter, ed. *A Companion to Ethics*. Oxford: Basil Blackwell, 1991.

Sithole, Ndabaningi. *African Nationalism*. Cape Town: Oxford University Press, 1959.

Skolimowski, Henryk. "The Cultural Model of Development: Alternative to Faustian Technology." *Alternatives: A Journal of World Policy* 5, no. 4 (January 1980): 477–88.

Smith, Anthony D. *The Ethnic Origins of Nations*. Oxford: Basil Blackwell, 1986.

———. *State and Nation in the Third World*. New York: St. Martin's Press, 1983.

———. *National Identity*. Reno: University of Nevada Press, 1991.

———, ed. *Ethnicity and Nationalism*. Leiden: E. J. Brill, 1992.

Taylor, Charles. "Atomism." In *Philosophy and the Human Sciences: Philosophical Papers*, 2. Cambridge: Cambridge University Press, 1985.

———. *Sources of the Self*. Cambridge: Cambridge University Press, 1990.

Thompson, Dennis F. *Political Ethics and Public Office*. Cambridge, Mass.: Harvard University Press, 1987.

Thucydides. *History of the Peloponnesian War*. Trans. Rex Warner. Harmondsworth, U.K.: Penguin Books, 1954.

Todd, Lord. *Problems of the Technological Society*. Aggrey-Fraser-Guggisberg Memorial Lectures. Accra: Ghana Publishing Corporation, for the University of Ghana, 1973.

Towa, Marcien. *Essai sur la problematique philosophique dans l'Afrique actuelle*. Yaounde, Cameroun: CLE, 1971.

Twum-Barima, K. *The Cultural Basis of Our National Development*. J. B. Danquah Memorial Lectures, 25th Series, February 1982. Accra: Ghana Academy of Arts and Sciences, 1985.

Urmson, J. O. "Saints and Heroes." In A. I. Melden, ed., *Essays in Moral Philosophy*. Seattle: University of Washington Press, 1958.

Vaughn, Karen I. *John Locke: Economist and Social Scientist.* Chicago: University of Chicago Press, 1980.

Verhelst, Thierry G. *No Life Without Roots: Culture and Development.* Trans. Bob Cumming. Atlantic Highlands, N.J.: Zed Books, 1987.

Verma, Roop Rekha. "The Concept of Progress and Cultural Identity." In Eliot Deutsch, ed., *Culture and Modernity: East-West Philosophic Perspectives.* Honolulu: University of Hawaii Press, 1991.

Walzer, Michael. "Philosophy and Democracy." *Political Theory* 9, no. 3 (August 1981): 379–99.

———. *Spheres of Justice.* New York: Basic Books, 1983.

Wamala, E. "The Socio-Political Philosophy of Traditional Buganda Society: Breaks and Continuity into the Present." In A. T. Dalfovo et al., eds., *The Foundations of Social Life: Ugandan Philosophical Studies,* 1. Washington, D.C.: Council for Research in Values and Philosophy, 1992.

Watt, Montgomery W. *Muhammad at Medina.* Oxford: Clarendon Press, 1956.

Wauthier, Claude. *The Literature and Thought of Modern Africa.* London: Heinemann, 1978.

Weber, Max. *Economy and Society.* Vol. 1. Eds. Gunther Roth and Claus Wittich. New York: Bedminster Press, 1968.

Werlin, Herbert H. "The Roots of Corruption: The Ghanaian Enquiry." *Journal of Modern African Studies* 10, no. 2 (1972): 247–66.

White, Lynn. *Medieval Religion and Technology: Collected Essays.* Berkeley: University of California Press, 1978.

Wilks, Ivor. *Asante in the Nineteenth Century: The Structure and Evolution of a Political Order.* Cambridge: Cambridge University Press, 1975.

Wilson, Brian R., ed. *Rationality.* Oxford: Basil Blackwell, 1974.

Wiredu, Kwasi. *Philosophy and an African Culture.* Cambridge: Cambridge University Press, 1980.

Wiredu, Kwasi, and Kwame Gyekye. *Person and Community: Ghanaian Philosophical Studies,* 1. Washington, D.C.: Council for Research in Values and Philosophy, 1992.

Wittgenstein, Ludwig. *Tractatus Logico-Philosophicus.* Trans. David F. Pears and B. F. McGuinness. London: Routledge and Kegan Paul, 1961.

———. *Zettel.* Ed. G. E. M. Anscombe and G. H. von Wright. Trans. G. E. M. Anscombe. Berkeley and Los Angeles: University of California Press, 1967.

Wright, Richard A., ed. *African Philosophy: An Introduction.* 3d ed. Lanham, Md.: University Press of America, 1984.

Index of Names

Index of Subjects